D1400333

*Varieties of Spanish
in the United States*

Georgetown Studies in Spanish Linguistics series
John M. Lipski, Series Editor

Sociolingüística y pragmática del español
    Carmen Silva-Corvalan
Sonido y sentido: Teoría y práctica de la pronunciación del español contemporáneo con audio CD
    Jorge M. Guitart
Varieties of Spanish in the United States
    John M. Lipski

Varieties of Spanish in the United States

JOHN M. LIPSKI

Georgetown University Press / Washington, D.C.

Georgetown University Press, Washington, D.C. www.press.georgetown.edu

© 2008 by Georgetown University Press. All rights reserved. No part of this
book may be reproduced or utilized in any form or by any means, electronic or
mechanical, including photocopying and recording, or by any information
storage and retrieval system, without permission in writing from the publisher.

Library of Congress Cataloging-in-Publication Data
Lipski, John M.
   Varieties of Spanish in the United States / John M. Lipski.
      p. cm.—(Georgetown Studies in Spanish Linguistics)
   Includes bibliographical references and index.
   ISBN 978–1–58901–213–4 (alk. paper)
1. Spanish language—United States.   I. Title.   II. Series.
   PC4826.L56 2008
   460.973—dc22

                                                            2008000084

∞ This book is printed on acid-free paper meeting the requirements of the
American National Standard for Permanence in Paper for Printed Library Materials.

15 14 13 12 11 10 09 08   9 8 7 6 5 4 3 2

First printing
Printed in the United States of America

This book is dedicated to the memory of
my parents, Victor Lipski and Rosaline Pozarzycki Lipski—
proudly bilingual, proudly bicultural, proudly American.

Contents

Introduction

This book is the result of an entire academic career spent observing, evaluating, investigating, and promoting the Spanish language in the United States. It is intended to serve as a reference work for teachers, scholars, and interested bystanders, a testimony to the vitality of the Spanish language in the United States, its legitimacy as a means of self-expression, and the considerable scholarship that documents the variation and richness of Spanish in the United States. Well into the twenty-first century, the topic needs no introduction; the chapters speak for themselves. Nonetheless, my more than three decades of work on U.S. Spanish induces me to indulge in a bit of reflection on the growth of interest in Spanish within the United States as reflected in my own unforeseen career trajectory.

Like many linguists of my generation, my current research agenda bears little resemblance to my graduate training. An apostate electrical engineering student with a B.A. in mathematics, I entered graduate school in Romance linguistics at the University of Alberta. My graduate training was evenly divided between classic Romance philology and European structuralism (one of my professors was a former student of André Martinet) and general linguistics within the then-radical transformation–generative paradigm. My first love was historical linguistics, particularly phonology, and my doctoral dissertation (1974) dealt with the comparative historical phonology of Spanish, Italian, and Portuguese. Romance linguistics has never been a North American pastime, and even before finishing graduate school I realized that my only opportunity for employment in the cutthroat academic job market of the 1970s was in a language department. Because Spanish was the Romance language I knew best, I landed a predissertation job (one of the terrible "all-but dissertation" jobs we enjoin our students against taking) at a small urban college in New Jersey. My theoretical and historical training were immediately shown to be useless in this setting, as was the Spanish that I had picked up by the seat of my pants during my undergraduate years in Texas, and from formal grammars. All my colleagues were Cubans, and a large number of my students were Puerto Rican, all speaking varieties of Spanish that bore little resemblance to anything found in textbooks and spoken at a rate of speed and with phonetic patterns that did not fit into the "ideal speaker–listener" and "ideal speech community" of my graduate training. Following this baptism by fire (which left more than a few scorch marks but also a great love for Caribbean Spanish) I landed a tenure-track job at Michigan State University in 1975, a year after the state of Michigan had passed a bilingual education law. My new job required me (in addition to coordinating all basic and intermediate Spanish courses) to aid in the development of materials for bilingual education, and to teach "about" bilingualism at the university level. At this time there was precious little bibliography, and what little there was had not figured in my graduate training. Nor had the Spanish of rural Mexican farmworkers, the "Michicanos" who represented our immediate constituents in the emerging bilingual education efforts. So primitive were the conditions at the time that a colleague specializing in Spanish literature and I were charged with developing the Spanish language proficiency test for the certification of all Spanish bilingual education teachers in the entire state. During my own bootstrapping I learned much through interviewing, observing, and advising Spanish-speaking workers, professionals, and students. I also came face to face with the cruel realities of migrant camps, the laws that deprived children of the right to public education and families of winter weatherization protection if the families did not spend more than six months of the year in the same state, and the persecution of the Spanish language.

This situation was not unlike the experiences of my immigrant grandparents a few generations before, or even of my parents (both U.S.-born nonnative speakers of English, who were thrown into a school system with no knowledge of English and subsequently humiliated and harassed to the point of refusing to pass their native language on to their offspring). There is nothing noble about needless suffering and humiliation; I am one language short because of the intolerance of previous generations.

While at Michigan State I taught one of the first classes on the Spanish language in the United States, scrambling to find bibliography and basing most of the readings on Fishman, Cooper, and Ma's *Bilingualism in the barrio* and Hernández Chávez, Cohen, and Beltramo's *El lenguaje de los chicanos*. A high point of that first class was the visit to our classroom by the emerging Chicano writer—now a distinguished prize-winning author and scholar—Rolando Hinojosa. During the same time period a colleague proposed to the department chair a course in Chicano literature, a daring new topic that had never before been proposed in the conservative Midwest. The response was that there was "not enough" Chicano literature to fill even a ten-week quarter; after some haggling it was decided that if some Puerto Rican literature were thrown in for good measure there would probably be sufficient material. Thus two unlikely suspects cobbled together this pioneering "Chicano-Riqueña" course: Malcolm Compitello (a respected literary scholar) taught the Chicano half, and *un humilde servidor* did his best to present island-based and U.S. Puerto Rican literature. I am delighted to say that this experience could never occur nowadays, and for all the right reasons.

Thus began an enduring relationship not only with the Spanish language as used in the United States but also with the people who use the language, and with the circumstances in which Spanish is taught and respected. Subsequent career moves took me first to Houston, where I worked with Mexican American and Central American communities as well as with Spanish-speaking groups in neighboring Louisiana, then to Florida, where work with Cuban and Nicaraguan speakers formed part of my research and teaching profile, and finally to the beautiful highlands of New Mexico, home to the Americas' oldest variety of Spanish. Even my current venue, rural central Pennsylvania, with more cows than people, is receiving a significant new influx of Spanish speakers from Mexico, Central America, and the Caribbean; as a sign that times are indeed a-changin', children of undocumented farmworkers are receiving scholarships to Penn State, soon to join the next generation of professionals contributing to the nation that generously received them.

Most of the material in the following chapters is based on factual research or on demographic data. However, I warn potential readers that I am not a dispassionate observer when it comes to the treatment that the Spanish language and its speakers have received in the United States. The very name of the nation is both linguistically plural and semantically singular, a good metaphor for what we have always been as a people: one nation, indivisible, with liberty and justice for all. I am an unrepentant believer in the fundamental human right of self-expression in the language of one's choice, and I reject the notion that the United States is a great nation because people speak English. Just for the record, (1) the United States is a great nation; (2) English is spoken in the United States, but only due to an accident of colonization; (3) there is not a shred of evidence that supports the idea that allowing immigrants and their offspring to continue to use their native languages dissuades them from learning English; (4) harassing people into abandoning their native or heritage language is every bit as much of a human rights abuse as binding the left arms of children born left-handed in an attempt to make them right-handed. The latter practice, once common, today causes us to shudder; the former practice is equally repugnant; and (5) "English only," "official English," and all other forms of linguistic bigotry do not jibe with our Constitution, our Declaration of Independence, nor with any sacred text I have ever read. Young children about to acquire siblings often fear that their parents will love them less because parental love will be diluted among all the children. Mexicans say *entre menos burros más elotes*. All loving parents know that love always multiplies and never divides. I believe that the same lemma holds true of the respect for peoples and cultures in these wonderful United States.

Although I alone bear responsibility for the contents of this book, it by no means developed in a vacuum. Over the years I have had the good fortune to count among my friends and colleagues many of the leading researchers on Spanish in the United States, and from them I have learned much and have drawn omnivorously from their collective wisdom. I am indeed privileged to have enjoyed the friendship and good counsel of the following people, among many others too numerous to name: Frances Aparicio, Samuel Armistead, Sandra Baumel-Schreffler, John Bergen, Garland Bills, Esther Brown, Richard Cameron, D. Lincoln Canfield, Isabel Castellanos, John Chaston, René Cisneros, Halvor Clegg, Anthony Cohen, Felice Coles, Cecilia Colombi, Jerry Craddock, Paola Dussias, Lucía Elías-Olivares, Mary Beth Floyd, MaryEllen García, Ofelia García, Chip Gerfen, Erlinda Gonazles-Berry, George Green, Jorge Guitart, John Gutiérrez, Robert Hammond, James Harris, José Esteban Hernández, Eduardo Hernández-Chávez, Margarita Hidalgo, Jane Hill, Alan Hudson, June Jaramillo, Nicolás Kanellos, Gary Keller, Carl Kirschner, Carol Klee, Judith Kroll, James Lantolf, Elizabeth Leone, Juan Lope Blanch, Raymond MacCurdy, Elizabeth Martínez-Gibson, Joseph Matluck, Carol Meyers-Scotton, Amparo Morales, Pieter Muysken, Rafael Núñez-Cedeño, Francisco Ocampo, Julián Olivares, Jacob Ornstein, Luis Ortiz López, Ricardo Otheguy, Fernando Peñalosa, Shana Poplack, Kim Potowski, Florence Rigelhaupt, Susana Rivera-Mills, Ana Roca, Mario Saltarelli, Rosaura Sánchez, Armin Schwegler, Carmen Silva-Corvalán, Robert Smead, Carlos Solé, Yolanda Solé, Tracy Terrell, Richard Teschner, Roger Thompson, Almeida Jacqueline Toribio, Lourdes Torres, Rena Torres-Cacoullos, Guadalupe Valdés, María Vaquero, Beatriz Varela, Neddy Vigil, and Ana Celia Zentella.

1

The Importance of Spanish in the United States

Spanish in the United States

After English, Spanish is the most commonly used language in the United States, and its speakers represent the fastest-growing language minority in the country. On a worldwide scale, the United States is home to the fifth largest Spanish-speaking population and is well on its way to fourth place—a position it may already hold if uncounted and undocumented Spanish speakers are added into the mix. This ranking occurs despite the fact that Spanish is not the official language of the country, or of any state, and that Spanish is the principal language in only a few exceptional areas such as Miami and some towns along the U.S.-Mexican border. Moreover, the aforementioned facts refer only to those individuals who declare Spanish as their native language; there are untold millions of proficient and not-so-proficient Spanish speakers who have learned this language, not as part of their birthright, but through formal instruction, residence in Spanish-speaking regions, work, travel, and other means of acquiring a second language.

At one time regarded as merely an ethnographic curiosity, the subject of word lists, and the butt of jokes, U.S. Spanish is now the focus of a major research and teaching paradigm. The first variety to be studied in any depth was also the one that enjoys historical precedence, namely Spanish of Mexican origin. Within this category we can further distinguish the traditional dialects of New Mexico and southern Colorado, and also some isolated varieties in Arizona and possibly California and Texas. Some of these early Spanish-language isolates have remained relatively untouched by later developments affecting Mexican Spanish, and they embody some—though not all—of the linguistic features that were present in colonial Latin American Spanish of the eighteenth century. The early work of Espinosa (1909, 1925, 1946) and Hills (1906) on the Spanish of New Mexico and Colorado, and of Rael (1939) on the Spanish of New Mexico and Arizona are exemplars of the early work on U.S. Spanish.

What might more legitimately be called Mexican American Spanish came about in several different ways, each of which has left its own mark on the corresponding varieties of the language. After the Texas war of independence (1836) and the Mexican-American War (1848), many Spanish-speaking Mexicans changed countries without ever moving an inch; as the popular saying has it, "they didn't cross the border; the border crossed them." This fact accounts for the smooth dialectal continuity between northern Mexican Spanish and the Spanish used in the southern areas of California, Texas, Arizona, and New Mexico. The Mexican Revolution brought thousands of Mexicans to the United States in the first decades of the twentieth century, not all of whom settled along the border. Moreover, the sociodemographic profile of twentieth-century refugees did not always parallel that of earlier Mexicans; many were middle-class and educated, as opposed to the rural groups with little formal education that had constituted much of the earlier Mexican immigration to the United States.

Shortly thereafter, labor shortages in the United States prompted the recruitment of thousands of Mexican laborers in Mexico's poorest states—in the southern region of Mexico—during the *bracero* program. This migration continues to the present, and it accounts for the fact that many migrant farmworkers in the midwestern and northern states trace their families to the southernmost zones of Mexico. Other Mexicans followed the economic opportunities offered by railroad expansion, ending up in Chicago, Milwaukee, and other northern industrial areas. Finally, Mexican immigration, both temporary and permanent, continues along the U.S.-Mexican border, all of which places contemporary Mexican American Spanish in the linguistic spotlight throughout the United States. To date, this is the variety of Spanish that has received the greatest amount of scholarly attention in terms of research monographs, theses and dissertations, major data-collection projects, and interfacing with the public schools and governmental sectors.

The next Spanish in terms of quantity of research is that of Puerto Rican origin, particularly as spoken in the New York City area and in other northeastern cities. The first large groups of Puerto Ricans came to the U.S. mainland just before World War II, and they settled in urban industrial areas in search of greater economic opportunities. In subsequent decades, immigration to and from Puerto Rico has moved in cycles, depending upon the relative economic conditions in Puerto Rico and the northeastern United States. Until recently, Puerto Rican Spanish was the major variety throughout the New York City area, and Spanish in the northern industrial cities east of Detroit was synonymous with Puerto Rican Spanish. Today this situation has changed somewhat, because the Dominican Spanish-speaking population is beginning to outnumber, and in some areas of New York City already does outnumber, the Puerto Rican Spanish-speaking population.

The third largest Spanish-speaking group, both in terms of numbers and with regard to linguistic studies, is the Cuban community. Cuban colonies in the United States were in existence even before the Spanish-American War of 1898, but it was not until after the Cuban Revolution of 1959 that Cubans flocked to the United States in large numbers. Until the Mariel boatlift of 1980, most Cuban Americans represented educated middle-class sectors of Cuban society; as a result, the linguistic study of Cuban Spanish has taken different sociolinguistic perspectives from the study of the largely rural varieties exemplified in the Mexican American communities, and from the study of the working-class Spanish of Puerto Ricans and Dominicans. It is also the variety most closely associated with a single geographical region (Dade County, Florida), even though large Cuban American communities are also found in the metropolitan New York area and in other large American cities.

Beginning in the 1980s, political turmoil in Central America caused hundreds of thousands of Central Americans to migrate to the United States, and many formed stable colonies there. The civil war in El Salvador resulted in the largest Central American refugee population (Speed 1992), most of whom entered the United States illegally because of the U.S. government's refusal to recognize them as political refugees. Salvadoran communities sprang up in Houston, Chicago, and Los Angeles, with smaller groups in Washington, D.C. (Jones 1994), Miami, and New York City.

Salvadorans were at first an invisible minority within a minority in the Southwest, because most blended in with the Mexican American population. For many Salvadorans, this was a conscious decision, because law enforcement and immigration officials were less likely to challenge Mexican Americans for proof of legal residence, whereas police targeted Salvadorans as illegal aliens, and landlords and utility companies exacted huge deposits. Although the current political situation in El Salvador is more promising—though far from resolved—the large Salvadoran communities in the United States have become integrated into the overall Spanish-speaking population of the country. In many cities, Salvadoran businesses are prominently visible, and Salvadoran Spanish has come to the attention of educators, advertisers, and journalists.

In 1979, the Nicaraguan people rose up against the forty-year dictatorship of the Somoza family. The Sandinista National Liberation Front, named after national hero Augusto César Sandino, who had fought the U.S. Marines during their occupation of Nicaragua earlier in the century, viewed the Nicaraguan revolution in terms of the earlier Cuban revolution. A socialist economy was the operative plan, and Cuban advisors arrived to help put the Sandinistas' vision into tangible form. The Nicaraguan bourgeoisie, aided by the sympathetic anti-communist government of the United States, began an armed counterinsurgency. Those who carried it out were known in Spanish as *contrarrevolucionarios* (counterrevolutionaries), or just *Contras*; the latter name was the one used in the United States.

The initial fear of a communist takeover following the Sandinista revolution had prompted thousands of Nicaraguans to flee to the United States, and the renewal of the armed struggle between Sandinistas and Contras spurred even more outward immigration. By far the largest Nicaraguan community was formed on the western edge of Miami, with another large colony in Los Angeles. Smaller groups of Nicaraguans are found in Houston, Atlanta, New Orleans, and other southern and southwestern cities. It is in Miami, however, where the Nicaraguan linguistic and cultural presence is most strongly felt. Although overshadowed by the dominant Cuban culture citywide, Nicaraguan Spanish and culture predominate in the Nicaraguan neighborhoods, and few Cubans in Miami are unaware of the speech and cultural patterns of Nicaraguans.

Smaller communities of Spanish speakers, some ethnically homogeneous, many more diverse, are found throughout major cities and agricultural areas of the United States. New York City and Miami have large Colombian communities; the Ecuadoran community in New York City is also sizable. Guatemalans are found in large numbers in rural southern Florida and in greater Los Angeles. New Orleans is home to a long-standing Honduran community; a more recent Honduran community is found in Yonkers, New York. Port Arthur, Texas, contains a group of Miskito fishermen from the Caribbean coast of Nicaragua; creole English-speaking Nicaraguans from the same area live in Opa Loka, Florida, just to the north of Miami. The country is also dotted with tiny pockets of isolated or vestigial Spanish-speaking communities, carryovers of once more-extensive settlements that have been washed over by Anglo American settlements during the past 150 years and which have been left as tide pools to be discovered by fieldworkers, who use them to fit in the pieces of the puzzle represented by the historical dialectology of Spanish in the United States.

Demographics of U.S. Spanish

Studying the demographics of Spanish speakers in the United States is confusing and torturous, because the population is ever changing, return migration to countries of origin is a frequent occurrence, underrepresentation in census counts is the rule rather than the exception, and undocumented members of the Spanish-speaking population may elude any attempts to study them. Moreover, the data, both official and unofficial, embody apparent paradoxes. On one hand, the total number of Spanish speakers in the United States is steadily growing, particularly in urban areas of the Southwest, in New York City, and in southern Florida. On the other hand, in many communities the retention of Spanish by U.S.-born speakers is at an all-time low, and the shift from Spanish to English is often complete after only two generations.

Thus the issue of the "future of Spanish" in the United States requires a two-pronged approach. First, barring some totally cataclysmic circumstance, Spanish speakers will continue to migrate to the United States, and the preeminence of Spanish as the second language of the United States (and as the first language in some areas) is guaranteed for the foreseeable future. At the same time, there is evidence that the pace of ethnic and linguistic assimilation to Anglo American culture is increasing in many parts of the country, both through pulls, such as the perception that upward socioeconomic mobility is associated with English, and by pushes, such as xenophobic "English only" movements (Bills 1997b; Bills, Hernández-Chávez, and Hudson 1995; Hernández-Chávez, Bills, and Hudson 1996; Hudson, Hernandez-Chávez, and Bills 1992, 1995).

The staying power of Spanish in a given U.S. community is dependent on political and economic events outside the borders of the United States, as well as on changing currents of thought and demographic trends within the country, and assessments should keep this in mind. Census data and other inquiries provide only a rough approximation to the total perspective, because self-reporting is notoriously inaccurate regarding matters linguistic and cultural, and many members of the Spanish-speaking population of the United States do not appear on census rolls. Confusion of Hispanic heritage with linguistic abilities in Spanish also clouds the picture, as does the failure to distinguish domains of usage of Spanish, English, and other languages. The following chapters will provide current data on the linguistic characteristics of the largest Spanish-speaking groups in the United States, together with brief historical and demographic profiles. Of necessity, the latter data are somewhat outdated, tentative, and in constant need of refinement. The linguistic traits of the groups involved tend to be more stable across time, and the data on individual dialects should provide a useful—if simplified—introduction to these communities.

Among comprehensive studies of the demographics of Spanish-speaking groups in the United States, Veltman (1988) offers a good point of departure. This study is based on U.S. Census Bureau studies carried out between 1975 and 1980, and therefore it does not accurately reflect the consequences of later events (for instance, the 1980 Cuban boatlift from Mariel and the continued arrival of Cuban *balseros* [raft people], the immigration of large numbers of Salvadorans and Nicaraguans that occurred during the 1980s, and the increasingly large Dominican and Colombian presence in New York City). Still, the figures are telling, and extrapolation to current levels is not entirely out of the question.

In figures provided by the U.S. Census Bureau in 1975, there were some 7.4 million "persons of Spanish language origin" over four years of age in the United States, and another 2.9 million English speakers lived in households where Spanish was also used. An estimated 2.2 million individuals (some 21.5% of the total Spanish language origin group) were presumed to speak little or no Spanish. Of the total Spanish language origin group, some 1.2 million were Spanish monolingual, 2.9 million were Spanish bilingual, and 4.2 million were English (dominant) bilingual, making for a total of at least 8.3 million Spanish speakers.

The 1980 census reported some 11.7 million individuals in the United States who spoke Spanish at least some of the time. Of this group, nearly 4.9 million were born outside of the United States. Some 43% of the foreign-born Spanish speakers were from Mexico, 19% from Puerto Rico, 8.4% from South America, 6.2% from Central America, 12% from Cuba, and 10.8% from other countries. If immigration is taken across time periods, from before 1950 until 1980, the Mexican total oscillates from a low of 32% in 1960–64 to a high of 53% in 1975–80. Puerto Rican immigration peaked in 1950–59, representing 45% of foreign-born Spanish-speaking immigrants, whereas the lowest period was 1970–74, when Puerto Ricans represented only 10.6% of the total. Similarly, Cuban immigration, which was only 3.5% of the total before 1950, shot up to 27% of the total in 1960–64 and 24% of the total in 1965–69, before dropping to 3.4% of the total in 1975–80 (just before the Mariel boatlift).

Among the approximately 5.7 million American-born Spanish speakers documented in 1979, about 52% had both parents born in the United States, 15% had both parents born in Mexico (12% had one parent born in Mexico), 7.6% had both parents born in Puerto Rico (1.4% had one parent born in Puerto Rico), and only 1.9% had both parents born in Cuba (0.6% had one parent born in Cuba).

In terms of geographical location, in 1976, of the roughly 11 million–strong Spanish-language origin group in the United States, 28.6% were found in California; 23.5% in Texas; 18.4 in the Northeast; 6.5% in Florida; 3.7% each in Illinois, Indiana, and New Mexico; 3.2% in Arizona; and 2.1% in Colorado. The remaining 10.3% were distributed among the other states. The mother tongue of these groups also varied widely: in California, 64% claimed Spanish as a mother tongue; in Texas the figure was 71%, in the northeast and in Florida 80%, in Illinois 73%, in New Mexico 63%, in Arizona 57.5%, and in Colorado 45%. The average claiming Spanish as a mother tongue in the remaining states was 56%. Taken as a nationwide average, nearly 69% of the group claimed Spanish as a mother tongue, and 30% claimed English.

The figures reported above do not correlate precisely with ethnicity because of the cross-generational shift from Spanish to English that has occurred in nearly all Hispanic communities within the United States. Veltman (1988) reports the well-documented trend for immigrants arriving young to adopt English as their primary language. Rates of English monolingualism rise sharply among immigrants who arrived in the United States before the age of 15. Spanish monolingualism rises most sharply in correlation with age in California, Texas, the Northeast, and Illinois, for the period 1950–76. In Florida and the remaining states, the switch to bilingualism was more pronounced even among immigrants who arrived at an older age. Among native-born Hispanics, the shift to English monolingualism or English-dominant bilingualism was most pronounced in Colorado, Illinois, the Northeast, and California. In New Mexico, Arizona, and Texas, this trend was not as striking.

The percentage of (identified and usually legally immigrated) Hispanic residents of the United States was about 6% in the 1980 census. New Mexico had the highest relative proportion (37%), followed by Texas (21%), California (19%), Arizona (16%), Colorado (12%), Florida and New York (9% each), and Illinois (6%). The Hispanic population averaged out across the remaining states was about 2% in 1980. In 1980, there were an estimated 11.6 million Spanish home speakers in the United States, some 5.3% of the total population. Of these, 28.3% lived in California (representing 14.5% of the population of the state). Texas had 22.5% of the Spanish speakers (19.2% of the state population); New York had 12.6% of the Spanish speakers (8.6% of the total state population); Florida had 7% of the Spanish speakers (8.6% of the state population); Illinois had 4.5% of the Spanish speakers (4.8% of the state population); New Jersey had 3.7% of the Spanish speakers (6.1% of the total state population); New Mexico had 3.1%

of the Spanish speakers (29.4% of the total state population); Arizona had 3% of the Spanish speakers (13.3% of the total state population); and Colorado had 1.6% of the Spanish speakers (6.7% of the total state population).

Data from the 1990 census document the increasing number of Hispanic residents, and of Spanish-speaking residents, in the United States. This census reported a total of some 21.9 million individuals of Hispanic origin, of whom 14.1 million were born in the United States. Individuals of Mexican origin constitute the largest single group: 13.9 million (8.9 million U.S.-born). Some 2.65 million Puerto Ricans live in the United States, as do some 1.05 million Cubans, of whom 298,000 are U.S.-born. Salvadorans form the next largest (self-reported) group: 565,000 Salvadorans appear in the 1990 census, of which 106,000 were born in the United States. The census reported 520,000 Dominicans (153,000 U.S.-born), 379,000 Colombians (98,000 U.S.-born), 269,000 Guatemalans (53,000 U.S.-born), 203,000 Nicaraguans (38,000 U.S.-born), 191,000 Ecuadorans (50,000 U.S.-born), 131,000 Hondurans (30,000 U.S.-born), 92,000 Panamanians (30,000 U.S.-born), 57,000 Costa Ricans (18,000 U.S.-born), and 48,000 Venezuelans (13,000 U.S.-born). Populations from other Spanish-speaking countries were considerably smaller.

The data from the 2000 census show a dramatic increase in the Hispanic presence in the United States—and probably also an improvement in counting techniques—showing a total of some 32.8 million Hispanics (not including Puerto Rico), or 12% of the national population. The chart and map in the appendix to this chapter, from the U.S. Census Bureau, illustrate some of the most important tendencies. Within the Hispanic population, the breakdown by national origin is as follows:

Mexico	58.5%
Puerto Rico	9.6%
Cuba	3.5%
Dominican Republic	2.2%
El Salvador	1.9%
Colombia	1.3%
Guatemala	1.1%
Ecuador	0.7%
Peru	0.7%
Honduras	0.6%
Nicaragua	0.5%
Spain	0.3%
Panama	0.3%
Venezuela	0.3%
Argentina	0.3%

Costa Rica	0.2%
Chile	0.2%
Uruguay	0.1%
Bolivia	0.1%
Paraguay	0.04%

Particularly noteworthy is the jump of the Dominican population to the nation's fourth largest Hispanic community, substantially concentrated in the New York City area (and extending into other urban centers of New York, New Jersey, and Pennsylvania) and in south Florida. The large Colombian and Ecuadoran populations are also striking, especially considering that these Hispanic groups do not form coherent neighborhood-based speech communities as do the more populous groups (as well as Hondurans and Nicaraguans in some cities). Moreover, Colombians and Ecuadorans in the United States come from a broad cross-section of geographical areas and dialect zones within their respective countries, thus making the retention of Colombian or Ecuadoran Spanish in the United States less viable than with many of the other varieties.

To give a sense of the demographic clumping of Latinos in the United States, the 2000 census recorded Latino populations of over 100,000 (in descending order) in the following cities: New York City (2.2 million); Los Angeles (1.7 million); Chicago (754,000); Houston (730,000); San Antonio (671,000); Phoenix (450,000); El Paso (432,000); Dallas (423,000); San Diego (311,000); San Jose, CA (270,000); Santa Ana, CA (257,000); Miami (238,000); Hialeah, FL (205,000); Laredo, TX (166,000); Brownsville, TX (128,000); Philadelphia (129,000); East Los Angeles (120,000); Oxnard, CA (113,000). (Additional census information can be found at www.census.gov/population/www/cen2000/briefs.html.) This list contains all of the ten largest U.S. cities except for Detroit, but also some "surprises" in regard to U.S. Latino demographics.

Not all Latinos in the United States speak Spanish, but some approximate figures of actual Spanish language usage can be deduced from census data, with due allowances for under reporting. The 2000 census reported 35.3 million Latinos (classified as "Hispanic") in the United States, of which 28.1 million or 79.6% reported using Spanish at home (with no indication of level of proficiency). Of the latter figure, 47.5% were born in the United States and the rest were foreign-born. The latest official population estimate for the Latino population is from mid-2006, indicating some 44.3 million Latinos out of a total U.S. population of 299.4 million; this represents a 25.5% increase in the Latino population from 2000. The U.S. population grew some 6.4% during the same interval, indicating that the reported Latino population is increasing at four times the rate of the overall U.S. population. As of the date of writing this chapter (May 2008), the estimated population of the United States is 303.5 million, or a 1.4% increase from 2006. Extrapolating a 5.6% increase in the Hispanic population from mid-2006 to mid-2008 gives an estimated total Latino population of 48.6 million. If one assumes the same ratio of reported Spanish-language usage as found in 2000, this produces a figure of 37.3 million Spanish speakers. The real numbers are probably higher, due to the well-known underreporting of minority groups, the fact that only speakers age 5 and older were considered in the U.S. census figures, and the fact that the increase in the Latino population from outside the United States is larger than the increase in the native-born group. Overall the United States contains approximately 9.3% of the world's estimated 400 million native speakers of Spanish, and depending on how speakers of Spanish are counted, is in a dead heat with Colombia as the world's fourth-largest Spanish-speaking nation (behind Mexico, Spain, and Argentina).

The Teaching of Spanish as a Second Language in the United States

Not only is Spanish the second language of the United States in terms of native speakers, but it is also the most frequently taught language, several times more popular in terms of student enrollments than its closest competitor (usually French, but in some regions of the country other languages). Matters were not always so; until the 1970s and in some areas well into the 1980s Spanish was regarded exclusively as a "foreign" language, which in the U.S. educational context meant a language exclusively designed for reading literary classics and for "high-culture" travel (e.g., to European museums and cathedrals). As such, Spanish was often overshadowed by French, German, and sometimes even Latin, all seen as having a greater impact on Anglo American intellectualism than Spanish, for whom Cervantes's *Quixote* was often the only cultural referent for prospective second-language learners.

Matters began to change with the growing awareness of Spanish as a language permanently embedded in the United States and essential to daily life in many regions of the country. The overwhelming predominance of Spanish over other foreign language classes at the university level is illustrated in figure 1.1, from the Modern Language Association (www.mla.org). These figures, representing surveys conducted in 2006, show that some 823,000 university students matriculated in Spanish language courses, out of a total of 1,577,810 foreign language students nationwide.

Some more representative data put the matter in even sharper perspective. At Penn State University Park (the main campus, not counting the other 23 campuses),

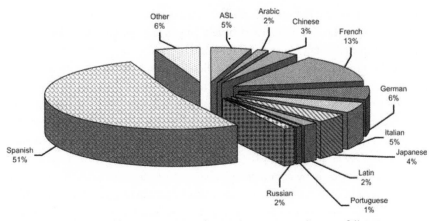

Figure 1.1 Percent of higher education foreign language enrollments, fall 2006.

where the typical language requirement is for three semesters (and where the first three semesters normally do not count toward majors and minors) for fall 2006 there were 152 sections of Spanish 1, 2, and 3 (the first three semester courses). This enrollment comes despite intensive efforts to encourage students to opt out of requirements through placement exams, and despite the availability of equivalent courses online or by correspondence, and it does not include classes for bilingual or heritage language speakers, which are taught at a higher level. This compares with 33 sections of the same levels of French; 22 of German; 18 of Italian; 10 of Japanese; 7 of Chinese; 5 each of Latin, Arabic, and Russian; 4 of Korean; 3 of Hebrew; 2 of Portuguese; and 1 of ancient Greek. Moreover, all sections of the first three semesters of Spanish were filled by the time classes began, which was not true of many of the other language classes.

Attempts at social engineering—for example, choking off the number of sections of Spanish in hopes that students will opt for other languages—have met with resounding failure. Students and their parents barrage departments, deans, university presidents, and state legislators with such vehemence that more sections of Spanish miraculously appear (although the waiting lists seem never to disappear). In other words, Spanish sections outnumber their closest neighbor by some four to one, and they represent more than half of all basic language class sections taught at Penn State. The figures are similar at other Big Ten universities. For purposes of comparison, at Penn State University Park there are 141 sections of the various flavors of obligatory freshman English—although to be fully accurate, it must be acknowledged that many entering students place into higher English classes, in which an additional 50 or more sections are available. Basic English courses, however, are required of all Penn State students, and usually more than one course, whereas not all colleges have a language requirement, and some college requirements entail fewer than three semesters.

Relative proportions vary widely at colleges and universities across the country, but the Penn State numbers are representative of national trends. In regions of the country where large Spanish-speaking communities are intermingled with universities, the proportion of students taking Spanish is even higher, whereas in colleges in rural inland regions far removed from Hispanophone populations, proportionately fewer students opt for Spanish. Even there, Spanish is invariably in first place, and usually by a wide margin. The reasons for the overwhelming push to study Spanish are many and are not always encouraging (Lipski 2002 offers some musings), but the fact remains that the combined secondary and postsecondary language programs produce an output of several million new learners of at least some Spanish every year, all of which adds significantly to the prominence of Spanish as an essential language within the United States.

Purpose of This Book

Throughout the United States, courses in Spanish for native or heritage language speakers continue to expand, and Spanish linguistics programs at colleges and universities offer courses on Spanish in the United States. In some regions, only a single variety of Spanish predominates, whereas in others, students and professors are faced with an array of regional and social variants of Spanish. Spanish of Mexican, Puerto Rican, and Cuban origin is represented by a substantial research bibliography, although monographic treatments suitable for classroom use are fewer.

Dominican and Central American dialects, which have risen to demographic and sociolinguistic prominence within the past fifteen years, are at best sparsely treated in the available bibliography. The purpose of this book is to compile in a single volume useful descriptions of the major varieties of Spanish found in the United States at the beginning of the twenty-first century. The treatment of each variety is of necessity brief and incomplete, as a result of limitations of space and bibliography, and of the inherent variability of some of the nation's largest and most diverse minority-language communities. Each of the following chapters contains a concise historical sketch of the events leading to the presence of the various Spanish-speaking groups in the United States, when necessary also making passing mention of important historical moments in the countries of origin. The most current demographic information is included, together with what is known about the sociolinguistic configurations in which each of the Spanish varieties is embedded.

Finally, each chapter contains descriptive material about the Spanish varieties, including phonetics, morphology, syntax, lexicon, and interactions with English and other dialects of Spanish. Although considerable material is drawn from the work of other scholars, the present author has personally conducted research—in varying degrees, depending upon the group—involving each of the varieties of Spanish treated in this book, thereby providing a measure of internal consistency. The following descriptions should be taken with the caveat that all research inevitably leaves some facets of language usage unexplored, or at best incompletely accounted for. The Spanish-speaking communities of the United States are dynamic entities, whose language is continually evolving through immigration, sociolinguistic modifications, interaction with English and other varieties of Spanish, and language-internal factors. A snapshot of these communities taken today will already appear to contain some inaccuracies when printed a year later, although to the extent that the original research has been thorough and well founded, the essential characteristics of the language will still emerge clearly. A treatise such as this one can never be definitive; it is simply a survey of major linguistic features, a bibliographic rallying point, and a call to arms for the next generation of scholars to continue the research on this country's Spanish-speaking communities.

2

Overview of Scholarship on Spanish in the United States

Introduction

The bibliography of research and scholarship on the Spanish language in the United States is large and is growing rapidly. It is also scattered across a wide range of monographs, anthologies, periodicals, and conference proceedings, spanning a period of more than a century. To a great extent, the course of scholarship on U.S. Spanish has followed the social and political currents that molded twentieth—and early twenty-first—century America, and it is most productively approached from the perspective of attitudes towards diversity and difference in a nation beset by war, depression, civil unrest, and the struggle for basic human rights. Each of the remaining chapters contains an appendix of fundamental bibliographical references, but given the inextricable bond between scholarship on U.S. Spanish and U.S. social history, the present chapter offers a necessarily brief but hopefully useful journey through the research milestones that culminate in the broad spectrum of scholarly writing about U.S. Spanish found in the first decade of the twenty-first century.[1]

Early Twentieth-Century Scholarship on U.S. Spanish

Writings on the Spanish language in the United States appeared sporadically in the late nineteenth century, in the form of newspaper columns and comments in popular magazines (e.g., Bourke 1896), but linguistic scholarship on U.S. Spanish as known in academe is a twentieth-century phenomenon. The fact that Spanish was not officially acknowledged, and that it was in effect a "captured" language at times under siege, had little impact on early scholarly treatments, with a few noteworthy exceptions.

In 1906 E. C. Hills published in the newly founded periodical *Publications of the Modern Language Association (PMLA)* an extensive article on "New Mexican Spanish," appropriately situated in a journal which then as now combines studies of the English-speaking "self" and the xenoglossic "other." Following this well-written but little-cited beginning, the most complete linguistic descriptions of a U.S. variety of Spanish came in the pioneering studies of Aurelio Espinosa (1909, 1911, 1911–12, 1914–15, 1925, 1946, 1975). Espinosa did most of his research before New Mexico became a state; as an exotic territory unknown to most Americans—even today people in other regions of the country believe that New Mexico is a foreign nation—New Mexico was unabashedly Spanish speaking. Espinosa's first scholarship, derived from his doctoral dissertation completed the same year, was published in the inaugural issue of the *Bulletin of the University of New Mexico* (1909), the organ of a university that itself was in its infancy and that was founded by and for the newly arrived Anglo American settlers. Two years later (1911) Espinosa published a popularizing description of New Mexico/southern Colorado Spanish in Santa Fe. Significantly, these seminal studies were written in English and directed at a non-Spanish-speaking readership; the scholarship is nonetheless first-rate, and at no point is Spanish referred to as anything but the natural and inevitable language of New Mexico. Astoundingly, in the year New Mexico gained statehood (1912), the president of the University of New Mexico, Edward Gray, published an article in the *University of New Mexico Bulletin* titled "The Spanish Language in New Mexico: A National Resource," assuming a stance that moved beyond academic curiosity-seeking and liberal posturing. That few others shared his views is exemplified by an article that appeared in another New Mexico journal just a few years later (Morrill 1918) titled "The Spanish Language Problem in New Mexico." This was the year after Puerto Ricans were granted U.S. citizenship, after having lived in political limbo for nearly twenty years.

In the first issue of *Language*—the journal of the recently founded Linguistic Society of America (1925)—Espinosa, the theoretical linguist, published an article on syllabic consonants in New Mexico Spanish, a tantalizing phenomenon that was not taken up again by linguists until Lipski (1993b) and then Piñeros (2005), by that time operating at a level of theoretical abstraction unheard of in the roaring twenties. Two years later Espinosa (1927–28) again published an article in

Language, this time a linguistic description of New Mexico Spanish based on folk tales, which reflected the founding of the LSA, with its strong admixture of anthropological orientations and descriptive linguistics. That New Mexico Spanish was not regarded as anything other than a de facto "national" language (taking "nation" in the demographic sense rather than adhering to the strictly hegemonic criteria of passport, flag, and military allegiance) is attested by the translation into Spanish of Espinosa's masterful works on the phonology (1930) and morphology (1946) of New Mexico Spanish in the *Biblioteca de Dialectología Hispanoamericana,* a prestigious collection of monographs edited by the linguists Amado Alonso (Spain) and Angel Rosenblat (Venezuela) and published by the University of Buenos Aires, all of whose other titles represented studies of Spanish as the indisputable national language of independent countries. Espinosa (1909–15, 1913, 1934, among others) also published specialized articles in Spanish in linguistics journals overseas.

The closest that Espinosa ever came to casting New Mexican Spanish as a language on the defensive came in 1917, in a mainstream historical anthology, when he wrote of "Speech Mixture in New Mexico: The Influence of the English Language on New Mexican Spanish." In the same year that the American Association of Teachers of Spanish celebrated its first annual meeting, Espinosa openly acknowledged that "race antagonism has always been very pronounced," and that although in the first years of the American occupation newly arrived Americans married Spanish women, "with the introduction of the railroads and the very rapid commercial progress of the last thirty years, . . . there has come a check in the race fusion and the mutual contact and good feeling between the two peoples . . . in the new cities . . . where the English speaking people are numerically superior, the Spanish people are looked upon as an inferior race." However, "outside of a few of these very recent American cities . . . the Spanish element is still the all important and predominant one, . . . and in these places the English influence in language, customs and habits of life is very insignificant." Although his predictions missed the mark geographically, Espinosa was surely prescient when he postulated that "some of the very isolated places like Taos and Santa Fe are yet thoroughly Spanish and will continue so, perhaps, for more than a century." Espinosa's comments came at a time when English-language schooling (for that matter schooling in *any* language) was just beginning to make significant inroads in the newly minted state, but his candid acknowledgment of racist repression is unique among early scholarship on U.S. Spanish. Most such research was written by out-group scholars for the consumption of other academicians who had yet to fully appreciate the fact that Spanish was now a permanent facet of the U.S. linguistic profile, not a struggling urban immigrant language that could—in the minds of working class Americans of the time—eventually be eliminated by ordering its speakers to "get back on the boat." The fact that New Mexico already contained an established and relatively prosperous Hispanophone population could give the state a respected spokesman such as Aurelio Espinosa in an era when most work on languages other than English in the United States was being done without the participation of in-group members. Much time was to pass before matters were to return to this configuration.

As statehood overtook New Mexico, other native or adopted New Mexicans continued to describe New Mexican Spanish—always in scholarly terms and directed at academic specialists. Kercheville (1934) offered a glossary of New Mexico Spanish terms, and McSpadden (1934) briefly described a rather unusual dialect spoken in an isolated New Mexican village. Juan Rael (1937), in a dissertation completed at Stanford University, described New Mexican Spanish based on a corpus of oral folktales, a brilliant work that unfortunately was never to slip beyond the pale of obscure university microfilm collections. It is perhaps not coincidental that although a brief note by Rael (1934) in *Modern Language Notes* (curiously published in Spanish) took a neutral tone, when Rael presented his work in the strait-laced *Hispanic Review* (1939, 1940) the title was the ominous "Associative Interference in New Mexican Spanish." The "interference" was not from English but rather was a language-internal analogy: *cuerpo espín <puerco espín* "porcupine," *nublina <neblina* "fog," *descudriñar <escudriñar* "to scrutinize," and the like, and the article is strictly philological as befits the journal's editorial standards. Nearly all the items mentioned by Rael are found in rural dialects of Spanish throughout Spain and Latin America. Nonetheless, the focus is exclusively on forms that were sure to arouse hilarity and derision among the normatively trained perusers of this periodical, and New Mexico Spanish was inadvertently portrayed to outsiders as an infelicitous patchwork of all the bleeding stigmata of *la lengua de Cervantes:* "it is quite remarkable that so many of the blends and malapropisms . . . should have found such a wide acceptance in New Mexican Spanish, in view of the fact that blends and malapropisms are generally considered individual peculiarities which are not repeated by others" (Rael 1939).

Post–World War I Scholarship: A Retreat into Isolationism

The 1930s and early 1940s saw a number of articles, theses, and dissertations dealing with Southwest Spanish centered on New Mexico; these almost inevitably dealt with perceived deficiencies of Spanish speakers, in school achievement, in learning English, and when taking intelligence tests.[2] Many of these studies were written by educators seriously preoccupied by the educational difficulties of

Spanish-speaking children, even though bilingualism was often hopelessly entangled with ethnocentric views of mental disabilities. Because the work was undertaken primarily by educators and psychologists, there was little denigration of the characteristics of Spanish, but the entire discourse was permeated with the notion that knowledge of Spanish was a cognitive liability. That such notions did not disappear with war ration coupons and Al Capone's gangs is illustrated by a 1950s study (Marx 1953) referring to the "problem" of bilingualism among Spanish-speaking Americans and a 1960s thesis addressing the "handicaps of bi-lingual Mexican children" (Marcoux 1961). One departure from this tendency was a brief article on Tampa Spanish (Ramírez 1939) published in a newly founded Puerto Rican journal.

Arizona achieved statehood even later than New Mexico, and when Anita Post presented her work to the professional organization American Association of Teachers of Spanish (now AATSP) in 1932 and published in the journal *Hispania* in 1933, Spanish was still the dominant language in most of the state. Aware of the growing Anglicization of Arizona, Post remarked, "It is difficult to predict what the Spanish of the future will be. Many archaic forms are disappearing; new words are coming in from Mexico; many more are being formed from English words. The Spanish of the future may be purer or it may disappear." In fact, neither has occurred: much of the archaic Spanish of the turn of the century has been supplanted by modern Mexican reintroductions, whereas bilingualism with English characterizes all but the state's most recent Spanish-speaking immigrants. Post's article briefly describes phonetic traits widely found in other vernacular varieties of Spanish and offers some oral folktales and songs; there is little in the article to distinguish Arizona Spanish from other rural dialects.

From World War II to Vietnam: Spanish Emerges as a National Language

The end of World War II and the immediate postwar years brought little research on Spanish-speaking groups (Woodbridge 1954). A few exceptional studies stand out in this period; in the middle of World War II, Keniston (1942) summarized research to date on U.S. Spanish based on a paper originally delivered in 1940. Porges (1949) studied Anglicisms in "New York Spanish"; Patterson (1946) provided information on the Spanish of San Antonio, Texas; and Díaz (1942) described Anglicisms in California Spanish.

Scholarship on Spanish in the United States generally followed the social and political contours of the two-decade gap between World War II and Vietnam. Several descriptive studies of U.S. varieties of Spanish were written during the

1950s and early 1960s; most were coolly objective and described dialects of Spanish with a degree of detachment that implied that they were entirely foreign and separated from the rest of American society by an impermeable membrane. Groups purportedly descended from "Spaniards" (implicitly white European, with no New World admixture) received ample treatment.[3] Several key articles, and many other theses and dissertations, although not unsympathetic to Spanish, described particular U.S. Spanish communities with the same insurmountable distance as did dialect studies of far-flung speech communities in foreign lands. Lozano (1961) was an early testimony to the fact that Spanish and English were in a symbiotic relationship throughout the Southwest, in a precocious article on code switching, while Tsuzaki (1963, 1971) and Beck (1970), although not overly helpful in defining English influence on Spanish, acknowledged the growing Hispanophone population in the urban Midwest. [4] Only Decker (1952), who described Puerto Rican Spanish in Lorain, Ohio, and Maravilla (1955), who dealt with Spanish in Indiana, antedated the Detroit study of Tsuzaki (1963), whereas Humphrey's (1943–44) was a very early precursor to work on midwestern Spanish. Kreidler (1958) continues the tradition of describing immigrant varieties of Spanish—in this case Puerto Rican Spanish in New Jersey—in terms of influence from English.

This decade witnessed perhaps the first commercially published textbook for native Spanish speakers in the United States: Paulline Baker's *Español para los hispanos* (1953), reprinted many times in the following four decades. Baker, teaching in rural New Mexico, offered the book as a supplement to traditional Spanish courses; discussing U.S. Spanish speakers she notes that *"estamos presenciando una decadencia lamentable del español de los Estados Unidos"* (we are witnessing a lamentable decline of Spanish in the United States), and *"Cada día se hace sentir más la necesidad de corregir los errores del mal español que se deben evitar y desarrollarse el buen uso del español que se debe emplear"* (every day it becomes more necessary to correct the errors of poor Spanish that should be avoided and to develop the proper Spanish that should be used) (introduction). The book, in her words, *"trata de los equívocos gramaticales o las faltas en el vocabulario de la gente de habla española de los Estados Unidos"* (deals with grammatical mistakes or gaps in the vocabulary of Spanish speakers in the United States) (introduction), and chapter headings include *"barbarismos"* (barbarisms), *"pachuquismos"* (Pachuco slang), and *"faltas gramaticales"* (grammatical errors). The book contains sections on letter writing and parliamentary procedure in Spanish, for setting up and conducting a Spanish club. Although seeming heavy-handed more than forty-five years later, many of the observations and recommendations contained in this book continue to figure prominently in Spanish courses for native speakers. In a 1975 bibliography Richard Teschner compares this work to the *Appendix Probi* in that it gives a wealth of authentic examples of vernacular speech all the while purporting to "correct" such language (Teschner, Bills, and Craddock 1975, 46).

The study of social registers of Spanish made its first appearance in the 1950s, invariably choosing socially marked underclass speech for individual attention. It was during the 1950s that Pachuco Spanish was first studied by scholars, almost all of whom were from outside the Mexican American community. Barker (1950) described Pachuco in Tucson as "an American-Spanish argot" (also the designation used by the German scholar Max Wagner 1953), a term that Barker extracts from Webster's dictionary as "a secret language or conventional slang peculiar to a group of thieves, tramps or vagabonds; or, more broadly, a cant or class jargon." Although not fully committing himself to the criminal or noncriminal connotations of Pachuco language, Barker inclines toward the former by citing informants' accounts that Pachuco originated among *grifos*, or marijuana smokers and dope peddlers in the El Paso underworld. It seems probable that these individuals, in turn, obtained a substantial part of their vocabulary from the *Caló* or argot of the Mexican underworld. He cites sources that claim that the language first reached Los Angeles when a group of El Paso hoodlums received suspended prison sentences in return for self-banishment. Although describing Pachucos as, in effect, youth gangs, Barker is judicious in describing the Sleepy Lagoon fights and the Zoot Suit riots and the kangaroo court justice that befell many of the participants. He also acknowledges that many young Chicano war veterans became disillusioned by the shabby treatment afforded by a society whose freedom they had risked their lives to protect. There remains an undercurrent of disapproval: "the habitual use of the argot, then, may be taken to indicate that the speaker is not interested in raising his social status above that of the laboring group. Such usage may also indicate his rejection of some of the conventional values of Mexican and American culture." Barker concludes—not without some justification—that "only when the goals of American society can be demonstrated as obtainable to him—perhaps then through such means as vocational education—will the pachuco as a linguistic and social type disappear."

Paulline Baker's textbook for native Spanish speakers in the United States (Baker 1953, 49) uncompromisingly refers to Pachuco language as "the slang of the dead-end kids," and cautions that *"A veces se expresa por medio del caló un muchacho de una familia buena y culta, . . . Pero nunca una señorita!"* (at times a boy from a good family may use caló slang, but never a young lady!). In addition to unequivocal *Pachuquismos* of the time, Baker also includes such tried and true Mexicanisms as *chamaco* (child), *feria* (small change), *Hórale!* [sic] (let's go), and even *chicano*. The chapter also contains an exercise titled *"Para ser tonto no es necesario estudiar"* (being a fool doesn't require study).

Lurline Coltharp's monograph *The Tongue of the Tirilones* (1965) was first presented as the author's doctoral dissertation in 1964, and then published the following year by the University of Alabama Press. Coltharp was the first woman to publish research on *caló,* which was then regarded exclusively as a male-oriented language: "It was and is a male language. The females who use it are the prostitutes of the area or the mates of the gang members. While law-abiding males use the language, no female of this level would admit that she even understood one word of the language. I have watched girls listening to boys who were speaking this *caló.* Their reactions assured me that they understood the language, but they were horrified by my suggestion that they help by taping. They were adamant that they neither spoke nor understood a single word" (32). Indeed, it was not until the work of the late Letticia Galindo (1992, 1995) that the role of women as speakers and researchers of *caló* was readdressed. Coltharp describes the El Paso Pachuco culture in strictly anthropological terms, stressing the poverty and alienation in the key neighborhoods covered by her research. In dealing with the topics of crime, drugs, sexuality, and gang activities, Coltharp largely refrains from value judgments, reiterating instead the rejection of El Paso's Chicano youth by the rest of American society. Although nearly all her informants were bilingual, "Spanish is rated as the school subject in which the children do most poorly. They are ashamed of the level of their Spanish" (30). In contrast to Barker, Coltharp cites evidence that *caló* had noncriminal beginnings, and "is in reality an inoffensive type of jargon that started during the time of World War I." In addition to serving as a shield by means of which criminal elements can verbally disguise their activities, "this language also provides protection to the law-abiding element. These people knowingly learn and use the language as an identification with the group so that they will not suffer physical harm at the hands of the unlawful element" (31). However, she does affirm that "this language was used originally as a cover for illegal activities, mainly fighting, smuggling and dope peddling" (32).

At the same time that William Labov was first struggling with the difficulties faced by out-group observers in obtaining linguistic material from inner-city black youth, Coltharp managed to secure the cooperation—if not necessarily the most authentic language—from her informants: "The fact that I am a female had surprisingly few drawbacks in this endeavor . . . during the recording and listening sessions I maintained a detached attitude as though I did not understand the language. Because of this, they did not have to worry about the propriety of what they were saying. In fact, they could maintain a male superiority in front of the uncomprehending female." Eventually Coltharp gleaned enough information to enable her to participate in the conversations and carry out a vocabulary survey. Although today's researchers might find Coltharp's advantageous use of stereotypes demeaning and insincere, the fact remains that the ensuing dictionary is both accurate and thorough—although by no means exhaustive—and *caló* is stripped of much of its threatening connotation.

That this was—and still remains—a minority opinion regarding Pachuco and contact-induced varieties of Southwest Spanish is revealed by considering other studies that appeared during the same time period. Braddy (1953, 1956, 1965) wrote of "Pachucos and their argot" together with "smugglers argot" and "narcotic argot" in Texas. R. J. González (1967) believed that Pachuco was becoming a creole (taking this term to entail language degeneration), a view also shared by Webb (1976, 1980). Griffith (1947) referred to the "Pachuco *patois*," whereas May (1966) wrote of "Tex-Mex," and Ranson (1954) wrote of *"viles pochismos"* (terrible *pocho* expressions).

In 1966, Jane and Chester Christian described Spanish–English bilingualism in the Southwest, couched in terms that may seem patronizing some three decades later, but which vividly paint the social dilemma faced by a population torn between maintaining its ethnic heritage and achieving economic survival through assimilation. In 1968 Joshua Fishman, Robert Cooper, and Roxanna Ma delivered to the U.S. Department of Health, Education, and Welfare the final report of a project titled "Bilingualism in the Barrio: Measurement and Description of Language Dominance in Bilinguals." A refined version of the report was published by Indiana University in 1971, and an expanded edition appeared in 1975. This study, based on the Puerto Rican community of Jersey City, New Jersey, exemplified the newly emerging intersection of sociology, linguistics, and quantitative analysis. It would not be an exaggeration to suggest that this study, together with the early work of William Labov, established the framework for much of the subsequent sociolinguistic research on Spanish-speaking communities in the United States. For the first time the full human scope of a bilingual community was coherently discussed by a multidisciplinary group of scholars, and language usage was integrated into a total community perspective; ghettoized Puerto Ricans were portrayed with the same care and equality as more prestigious groups of French, Scandinavian, and German speakers.

The Study of U.S. Spanish in the Era of Civil Rights and Civil Struggle

The 1970s was the decade when Chicano literature entered the canon with great fanfare, including Rodolfo Anaya's *Bless me Ultima*, Rolando Hinojosa's *Estampas del Valle*, Miguel Méndez's *Peregrinos de Aztlán*, Tomás Rivera's *Y no se lo tragó la tierra*, Alejandro Morales's *Caras viejas y vino nuevo*, Alurista's *Floricanto en*

Aztlán, Sabine Ulibarrí's *Tierra Amarilla,* and many others. It was also the time when the study of Spanish in the United States as a major scholarly pursuit was initiated.

In 1974 the United States Supreme Court handed down the landmark *Lau v. Nichols* decision. Bilingual education had come of age. One by one, individual states began to pass bilingual education legislation, and more important, they began to take concrete steps toward providing the services required by the law, the groundwork for which had already been laid by Title VI of the Civil Rights Act of 1964. School systems throughout the nation scrambled to cobble together bilingual education programs, and colleges and universities were besieged with requests to provide guidance and training in a discipline that still did not exist. Many Hispanists and linguists, myself included, were pressed into service to design courses, certify teachers, and ensure compliance with the new mandates. As desperate searches for bibliographies yielded meager gleanings, scholarship on U.S. Spanish began a gradual upsurge that was to become a torrent by the end of the decade, spurred in part by bilingual education programs but also by the growing power and social consciousness of underclass groups, many of whom spoke Spanish. Latino scholars entered the discussion in ever-increasing numbers, representing not only elitist perspectives but also the reality of the *barrios,* the migrant farmworker communities, and the ever-permeable southern borderlands. U.S. Spanish gradually ceased to be described as a museum specimen—complete with phonology, morphology, syntax, and lexicon—and was instead portrayed as a living entity vital to the communities in which it was used and as an instrument of social change in an America that was once again agonizing over the spectre of imperialism that never seemed to be permanently banished. Several journals that would become instrumental in spreading the appreciation and study of U.S. Spanish were founded in the 1970s: *Aztlán* in 1970, the *Revista Chicano-Riqueña* in 1973, and the *Bilingual Review/Revista Bilingüe* in 1974. The last two journals contributed immensely to scholarship on Puerto Rican and Cuban Spanish in the United States, as well as expanding the study of Mexican and Mexican American varieties. The *Journal of the Linguistic Association of the Southwest (LASSO),* later to become the *Southwest Journal of Linguistics,* began publication in 1975. The Southwest Area Languages and Linguistics Workshops (SWALLOW) were begun in 1971, and several influential sets of conference proceedings added to the bibliography on the linguistic behavior of Spanish–English bilinguals, beginning with Bills (1974).

The year 1973 also marked the founding of the Academia Norteamericana de la Lengua Española (North American Academy of the Spanish Language); its inaugural meeting was held the following year. At least half of the members were originally from outside the United States, and the list of academicians contained more literary scholars than linguists. That U.S.-born Spanish speakers or working-class immigrants were not the primary intended beneficiaries of the academy is suggested by the tone of the president's inaugural remarks:

> *Los españoles e hispanoamericanos residentes en este país forman un verdadero pueblo dentro de la gran familia norteamericana . . . este conglomerado étnico naturalmente se identifica con todas las modalidades idiomáticas del español que se habla en sus países de origen y necesita más que ningún otro un idioma castellano claro, libre de localismos y provincialismos, que le sirva como instrumento de fácil comunicación con sus hermanos de idioma y destino* (Spaniards and Latin Americans residing in this country form a true nation within the great American family . . . this ethnic conglomeration naturally identifies with all the idiomatic varieties of Spanish spoken in the countries of origin and needs more than anything else a clear Spanish, free from regionalisms and provincialisms, that serves as an instrument of easy communication with those who share their language and destiny) (McHale 1976, 91).

In 1976 the first number of the academy's *Boletín* appeared. The academy's own statement of purpose declares that the members will work for *"la preservación de la unidad, universalidad, pureza, belleza y mayor difusión del idioma español en los Estados Unidos"* (the preservation of the unity, universality, purity, beauty, and greater dissemination of the Spanish language in the United States) (Academia Norteamericana de la Lengua Española 1976, 99). The editor's introduction (Chang-Rodríguez 1976, 5–6) notes that *"los estatutos de nuestra Academia señalan una serie de tareas en defensa de la pureza de nuestro castellano"* (the statutes of our Academy set forth a series of tasks for the defense of the purity of our Spanish), and concludes by saying *"Ante estos múltiples retos lingüísticos, agravados por el actual prestigio del inglés, ofrecemos amor al castellano y nuestra propia interpretación de la ardua tarea de limpiarlo, fijarlo y darle esplendor"* (faced with these linguistic challenges, aggravated by the prestige of English, we offer our love of the Spanish language and our own interpretation of the arduous task of cleansing it, straightening it, and giving it brilliance). Despite these inauspicious words, the first number contains a bibliography of studies on U.S. Spanish (Beardsley 1976) and an overview of the phonetics of U.S. Spanish varieties (Canfield 1976), as well as the more usual fare of literary studies and lists of "approved" words. Subsequent numbers would reflect this ambivalence, combining objective linguistic studies with literary accolades and official pronouncements.

The 1970s was the decade when canonical works on U.S. Spanish became widely available for the first time, and when university departments began to include mention of U.S. Spanish language and literature. In 1970 Daniel Cárdenas published a brief document in the ERIC/Center for Applied Linguistics series describing the most salient linguistic characteristics of some U.S. Spanish dialects. The Fishman, Cooper, and Ma (1975) study of a bilingual Puerto Rican neighborhood first became widely disseminated through the Indiana University editions of 1971 and 1975. Also appearing in 1975 is Casiano Montañez's (1975) phonological study of New York Puerto Rican Spanish, a little-known monograph that gives sparse variational data. In 1972 Rosaura Sánchez, then a graduate student, published in a journal directed at socially committed Chicano intellectuals "Nuestra circunstancia lingüística," an impassioned if ingenuous description of rural and urban varieties of Chicano Spanish. It is the *nuestra* (our) of the title that presages what was to become one of the most compelling voices in Chicano social and linguistic scholarship, for Sánchez unabashedly juxtaposes her university training with her membership in a community whose language had been ignored or mistreated—by speakers of English and Spanish alike—for more than a century. Although having done master's work in Latin American literature and being in the process of writing a doctoral dissertation in the fashionable generative grammar paradigm, Sánchez took a strong stance in defense of the *circunstancia* (circumstance) of Chicano Spanish, using the intersection of her graduate training and activist credentials to add weight to her arguments. The fact that the article is written in Spanish is also of significance, because Sánchez observes (1972, 47):

> *Un pueblo que participa en la economía de este país sin gozar de los bienes materiales que disfrutan los adinerados o los de la clase media necesita un esfuerzo colectivo para cambiar una situación que puede compartir con gran parte del mundo. Nuestra lengua, lo que podríamos denominar un dialecto popular del español, nos une a un gran número de personas por todo el sudoeste de EEUU y por toda la América Latina. No vamos a dejar perder este vínculo, convirtiéndonos en un pueblo monolingüe, agringado. Ahora que nuestro idioma se ve amenazado con la desaparición, es imprescindible llegar a un acuerdo en cuanto a fines lingüísticos* (a people that participates in the economy of this nation without enjoying the material goods of the wealthy or the middle class requires a collective effort to alter a situation shared by much of the world. Our language, which can be called a popular dialect of Spanish, unites us with many people in the southwestern United States and in Latin America. We will not lose this link, becoming a monolingual gringoized people).

Sánchez's article became required reading for students of U.S. Spanish and is still included in core bibliographies of Chicano studies.

Craddock (1973) published a comprehensive article on U.S. Spanish in the *Current Trends in Linguistics* series, bringing the topic to the attention of linguists throughout the world and legitimizing the study of U.S. Spanish as a major research domain. The volume is titled *Linguistics in North America,* and Spanish is grouped together with English and French in the category "Major languages of North America." Reflecting the available bibliography of the time, Craddock makes brief mention of Puerto Rican, Sephardic, and Louisiana Spanish, makes even briefer mention of Cuban American Spanish (citing only articles on traditional Tampa Spanish), and gives considerable attention to Spanish in the Southwest. Craddock presciently speaks of "a good reason to expect a resurgence of interest in MA [Mexican American] Spanish" (475), while cautioning (476) that "unless a much larger proportion of the basic research and development is taken over by the Mexican Americans themselves, many current efforts to expand our knowledge of the varieties and vicissitudes of MA Spanish may be doomed to sterility." He was perhaps prematurely optimistic when he observed that "it may be possible to foresee the disappearance of the insane spectacle of our schools' systematic attempts to eradicate native speakers' Spanish while vainly striving to teach the language to countless unwilling and incompetent Anglo youths" (476). All in all, Craddock gives a penetrating review of previous scholarship on Southwest Spanish.

In 1975 the Center for Applied Linguistics (CAL), a growing clearinghouse for scholarly work on the languages of the United States, published the anthology *El lenguaje de los Chicanos,* compiled by Eduardo Hernández-Chávez, aided by Andrew Cohen and Anthony Beltramo (1975). The CAL had contacted Hernández-Chávez several years earlier, in response to a growing awareness of the need for a sourcebook on Mexican American language. The book contains twenty articles, ranging from the classic studies reviewed previously to more recent work, plus a thorough bibliography of works on U.S. Spanish and an extensive editors' introduction. For more than a decade this anthology served as the primary reader for courses on Mexican American Spanish throughout the country, gradually supplanted by studies with a more modern orientation. The latter, however, have never been anthologized, thus making *El lenguaje de los Chicanos* the most comprehensive collection of research on a single variety of U.S. Spanish ever published. The editors end their introduction (1975, xvii) with a plea for the integration of academic research and social concerns: "There is the strong feeling among Chicanos, not entirely unjustified, that much of the research in their communities has not been for the benefit of the communities themselves. It has benefited scholars who have used the results of studies in their publications or, less unkindly, it has been of general benefit to human knowledge. Even so, a flaw in much of the work is a profound lack of understanding on the part of researchers of the people and of their culture." Although the editors acknowledge that matters were changing even as they were writing these words, their concerns are still a relevant mirror in which to examine ourselves as we continue the research enterprise a quarter century later.

In the same year, Richard Teschner, Garland Bills, and Jerry Craddock (1975) published a comprehensive and richly annotated bibliography on the language behavior of Spanish–English bilinguals in the United States, also published by the Center for Applied Linguistics. This bibliography includes work on Cuban, Puerto Rican, Mexican American, and some isolated varieties of U.S. Spanish and constitutes the most comprehensive bibliography published to date on the Spanish language in the United States.[5] The compilers' introduction traces the evolution of scholarship on U.S. Spanish, which was only then appearing over the horizon in academic departments.

Also in 1975 Roberto Galván and Richard Teschner (1975) published their *Diccionario del español tejano,* the first commercially published dictionary of an explicitly U.S. variety of Spanish, not a dictionary of Mexicanisms published in Mexico, nor a glossary of forms found in a single Spanish-speaking community in the United States. In the second edition (1977), the authors included data from California, Arizona, New Mexico, Colorado, and even Florida, thus turning the dictionary into the *Diccionario del español chicano.* The year 1976 saw the publication of another important anthology, *Studies in Southwest Spanish,* edited by J. Donald Bowen and Jacob Ornstein (1976). The nine articles cover dialectology, grammatical systems, phonology, lexicon, and bilingual language switching, and many of the studies continue to figure in the core bibliography of U.S. Spanish. In the same year the volume *Bilingualism in the Bicentennial and Beyond* (Keller, Teschner, and Viera 1976) provided a diverse collection of articles spanning a larger range of issues and bilingual groups in the United States. Jorge Guitart (1976) published a scholarly treatise on Cuban Spanish phonology, in reality representing the first monograph on Cuban Spanish in the United States.[6] Hammond (1976) also used Miami Cuban-Spanish data to bolster a theoretical phonological model, whereas Domínguez (1974) offered a scheme for classifying dialect variants in New Mexican Spanish.

For linguists, sociologists, and bilingual educators, the 1970s marked the beginning of serious inquiry into the linguistic and social constraints on Spanish–English code switching, which had hitherto become regarded as a degenerate practice symptomatic of the undesirability of bilingualism and the confounding effects of language contact. It was during this time period that poetry and narratives incorporating code switching appeared prominently, as U.S. Latino writers emerged as a new literary voice. Intertwined language was a defining characteristic of many U.S. writers, creating a third code in defiance of the colonialist literary canon that had held bilingual authors hostage to a single language or at best to the use of one language per work. The dual languages of bilingual communities were studied as a coherent system rather than as language deterioration punctuated by slips and errors. A great number of individual studies rapidly transformed the perception of language switching from a sociopathic behavior to fodder for a mainstream research paradigm, a vehicle of literary expression, and an instrument of ethnic pride.[7] So powerful were the effects of this first major scholarly thrust into bilingual language switching that the next decade of code switching research was dominated by the Spanish–English findings from the United States, only gradually moving beyond the linguistic and social configurations of U.S. Latino bilingualism to discover the relative uniqueness of Chicano and U.S. Puerto Rican code switching, particularly in regard to the density and flexibility of intrasentential shifts. Although derogatory comments about Spanglish, *pocho,* Tex-Mex and other content-free misnomers for fluid code-switched language continue to this day to appear in the media and in public forums, it is now possible to rebut ignorance and bigotry with solid research that has finally trickled out of the sterile academic laboratory and into the consciousness of the more enlightened sectors of the general public.

By the mid-1970s the generative grammar paradigm was in full swing, and linguists were surging beyond the study of English and standard varieties of western European languages to incorporate data from regional and social dialects as well as less commonly studied languages. Harris (1974) employed data from Chicano Spanish (taken from some of the classic descriptive accounts) to refine theoretical proposals in generative phonology; Reyes (1976a) did the same for grammatical patterns, whereas Saltarelli (1975) included mention of analogical verb forms in Southwest Spanish in a comparative morphological analysis.

Yet another landmark of the 1970s was the publication of the first commercially successful textbooks designed to teach Spanish grammar and literacy to bilingual native speakers in the United States. As textbook publishers ventured into the "Spanish-for-native-speakers" market, the first steps sometimes resulted in smashed toes. For example, one of the early textbooks designed specifically for Spanish-for-native-speakers courses (first published in the 1960s, with subsequent editions stretching into the 1980s) states in the introduction that nonstandard speech is not to be despised, although it is recommended that "educated" language be used. However, throughout the book the author mentions *barbarismos* (barbarisms) and *expresiones viciosas* (terrible expressions), most of which are socially unaccepted Anglicisms, popular pronunciations, or morphological variants such as *asigún* (*según* [according to]), *truje* (*traje* [I brought]), and *maiz* (*maíz* [corn]). This book (Barker 1966) was written by an individual who learned Spanish as a second language, presumably in the strait-laced tradition described earlier. In a preface to this book, Christian (1971, vi) speaks approvingly of the author's stance: "In an era which attempts to be so linguistically democratic that the jargon of adolescents is as nearly 'correct' as that of the most universally recognized writer, and in which the academician feels free, like the adolescent, to create a jargon that only he and a few of his colleagues can understand, this book goes against one of the strong currents of contemporary culture. The author assumes that standards are proper to a language, and should be imposed upon students. This is still, in spite of protestations to the contrary, a universal process. When authorities in general were more nearly sacrosanct, teachers had stronger convictions regarding the propriety of their beliefs and viewpoints, and were less hesitant about making them clear." The "contemporary" culture referred to in this lament for the loss of canonical authority existed thirty years ago, at a time when few Spanish courses for native speakers existed, and even fewer teachers were so enamored of "adolescents' jargon." Today's bilingual educators, although not denying the importance of literacy in the educated standard dialect and of awareness of literary texts, see the home-versus-school language dichotomy as symbiosis rather than antagonism.

Although a few educators had addressed the issue of teaching Spanish to bilingual students in the United States during the 1960s, the convergence of linguists and educators in developing materials for university-level teaching of Spanish to Spanish-speaking students occurred during the 1970s.[8] In 1970 the American Association of Teachers of Spanish and Portuguese commissioned a report on teaching Spanish to native speakers in high school and college (AATSP 1970). Two years later the U.S. Office of Education (1972) issued a similar report. A number of school districts, especially in the Southwest, prepared reports and teaching materials directed at bilingual Spanish-speaking students.[9] In 1976 Guadalupe Valdés and Rodolfo García-Moya edited an important collection of articles on teaching Spanish to Spanish speakers in a U.S. setting. In the following year the first major textbook for bilingual students in the United States, Valdés and Teschner's *Español escrito* (1977a), was published. Valdés and Teschner (1977b) also published a bibliography of materials on teaching Spanish to bilinguals in the same year. *Español escrito* was, as the title indicates, primarily devoted to teaching literacy and standard grammatical forms to students who were already fluent native speakers of some vernacular variety of Spanish. Although written by authors based in the Southwest, *Español escrito* does not incline toward Mexican/Chicano Spanish in particular. Rather, in the introduction the authors briefly mention Mexican, Cuban, and Puerto Rican regional expressions, while stressing three key components of the pedagogical approach. First, they stress differences in style, underscoring the need to apply formal styles in formal contexts while fully accepting the home vernacular in the appropriate domains. Second, irrespective of phonetic differences of style, register, and region, there is a single correct spelling for Spanish words, which the educated speaker must master. Finally, bilingual speakers are warned that use of noninternationalized Anglicisms with interlocutors from other countries may impede comprehension. And all of this is stated without undermining the fundamental integrity of the home language, which as the authors point out, is not "bad Spanish," whatever else it may be.

Appearing at nearly the same time was Quintanilla and Silman's textbook (1978), which offered basic Spanish grammar and orthography as well as frequent Anglicisms but made no mention of the characteristics of Spanish varieties spoken in the United States. The authors suggest that the book be accompanied by a book of Mexican American readings when used in bilingual programs. De la Portilla and Varela's (1979) book is titled *Mejora tu español* and implicitly includes the by then substantial Cuban American population, many of whose members were already literate in Spanish and required less primary instruction and more fine tuning to achieve parity with educated Spanish speakers in other countries.

In 1979 the first conference *Spanish in the United States/El español en los Estados Unidos* was held at the University of Illinois–Chicago Circle. The presentations covered a range of topics and varieties of U.S. Spanish and provided the most comprehensive forum to date for discussing U.S. Spanish as a national and not simply a regional concern. The venue itself was striking, because Chicago (whose Latino population was then almost evenly divided between Mexican and Puerto Rican) is the quintessential city of immigrants, a reflection of the growing presence of U.S. Spanish as a language of recent immigration in addition to an already present imperialist inheritance. For several years the conveners of this seminal conference were deliberately held in northern cities—in Indiana, New York, Illinois, and Iowa—highlighting the fact that U.S. Spanish was not just the concern of the Southwest and New York City.

The 1980s and 1990s, U.S. Spanish Scholarship Takes Center Stage

Despite the increasingly fractious political climate in the United States, the 1980s produced some of the most incisive scholarship on U.S. Spanish. Fernando Peñalosa's monograph *Chicano Sociolinguistics* (1980) offered the balanced perspective of a sociologist who was also an in-group member, giving a full overview of the linguistic and sociocultural issues facing the Chicano community. The year 1981 saw the publication of two anthologies that became required reading for research and teaching on U.S. Spanish. Roberto Durán's *Latino Language and Communicative Behavior* (1981) contains original scholarship on Chicano and Puerto Rican bilingualism, including code switching and grammatical contact. In the same year, Guadalupe Valdés, Anthony Lozano, and Rafael García-Moya (1981) edited *Teaching Spanish to the Hispanic Bilingual,* a volume that specifically addressed issues related to language teaching in bilingual communities. Maintenance of Spanish, rather than acquisition of English, was the focus of this collection, which includes theoretical studies in dialectology, recommendations for classroom implementation of Spanish for bilingual student courses, sample course designs, and evaluation procedures. Although Spanish had been taught to bilingual students for decades, the unique sociolinguistic constraints on U.S. Latino bilingual communities were never fully acknowledged until the publication of this volume. During this decade several more Spanish textbooks for bilingual students appeared: Mejías and Garza-Swan's (1981) *Nuestro español,* Burunat and Starčević's *El español y su estructura,* and Marqués's (1986) *La lengua que heredamos.* All three go beyond the implicit Southwest focus of the first textbooks for Spanish–English bilinguals, and all continue to stress literary, standard grammar, elimination of or at least conscious awareness of Anglicisms, and cultural awareness of the Spanish- speaking world, within the United States and abroad. Except for the fact that they are written in Spanish and offer introductory comments aimed at bilingual students, these books are not easily distinguishable from intermediate-level textbooks aimed at second-language learners of Spanish. However, linguists offered explicit comparisons of U.S. Spanish varieties and dialects from other countries with an eye to legitimizing the pedagogical use of the former; Hidalgo (1987) is among the best examples, building on earlier work (e.g., García 1975).

In 1982 Jon Amastae and Lucía Elías-Olivares (1982) edited *Spanish in the United States: Sociolinguistic Aspects,* the first comprehensive sourcebook on a broad range of issues and dialects of U.S. Spanish, including Chicano, Puerto Rican, and Cuban varieties. Most of the articles are reprints of work done in the 1960s and 1970s, and the prestige of the Cambridge University Press imprint added further impact to a field of study that by this time had indisputably established itself as a major domain of scholarship and pedagogy. Particularly noteworthy are the reprints of several influential articles on code switching. In the same year Joshua Fishman and Gary Keller (1982) published the anthology *Bilingual Education for Hispanic Students in the United States,* which also contained reprints of recently published articles and reports as well as studies appearing for the first time. There is considerable emphasis on child language acquisition and language attitudes, in addition to studies on language variation and educational techniques.

In 1983 Rubén Cobos published his *Dictionary of New Mexico and Southern Colorado Spanish,* the first modern dictionary of a nonimmigrant variety of Spanish in the United States. In the same year Rosaura Sánchez published *Chicano discourse,* which combines a sociolinguistic analysis of Chicano Spanish with a scathing portrayal of the treatment of Chicano society by the Anglo American majority, situating Chicanos at the heart of a ruthless class struggle. Sánchez takes the stance that Chicano language and culture are under assault, and she views with pessimism the possibilities for significant linguistic and cultural retention in view of the heavy pressure to assimilate to Anglo American society. Cast in a neo-Marxist framework, Sánchez's monograph examines the root causes of Chicano language behavior, rather than confining herself to simply describing the end product. Her description of Chicano Spanish is considerably more mature than the "Nuestra circunstancia" article (Sánchez 1972), both in terms of descriptive detail and in encompassing the entirety of Mexican American language usage. She distinguishes among standard Spanish, popular urban Spanish, and popular rural Spanish in describing Mexican American speech, and treats all Chicano language usage from a discourse perspective. Language usage is set in terms of usage domains, integration into distinct strata of U.S. society, linguistic and cultural attitudes, and rural or urban origin. Particularly useful is her careful delineation of rural versus urban variants, based on field data. Sánchez convincingly demonstrates that not all Mexican American Spanish is archaic or even nonstandard—that despite relative socioeconomic disadvantage with respect to the Anglo American population, the Mexican American community contains a variety of styles and registers comparable to those used by monolingual native speakers of English.

Other influential anthologies, many stemming from the *Español en los Estados Unidos* conferences, were to appear in the 1980s: Bixler-Márquez, Green, and Ornstein (1989) and Green and Ornstein-Galicia (1986) with pieces on Mexican American Spanish; Elías-Olivares (1983) with articles on several U.S. Spanish dialects; Elías-Olivares, Leone, Cisneros, and Gutiérrez (1985), with emphasis on language planning and public policy; Barkin, Brandt, and Ornstein-Galicia (1982) on bilingual language contacts; Aguirre (1985) on Chicano Spanish; Wherritt and García (1985) on U.S. Spanish; McKay and Wong (1988) with articles on Cuban, Mexican American, and Puerto Rican communities in the United states, in addition to other bilingual groups; Ornstein-Galicia, Green, and Bixler-Márquez (1988) on several U.S. Spanish dialects; Blansitt and Teschner (1980) with several articles on U.S. Spanish; and Ferguson and Brice Heath (1981) with articles on U.S. Spanish.

During the 1980s most research on U.S. Spanish concentrated on Chicano and Puerto Rican varieties, with comparatively little work done on Cuban American

Spanish (what little research was done was still largely based on Cuban-born expatriates).[10] Noteworthy exceptions, including work on Cuban American communities, include Fernández (1987), García and Otheguy (1988), Solé (1979, 1980, 1982), and Roca (1988). As hundreds of thousands of Central Americans poured into the United States, a few studies on Central American Spanish in the U.S. setting became available.[11]

The furthest-reaching linguistic survey of any U.S. variety was conceived in the late 1980s and carried out in the following decade. Garland Bills and Neddy Vigil received funding from the National Endowment for the Humanities to collect materials for an atlas of the traditional Spanish of northern New Mexico and southern Colorado, a region in which relatively little demographic turmoil has occurred over the past three centuries. Over a three-year period, over 1,000 hours of field recordings were made, covering all Spanish-speaking areas of New Mexico and Colorado; focusing on persons of all age ranges and backgrounds; and including free conversation, lexical and grammatical surveys, stories, and oral folklore. Numerous reports have already emerged from the survey, and funding is now being sought to convert the recordings to digital format, which would facilitate the use of these recordings by other scholars.[12] Bills and Vigil (forthcoming) offer a comprehensive linguistic atlas of regional and social variation in the traditional Spanish of New Mexico and southern Colorado. Similar projects have been contemplated in other southwestern states, but to date this New Mexico/Colorado survey is the only comprehensive linguistic atlas of a language other than English carried out in the United States.

The decade of the 1990s was one of business as usual for the study of U.S. Spanish, although the publication of anthologies and monographs slowed down a bit. Several of the major publishers that had produced volumes on U.S. Spanish showed reluctance to accept new collections, arguing that the topic was no longer innovative, and therefore that matters were sufficiently settled. Among the anthologies that overcame that reaction are Bergen (1990) and Roca and Lipski (1993), which are derived from the *Español en los Estados Unidos* conferences; other anthologies stemming from conference presentations include Klee and Ramos-García (1991), a collection of articles on the sociolinguistics of the Spanish-speaking world containing articles on U.S. Spanish, and Colombi and Alarcón (1997), a collection devoted to teaching Spanish to native speakers. Silva-Corvalán (1995) and Roca and Jensen (1996) cover Spanish in bilingual contact environments, including the United States. Galindo and Gonzales (1999) offer an anthology of Chicana language studies. Coulmas (1990) contains overview articles on U.S. Spanish.

In contrast to the relative scarcity of U.S. Spanish anthologies during the 1970s and 1980s, several important monographs on the sociolinguistic setting of

U.S. Spanish varieties were published during the 1990s. Varela (1992) published the first comprehensive monograph on Cuban American Spanish. Silva-Corvalán (1994) models the highly complex Los Angeles bilingual community. Zentella (1997) covers developmental bilingualism among Puerto Ricans in New York, and Torres (1997) offers a discourse analysis of a suburban Puerto Rican community, the first monograph on suburban Spanish in the United States. Gutiérrez González (1993) provides a lexical survey of New York Puerto Rican Spanish. The vestigial dialects of Louisiana once more returned to the spotlight,[13] and the linguistic significance of semifluent bilinguals or isolated vestigial language speakers was also a recurring research topic.[14] Arnulfo Ramírez (1992) published *El español de los Estados Unidos: el lenguaje de los hispanos.* This book combines a brief overview of the linguistic characteristics of Chicano, Cuban, Puerto Rican, and Louisiana Isleño Spanish with more extensive chapters dealing with the sociolinguistics of language contact. Dominican Spanish, the burgeoning new kid on the block in the barrios of *Nueva York,* is beginning to accrete a research bibliography (e.g., García and Otheguy 1997), which has yet to grow in proportion to the Dominican-American population.

During the 1990s several of the principal textbooks of Spanish for bilingual students have come out with revised editions, and a number of important new books have been published. Some of the most noteworthy new books are DeLeon's (1993) *Español: material para el hispano,* Alonso-Lyrintzis's (1996) *Entre mundos,* Schmitt's (1997) *Nosotros y nuestro mundo,* and most recently Roca's (1999) *Nuevos mundos.*

Research on U.S. Spanish from Scholars Abroad

U.S. Spanish has typically not been a topic of scholarly interest in the countries of origin of the principal U.S. Hispanophone populations. Puerto Rican linguists on the island have traditionally not included mainland U.S. Puerto Rican varieties in their studies, possibly because they are discouraged by prevailing sentiments that stigmatize Nuyoricans for their language and cultural behavior. In the Dominican Republic, whose expatriates now rival Puerto Ricans as the largest Spanish-speaking group in New York City, "Dominican-York" speech has never been seriously broached as a research topic. Within Cuba the entire Cuban American population is regarded simply as expatriate counterrevolutionaries, ignoring the fact that the second and third generations of U.S.-born Cuban Americans have already emerged, speaking a language that is no longer the unaltered Spanish of Cuba. The Central American nations that have contributed the largest numbers of expatriates to the United States—El Salvador, Nicaragua, and Guatemala—have been too burdened by political, social, and economic challenges to address the linguistic dimensions of Central American communities in the United States.

Within Spain, and despite a growing interest in Chicano literature, research on Spanish in the United States has centered on demographic concerns, the need to preserve the language, and the maintenance or establishment of cultural links between Spain and Spanish-speaking groups in the United States. Peñuelas (1964, 1978) gives a sociohistorical perspective on Chicanos from a Spanish perspective, including mention of language, folklore, and literature. Montero de Pedro (1979) describes the remnants of Spanish language and culture in New Orleans. The first panoramic book on Spanish in the United States from a scholar outside of the United States appeared in 1980. This book was Ernesto Barnach-Calbó's *La lengua española en Estados Unidos* (1980). The focus is exclusively historical, legislative, and demographic; there are no linguistic details, and the author's stated intention is the defense of Spanish as a legitimate language in the United States.

In Mexico, where the term "Chicano" traditionally has negative connotations, interest in Chicano Spanish has not surprisingly been a late-blooming phenomenon. A noteworthy exception to this trend is the interest of Mexican dialectologists and sociolinguists, headed by Juan Lope Blanch (himself an expatriate Spaniard) in documenting the traditional Spanish spoken in the U.S. Southwest. The Universidad Nacional Autónoma de México (UNAM) held a conference in 1988 (already adumbrated in Lope Blanch 1987) at which plans were laid for systematic collection of samples of "traditional" Spanish dialects in New Mexico, Colorado, California, Arizona, and Texas. The results of the symposium are summarized in Lope Blanch (1990b). Lope Blanch himself made several trips to the U.S. Southwest in the 1980s, collecting speech samples and writing brief analyses of several dialects (Lope Blanch 1990a, 1990c). Although explicitly referring only to "traditional" Southwest Spanish, and therefore presumably leaving out the thousands of more recent Spanish-speaking arrivals and their descendants, the ambitious "Proyecto de estudio coordinado del español del Suroeste de los Estados Unidos" promises to place the study of Southwest Spanish on the same firm dialectological footing as the masterful *Atlas lingüístico de México* (Lope Blanch 1990). A possible shortcoming of this project is the fact that it is modeled after dialect atlases of sedentary populations, which allows stable regional varieties and isoglosses to be easily traced. With the exception of northern New Mexico and southern Colorado, the "traditional" (i.e., colonial) Spanish of the U.S. Southwest has been so completely overlaid by immigration from many regions of Mexico as to render the regionalist/isogloss approach untenable. As the data are collected researchers will face the challenge of developing dynamic models of U.S. Spanish that go beyond the classic European dialect atlas format, particularly in urban and suburban areas marked by a highly heterogeneous immigrant population.

Into the Twenty-first Century

Although dotted with a considerable number of maverick authors and topics, the bibliography on U.S. Spanish studies converges handily with the social and political undulations of the past century. As the nation iterated backwards into replayed scenarios of intolerance and xenophobia, so did scholarship on U.S. Spanish contract and retreat, but a true forward momentum was never lost. Every progressive societal thrust was accompanied by a surge in the quantity and quality of research on Spanish in the United States.

The following chapters contain specific references to each of the Spanish language varieties under study. To date no comprehensive overview of U.S. varieties of Spanish has emerged, although the articles on Spanish-speaking groups in the collection edited by McKay and Wong (1988, 2000) provide an excellent starting point. Information on the Latin American dialects brought to the United States through immigration can be found in Lipski (1994b) (from which, not surprisingly, much of the background for the following chapters was derived), Cotton and Sharp (1988), Moreno de Alba (1988), Lastra de Suárez (1992), Fontanella de Weinberg (1992), and the articles anthologized in Alvar (1996).

Notes

1. Lipski (2001a) offers a more thorough survey.
2. Ajubita (1943), Baugh (1933), Blackman (1940), Callicut (1934), Coan (1927), Conway (1942), Fickinger (1930), Flores (1926), Hanson (1931), Haught (1931), Herriman (1932), Hoben and Hood (1937), Jackson (1938), Johnson (1938), Kelly (1935), Mahikian (1939), Manuel and Wright (1929), Montoya (1932), O'Brien (1937), Page (1931), Sánchez (1931, 1934a, 1934b), Vincent (1933), inter alia.
3. For example, MacCurdy (1950, 1959) for Louisiana, Ortiz (1947, 1949), Hayes (1949), and Canfield (1951b) for Tampa, Friedman (1950) for Minorcans in St. Augustine.
4. For example, Bowen (1952), Hardman (1956), Ornstein (1951, 1972, 1975a), Cherry (1966), Galván (1955), Phillips (1967), Sawyer (1958, 1964).
5. Solé (1970) had previously included U.S. dialects in his bibliography of Latin American Spanish dialectology.
6. Castellanos (1968) and Lamb (1968) are unpublished descriptions of the first wave of Cuban immigrant Spanish.

7. These include Aguirre (1978, 1981), Anisman (1975), Barkin (1976, 1978a, 1978b), Dearholt and Valdés-Fallis (1978), DiPietro (1978), Gingras (1974), Gumperz and Hernández-Chávez (1975), Jacobson (1977a, 1977b, 1978a, 1978b), Lance (1975a, 1975b), Lipski (1977, 1978, 1979, 1982, 1985b), McClure and Wentz (1975), McMemenamin (1973), Pfaff (1979), Poplack (1980), Redlinger (1976), Sánchez (1978), Timm (1975), and Valdés-Fallis (1975, 1976a, 1976b, 1978, 1979).

8. For example, Barker (1966), Whittier Union High School District (1966).

9. For example, Corpus Christi Independent School District (1975).

10. Alvarez (1989), Attinasi (1978, 1979), Flores, Attinasi, and Pedraza (1981, 1987), Milán (1982), Pousada and Poplack (1982), Reyes (1981), Torres (1989), Zentella (1981a, 1981b, 1981c, 1983, 1985, 1988) for samples of the latter.

11. Lipski (1986d, 1989b) for Salvadoran Spanish; Peñalosa (1984)'s survey of Central Americans in Los Angeles stands as the only monographic treatment; Varela (1998–99) updates the still scanty bibliography). Lipski (1984b, 1989a, 1991a, 1992, 2000a) provides additional details.

12. For example, Bills and Vigil (1998), Vigil and Bills (1997), Vigil et al. (1996).

13. Armistead (1992), Coles (1991a, 1991b, 1993), Lipski (1990) for the Isleños; Holloway (1999) for the Brulis.

14. For example, Harris (1994), Lipski (1985b, 1986a, 1987a, 1987c, 1987d, 1993a, 1996b, 1996c), Martínez (1993).

3

Spanish, English, or . . . Spanglish?

Introduction

When referring to racial and ethnic minorities in the United States, a number of words and expressions once used frequently and insensitively have fallen out of favor, and they are now shunned in favor of more accurate designations. Words once openly spoken in reference to African Americans, Jews, Italians, Asians, Native Americans, Latinos, and those with mental and physical disabilities, and found in radio and television programs, popular literature, films, and public discourse in general, are now socially and politically unacceptable. One particular subset of these terms refers to racially or ethnically mixed individuals or groups, generally included in ersatz cover terms such as *half-breed*. Of the racial/ethnic terms that have survived the enhanced focus on civil rights and social conscience, only one refers simultaneously to language use and—by inference rather than by direct indication—to specific ethnic groups: Spanglish. An obvious blend of English and Spanish, this word has become the less transparent *espanglish* in the Spanish-speaking world. Although Spanglish has at times been used to refer to a wide variety of phenomena (see Lipski 2004b for a representative survey), in the vast majority of instances Spanglish targets the language usage of Latinos born or residing in the United States. In a few instances Spanglish is a strictly neutral term, and some U.S. Latino political and social activists have even adopted Spanglish as a positive affirmation of ethnolinguistic identity. In the usual circumstances, however, Spanglish is used derogatorily, to marginalize U.S. Latino Spanish speakers and to create the impression—not supported by objective research—that varieties of Spanish used in or transplanted to the United States become so hopelessly entangled with English as to constitute a "third language" substantially different from Spanish and English. This "third language" in turn is seen as gradually displacing Spanish in the United States, thereby placing U.S. Latino Spanish speakers at a disadvantage vis-à-vis their compatriots in Spanish-speaking countries and, ultimately, causing the deterioration of the Spanish language.

Within the United States the designation Spanglish is most commonly used by non-Latinos (or by Latinos who are openly critical of nonstandard language usage), in reference to the speech patterns of resident Latino communities. The most frequent targets are the nation's two oldest Hispanophone communities: those of Mexican and Puerto Rican origin. In the southwestern United States, Tex-Mex is often used (by non-Latinos) as a synonym of Spanglish, as is *pocho* among Mexican Americans. Spanglish is occasionally used to refer to the language spoken by Cuban Americans and increasingly by resident Dominicans; rarely if ever does one hear Spanglish used in conjunction with expatriates from Spain or Southern Cone nations, whose population is perceived as "white," thus suggesting an element of racism coupled with the xenophobia that deplores any sort of linguistic and cultural hybridity.

Despite the lack of empirical evidence, the view that Spanglish constitutes a specific type of language is widespread; one can find dictionaries, grammar sketches, greeting cards, t-shirts, bumper stickers, and an enormous number of editorial comments and references in popular culture, all suggesting that Spanglish has a life of its own.[1] One common thread that runs through most accounts of Spanglish is the idea that Latinos in the United States—and perhaps in Puerto Rico and border areas of Mexico—speak this "language" rather than "real" Spanish. Given that upwards of 50 million speakers are at stake, the matter is definitely of more than passing interest. The ambivalence and ambiguity that shrouds all things Spanglish is nowhere better illustrated than in definitions found in two of the most widely used and presumably authoritative dictionaries of the English language. The *American Heritage Dictionary* gives the generic and neutral definition "Spanish characterized by numerous borrowings from English." On the other hand, the prestigious and etymologically well-researched *Oxford English Dictionary* defines Spanglish as "a type of Spanish contaminated by English words and forms of expression, spoken in Latin America." Thus, from the outset, we are confronted with the ever-shifting and potentially insidious manipulation of hybrid terms designed to undermine the credibility and human capital of internally colonized groups.

In Search of the Origins of Spanglish

A transparent linguistic blend such as Spanglish is likely to arise spontaneously whenever contacts between English and Spanish are under discussion, and therefore, to assign the creation of this term to a single individual or event is unrealistic. Spanglish takes its place among a plethora of language-contact blends, including Taglish (Tagalog-English in the Philippines), Hinglish (Hindi-English in India), Franglais (mixture of French and English), Portuñol/Portunhol (Portuguese-Spanish), Guarañol (Guaraní-Spanish), and many others. Despite the unlikelihood that Spanglish has a unique parentage, the *Oxford English Dictionary* places the first known written attestation of this word—in Spanish rather than in English—in a setting that represents the quintessence of conflicting linguistic attitudes: Puerto Rico. The ambiguous status of Puerto Rico—at once a Spanish-speaking Latin American nation and a colony of the world's most powerful English-speaking society—has caused concern about the purity of the Spanish language and an ambivalence toward the English language unmatched in the Spanish-speaking world. The number of popular works that purport to describe and decry the "contamination" of Puerto Rican Spanish by English is enormous; serious linguistic studies are much fewer, but a pair of prominent monographs have kept the debate alive. The Spanish linguist Germán de Granda (1972), who resided briefly in Puerto Rico, described the *transculturación* (transculturation) of Puerto Rican Spanish in terms that would give credence to the spread of an epidemic. Granda is by no means a purist; his studies of Afro-Hispanic creole languages and the languages of Equatorial Guinea are legendary, as is his work with Paraguayan and Andean varieties of Spanish, all based on rigorous fieldwork and a deep sense of appreciation and respect for the communities in which he lived. Granda's perspective on Puerto Rican Spanish therefore cannot be summarily dismissed as an elitist neocolonial diatribe, although few scholars of Puerto Rican sociolinguistics would agree with his portrayal. The exiled Cuban linguist Paulino Pérez Sala (1973), a professor at a Puerto Rican university, spoke of the *interferencia lingüística del inglés* (linguistic interference from English) in Puerto Rican Spanish. Such interference no doubt occurs, especially under the avalanche of English-language advertising, technical language, and school discourse, but many of Pérez Sala's examples are typical of English-dominant bilinguals, and not of the Spanish-dominant population of the island.[2]

The term Spanglish (*espanglish* in Spanish) appears to have been coined by the Puerto Rican journalist Salvador Tió (1954) in a newspaper column first published in 1952. Tió—who certainly considers himself the inventor of this word (an opinion largely shared by others in Latin America)—was concerned about what he felt to be the deterioration of Spanish in Puerto Rico under the onslaught of English words, a situation that led him to wage a campaign against it with a series of polemical and satirical articles over the course of more than half a century. Tió (1954, 60) stated his position unashamedly: *"No creo ni en el latín ni en el bilingüismo. El latín es una lengua muerta. El bilingüismo, dos lenguas muertas"* (I don't believe either in Latin or in bilingualism. Latin is a dead language, bilingualism, two dead languages). Many of Tió's examples are legitimate borrowings from English—some in unassimilated form—that are found in modern Puerto Rican speech, most of which refer to consumer products marketed in the United States or to aspects of popular youth culture. But Tió felt that Puerto Rican Spanish could suffer a far worse fate than simply absorbing foreign borrowings—which, after all, had been occurring in Spanish for more than a thousand years. Evidently not understanding that creole languages are formed under conditions far different from the bilingual borrowing found in Puerto Rico, he examined Papiamentu—an Afro-Iberian creole language spoken mainly in Aruba and Curaçao—and concluded that it was a degenerate form of Spanish. He warned that the same fate could befall Puerto Rican Spanish (Tió 1992, 91):

"Si en ese estado de postración cayó el español de Curazao y Aruba, también podría ocurrir algo similar en Puerto Rico si no se extrema el rigor para evitarlo. Puede tardar más tiempo por muchas razones pero si le ha ocurrido a otras lenguas en todos los continentes no hay razón para creer que somos indemnes al daño" (If the Spanish of Curaçao and Aruba could sink to such depths, something similar could occur in Puerto Rico if stiff measures are not taken to avoid it. This could take longer for various reasons, but if it has happened to other languages in every continent, there is no reason to believe that we are exempt from this danger) (Tió 1992, 25).

Tió's early article also contained humorous Spanglish words of his own invention, which were not used at the time and have not been used since, thereby creating some confusion between legitimate examples of language contact and sarcastic parodies. Although Tió had lived in New York City, and therefore had experienced firsthand true bilingual contact phenomena, he accepted uncritically others' parodies of Spanish-English interaction (Tió 1992, 91): *"[El español] se pudre en la frontera nuevo-mejicana donde, como dice* H. L. Mencken *en su obra* The American Language, *dos nuevo-mejicanos se saludan con esta joya de la burundanga lingüística: '¡Hola amigo! ¿Cómo le how do you dea?' 'Voy very welldiando, gracias'"*

(Spanish is rotting on the New Mexican border [*sic*] where, as H. L. Mencken says in *The American Language,* two New Mexicans greet each other with this gem of linguistic nonsense. . . .). This example, from Mencken (1962, 650–51), does not actually come from the latter author, whose other observations on Spanish in the United States and its influence on English are in general well documented and factually accurate. Rather, Mencken quotes (uncritically, it appears) a "recent explorer" (McKinstry 1930, 336), whose concern for linguistic accuracy was highly questionable. McKinstry wrote during a time when Mexican-bashing was an acceptable literary pastime, and although his witty anecdotes about his linguistic experiences on the U.S.-Mexican border suggest that he actually spoke Spanish, his factual account of borrowed Anglicisms stands in stark contrast to his mocking account of the language skills of Mexicans living near the border:

> While the Mexican of the border appropriates the words of his neighbor in a truly wholesale manner, there is neither hope nor danger that he will ever become English-speaking. It is only the bare words that are adopted. They are woven ingeniously into a fabric of grammar and pronunciation which remains forever Mexican. Although every other word your Nogales or Juárez peon uses may be English, he could not, to save his sombrero, put them together into a sentence intelligible to an American, that is, beyond such simple household phrases as *all right* and *goddam.* . . . This mongrel jargon of the border is naturally shocking to the ears of the well-bred Mexican of the interior.

By uncritically quoting this crude parody together with legitimate examples of borrowing and calquing, Tió (and Mencken) contributed to the false impression of a "mongrel" language teetering on the brink of total unintelligibility.

Despite his concern about the status of Spanish in Puerto Rico—and by extension in other areas where English threatens to overwhelm it—Tió (1954, 64) offers his own version of Spanglish, a travesty of bilingual behavior that sets the stage for later debates on Spanglish. As an example, Tió creates new verbs based on whimsical convergences between Spanish and English:

> Tree—*árbol.* To climb—*trepar.* To climb a tree—*treepar un árbol. ¿Por qué no formar una palabra que exprese en ambos idiomas el mismo sentimiento? Para nosotros que somos bilingües la cosa es clara. Se acuña una palabra nueva y se atacuña bien. Y ha nacido un nuevo idioma . . . Treepar. He aquí una palabra llena de movimiento. Es una especie de taquigrafía lingüística cuya única dificultad consiste en que es más rápida que el pensamiento. Es una palabra que puede expresar, en dos idiomas a un tiempo, no ya dos palabras, dos oraciones completas. Y lo grande de esta idea, lo original, es que se pueden conjugar a un tiempo, no dos verbos, sino dos pensamientos completos en dos lenguas distintas. La lengua queda recogida en el verbo, y paradoja, se acaba la verborrea . . . Para decir "Me subí a un árbol"* (I climbed a

tree), *basta decir: treepé.* (Why not form a word that expresses the same feeling in both languages? For us bilinguals it's clear. You coin a new word and "rub it in." And so a new language is born . . . *Treepar.* Here's a word full of movement. It's a kind of linguistic shorthand whose only problem is that it is faster than thought. It's a word that can express in two languages at the same time not just two words, but two complete sentences. And the best part, the most original, is that one can conjugate at the same time not two verbs but two complete thoughts in two different languages. The language is contained in the verb, and, paradoxically, verbage is eliminated . . . To say "I climbed a tree" it's enough to say *treepé*).

Tió (1954, 64–65) continues in this fashion, creating other neologisms via similar leaps of logic; for example "Rocking chair—*sillón. De ahí formamos el sustantivo:* rollón *y el verbo:* rollar (to rock—*mecerse*) . . . *y para decir:* "I get up from the rocking-chair" (*Yo me levanto del sillón), basta decir: "Yo me desenrollo."* (From this we form the noun *rollón* and the verb *rollar* . . . and to say "I get up from the rocking-chair" one just says "I unroll.")

Tió (1954, 65) then offers some lexical neologisms, for example from *piscina/swimming pool* come *pipool, polina, swicina;* from *mattress/colchón/colchoneta* come *machón/machoneta;* the mixture of *pull* and *influencia* gives *opulencia,* and so on. Tió—perhaps inspired by McKinstry's grotesque parody—then illustrates what a dialogue in such Spanglish might sound like (Tió 1954, 65): *Espiblas Espanglish? — Yi, Minor. Yi* is a blend of *yes* and *sí; espiblar* combines *speak* and *hablar,* and *Minor* is derived from *Mister* and *Señor.* Tió then echoes the affirmation that anyone can speak Spanglish by just making things up as he/she goes along. This xenophobic diatribe is frequently voiced in reference to creole languages—such as Papiamentu, Lesser Antilles French Creole (known locally as *patois)* and Philippine Creole Spanish (known as *Chabacano)*—which are instantly created by simply "mixing together" two or more languages in a polyglot free-for-all. For Tió (1954, 65),

Éste es un idioma que se aprende en tres lecciones. El resto lo pueden hacer ustedes por su cuenta. Por su cuenta y riesgo. . . . Esta lengua que surge del choque de dos culturas es la única solución al problema de las Américas. No nos entenderemos mientras no hablemos el mismo idioma. . . . Hay que crear una nueva lengua que no se preste a engaños. Por ahora sólo está en teoría, la teoría del "espanglish," la teoría para acabar con el bilingüismo en nombre del bilingüismo. (This is a language that can be learned in three lessons. You can do the rest on your own. On your own and at your own risk. . . . This language that arises from the clash of two cultures is the only solution to the problem of the Americas. We will never understand one another as long as we don't speak the same language. . . . We must create a new language that can't be tampered with. For now this language only exists in theory, the "Spanglish" theory, the theory that will get rid of bilingualism in the name of bilingualism.)

Although Tió offers this wry "if you can't beat 'em, join 'em" pseudosolution to language and culture clash, his bitter refutation of English comes through clearly. Tió's many remarks about Spanglish—scattered across several articles and four decades—present an ambiguous picture. On the one hand, Tió shared with many other Puerto Rican intellectuals of the time the fear that U.S. cultural imperialism and the crushing weight of English would eventually displace a language that had landed with Columbus and had survived unaltered until only a few decades previously. After all, Tió could remember the English-only schools that arrived with the American occupation of Puerto Rico. His first comments on Spanglish were written just after Puerto Rico had finally wrested from the U.S. government the right to elect its own governor and representatives. By the middle of the twentieth century, worldwide Spanish already contained numerous well-integrated Anglicisms, and Puerto Ricans used them even more—including those that had entered via the American school system, consumer advertising, and American businesses located in Puerto Rico, and those resulting from the increasing tide of Puerto Ricans who emigrated to the mainland to work and returned with new English expressions. All these Anglicisms were either assimilated unaltered—except for the basic phonetic adaptations in such words as *welfare, teacher, míster,* and *miss*—or were morphologically adapted to Spanish patterns (*leak > liquiar, spell > espeliar*).

False cognates might become true cognates in a language-contact environment (whence *aplicar* could mean "to apply for a job" and *registrar* "to register for a class"), the use of the gerund or progressive verb tenses might be more frequent than in monolingual Spanish (e.g., *le estamos enviando el paquete mañana* instead of *le enviamos/enviaremos el paquete mañana*), and occasional idiomatic expressions from English might be calqued into Spanish—on the mainland but seldom on the island, except among returning Nuyoricans (e.g., *llamar para atrás* calqued from "to call back").[3] But nowhere did one find—in Puerto Rico or elsewhere among Spanish speakers in contact with English—bizarre linguistic chimeras like *treepar* (from English *tree* and Spanish *trepar*), *rollón* (from *rocking chair* and *sillón*), *pipool* (from *swimming pool* and *piscina*), or *machoneta* (from *mattress* and *colchoneta*). Tió had clearly never heard such items, nor was there any danger of his ever hearing them. He deftly avoided any discussion of true language-contact phenomena, which have enriched Spanish for at least thirteen centuries, in favor of creating a xenoglossic straw man emblazoned with the epithet Spanglish, with which to bludgeon those who might not share his abhorrence of Spanish-English bilingualism. Tió, like McKinstry and scores of nameless commentators before and since, deliberately invented pseudo-bilingual monstrosities into order to denigrate legitimate bilingual speech communities individually and collectively. For

McKinstry the prime motivation was racist supremacy: Mexicans were regarded as inferior to Anglo Americans, and hence incapable of adequately acquiring English but all too capable of losing their grip on their own native language once confronted—even at a distance and separated by a national border—with the English-language juggernaut. Tió may well have harbored racist sentiments against Anglo Americans—his scorn for the Afro American language Papiamentu provides a possible bit of evidence—but his harshest broadsides are directed at his fellow citizens for their failure to embrace monolingualism, which for Tió was a primordial virtue. Tió foreshadows a viewpoint that would later be taken up in the continental United States by expatriate intellectuals like Roberto González Echeverría (to be discussed below): namely, that even educated Latinos willingly allow their language to be overrun by English in the mistaken view that this increases their upward social mobility.

Other Viewpoints and Definitions

But not all regard Spanglish with animosity. Nash (1970, 223–25) offers a somewhat different definition and set of observations on Spanglish in Puerto Rico:

> In the metropolitan areas of Puerto Rico, where Newyorricans play an influential role in the economic life of the island, there has arisen a hybrid variety of language, often given the slightly derogatory label of Spanglish, which coexists with less mixed forms of standard English and standard Spanish and has at least one of the characteristics of an autonomous language: a substantial number of native speakers. The emerging language retains the phonological, morphological, and syntactic structure of Puerto Rican Spanish. . . . Spanglish as defined here is neither language containing grammatical errors due to interference nor intentionally mixed language.

Most of Nash's examples represent the sort of lexical borrowing found in all bilingual contact situations.

In a recent survey of attitudes and inquiries about Spanish in the United States, Fairclough (2003, 187) defines Spanglish as simply *"la mezcla del inglés y del español"* (the mixture of English and Spanish). Odón Betanzos Palacios (2001, 2), president of the North American Academy of the Spanish Language, is of the *opinión* that

> *El* espanglish *y el* engliñol *han sido y son dos problemas normales en comunidades donde conviven los de lengua española y los estadounidenses, comunidades en las que sus hablantes*

son monolingües y tienen necesidad de comunicarse. El de lengua española ha recogido palabras del inglés, de las que entiende su significado y, sencillamente, las españoliza; igualmente hará con las formas verbales y así, en su variedad de injertos, se aproximará a la comunicación con el de la otra lengua . . . el espanglish *es, sólo, medio de comunicación temporal . . . Creo que [los que promueven la enseñanza del spanglish] no se han percatado del enorme error que cometen al querer hacer de amplitudes y querer enseñar una jerga de comunidades que ni siquiera podrán entender otras comunidades de sus cercanías.* (Spanglish and Engliñol have been and continue to be two normal problems in communities where Spanish speakers and Americans live together. The Spanish speaker has taken those English words whose meaning is understood and, simply, has Hispanized them; the same is done with verbal forms and with such hybrids, and in this way, some approximation to communication in the other language will be achieved . . . Spanglish is only a temporary means of communication . . . I believe that those who promote the teaching of Spanglish are not aware of the huge mistake in teaching this jargon that cannot even be understood in neighboring communities.)

Adopting an anti-imperialistic stance and considering Spanglish to consist primarily of the use of Anglicisms by Spanish speakers, the distinguished literary critic Roberto González-Echeverría (1997, 1) laments the negative implications of Spanglish:

Spanglish, the composite language of Spanish and English that has crossed over from the street to Hispanic talk shows and advertising campaigns, poses a grave danger to Hispanic culture and to the advancement of Hispanics in mainstream America. Those who condone and even promote it as a harmless commingling do not realize that this is hardly a relationship based on equality. Spanglish is an invasion of Spanish by English. The sad reality is that Spanglish is primarily the language of poor Hispanics, many barely literate in either language. They incorporate English words and constructions into their daily speech because they lack the vocabulary and education in Spanish to adapt to the changing culture around them. Educated Hispanics who do likewise have a different motivation: Some are embarrassed by their background and feel empowered by using English words and directly translated English idioms. Doing so, they think, is to claim membership in the mainstream. Politically, however, Spanglish is a capitulation; it indicates marginalization, not enfranchisement.

This condemnation of Spanglish as a manifestation of defeat and submissiveness by Hispanic communities in the United States recalls Odón Betanzos Palacios's lament, when he speaks of *"el problema de algunos hispanos en Estados Unidos, de los que no han podido ni tenido la oportunidad de aprender ninguna de las dos lenguas (español e inglés)"* (the problem of some Hispanics in the United States, who have not had the opportunity to learn either of the languages [Spanish or English]). In another commentary on Spanglish, the Spaniard Joaquim Ibarz (2002, 3) offers the following observation, which clearly confuses regional and social dialects, youth slang, and language-contact phenomena:

> *Hablar medio en español, medio en inglés, no es tan descabellado si se piensa en la mezcla de las culturas, las migraciones y todas las circunstancias que han hecho que estos dos idiomas puedan combinar. . . . La lengua resultante del mestizaje entre español y el inglés, conocida como "spanglish," es hablada por más de 25 millones de personas a ambos lados de la frontera entre México y Estados Unidos, zona en la que residen cerca de 40 millones de latinos. La mayoría utiliza formas diferentes de este dialecto, que cambia según el país de origen de quién lo utiliza, como el cubonics de Miami, el nuyorrican de los puertorriqueños de Manhattan y el caló pachuco de San Antonio.* (Speaking half in Spanish, half in English, isn't so crazy if we think about cultural mixture, migrations, and other circumstances that have brought these two languages together. . . . The language resulting from the mixture of Spanish and English, known as "Spanglish," is spoken by more than 25 million people on both sides of the U.S.-Mexican border, an area in which some 40 million Latinos live. Most use some variety of this dialect, which changes according to its country of origin, like Cubonics in Miami, Nuyorican for Puerto Ricans in Manhattan, and Pachuco caló in San Antonio).

Another Spaniard, Xosé Castro (1996, 3), gives a similar appraisal:

> *El* espanglish *tiene una lógica forma de ser y un origen explicable y comprensible. Su función es claramente comunicadora, pero sólo puede darse cuando existe una carencia de vocabulario en alguna de las dos partes que forman un diálogo. Cuando existe alguna duda o algo que obstaculice la comprensión, se echa mano de la versión inglesa, idioma que ambos interlocutores comprenden, y la comunicación, por fin, se completa. . . . La marginalidad del* espanglish *. . . excluye al hispano que no entiende inglés, y al angloparlante que no entiende español. Se restringe, por tanto, a una reducida comunidad de hablantes.* (Spanglish has its own logic and a logically explained origin. It serves a clear communicative function, but it can only occur when one of the dialogue partners lacks a vocabulary item. When in doubt, to eliminate any obstacle to communication, one reverts to the English version, understood by both interlocutors, and communication takes place. . . . The marginal status of Spanglish . . . excludes Latinos who don't understand English and English speakers who don't understand Spanish. It is therefore restricted to small speech communities.

For the Cuban linguists Valdés Bernal and Gregori Tornada (2001, 5), Spanglish is in essence a phenomenon peculiar to Puerto Ricans living in New York, but these linguists, unable to travel to Miami to observe the situation firsthand, assert that

> *El* spanglish *queda para los puertorriqueños en sus barrios neoyorquinos. Sin embargo, esto ya es historia, y el spanglish, como era de esperar, ha hecho su aparición en Miami entre la nueva generación de los cubanoamericanos—los yacas—quienes se "divierten" hablando esta variedad de lengua "en parte español anglosajonizado, en parte inglés hispanizado, y en parte giros sintácticos, que usan niños y adultos, a veces casi sin darse cuenta."* (Spanglish was used by Puerto Ricans in their New York neighborhoods. But this is now history, and Spanglish, as might be expected, has made an appearance in Miami among the new generation of Cuban Americans—*yacas*—who "mess around" speaking this dialect, which is "partly Anglicized Spanish, partly Hispanicized English, and partly syntactic combinations used unconsciously by children and adults.")

Most of the cited examples include code switching, but in some cases, the results of language erosion among increasingly English-dominant bilinguals is taken as an indicator of Spanglish (for example, the use of the familiar pronoun *tú* in conjunction with deferential address forms such as *señor alcalde* [honorable mayor]).

A website devoted to the teaching of Spanish to Americans defines Spanglish as "an entity that is not quite English, not quite Spanish but somewhere in between; the 'language' spoken by an English-speaking person when attempting to speak in Spanish."[4] In a few cases (e.g., García Rojas and Molesworth 1996), Spanglish is understood to be spoken by native speakers of Spanish whose second language is English, a phenomenon that Nash (1971) has dubbed "englañol." Finally, the president of the Spanish Royal Academy (RAE) has declared succinctly that *"el 'spanglish' no es un idioma."* (Spanglish is not a language.)

Many professional educators have viewed terms like Spanglish with alarm. Milán (1982, 202–3) specifically recommends that researchers and educators in New York City refrain from using the term "Spanglish" and use instead neutral designations such as "New York City Spanish." Acosta-Belén (1975, 151) observes that "speakers of the nondefined mixture of Spanish and/or English are judged as 'different' or 'sloppy' speakers of Spanish and/or English, and are often labeled verbally deprived, alingual, or deficient bilinguals because supposedly they do not have the ability to speak either English or Spanish well." On the other hand, the linguist and Latina activist Zentella (1997, 82) demonstrates that younger Puerto Ricans in New York and other cities of the northeastern United States are beginning to adopt the word Spanglish with pride, to refer explicitly to code switching: "More NYPR's [New York Puerto Ricans] are referring to 'Spanglish' as a positive way of identifying their switching." She concludes

(112–13) by stating that "contrary to the attitude of those who label Puerto Rican code switching 'Spanglish' in the belief that a chaotic mixture is being invented, English-Spanish switching is a creative style of bilingual communication that accomplishes important cultural and conversational work." Zentella's proposed grammar of Spanglish is in reality a compilation of grammatical and pragmatic constraints on code switching.

Latino Activism and the New Spanglish

The evolving social and political identity of U.S. Latino communities and the upsurge in dialogue between intellectuals and activists have resulted in a rebirth of the notion of Spanglish in new guises. Just as the word *Chicano* in Mexico and the southwestern United States now has vastly different connotations and implications compared with a few decades ago, so has Spanglish been deliberately claimed as linguistic and cultural patrimony, albeit with no single unifying thread. To illustrate the range of ideas and viewpoints encompassed by "neo-Spanglish," the writings of two well-known will be examined next.

Ed Morales (2002, 3) takes a politically grounded stance, linking Spanglish with the notion that

> Latinos are a mixed-race people . . . there is a need for a way to say something more about this idea than the word "Latino" expresses. So for the moment, let's consider a new term for the discussion of what this aspect of Latino means—let us consider Spanglish. Why Spanglish? There is no better metaphor for what a mixed-race culture means than a hybrid language, an informal code; the same sort of linguistic construction that defines different classes in a society can also come to define something outside it, a social construction with different rules. Spanglish is what we speak, but it is also who we Latinos are, and how we act, and how we perceive the world. It's also a way to avoid the sectarian nature of other labels that describe our condition, terms like Nuyorican, Chicano, Cuban American, Dominicanyork. It is an immediate declaration that translation is definition, that movement is status quo.

While acknowledging that many observers—particularly those from other Spanish-speaking nations—regard Spanglish as "Spanish under siege from an external invader" (Morales, 5), he goes on to celebrate the emerging Latino language as an affirmation of resistance and the construction of a powerful new identity. The remainder of his work deals with manifestations of the Spanish-English interface in literature, popular culture, and political discourse; and it is the most eloquent manifesto showing that Spanglish, an originally derogatory term, has been co-opted by its former victims as a badge of pride and courage.

A very different perspective comes from Ilan Stavans, an expatriate Mexican writer now teaching in Massachusetts who is also a self-declared admirer and promoter of Spanglish. Stavans's prolific popular writings on Spanglish and his purported specimens of this "language" have made him a lightning rod for polemics as well as a widely cited source among international scholars unfamiliar with the reality of Spanish-English bilingualism in the United States. Rather than applying Spanglish to an already existent discourse mode or sociolinguistic register (as done, for example, by Ed Morales or by the New York Puerto Ricans cited by Zentella 1997), Stavans invents his own mixture of Spanish and English, loosely modeled after true intrasentential code switching typical of U.S. Latino communities. Stavans (2003, 6) initially defines Spanglish innocuously as "the verbal encounter between Anglo and Hispano civilizations." His anecdotal accounts of learning Spanglish upon arriving in New York City from Mexico reveal an often less-than-affectionate reaction: "But to keep up with these publications [Spanish-language newspapers in New York City in the 1980s] was also to invite your tongue for a bumpy ride. The grammar and syntax used in them was never fully 'normal'; for example, it replicated, often unconsciously, English-language patterns. It was obvious that its authors and editors were *americanos* with no connection to *la lengua de Borges*."

Although perhaps initially offended by varieties of Spanish that seemed exotic to one coming from Mexico as well as by the frequent code switching, loan translations, and assimilated Anglicisms characteristic of these bilingual environments, Stavans came to profess a deep admiration for code-switched discourse, which for him forms the essence of Spanglish. Stavans appears to regard all code switching as a deliberate act of creativity, whereas most linguists who have studied code switching in a wide variety of language-contact environments throughout the world analyze spontaneous code switching in spoken language as a loosely monitored speech mode that is circumscribed by basic syntactic restrictions and is largely below the level of conscious awareness. Only in written language, particularly in creative literature, is deliberate manipulation of code switching to achieve specific aesthetic goals a viable option. In the 1970s, the use of code switching in U.S. Latino literature began to become increasingly common in poetry and in narrative texts as well. Such writers as Alurista, Tato Laviera, Roberto Fernández, and Rolando Hinojosa have fine-tuned the language of U.S. Latino communities to create a striking "third language" in their innovative literary texts. Even in their most creative flights of fancy, these writers almost always adhere to the syntactic and pragmatic rules that govern spontaneously produced bilingual speech. The most general restriction on mixing languages within the same sentence is that the material from the second language is in some way as likely a combination as a continuation in the first language. Fluent code switching may therefore produce combinations in which a switch occurs, for example, between an article and a noun, between a complement and a subordinate clause, or between a conjunction and one of the conjuncts.[5] Spontaneous code switches not accompanied by hesitations, pauses, or interruptions are normally unacceptable in the following environments: (1) between a pronominal subject and a predicate; (2) between a pronominal clitic and a verb; (3) between a sentence-initial interrogative word and the remainder of the sentence; and (4) between an auxiliary verb (especially *haber*) and the main verb. Moreover, adverbs of negation are normally in the same language as the verbs they modify. These restrictions reflect the general need to maintain the grammatical rules of each language, following the linear order both in English and in Spanish, and to retain easily identifiable chunks of discourse.

Although surrounded by bilingual discourse since arriving in the United States, Stavans reports on a particularly apocryphal experience that revealed the creative potential of written code switching. During an early teaching assignment, some Latino students frustrated with the treatment of Latinos by the American "system" expressed their alienation by rendering the Pledge of Allegiance, the United States Constitution, and the Declaration of Independence into a humorous but obviously inauthentic mixture of languages (Stavans 2003, 15):

(a) *Yo plegio alianza a la bandera de los Unaited Esteits de America.* (I pledge allegiance to the flag of the United States of America.)

(b) *Nosotros joldeamos que estas truths son self-evidentes, que todos los hombres son creados equally, que están endawdeados por su Creador con certain derechos unalienables, que entre these están la vida, la libertad, y la persura de la felicidad.* (We hold these truths to be self-evident, that all men are created equal, that they are endowed by their Creator with certain inalienable Rights, that among these are Life, Liberty, and the pursuit of Happiness.)

(c) *We la gente de los Unaited Esteits, pa' formar una unión más perfecta, establisheamos la justicia, aseguramos tranquilidá doméstica, provideamos pa' la defensa común, promovemos el welfer, y aseguramos el blessin de la libertad de nosotros mismos y nuestra posterity, ordenando y establisheando esta Constitución de los Unaited Esteits de América.* (We the people of the United States, in order to form a more perfect union, establish justice, insure domestic tranquility, provide for the common defense, promote the general welfare and secure the blessings of liberty to ourselves and our posterity, do ordain and establish this Constitution for the United States of America.)

Although these cynical parodies do not violate any major grammatical restrictions on language mixing, they contain unlikely Anglicisms (*joldeamos, endawdeados, establisheamos*) and an admixture of colloquial speech forms (*pa'* for *para, tranquildá* for *tranquilidad*) that clash with the solemn and formulaic language of these iconic texts. For Stavans, these parodies constitute "an exercise in ingenuity . . . show[ing] astuteness, a stunning capacity to adapt, and an imaginative aspect . . . that refuses to accept anything as foreign." He was inspired to try his hand at similar recastings of classic literary texts, with the following results (Stavans 2003, 16):

(a) *Sudenmente fuera del air estéril y drowsy, el lair de los esclavos como un lightning Europa dió un paso pa'lante* (Walt Whitman, *Leaves of Grass*)

(b) *You no sabe de mí sin you leer un book by the nombre of The Aventuras of Tom Sawyer, pero eso ain't no matter* (Mark Twain, *The Adventures of Huckleberry Finn*)

(c) *La tierra was ours antes que nosotros were de la tierra. It was nuestra tierra más de cien años pa'tras* (Robert Frost, "The Gift Outright")

Like his students' parodies, Stavans's imitations combine improbable Anglicisms (*sudenmente*) and rapid speech forms (*pa'lante, pa'tras*). In addition, there are violations of basic code switching restrictions, that is, between pronominal subject and verb (*sin you leer, you no sabe*) as well as inappropriate combinations in Spanish (*sabe de mí*). The linguistic differences between Stavans's bilingual texts and those of his students underscore the fact that fluent code switching forms part of the basic competence of native bilingual speakers and that it is not easily acquired among second-language learners.

Stavans's early attempts at creating a literary Spanglish were largely unknown, until he revealed them in his 2003 book. But the end result of his linguistic manipulations have made Stavans and his definition of Spanglish much-quoted commodities among intellectuals in other Spanish-speaking countries who decry the state of Spanish in the United States. In a tour de force that—thanks to the World Wide Web—has reached untold thousands of readers, Stavans (2002, 5–6) has offered a purported translation of the first chapter of *Don Quixote* into Spanglish:

In un placete de La Mancha of which nombre no quiero remembrearme, vivía, not so long ago, uno de esos gentlemen que always tienen una lanza in the rack, una buckler antigua, a skinny caballo y un grayhound para el chase. A cazuela with más beef than mutón, carne choppeada para la dinner, un omelet pa los sábados, lentil pa los viernes, y algún pigeon como delicacy especial pa los domingos, consumían tres cuarters de su income. El resto lo empleaba en una coat de broadcloth y en soketes de velvetín pa los holidays, with sus slippers pa combinar, while los otros días de la semana él cut a figura de los más finos cloths. Livin with él eran una housekeeper en sus forties, una sobrina not yet twenty y un ladino del field y la marketa que le saddleaba el caballo al gentleman y wieldeaba un hookete pa podear. El gentleman andaba por allí por los fifty. Era de complexión robusta pero un poco fresco en los bones y una cara leaneada y gaunteada. La gente sabía that él era un early riser y que gustaba mucho huntear. La gente say que su apellido was Quijada or Quesada—hay diferencia de opinión entre aquellos que han escrito sobre el sujeto—but acordando with las muchas conjecturas se entiende que era really Quejada. But all this no tiene mucha importancia pa nuestro cuento, providiendo que al cuentarlo no nos separemos pa nada de las verdá.

This text contains numerous syntactic violations of code switching, phonetically unlikely combinations (e.g., *saddleaba*), and hints of popular or uneducated Spanish (e.g., *pa* < *para* "for," *verdá* < *verdad* "truth") that implicitly reinforce the notion that only uneducated people speak Spanglish. That Stavans's *Quixote* is not simply a foreigner's innocent attempt to mimic authentic bilingual speech is amply demonstrated by his considerable proficiency in producing realistic code-switched language in his expository prose writings (e.g., Stavans 2000, 2003). Regardless of Stavans's motivations, his *Quixote* rendition has been widely cited—always disapprovingly—as evidence of the deplorable state of Spanish in the United States.

Enumeration of the Uses of Spanglish and Major Research Questions

The preceding remarks demonstrate that there is no universally accepted definition of Spanglish. The term Spanglish has variously been used to describe the following distinct phenomena:

- The use of integrated Anglicisms in Spanish
- The frequent and spontaneous use of nonassimilated Anglicisms (i.e., with English phonetics) in Spanish
- The use of syntactic calques and loan translations from English in Spanish
- Frequent and fluid code switching, particularly intrasentential (i.e., within the same clause) switches
- Deviations from standard Spanish grammar found among vestigial and transitional bilingual speakers whose productive competence in Spanish falls below that of true native speakers, as a result of language shift or attrition
- The characteristics of Spanish written or spoken as a second language by millions of Americans of non-Hispanic background who have learned Spanish for personal or professional motives
- The humorous, disrespectful, and derogatory use of pseudo-Spanish items in what anthropologist Jane Hill (1993a, 1993b, 1998) has called *junk Spanish*

The principal research questions surrounding Spanglish, irrespective of how this term is defined, include the following:

- Who uses Spanglish and in what circumstances?
- When and where is Spanglish used and not used?
- How is Spanglish acquired?

- Is Spanglish a language distinct from English and Spanish?
- Can Spanglish be characterized technically as a jargon, a pidgin, or a creole language?
- Does Spanglish have native speakers? If so, are there monolingual speakers of Spanglish?
- Does Spanglish have a common linguistic core, understood and used by all speakers/listeners?
- Do regional or social dialects of Spanglish exist?

It is impossible to adequately address all these issues in a single forum, but an overview of the issues and observations will bring matters into a clearer perspective. In the following remarks, attention will be confined to the interface of Spanish and English in the United States. The issue of whether cyber-Spanglish and other English-laden Spanish discourse modes used by monolingual Spanish speakers in other countries will, except for one case, henceforth be kept out of the discussion. The possible exception would be Spanish-English contact phenomena in Gibraltar, a speech community whose sociolinguistic profile closely mirrors that of many parts of the United States: in Gibraltar English is the sole official and prestige language, whereas Spanish is the native and preferred language of the majority of the population (Lipski 1986g; Moyer 1992). Data on code switching, calquing, and borrowing in Gibraltar is strikingly convergent with similar data in the United States, and most of the observations relating to U.S. Latino bilingualism can be extrapolated to include Gibraltar.

Setting the Scene: Spanish-to-English Language Displacement in the United States

Language shift from Spanish to English occurs in Hispanic communities in the United States even as the total number of Spanish speakers continues to grow through immigration. Bills, Hernández-Chávez, and Hudson have demonstrated a pattern of second-generation language shift in the Southwest (Texas, New Mexico, Arizona, California, and Colorado) amid continuing growth in the total number of Spanish speakers.[6] The 1970 census indicated that the Spanish language was lost in the Southwest after one or, at most, two generations (Thompson 1974). A comparison between the 1980 and 1990 censuses reveals that Spanish is maintained only in those regions where recent immigration from Spanish-speaking countries is intense (Hudson, Hernández-Chávez, and Bills 1995). These conclusions have been confirmed by Y. Solé (1990) and Hart-González and Feingold (1990). Veltman (1988, 3) concludes that "Spanish cannot survive in any area of the United States in the absence of continued immigration." Bills (1990, 24) adds, "With a halt to immigration, a complete shift to English would likely occur within a generation or two." Distance from the Mexican border as well as opportunities for using Spanish on a daily basis at home and in the workplace are key parameters for Spanish language retention. Sadly, there is a negative correlation between (1) level of formal schooling and socioeconomic achievement and (2) loyalty to the Spanish language in the Southwest. In other words, those who achieve success have done so within social and educational systems that favor the use of English over Spanish. Bills (2000) also establishes an inverse correlation between proficiency in English and retention of Spanish in the home: those who exhibit higher absolute levels of proficiency in English—although they may have immigrated into the United States from Spanish-speaking countries—tend to abandon the use of Spanish for daily needs even at home.[7] In contrast, García and Cuevas (1995) have determined that among Puerto Ricans in New York, the factor that most strongly favors maintenance of Spanish is the status of the individuals in their own community. The authors find that Spanish is used more frequently among young Nuyoricans than among older speakers, suggesting that younger generations of Puerto Ricans no longer associate use of Spanish with socioeconomic failure. Unlike in the Southwest, there is a positive correlation between educational attainment (particularly at the university level) and the retention and active use of Spanish.

The rapid shift to English within Latino communities in the United States has accelerated the incorporation of Anglicisms, intensified code switching, and created large numbers of semifluent transitional bilinguals whose incomplete active competence in Spanish—a stage that typically lasts no more than one generation—has at times been confused with the speech of stable bilingual communities.

Code Switching as Spanglish

Much of the discourse surrounding Spanglish is in effect a discussion of language switching within a single discourse or, as more commonly described by linguists, code switching. The grammatical and pragmatic constraints implicated in fluent code switching are described further in chapter 13. In general, there is an overarching requirement that no grammatical rule in either language be violated, particularly after the point of the switch. There are circumstances that favor code switching among fluent bilinguals, such as the anticipation of an upcoming proper noun in the other language as well as the presence of fulcrum words (e.g., conjunctions and complimentizers—*que* in Spanish, *that* in English—introducing subordinate clauses). The most cursory examination of pseudo-Spanglish inventions, such as Stavans's translation of the *Quixote* fragment, suffices to demonstrate both qualitative and quantitative deviations from legitimate code switching as it occurs in bilingual Latino communities in the United States, and it underscores the fact that much of the debate on Spanglish is based on misleading or erroneous information.

The Spanish of Vestigial and Transitional Bilingual Speakers

The debate on Spanglish and on the general status and vitality of Spanish in the United States is complicated by the existence of thousands of individuals who consider themselves Latinos and whose passive competence in Spanish is considerable, but whose productive competence may fall short when compared to that of fluent native speakers. Educational programs have come to refer to such individuals as "heritage language speakers," and the impact of such educational programs on the assessment of Spanish in the United States has yet to be charted. In classic studies of language attrition in minority communities, the technical term *semi-speaker* has been used, as distinguished both from the fluent bilingual or monolingual speaker of the language in question, and from foreign or beginning speakers of the language. In the ontogenesis of semifluent speakers, there is usually a shift away from the minority language and toward the national/majority language within a single generation or two, at most. This shift is signaled by a transitional generation of vestigial speakers who spoke the language in question during their childhood, but who have subsequently lost much of their native ability and their standing as true *transitional bilinguals* (TB), a term more neutral than *semi-speaker* and preferred by the author of the present work (Dorian 1977, 1981; Lipski 1985d, 1993a, 1996b, 1996c).

In the United States, the rapid displacement of Spanish in favor of English after at most two generations has created a large and ever-changing pool of transitional bilinguals who represent various national varieties of Spanish and a wide range of active and passive language proficiency. Although there are a few tiny communities of long standing in which Spanish as an ancestral language is rapidly disappearing, Spanish as a viable language is widespread in the United States. And even within Spanish-speaking groups living in areas geographically removed from larger Spanish-speaking communities, speakers have access to various forms of the Spanish language through public media, travel opportunities, and a nationwide awareness of some aspects of Spanish. At the same time, within individual families, in entire neighborhoods, and even in larger communities, shifts away from Spanish are commonplace in many regions of the United States, including areas with large, stable Hispanic populations and areas into which immigration from Mexico, Central America, and the Caribbean continue.[8]

Despite studies on marginal Spanish speakers in the United States (e.g., the *isleños* of Louisiana and the Sabine River Spanish speakers of Texas and Louisiana) and overlapping studies on Spanish-to-English shifts among larger Hispanic populations, theoretical assessments derived from vestigial and TB speakers have rarely been applied to the Spanish language as used by individuals of Mexican, Puerto Rican, and Cuban origin who, for whatever reasons, fall into the TB category. There is not even a rough estimate of the proportion of TB Spanish speakers in the United States, either in the school systems or in society as a whole, nor is there an adequate linguistic definition of vestigial or transitional bilinguals.

There is no preferred geographical locus for TB speakers; many are naturally found in regions into which immigration of Spanish speakers has been sporadic and has not occurred recently (as in many midwestern states), or in isolated groups where monolingual Spanish usage has given rise to English dominance. Even larger numbers of TB speakers are found in rural regions of the Southwest—where Spanish language usage is still strong—and in the major cities of the same region.

It is difficult to arrive at a noncircular definition of a TB Spanish speaker if one considers certain speech forms or error-types as defining aspects for this category. The only reasonable approximation to a usable, working definition involves external observations or self-assessed Spanish language ability as well as longitudinal behavior. In a typical U.S. setting (e.g., urban or suburban environment, availability of at least a small Hispanic population in the midst of a predominantly Anglo American setting, no bilingual or Spanish-dominant educational programs), the following combination of features helps us identify TB Spanish speakers:

1. The speaker had little or no school training in Spanish; in the case of little school training, classes taken were designed for English-speaking students.
2. Spanish was spoken in early childhood, and either it was the only language used at home or it was spoken in conjunction with English.
3. A rapid shift from Spanish to English occurred before adolescence, involving the individual in question, his or her immediate family members, and/or the surrounding speech community.
4. Subsequent use of Spanish is confined to conversation with a few relatives (typically quasimonolingual Spanish speakers of the grandparents' generation).
5. When addressed in Spanish by individuals known to be bilingual, TB speakers often respond wholly or partially in English, thus giving rise to asymmetrical conversations.

6. There is no strong perception of the Spanish language as a positive component of Hispanic identity. Individuals' feelings toward the latter ethnic group range from mildly favorable (but with no strong desire to retain the Spanish language) to openly hostile and pessimistic.

Naturally, these features are neither necessary nor sufficient to define TB speakers, but the above-mentioned characteristics overlap to a great extent with the linguistic behavior typical of vestigial Spanish speakers. True native Spanish speakers or fluent bilinguals differ systematically from the latter group in the following fashions:

1. The native Spanish speaker and his or her immediate family have never totally shifted from Spanish to English, although the linguistic profile of the surrounding environment may have changed through language shift or geographic displacement.
2. The native Spanish speaker's knowledge of English may be quite limited, although completely fluent bilinguals can also fall into this category.
3. The native Spanish speaker routinely holds conversations in Spanish with friends and family members, and he or she takes advantage of Spanish-language radio, television, films, and community events.
4. The native Spanish speaker's self-concept is usually positive with regard to his or her Hispanic identity; although there may be no active drive to retain the Spanish language, these speakers use it naturally and spontaneously.

True native Spanish speakers and fluent bilinguals are naturally separated from those who learned Spanish as a second language because of the different circumstances surrounding initial language acquisition, although many individuals who have learned Spanish as a true second language speak it as frequently as do native speakers.

It is difficult to offer an empirically sustainable linguistic definition of vestigial or TB Spanish speakers—as opposed to fluent bilinguals—although cases of skilled TB usage are readily recognized as such by fluent speakers of Spanish. A nonexhaustive, but highly representative, set of linguistic characteristics of vestigial Spanish usage—characteristics that can be found in the speech of nearly all individuals regarded as TB speakers of Spanish—includes the following:

Instability of Nominal and Adjectival Inflection

One of the most difficult aspects for learners of Spanish as a second language to master is the inflection of adjectives for gender and number. Native Spanish speakers, including true bilinguals whose Spanish exhibits massive English structural and lexical interference, virtually never commit errors of adjectival inflection. Vestigial Spanish speakers are aligned more with second language learners as regards adjectival inflection because they frequently make mistakes in gender and number concord. Typical examples include the following:

> *Mi blusa es blanco.* (My blouse is white.) (MX)
> *Tenemos un casa allá.* (We have a house there.) (MX)
> *¿Cuál es tu favorito parte?* (What's your favorite part?) (CU)
> *Decían palabras que eran ingles.* (They said words that were English.) (PR)
> *Ehta décima fue composío [compuesta] pol mi tío.* (This *décima* was composed by my uncle.) (IS)
> *Un rata ansina* (A muskrat this big) (IS)
> *Hay cosas que son más común a francés.* (There are things that are more like French.) (PR)
> *Que me pegaran por ningún razón.* (They hit me for no reason.) (PR)

Incorrectly Conjugated Verb Forms

In TB Spanish, third-person verb forms are frequently substituted for first- or second-person forms; other less systematic substitutions also occur. Native Spanish speakers do not commit genuine paradigmatic errors of verb conjugation. Some Hispanic bilinguals in the United States have been gradually abandoning the subjunctive mood in favor of a uniform use of the indicative in certain constructions. However, only vestigial Spanish speakers (as well as foreign language learners) consistently commit errors of person, tending toward but never reaching the canonical use of third person singular and plural forms for all singular and plural verb forms. For example:

> *Yo bailo y come.* (I dance and eat.) (MX)
> *Viene mis tíos del rancho d'él.* (My aunt and uncle come from his ranch.) (MX)
> *Se m'olvida muchas palabra.* (I forget a lot of words.) (CU)
> *Yo tiene cuaranta ocho año.* (I am 48 years old.) (TR)
> *Yo no sabe bien.* (I don't know well.) (TR)
> *Nosotro saben trabajá junto.* (We know how to work together.) (IS)
> *Omar y yo no eh mucho amigo.* (Omar and I aren't good friends.) (CU)
> *Mi mamá y mi papá eh bueno.* (My mom and dad are good.) (PR)
> *Esos pajaritos se metió adentro.* (Those birds got inside.) (PR)
> *Un lugar tan grande donde nadie conozco a nadie* (A big place where no one knows anyone else) (MX)
> *Ellos fue allá.* (They went there.) (MX)

Incorrect Use of Definite and Indefinite Articles

The elimination of articles required in standard usage is common in TB Spanish. Popular Spanish worldwide is characterized by inconsistent use of articles in certain contexts, but cardinal cases are rarely altered. Fluent Spanish-English bilinguals maintain standard usage of articles, except for occasional introduction of superfluous indefinite articles to indicate simple existence (e.g., *mi tío es [un] médico* [my uncle is a doctor]). TB speakers, on the other hand, frequently employ articles in fashions which deviate significantly from usage among fluent native Spanish speakers, but which are at times found among foreign language learners (Plann 1979; Gonzo and Saltarelli 1979). Some examples include the following:

> *Cuando tú deja [la] música* (When you quit music) (PR)
> *[El] español es muy bonita[o].* (Spanish is very pretty.) (PR)
> *Me gusta [las] clases como pa escribir.* (I like classes like how to write.) (CU)
> *Yo iba a [la] escuela.* (I went to school.) (MX)
> *Lo único inglés que ellos saben aprendieron en [la] escuela.* (The only English they know they learned in school.) (MX)
> *Tengo miedo de [los] examens.* (I'm afraid of exams.) (MX)
> *No ponen [los] zapato en la mesa.* (Don't put your shoes on the table.) (IS)

Errors in Prepositional Usage

Nonstandard popular Spanish exhibits an extraordinary variety of deviations from standard prepositional usage, typically involving the substitution or deletion of prepositions. Fluent native Spanish speakers never delete prepositions, except in cases of phonetic erosion, and prepositional substitutions are usually constrained along regional lines. TB Spanish speakers frequently shift prepositions in fashions not found among fluent speakers, and they often eliminate *de, a,* and occasionally other prepositions. Some examples are as follows:

> *¿Tienes oportunidades en hablar el español?* (Do you have opportunities to speak Spanish?) (CU)
> *Hoy etamo [a] siete.* (Today is the seventh.) (PR)
> *Vamos a estar más cerca a la familia d'él.* (We're going to be closer to his family.) (PR)
> *Voy a hablar de las comidas [de] Bélgica.* (I'm going to talk about Belgian foods.) (MX)
> *Comenzaba [en] septiembre.* (It began in September.) (IS)
> *Ya recibirá carta [de] Ehpaña.* (He [or she] will soon get a letter from Spain.) (IS)

Categorical Use of Redundant Subject Pronouns

In theory, subject pronouns are redundant in Spanish in those cases where verb forms or other elements permit semantic identification of the subject; in practice, usage varies widely. For example, in the Caribbean and in southern Spain, where word-final consonants are frequently eroded, use of subject pronouns is considerably more common to compensate for lost morphological material (Rosengren 1974; Mondéjar 1970; Silva-Corvalán 1982). TB speakers differ even from speakers of phonologically radical dialects, in which massive loss of word-final consonants has been associated with a higher frequency of overt subject pronouns in compensation for the loss of some verbal distinctions, in their preference for categorical usage of subject pronouns, even using two non-coreferential pronouns in the same sentence, something virtually impossible among fluent Spanish speakers. Some examples include the following:

Yo *sé las palabras pero cuando* yo *tengo que encontrar las palabras es cuando* yo *tengo problemas.* (I know the words, but when I have to find the words, that's when I have problems.) (MX)

Ello[s] *venden y* ello[s] *van.* (They sell and they go.) (CU)

Yo *lo jablo onde* yo *quiero.* (I speak it wherever I want.) (PR)

Cuando ella *termina,* ella *tiene que tirá el agua.* (When she finishes, she has to throw out the water.) (IS)

Yo *tengo do sijo;* yo *tengo a Al y* yo *tengo a Paul.* (I have two sons, I have Al and I have Paul.) (IS)

Yo *fui la mayor y* yo *no me acuerdo que* yo *hablaba inglés cuando comencé la escuela.* (I was the oldest, and I don't remember speaking English when I started school.) (MX)

Yo *quiero decir cariño pero* yo *no sé si es eso.* (I want to say affection, but I don't know if that's what it is.) (MX)

Nojotros *tratamos de que vaya otra persona más que nosotros porque* nojotros *estamos para aquí.* (We try to get someone else other than us to go because we are supposed to be here.) (MX)

Yo *decidí ser maestra porque* yo *estuve trabajando con niños y* yo *pensé que* yo *podía hacer lo mismo.* (I decided to be a teacher because I was working with children, and I thought that I could do the same thing.) (MX)

Yo *aprendí francés,* yo *tomé francés por tres años, pero* yo *no sé hablar muy bueno porque* yo *lo perdí todo. Si* yo *pudiera,* yo *quería aprender todas las lenguas, para que* yo, *cuando* yo *vaya a un país,* yo *misma pueda hablar.* (I learned French, I took French for three years, but I don't know how to speak very well because I lost it all. If I could, I would learn all languages so that when I went to a country I myself could speak.) (PR)

Ella$_i$ *hablaba el inglés que* ella$_i$ *sabía.* (She always spoke the English that she knew.) (Please note the repeated use of *ella* as indicated by the subscript i) (CU)

Yo *voy y* yo *nado y* yo *visito mis amigos y mi abuela.* (I go, and I swim, and I visit my friends and my grandmother.) (CU)

Backwards Anaphora

Also found in the speech of many TB Spanish speakers is the use of a redundant subject pronoun that stands in anaphoric relation to a (usually preceding) dropped pronoun, a usage that is proscribed in fluent varieties of Spanish when no contrastive emphasis is intended. This behavior may reflect an interference from English usage, which is a result of mixing the English rule that makes the use of subject pronouns mandatory with the Spanish rule that allows for the deletion of subject pronouns. This linguistic behavior yields highly varied results, such as the following:

Alguien me habla en español y $\emptyset_i$ *puedo entender pero* yo$_i$ *contesto en ingles.* (Someone talks to me in Spanish, and I can understand, but I answer in English.) (MX)

$\emptyset_i$ *creo que* yo$_i$ *tengo bastantes problemas con la gramática.* (I think I have a lot of problems with grammar.) (MX)

$\emptyset_i$ *no pude creer que* yo$_i$ *ha hecho esos errores.* (I couldn't believe that I had made those mistakes.)

$\emptyset_i$ *tenía muy buena recomendación pa que* él$_i$ *siguiera con la carrera de electrónica.* (He had a good recommendation so that he could continue his career in electronics.) (MX)

Pa que $\emptyset_i$ *no le tengan miedo a uno y sigan* ellos$_i$ *adelante.* (So they aren't afraid and they keep on going.) (MX)

Allá $\emptyset_i$ *te pagan, y si* ellos$_i$ *no gustan cómo estás jugando,* $\emptyset_i$ *te dicen.* (There they pay you, and if they don't like how you're playing, they tell you.) (MX)

This departure from Spanish grammatical restrictions among TB speakers suggests an eventual parameterization of TB speech in terms of pronominal reference, but the high degree of interspeaker variability in this dimension makes it unlikely that a stable parametric difference will ever become established. Among TB speakers, the pronoun *yo* is more frequently retained in redundant contexts, followed by *nosotros*. These same pronouns are the most frequent in anaphoric violations, probably because they are very frequently used. The examples in the present corpus suggest not a totally random occurrence of redundant pronouns in conjunction with a preceding/c-commanding dropped pronoun but rather a variable insertion of redundant pronouns following what the speaker perceives as a pause, shift of topic, or momentarily emphatic construction. Objectively, a pause or other juncture is usually absent, which suggests yet another possibility, namely pronoun deletion in short, stereotyped combinations (e.g., *creo que* [I believe]). In light of the (admittedly limited) data collected to date, the most reasonable hypothesis is that TB speakers have acquired a rudimentary form of the pro-drop parameter in Spanish—namely the possibility to eliminate subject pronouns (and the obligatory dropping of subject pronouns with impersonal constructions involving *haber*)—but they have not acquired, or have partially lost, the ancillary co-occurrence restrictions that forbid the presence of an expressed pronoun with a dropped antecedent.[9]

The preceding sections show that vestigial and TB Spanish speakers consistently produce errors rarely, if ever, found among fluent native speakers, or even among fluent bilinguals whose Spanish contains much structural interference from English. The characteristics just described combine to define the linguistic behavior of vestigial Spanish speakers. Of these characteristics, the first and second appear to be exclusive to vestigial speakers (except in very occasional and well-monitored slips among fluent native speakers), and they are found among nearly all vestigial speakers. The fifth characteristic—involving categorical use of redundant subject pronouns, non-coreferential pronouns in the same sentence, and repetition of coreferential subject pronouns—is nearly exclusive to vestigial speakers (being found occasionally among fluent bilinguals who exhibit structural interference from English) but not found among all vestigial speakers. The characteristic representing anaphoric violations is normally found only among TB and foreign speakers of Spanish. The third and fourth characteristics occur very frequently among vestigial speakers and very infrequently among bilinguals whose Spanish experiences interference from English. Table 3.1 summarizes the interaction between these characteristics and the three

Table 3.1 Structural Features of U.S. Spanish Speakers

Feature	Fluent Spanish speakers	Bilingual with English	Vestigial/TB Spanish speakers
Unstable adjectival inflection	Never	Never	Always
Unstable verb agreement	Never	Never	Always
Categorical use of subject pronoun	Never	Sometimes	Frequently
Anaphoric pronoun violations	Never	Never	Frequently
Errors/elision of prepositions	Never	Rarely	Frequently
Errors/elision of articles	Never	Rarely	Frequently

principal groups of Spanish speakers represented in the United States: monolingual Spanish speakers or fluent bilinguals whose Spanish contains virtually no structural interference from English; bilinguals exhibiting significant structural interference from English; and vestigial Spanish speakers. The characteristics represent target values defining the ideal TB speaker.

The relationships defined in table 3.1 are subject to considerable intersubjective variation, but taken as a whole, they are effective in differentiating true bilingual Spanish speakers from the majority of TB speakers as well as from individuals who learned Spanish as a second language after adolescence. Refinement of the basic scales to include detailed quantitative data will provide more accurate measures of the true extent of bilingual abilities in given individuals, while delimiting the potential accuracy of the implicational scales for diagnostic and evaluative purposes.

Transitional bilinguals with greater fluency in Spanish may produce utterances that don't violate Spanish grammatical restrictions, but they may not possess the full range of syntactic and stylistic options found among fluent native speakers of Spanish. Transitional bilinguals—most of whom are regarded, and regard themselves, as true bilinguals—in business, politics, journalism, law enforcement, and the arts are frequently used as examples of U.S. Latino Spanish speakers, and much of the criticism directed at Spanglish as an impoverished language spoken in the United States stems from confusing the symptoms of transgenerational language attrition with stable bilingualism.

Second-Language Spanish as Exemplary Spanglish

In addition to the more than 35 million Hispanic residents of the United States counted in the 2000 census, most of whom speak Spanish, uncounted millions of Americans have learned Spanish as a second language, through formal education and through life experience. Many of these L2 Spanish speakers use Spanish on a regular basis—on the job and in their personal lives—and many are called upon for impromptu or even official translation and interpretation, in situations that frequently exceed their linguistic abilities. Over the past several decades, as Spanish became the language that could no longer be ignored, numerous official and unofficial documents, signs, instruction manuals, and notices have been translated into Spanish, and they have become cultural and linguistic icons readily available to anyone visiting or traveling in the United States. Unfortunately, those requesting the translations did not always see fit to look for qualified translators or even legitimate native speakers, often handing the task off to anyone who "knew a little Spanish." The results are not difficult to imagine, and a torrent of broken Spanish that ranged from slightly off-kilter to grotesquely unintelligible has greeted Spanish speakers in the United States. There are no data on the frequency with which such unintentional travesties of proper Spanish have been correctly attributed to careless or incompetent second-language learners rather than to bilingual Spanish speakers whose command of Spanish has become slipshod through contact with English. Anecdotal evidence, particularly from abroad, suggests that many first-time visitors to the United States are convinced that the barrage of made-up Spanish is tangible proof of the deplorable state of U.S. Spanish.

"Junk Spanish" in American Popular Culture

Most residents of the United States born before 1960 remember Western movies in which even the most loutish cowboy could muster enough lingo to safely navigate the forbidden territories of Old Mexico, and perhaps he could also parlay with friendly and hostile Indians with equal facility (speaking Indian lingo, of course). Peggy Lee could sing "Mañana" in a pseudo-Hispanic accent, and parodies of Spanish cluttered the airwaves, from *I Love Lucy* to *The Lawrence Welk Show*. Americans are immersed in a morass of what anthropologist Jane Hill (1993a, 1993b, 1998) has called "junk Spanish" (her original term was "mock Spanish"), which is typified by the menu items at Tex-Mex restaurants, by jokes and stereotypes found in mass media, and by the names of streets, buildings, and subdivisions even in the least Hispanic parts of middle America, which juxtapose real and invented Spanish words with total disregard for grammatical concord and semantic coherence. When the most difficult situation can be shrugged off with a wink and a conspiratorial *no problemo,* and when one gets business done by talking to the *head honcho,* bemoans a junky *el cheapo* product, and criticizes a teenager for *showing his macho,* who can doubt that full command of Spanish is as much within reach as a margarita or a breakfast burrito? Even the *X-Files'* normally sensitive and chivalrous Fox Mulder could only think to say "no-ho with the rojo" when trying to warn a monolingual Puerto Rican not to touch a red button.[10] Yesteryear's Frito Bandito has been replaced by today's "Spanish"-talking lapdog, and the media rail against Spanglish as though cross-fertilization in bilingual communities was not the common patrimony of English, French, Latin, Hebrew, Chinese—indeed of most of the world's languages. One does find—it is true—occasional parodies of other languages in American popular culture (although the most obvious examples are now socially unacceptable), but none even remotely approaches the torrent of gibberish that is tolerated as gentlemen's approximation to Spanish. In a society that has become increasingly intolerant of racial and ethnic slurs and offensive discourse disguised as "just plain fun," the continued acceptance of pseudo-Spanish is a stark reminder of the challenges that remain.[11]

Hill extends the rubric of junk Spanish to include legitimate Spanish words or constructions used derisively; thus not only are *el cheapo* and *no problemo* charter members of the junk Spanish fraternity, but also *no way, José; yo quiero Taco Bell;* and naturally *hasta la vista, baby.*[12] For Hill, junk Spanish is a racist affirmation of the superiority of white Anglo American culture and language, and it has no legitimacy as a merely humorous tip-of-the-hat to the language of neighboring countries. Matters are exacerbated by the fact that many detractors of Spanish in the United States have turned junk Spanish exemplars—including some of their own invention—into urban legends that are now widely believed to be actually occurring instances of Spanglish.

More than half a century ago, the Nobel Prize–winning Spanish author Camilo José Cela claimed that he had encountered stores in the northeastern United States that offered home delivery of groceries via the grotesque combination *deliveramos groserías,* literally (and taking into account spelling differences) "we think about dirty words." This same phrase has subsequently been attributed to stores in Florida, Texas, California, and elsewhere—as a brief Internet search will reveal—in all cases without a single eye-witness to the alleged impropriety. The proliferation of Internet sites devoted to commentary on the Spanish language has spawned numerous variants of this obvious urban legend, including a supposed grocery store employee—a truck driver—who told the visiting Cela *"me paso el tiempo deliberando groserías,"* which in anybody's Spanish can only mean "I spend my time thinking about dirty words."[13] Cela, the author of the infamous *Diccionario secreto,* the world's most scholarly treatise on Spanish obscene words, is said to have been duly impressed with this response. The chances that even the most precarious bilingual speaker has spontaneously produced such an expression seriously—and not as a deliberate parody—are virtually nil, and yet this example is brandished even today as proof of the deplorable condition of U.S. Spanish.

The continued belief in the existence of such linguistic gargoyles is reminiscent of the often-quoted notion that the Inuit (Eskimo) languages have numerous words for different types and textures of snow because their society depends so vitally on a snowbound environment. Only recently have anthropologist Laura Martin (1986) and linguist Geoffrey Pullum (1991) revealed this fallacy (in fact, Inuit languages have no more words for snow than other languages in contact with snow), propagated through careless repetition of a plausible but unverified assertion. It is plausible that a bilingual speaker whose languages leak into each other uncontrollably would blurt out *deliveramos groserías* in some unhappy moment, but the fact is that no such combination exists in bilingual communities, precisely because no such unconstrained leakage occurs in normal bilingualism. Because of the continued outpouring of junk Spanish in American popular culture and the elevation of some apocryphal specimens to worldwide cult status, humorous pseudo-Spanish constitutes one of the greatest impediments to the serious study of Spanish in the United States and to the determination of what Spanglish actually is.

Empirical Research on Spanish in the United States

Set against the backdrop of smokescreens, red herrings, scapegoats, straw men, and other metaphorical chimeras, serious empirical research on Spanish in sustained and disadvantageous contact with English in the United States does reveal some grammatical limitations of Spanish morphosyntactic resources in favor of those that coincide with English, although true cases of grammatical convergence are rare except among transitional or semifluent bilinguals (for example, Pousada and Poplack 1982). There is some variation in verb tense usage among some bilingual speakers, particularly the historically variable preterit-imperfect distinction, although this distinction is never obliterated, as in English (Floyd 1976, 1978, 1982; Chasten 1991; Klein 1980; Kirschner 1992). Similarly, the Spanish indicative-subjunctive distinction never disappears—except among nonfluent heritage language speakers—but some constructions that show variable subjunctive usage among monolingual speakers may gravitate toward the indicative among English-dominant bilinguals. Silva-Corvalán (1994) and others have documented a reduction in Spanish word-order possibilities in bilingual communities, which yields restricted combinations that match the canonical SVO order of English. Bilingual Spanish speakers in daily contact with English may prefer the analytical passive voice construction—congruent with English—to the pseudo-passive constructions with *se* that are peculiar to Spanish. In Spanish, overt subject pronouns are normally redundant and used primarily for emphatic or focus constructions, whereas English requires overt subject pronouns in nearly all finite verb constructions. Research on pronoun usage among bilinguals reveals a broad range of variation, with a clear tendency to use more overt pronouns in Spanish as a direct correlate of English dominance (Lipski 1996c).

Summary of Major Research Questions

To summarize the preceding discussion, coherent definitions of Spanglish cluster around two characteristics, both of which represent unremarkable language-contact phenomena found in virtually every bilingual society, past and present.

The first characteristic of Spanglish is the frequent use of unassimilated and assimilated borrowings and loan translations (calques). The second one is fluent code switching. Adopting this Janus-faced definition, let us return to the research questions posed at the outset.

Who Uses Spanglish and in What Circumstances?

Loan translations and calques are typically used by all bilingual speakers, including those for whom one of the languages is a second language, learned in adulthood. The frequency and density of calques and assimilated loans in Spanish is inversely proportional to formal instruction in Spanish and the ready availability of Spanish-language mass media produced from all over the Spanish-speaking world. The opposite situation occurs in speech communities—such as much of the Caribbean coast of Central America and some former enclaves in Argentina and Chile—in which Spanish is the official language and English a nonprestige home language. Code switching, on the other hand, predominates among native bilingual speakers born or raised in the United States. Attitudes vary widely, and not all bilingual speakers spontaneously engage in code switching. No true bilingual is unable to speak exclusively in Spanish if necessary (for example, when the interlocutor is monolingual or will not allow code switching), although borrowings and loan translations may still be used at all times.

When and Where Is Spanglish Used and not Used?

Loan translations and borrowings are found in all Spanish-English bilingual communities, and many have spread to monolingual Spanish-speaking areas, in the language of consumer products, popular culture, and the Internet. Fluent code switching is confined to speech communities in which Spanish and English are used on a daily basis; such communities include bilingual areas of the United States as well as Gibraltar and some regions of Central America (Lipski 1986c, 1986g).

Is Spanglish a Language Distinct from English and Spanish?

No variety of Spanish that has absorbed a high number of lexical Anglicisms is any less Spanish than before—nor is code-switched discourse a third language, although fluent code switchers have arguably augmented their monolingual grammars with a set of grammatical and pragmatic constraints on switch points. Knowing how to switch languages does not constitute knowing a third language any more than being ambidextrous when playing tennis constitutes playing a new sport when one switches the tennis racket to his or her other hand. Only in the unthinkable event that all immigration to the United States from Spanish-speaking countries were to cease—and that a bilingual enclave such as Miami, Los Angeles, or New York City were to be simultaneously cut off from the remainder of the English-speaking population—is it conceivable that after several generations the legacy of contemporary bilingualism would morph into a language empirically distinct from English and Spanish. In the world as we know it, Spanish and English will remain separate and distinct, although they will borrow and lend from each other whenever and wherever they come into contact.

Can Spanglish Be Characterized Technically as a Jargon, a Pidgin, or a Creole Language?

A variety of Spanish that has absorbed many Anglicisms is still Spanish (i.e., a complete, natural language), and consequently, it cannot be a reduced or partial form of a language, such as a jargon or pidgin. The same is true of code-switched discourse, which is predicated on fluency in two natural languages, albeit not always on prestigious varieties. As used by scholars of linguistics, the term *creole language* refers to a new language that arises when a reduced contact vernacular such as a pidgin—which, critically, is not spoken natively by anyone—is expanded in subsequent generations into a complete natural language (e.g., Holm 1988, 2000; Mühlhäusler 1986; Romaine 1988; Sebba 1997). In this sense, no manifestation of Spanglish qualifies as a creole language. If code switching were to coagulate into replicable patterns—in itself an unlikely possibility—then a permanently code-switched discourse might be considered an intertwined language. Outside of linguistics, the term creole is frequently used to refer loosely to the product of any language contact and mixing; in this sense U.S. Spanish can be called a creole language because it exhibits some hybrid traits; however, no creolization in the strict sense has occurred.

Does Spanglish Have Native Speakers? If So, Are There Monolingual Speakers of Spanglish?

There are certainly native speakers of Spanish varieties containing a large proportion of Anglicisms; so, if Spanglish refers to such dialects, then it has native speakers. Similarly, fluent code switching is most common among native bilinguals. However, because the product of code switching is not a language *per se,* it makes no sense to speak of native speakers of this bilingual discourse mode.

Does Spanglish Have a Common Linguistic Core, Understood and Used by All Speakers/Listeners?

The key word here is *common*, because most Spanish speakers in the United States recognize both assimilated and spontaneous Anglicisms, and all bilingual speakers can readily understand code-switched discourse irrespective of personal preferences. Although there are lexical Anglicisms and calques (e.g., *para atrás)* that are used by nearly all bilingual Latino speakers, spontaneous creations are more common, which thus undermines the notion of a stable Spanglish core. Purported dictionaries of Chicano Spanish (e.g., Galván and Teschner 1977) or Spanglish (e.g., Cruz and Teck 1998; Stavans 2003) usually include a potpourri of items gleaned from numerous sources and regions, but such items do not constitute the lexical repertoire of any known speech community.

Do Regional or Social Dialects of Spanglish Exist?

Regional and social dialects of U.S. Spanish continue to exist, representing the dialects of the countries of origin of speakers, as well as the results of dialect leveling in some urban areas. Sociolinguistic differences are found throughout U.S. Latino speech communities. Neither the frequency of Anglicisms nor the use of code switching varies regionally or socially in correlation with U.S. Spanish regional and social dialects; therefore it makes no sense to speak of dialects of Spanglish.

Conclusions

It is precisely the rapid shift to English after at most two generations that militates against the formation of any stable U.S. varieties of Spanish, let alone against any empirically replicable hybrid language such as Spanglish. In particular, Spanglish in any of its many avatars does not meet the definitions of true mixed or intertwined languages: that is, languages containing lexical category items (nouns, verbs, adjectives, etc.) from one language and functional elements (inflectional morphemes, prepositions, articles, etc.) from another.[14] Rather, Spanglish is an overly facile catchphrase that has been used to refer to so many disparate and inaccurately described language phenomena as to have become essentially meaningless. In speech communities where one Spanish-speaking group predominates, the corresponding regional variety of Spanish is retained, together with the inevitable introduction of lexical Anglicisms and some syntactic calques. In large urban areas where several Spanish-speaking groups converge (e.g., Chicago, Washington, New York, Houston, and parts of Los Angeles), some dialect leveling has taken place, again with some introduction of Anglicisms, but the specific linguistic features vary from city to city. In no instance has a homogeneous and consistent U.S. dialect of Spanish emerged, nor is such a variety likely to develop in the foreseeable future. As a consequence, whereas monolingual Spanish speakers in their respective countries of origin (Mexico, Puerto Rico, Cuba, etc.) can identify traits that differ from their own in the speech of their compatriots born or living extensively in the United States, each observer will come up with a somewhat different set of contrasts whose common denominators form a vanishingly small set. We may choose to designate as Spanglish the totality of the discrepancies between monolingual Spanish of other nations and the speech of Hispanophones in the United States, but to do so is to deprive this term of a place among the languages of the United States.

Who Needs Spanglish?

The bibliography of empirical research on varieties of Spanish in the United States is vast and continually growing, and all results converge on a single conclusion: there is no third language or cohesive Spanglish to be found anywhere in this country, nor can extrapolation from contemporary language contact environments project such a language in the foreseeable future. I suggest that Spanglish, as most commonly used, is no more than the latest addition to the list of epithets and slurs applied to the speech of the underclasses, and that the true nature of the Spanish-English interface must be sought from an additive rather than a subtractive viewpoint. Each Latino speech community retains the major dialect features of its country of origin, together with the inevitable dialect leveling in urban areas where several regional varieties of Spanish are in daily contact. In the aggregate, Spanish speakers living in the United States use more Anglicisms than their monolingual counterparts in other Spanish-speaking countries; these include loan translations, false and partial cognates, and assimilated borrowings. However, there are no instances in which basic grammatical principles of Spanish are violated among fluent speakers of Spanish, although patterns of usage may vary. Only among second- and third-generation English-dominant speakers is it possible to find combinations that would be grammatically unacceptable in fully fluent Spanish. This, however, is not Spanglish, but rather the natural consequence of the LANGUAGE SHIFT > LANGUAGE LOSS trajectory typical of most immigrant speech communities.[15] The implicit failure to distinguish between fluent bilinguals and semifluent heritage language speakers is partially responsible for misleading statements about the prevalence of Spanglish among U.S. Latino communities.

What is the future of Spanglish? Will it continue to be the whipping boy for purists and xenophobes, or will it emerge into the sunshine as the positive affirmation of U.S. Latino identity? To address these questions within an academic context is to engage in mere speculation, but some factual points may be brought to bear. First, despite the enormous bibliography of empirical research on U.S. varieties of Spanish—spanning nearly a century of scholarship and covering nearly every Spanish-speaking community residing within the United States— little of this knowledge has penetrated elementary and secondary education, the mass media, the entertainment industry, or the diplomatic service. Although there is greater reluctance to employ offensive terms in public discourse, popular notions about the language of U.S. Latinos differ little from those in vogue more than half a century ago. At the university level matters are much more salutatory: courses on U.S. Latino culture and literature and on Spanish language designed for native and heritage language speakers are encouraging portents, but seldom does this enlightenment penetrate the "town versus gown" barrier. It is therefore difficult to envision an eventual widespread acceptance of Spanglish as a proud affirmation of ethnolinguistic identity. In the history of U.S. sociocultural discourse, no term has risen from bigotry to splendor. It is true that within Mexico *Chicano* has often been used as a negative stereotype for Mexican Americans, but the word itself is simply a retention of the archaic pronunciation of *mexicano*. No racial or ethnic slur has been transformed into a favorable epithet across wide sectors of American society.[16] Items like *African American, physically challenged, Asian, Native American, domestic partner,* and the like are modern usages that bear no resemblance to the host of ugly tags once found in common parlance. If the term *Ebonics* survives unscathed—and it is very much up for grabs—it will be at least in part because of its lack of similarity to any of the popular or academic terms previously used to designate these language varieties.

Urgently needed is a greater public awareness of the reality of U.S. Latino language, and if Spanglish is allowed to creep into the (re)education of the American public, I fear the results of any remediation. As a term, *Spanglish* is as out of place in promoting Latino language and culture as are the words *crazy, lunatic, crackpot,* or *nut case* in mental health care, or *bum, slob, misfit,* and *loser* in social work. From the perspective of a linguist who has spent more than three decades studying the Spanish language in its U.S. setting, Spanglish will always be a signpost on the wrong road, a road whose many way stations range from misunderstanding to intolerance. The expression *"el que habla dos lenguas vale por dos"* (one person who speaks two languages is worth two people) does not admit qualifiers, and neither should our acceptance of the nation's largest bilingual community.

Notes

1. Spanglish has even made its way into children's literature, for example in a humorously didactic novel by Montes (2003) in which a Puerto Rican girl is teased by her classmates, who speak only English. The cover blurb sets the stage: "Maritza Gabriela Morales Mercado (Gabí for short) has big *problemas*. Her worst enemy, Johnny Wiley, is driving her crazy. . . . Gabí is so mad she can't even talk straight. Her English words keep getting jumbled up with her Spanish words. Now she's speaking a crazy mix of both, and no one knows what she's saying! Will Gabí ever make sense again? Or will she be tongue-tied forever?" The book provides a touching lesson in cultural sensitivity and a few examples of realistic code switching, although the idea that bilingual speakers "jumble up" their languages when they become angry is unlikely to score any points in the bilingual education arena.

2. Similar viewpoints have been expressed by the journalists Lloréns (1971) and Varo (1971). See Lipski (1975, 1976) and López Morales (1971) for a different viewpoint.

3. For a discussion of *pa' trás* and similar phenomena see Lipski (1985b, 1987d) and Otheguy (1993).

4. In one case (Avera 2001) Spanglish refers simply to an elementary textbook in conversational Spanish written in bilingual *en face* format. The author defines Spanglish as "the combination of the words Spanish and English. The two languages represent the form of communicating for millions of people in the Americas, Australia, England, Spain, and others." No mention of language mixing or interference is found in the textbook, although the use of available cognates is encouraged throughout.

5. The literature on the syntactic constraints that govern code switching is vast and still growing. Summaries of relevant theories and approaches are found in Lipski (1982, 1985d) and Toribio (2001a, 2001c).

6. Bills (1989, 1997a, 1997b); Bills, Hernández-Chávez, and Hudson (1995, 2000); Hernández-Chávez, Bills, and Hudson (1996); Hudson, Hernández-Chávez, and Bills (1992, 1995).

7. Chávez (1988, 1993) further documents the rate of language displacement and loss in relation to gender differences.

8. C. Solé (1979, 1982), Y. Solé (1975), Attinasi (1978, 1979), Peñalosa (1980), Sánchez (1983).

9. The issues of Spanish pro-drop in first- and second-language acquisition, and of backward anaphora in general, are immensely complex and are the subject of intensive research on several fronts. To the best of my knowledge, none of the results of research programs have been applied to TB speakers or vestigial speakers of any language. My own research is currently directed toward the interaction of Spanish TB speakers and the pro-drop parameter(s), and toward the interaction of anaphoric relations.

10. In the episode "Little Green Men," first aired on September 16, 1994.

11. Barrett (2006) provides numerous examples from a restaurant setting that illustrate the pervasiveness of racist language and attitudes well into the twenty-first century.

12. This is perhaps the best known of the many examples of this sort in popular culture. For another typical case, in the film *Night Shift*—a makeover of a Stephen King story by the same name and set in a Maine mill town with no Latino presence—the mad exterminator screams *"Adiós, motherf . . . s!"* as he flushes thousands of rats into a river.
13. Found at http://badhairblog.blogspot.com/2006/01/city-university-of-new-york-and.html
14. Such mixed languages include Michif (a mixture of Cree and French; Bakker 1996), and Media Lengua (a mixture of Spanish and Quechua, spoken in some villages in Ecuador; Muysken 1997).
15. See the examples in Bills (1989, 1997), Bills, Hernández-Chávez, and Hudson (1995, 2000), Lipski (1985a, 1992, 1993b, 1996b, 1996c), and Silva-Corvalán (1994).
16. It is true that *nigga* has positive attributes in African American hip-hop culture, but this term is not freely available for use by nonmembers of this community and is rejected by more conservative African Americans. *Queer* has become accepted in academic circles (to wit, queer studies, queer theory), but "on the street" it retains the traditional locker-room flavor.

4

Mexican Spanish in the United States

Introduction

Mexicans and Mexican Americans are by far the largest Latino group in the United States, making up nearly 59% of the total Latino population recorded in the 2000 census. They are also the group that has shared the longest history with the United States. For many Americans of all ages, terms such as "Hispanic," "Latino," "Latin American," and even "Spanish" are implicitly equated with "Mexican." In much of the Southwest the term "Mexican" is often used— more often than not with disparaging overtones—as a synonym for the Spanish language itself ("How do you say that in Mexican?"), and the proliferation of pseudo-Mexican fast food restaurants as well as numerous media stereotypes keep images of things Mexican and Mexican American before the American public. Once viewed popularly as being mostly migrant farmworkers and day laborers, Mexican Americans now occupy positions of power and prominence throughout the United States, although Mexicans from impoverished backgrounds continue to arrive in search of a better life. Popular notions notwithstanding, the Spanish of Mexican Americans is not monolithic, but covers a broad range of social and regional variants, reflective of the immense linguistic diversity of Mexico itself. In their totality, the varieties of Mexican American Spanish form a coherent dialect cluster, significantly different from the Caribbean dialects found in the eastern United States, and sharing some similarities with

Central American usage, particularly that of Guatemala and to a lesser extent El Salvador.

Together with Peru, Mexico was one of the main pillars of Spain's American empire. Mexico provided mineral wealth, an abundant indigenous labor force, fertile land for agriculture, and a nearly limitless territory for settlement. New Spain, as the colony was first known, was elevated to a viceroyalty in 1535, dominating a territory that stretched from the middle of the modern United States to Panama, and which also encompassed the Philippines. Following independence from Spain, Mexico broke with the short-lived Central American Union; Chiapas, originally part of Guatemala, was integrated into Mexico. Mexican boundaries remained stable until the Texas war of independence in 1836, spurred by American settlers in the region, caused the loss of this territory. A few years later, the Mexican-American War, settled in 1848, resulted in the loss of nearly half of Mexico's remaining territory, including the modern states of California, Arizona, Colorado, New Mexico, Nevada, and parts of Wyoming and Utah. This is the original source of Mexican Spanish as spoken in the United States.

Mexicans in the United States

The 1990 census detected almost 13.9 million residents of the United States who considered themselves to be of Mexican origin, of whom 8.9 million were born in the United States. The 2000 census registered 20.6 million Mexicans, a dramatic 53% increase in a single decade. Most of the largest concentrations of Mexican Americans are in states that traditionally have received heavy immigration from Mexico, but some concentrations have developed only recently. The following are representative figures, based on the 2000 census:

California	8,456,000
Texas	5,071,000
Illinois	1,144,000
Arizona	1,065,000
Colorado	450,700
Florida	364,000
New Mexico	330,000
Washington	330,000
Nevada	286,000
Georgia	275,000
New York	261,000
North Carolina	247,000
Michigan	221,000

Oregon	215,000
Indiana	153,000
Kansas	148,000
Utah	136,000
Oklahoma	133,000
Wisconsin	127,000
New Jersey	103,000

Although the vast majority of Mexican Americans are concentrated in Texas and California, these figures show considerable strength in regions of the country far removed from the U.S.-Mexico border. Among the ten U.S. cities with the largest Hispanic populations, Mexican Americans represent the largest Latino group in Los Angeles, Chicago, Houston, Phoenix, San Diego, Dallas, San Antonio, El Paso, and San Jose (California).

Not all of these individuals speak Spanish; on the other hand, an undetermined number of speakers of Mexican Spanish were not reported by the census. As unreliable as these numbers may be, they demonstrate the significant impact of Mexican and Mexican American varieties of Spanish on the U.S. linguistic profile. Despite noteworthy regional and sociolinguistic differences, the entirety of this language usage is often grouped under the label Mexican American or Chicano Spanish. The word *Chicano* is a shortening of the archaic *mexicano*, in which the letter *x* was pronounced as [ʃ] (like English *sh*) until the middle of the seventeenth century. When used in modern Mexico, it is a derogatory term for Mexicans born or raised in the United States, who live in poverty and exploitation, and are rejected by Anglo-Americans. Within the United States, the same connotation persists among older Mexican Americans and in rural regions, and like most vernacular ethnic designations is best avoided by those who do not belong to the group in question. Among younger Mexican Americans, *Chicano* has acquired a positive meaning, associated with social engagement, a group consciousness that has meant political enfranchisement and economic power. The range of viewpoints associated with *Chicano* extends from radical political activism to creative writing, custom automobiles ("low-riders"), and a musical blend of Mexican *ranchera* and American rock and roll.

Important Events in the Establishment of the Mexican American Community

The presence of Mexican Americans in the United States stems from a variety of sources, spanning several centuries, and the contemporary Mexican American population is scattered throughout the country, distributed among rural, urban, and suburban environments. Moreover, Mexican Americans differ from other Spanish-speaking groups in the United States in that they are divided into three groups (Valdés 1988): (a) permanent immigrants; (b) short-term immigrants, who spend an average of ten to twelve weeks in the United States before returning to Mexico; and (c) cyclical immigrants, who are typically migrant farmworkers. These differences have obvious consequences for language usage in both Spanish and English. Some Mexican Americans are fully bilingual, integrated members of U.S. society, whereas others live at the very margins of tolerable existence, unknown and unwanted. To lump the speech of all these groups under a general heading of "Mexican American" is as meaningless as to regard all Americans—of all races, ethnic groups, socioeconomic classes, and ages—as speaking a single form of English, although some rather substantial common denominators could be found. In tracing the development and spread of Mexican varieties of Spanish in the United States, several historical moments and sociogeographical configurations must be taken into consideration.

Texas was separated from Mexico following the Texas Revolution, which began in 1836, and the Mexican-American War of 1848 (and several subsequent small territorial adjustments) brought the remaining southwestern territories under U.S. control. In these regions, there are considerable populations descended from settlers who never relocated, from the time of the Spanish colony, through Mexican independence, and after annexation to the United States. In most parts of the country, the linguistic traits of this early population were overrun by later accretions from more recent Mexican immigration, but there are still pockets of relatively untouched colonial Mexican Spanish to be found in the United States. The largest single speech community spans northern New Mexico and southern Colorado, and is the subject of a separate chapter. Lope Blanch (1990a, 1990b) carried out exploratory studies in rural areas of Texas, Arizona, and California in search of similarly archaic colonial Mexican Spanish, with very ambiguous results. In most cases, it is impossible to definitively tag a particular configuration as stemming from colonial times, untouched by later migration, since what are at stake are archaic carryovers that are still to be found among untutored rural residents of Mexico, who make up the bulk of the immigrant population in much of the southwestern United States. Only a combination of linguistic reconstruction and careful sociohistorical analysis allows for the conclusion that a particular group of speakers represents a direct continuation of early colonial Mexican Spanish.

In the years immediately following the Mexican-American War, immigration from Mexico to the United States was relatively sparse because there was neither a push nor a pull of sufficient magnitude to compel Mexicans to abandon their country for an obviously foreign, if not overtly hostile, environment. The next major event in the Mexican-U.S. linguistic interface came with the Mexican Revolution of 1910–20, during which thousands of Mexicans of all social classes sought refuge from chaos and destruction by moving across the border into the United States. For the first time, Spanish was deliberately taken into areas where English had been the prevailing language, and for the first time Spanish as a "foreign" language entered the southwestern United States from outside its (new) borders. The varieties of Mexican Spanish brought into the United States as a direct result of the Mexican revolution were predominantly from the northern border states of Mexico. These dialects were similar in many ways to the varieties of Spanish that remained in the southwestern states after the Mexican-American War. Few Mexicans emigrated further than the U.S. border states at this point.

During and immediately after World War I (1918–30), there arose a shortage of farm laborers in the United States, particularly because many young male farmers had been sent to the battle front. To compensate for this diminished work force, the U.S. government initiated the *bracero* program, which involved actively recruiting Mexican laborers for "temporary" work in U.S. agriculture. Although workers from all over Mexico joined the emerging migrant labor force, most of the official recruiting stations were set up in Mexico's poorest states, those of the central-southern region, including Michoacán, Guerrero, and Guanajuato. At a time when the northernmost Mexican states were enjoying relative prosperity, southern Mexican workers entered the United States in large numbers, and most migrated to midwestern and northern states far from the Mexican border. Thus southern Mexican Spanish came to be the predominant variety in the northern United States, whereas northern Mexican Spanish predominated along the southern border of the United States.

As with other foreign labor recruitment movements, the perceived need for Mexican laborers quickly receded, but attempts at repatriation of Mexican immigrants during the labor-surplus years of the Great Depression (1930–42) met with little success. Quite to the contrary, the conduits opened by the bracero movement brought ever greater numbers of Mexican workers to the United States, following in the footsteps of the first recruits. This period marks the beginnings of the annual pilgrimages from the U.S.-Mexican border to midwestern and northwestern states during each summer's agricultural harvest season, a migratory trend which continues even today.

Not all Mexicans who arrived during this period worked in agriculture. An efficient railroad system connected southern Texas to midwestern industrial cities such as Chicago, Milwaukee, and Detroit, and Mexican immigrants began to obtain jobs in industry, often coinciding with the northward migration of African

Americans from the southern states. Although the annual migratory oscillation characterized the lives of many workers (who during the summers lived in the notorious northern migrant camps), an increasing number of Mexican arrivals found the means to survive the severe northern winters and became permanent residents of midwestern and northern states. Today, the Mexican population of these states is more varied in terms of regional origins within Mexico, with northern Mexicans being prominently represented along with those from more southern Mexican states.

World War II brought a new round of xenophobia, more strident and harsher than the isolationism that had followed World War I. On the west coast of the United States, Mexican Americans (many of whom were native-born U.S. citizens) were subject to harassment and sometimes forced deportation. At the same time, Mexicans and Mexican Americans made large-scale migrations to urban areas of the Southwest. From El Paso to Los Angeles, Mexicans settled in cities, and as stable Mexican *barrios* became established, the Spanish language enjoyed some measure of de facto legitimization. The period from 1942–70 marked another large increase in Mexican immigration to the United States, spurred by the need for unskilled labor in many parts of the country (Valdés 1988, 112); some 1.75 million Mexicans legally entered the United States during this period.

Mexican American Spanish again came to prominence in the 1960s, as political activism reached this community. The term *Chicano* became a badge of ethnic and political pride rather than a derogatory epithet; the quintessential homeland of Aztlán was recognized in the raised consciousness of many Mexican Americans; *La Raza* came to symbolize Mexican Americans in their struggle against discrimination and marginality. Social activists, labor leaders, writers, politicians, and academics combined to place the social and linguistic agenda of Mexican Americans before a larger audience, including Anglo Americans, Spanish speakers from other countries (including Mexico), and other U.S. Spanish-speaking groups. Universities established "Chicano Studies" programs and departments, and professional journals were founded bearing names such as *Revista Chicano-Riqueña, Aztlán,* and *El Grito,* as well as the more academic-sounding *Bilingual Review/Revista Bilingüe* and *Hispanic Journal of Behavioral Sciences.* All aspects of Mexican American language and culture received a wider airing, from the artistic, social, and political accomplishments of community leaders to counterculture manifestations such as the Pachucos, Low-Riders, *caló* slang, and the like.

In the 1990s, sizeable populations of Mexican origin arose in Florida and the Pacific Northwest, regions that continue to attract new immigrants. Within the past decade Mexicans have also immigrated in considerable numbers to southern states such as North Carolina, Georgia, and Alabama, as well as to rural Pennsylvania and Maryland.

Demographic Milestones of Mexican Americans

Early Mexican presence in what is now the United States long antedates the Mexican-American War, and both settlement and subsequent migration patterns have varied widely in the different states of the U.S. Southwest. Prior to the Mexican-American War, the number of Mexicans actually inhabiting the area that would be lost to the United States was relatively small, and they were scattered in largely rural agricultural holdings. It is estimated that 5,000 Mexicans lived in Texas, 7,500 in California, and only 1,000 in Arizona. Only New Mexico had a sizeable Mexican population—estimated at around 60,000, and this population was mostly concentrated around Santa Fe and in a few small northern communities (Moore and Pachon 1985, 18). Hostile Indian raids in Texas and Arizona kept the Mexican population small, whereas New Mexico and California were so far from the major Mexican population centers that little immigration occurred. Beginning with the declaration of the Texas Republic in 1836, the plight of Mexicans in Texas began to worsen. Following the Mexican-American War, despite the guarantees embedded in the Treaty of Guadalupe Hidalgo, many Mexicans in Texas and elsewhere lost their land to American ranchers and farmers, and racial discrimination became the order of the day. Despite these difficulties, immigration from Mexico was constant, particularly during and after the Mexican Revolution.

In New Mexico and southern Colorado, where the largest Mexican population had lived prior to annexation to the United States, the Spanish-speaking population held its own relatively well against the Anglo American newcomers. Alliances were as common as confrontations, and it was not until well into the twentieth century that ethnic and social tensions replaced more amicable relations. Little inward migration of Mexicans occurred in New Mexico until the advent of the railroads in the twentieth century, although in the southern part of the state the permeable land border with Mexico was constantly crossed by two-way migrations. Arizona's small Mexican population was further fragmented after the Mexican-American War, when the influx of Anglo American ranchers and miners, combined with the continued threat of Indian hostilities, kept the Mexican population marginalized. Discrimination against Arizona's Mexican minority began early and continued throughout the history of that region, from territory through statehood.

Spanish and Mexican ranchers in California found far greater prosperity than in the rest of the former Mexican territory, and relations with the new American occupiers were smooth for the first few years, until the 1849 advent of the gold rush in northern California. Anglo American miners imported Mexicans (mostly from Sonora) as well as thousands of Chilean laborers to work in the mines, all the while coercing or cheating many of the original landowners out of their holdings. The use of Mexicans as laborers increased the perception of Hispanics as fit for nothing but menial jobs and reinforced racial and ethnic discrimination. In southern California, the Mexican landowners were able to hold out somewhat longer, but eventually the Anglo American settlers outnumbered and outmaneuvered the Mexican residents. When the railroads arrived in the 1880s, the stream of American immigrants turned to a torrent; in 1887, for example, more than 120,000 Anglo American settlers arrived in southern California, where only 12,000 Mexicans lived (Moore and Pachon 1985, 23).

By the turn of the twentieth century, the Mexican population in the United States was increasingly poor, landless, and subordinate to Anglo American agricultural and commercial interests. From 1910–29, Texas was one of the most popular destinations for Mexican migrants. In later years, the migratory trends favored California. During 1960–64, almost 56% of the known Mexican immigrants relocated to California, 25% to Texas, 8% to Arizona, and only 2.5% to New Mexico. Only around 10% of Mexican immigrants traveled beyond the border states.

Legal Mexican immigration to the United States has closely followed the historical events mentioned above. Listed below are some representative figures that trace the historical profile (Portes and Bach 1985, 79):

Period	Number of Mexican Immigrants
1881–1890	2,000
1891–1900	1,000
1901–1910	50,000
1911–1920	219,000
1921–1930	459,000
1931–1940	22,000
1941–1950	61,000
1951–1960	300,000
1961–1970	454,000
1971–1978	512,000

When it is recalled that these figures reflect primarily legal immigration and do not take into account undocumented Mexicans in the United States, the magnitude and rapid growth of the migratory flux can be more fully appreciated. The authors of the study from which the above figures are drawn also note that emigration from

Mexico to the United States is not always or even principally from rural regions, but rather comes frequently from the urban working classes. Emigrants also do not necessarily come from the most economically depressed Mexican states, and the states that border the United States no longer overwhelmingly dominate Mexican migration. These facts are reflected in the profile of contemporary Mexican American Spanish in the United States, which is not entirely circumscribed by the rustic variants described in many classical studies. When rural residents of Mexico emigrate to the United States, they may congregate in rural agricultural areas. Matus-Mendoza (2002, 2004, 2005) describes one such cohesive Mexican American community in rural Pennsylvania, which characterized by considerable return migration to a single area of rural Mexico. As a result of these differences, linguistic probes among recently arrived Mexican farmworkers in the United States and their immediate descendents may well reveal a number of rustic forms. Urban working class Mexican immigrants are often more attracted to urban areas; hence, linguistic surveys of urban Mexican American communities will usually turn up fewer rustic Mexican elements. Although some rural residents of Mexico do end up in urban areas of the United States—just as rural-to-urban emigration within Mexico displaces many rural residents—the reverse trend is seldom observed. Most urban Mexican natives migrate directly to urban areas of the United States.

The "Dialects" of Mexican American Spanish versus Dialects of Mexico

The varieties of Spanish included in the Mexican American category have never been cut off from Mexico, and most are replenished by contact with Mexico, through family ties, travel, or continued immigration. Nonetheless, there is a tendency to describe Mexican American Spanish as though it were a discrete dialect with uniquely definable characteristics. A glance at the available bibliography reinforces this notion. In addition to studies of Mexican American Spanish as spoken in particular cities, there are dictionaries and glossaries that claim to represent "Chicano" speech. Among such works it is possible to discern at least three viewpoints. At one extreme is the opinion that Mexican American Spanish is indistinguishable from dialects in Mexico, except for the inevitable incorporation of lexical Anglicisms. At the opposite end is the notion that Mexican American Spanish is a degenerate Mexican Spanish, the result of imperfect bilingualism sometimes compared with creolization (e.g., Webb 1980). Proponents of this view claim that Mexican American Spanish is a conglomeration of errors, misperceptions, and unacceptable simplifications, as well as bearing an overwhelming structural influence from English: in other words, a language created by individuals who think in English while speaking Spanish. This pessimistic viewpoint, although supported by little empirical evidence, is widely diffused, known by such unflattering terms as *Tex-Mex, pocho, border Spanish, Spanglish,* and the like. In reality, Mexican American Spanish is not a discrete dialect, but a continuum of language-contact varieties encompassing a wide range of abilities in both English and Spanish. The sociodemographics of the Mexican American population in the United States reflect in the aggregate a predominantly rural population that has received little or no formal education in Spanish (Hidalgo 1987). Early descriptions such as Espinosa (1913), Ornstein (1951), Rael (1939), Post (1933), Sánchez (1972), and Peñalosa (1975, 1980) may create the misleading impression that Mexican American Spanish is a patchwork of nonstandard and archaic forms, highly reduced pronunciation, and transparent borrowings or loan-translations from English. Ironically, this is the only speech mode which might lay claim to being distinct from the speech of Mexico, but it fails to adequately describe hundreds of thousands of Mexican Americans whose speech is characterized by more prestigious forms convergent with those of educated Mexicans. Studies of wider scope, such as Bills and Ornstein (1976), García (1977), Hensey (1973, 1976), Hidalgo (1987), Ornstein (1972), Peñalosa (1980), and Sánchez (1978, 1983), give a more realistic perspective on the range of linguistic phenomena which can properly be called Mexican American.

In order to understand the specifics of Mexican American Spanish, it is necessary to take a closer look at dialect differentiation within Mexico, particular the speech of economically distressed regions, which have contributed the majority of Mexican immigrants to the United States in the last half century or so. A number of monographic studies, as well as countless articles, provide a core bibliography for Mexican Spanish. The basic facets of Mexican dialectology are summarized in Lipski (1994a). Regional features of Mexican pronunciation are treated in Moreno de Alba (1994). In general, Mexican Spanish is linguistically more conservative than the Caribbean dialects, in retaining in unmodified form many sounds that have been altered or eliminated in the Spanish-speaking Caribbean. There are a few regions of Mexico, primarily along the southern (Pacific) and Caribbean coasts, where pronunciation approximates varieties heard in the Caribbean, but these dialects are scarcely represented in Mexican American communities. Even to the untrained ear, Mexican Spanish of nearly any geographical origin "sounds" different than any Cuban, Puerto Rican, or Dominican variety. Mexican Spanish bears greater resemblance to Guatemalan Spanish, a not surprising fact given the common border between the two nations; similarities with Salvadoran Spanish are fewer but still considerable. At the same time the proportion of vocabulary items of non-Romance origin is proportionally higher in Mexican Spanish than in

Caribbean varieties; most such words are of Nahuatl origin. Mexican Spanish also presents some grammatical innovations not found in other Spanish dialects.

Although regional variation is considerable, a number of common linguistic traits are found in most of central and northern Mexico, the areas from which the majority of Mexican Americans derive their origins. All these traits can be found to varying degrees in every Mexican American speech community as well. There is little evidence of English interference in Mexican American pronunciation, except among semifluent speakers (Foster 1976; Phillips 1967, 1972, 1975, 1976). Common Mexican and Mexican American Spanish traits are described below:

Phonetics and Phonology

- The most striking feature of Mexican Spanish pronunciation as compared with Caribbean dialects is the strong sibilant pronunciation of syllable- and word-final /s/ (Lipski 1994c). Mexican Spanish shares this trait with northern Spain, central Colombia, and the Andean countries. Syllable- and word-final /s/ is often aspirated along the Caribbean states (particularly in the states of Tabasco and Chiapas, but also in Veracruz) and along the Pacific coast, from Oaxaca to Baja California. In the remainder of the country, significant reduction of final /s/ is largely confined to rural northwestern Mexico, including the state of Sonora (Brown 1989), and part of Sinaloa and Baja California Sur (Hidalgo 1990, López Chávez 1977). Among U.S. Spanish dialects of Mexican origin, /s/ does not normally reduce at significant rates, because these varieties are derived from dialects of central and northern Mexico in which word-final /s/ remains strong. In southern Arizona, bordering on Sonora, a weaker /s/ is sometimes observed. The weak final /s/ of traditional New Mexico Spanish evidently comes from much earlier times; this is covered in chapter 12.
- Word-final /n/ is alveolar in most of the interior, and velar [ŋ] in the Yucatán and coastal zones of the Caribbean and the Pacific. Virtually all Mexican Americans realize word-final /n/ as alveolar [n], in sharp contrast to Central Americans and speakers of Caribbean origin, who velarize word-final /n/ to [ŋ], as in English *sing*.
- The phoneme /r/ is an alveolar trill throughout most of Mexico. The velarized trill found in Puerto Rico and the preaspirated [hr] trill common in the Caribbean are not heard in Mexican Spanish.
- There is a tendency for /e/ to be laxed to [ɛ] as in English *let*, particularly in final closed syllables, as in *inglés* (Matluck 1963). This feature is found throughout Mexican American communities.
- Intervocalic /j/ is weak in many central and northern regions and tends to disappear in contact with /i/ or /e/, as in *gallina* (hen), *sello* (stamp), *milla* (mile), and so forth. Although the weakened pronunciation of /j/ by no means characterizes all varieties of Mexican Spanish (for example, the prestigious dialect of Mexico City does not

weaken /j/ appreciably), the weakened pronunciation of /j/ typifies much Mexican American speech, given the strong representation of northern dialects in most Mexican American communities.

- Much of central Mexico exhibits high rates of unstressed vowel reduction and elision. This process is most frequent in contact with /s/ and affects /e/ and /i/ with the highest degree of regularity. Thus, *entonces* (then) may emerge as *entons, presidente* as *presdente,* and *camiones* (buses) as *camions.* This pronunciation is not frequent in Mexican American dialects in the southwestern United States, where dialectal features of northern Mexican Spanish predominate. However, reduction of unstressed vowels can be heard with some frequency in Mexican American communities throughout the United States, particularly in midwestern states, where speakers of central and southern Mexican dialects are proportionately more numerous.

- Syllable-final /ɹ/ is often pronounced as a voiceless sibilant almost like [s] throughout central and southern Mexico. In the northern states, a flap or trill pronunciation predominates. As with unstressed vowel reduction, sibilant final /ɹ/ is not often heard along the U.S.-Mexican border, but occurs as an occasional variant in many Mexican American communities across the United States.

- In central Mexico, the posterior fricative /x/ (written as *j,* or as *g* before *e* and *i*) receives audible friction, particularly before front vowels, as in *México.* In the rest of the country, /x/ is weak, much like English *h.* Most Mexican Americans pronounce /x/ weakly, although a stronger velar fricative is always an acceptable variant.

- Pronunciation of /tʃ/ *ch* as a fricative [tʃ] (as in English *ship*) is a common feature of northwestern Mexican dialects, particularly in rural regions. This pronunciation is found throughout New Mexico, Colorado, and Arizona, where linguistic ties to the Mexican states of Chihuahua and Sonora are strong. In other Mexican American communities, fricative pronunciation of /tʃ/ is not common, although it does sometimes occur.

Morphological Characteristics

- Mexican Spanish, like Caribbean varieties, uses *tú* as the familiar subject pronoun, together with the normal *tuteo* verb conjugations. There are a few areas where *vos* and accompanying verb forms are still used, particularly in Chiapas, but this usage has not penetrated Mexican American speech.

- Although Mexico is *loísta* (use of the clitic *lo* for masculine direct objects, both animate and inanimate), Mexican Spanish frequently adds the clitic *le* to intransitive verbs or uses *le* as a generic direct object. This usage is particularly frequent in imperatives. In addition to the ubiquitous Mexican *ándale* (let's go, okay), *órale* (come on, let's go), *híjole/jíjole* (an expression of surprise), and *úpale* (said while lifting a heavy object), one hears commands like *ciérrale* (close [the door]), *dele* (do it, let 'em have it), and so forth. Police officers directing traffic say *pásele* (move on), and *apúrale* (hurry up) is a common way of urging haste. This use of *le* carries over into Mexican American varieties.

Syntactic Characteristics

- Mexican Spanish does not use noninverted questions such as those found in Caribbean Spanish, as in *¿cómo tú te llamas?* (what's your name?), nor are overt subject pronouns such as *tú* and *usted* used as frequently as in the Caribbean, particularly in tag phrases such as *tú sabes* (you know).
- Infinitives with subjects such as *antes de yo llegar* (before I arrived) occur occasionally, but not nearly with the frequency found in Caribbean Spanish varieties.
- Mexican Spanish prefers *qué tanto* to *cuánto* for "how much," and uses *qué tan* + ADJECTIVE in expressing degree, as in *¿qué tan grande es?* (how big is it?).
- The colloquial superlative of adjectives is formed with *mucho muy*, as in *es mucho muy importante* (it is very important).
- Mexican Spanish is noted for frequent use of *no más* for "only, just" as in *no más quería platicar contigo* (I just wanted to talk to you).
- The Spanish word *mero* is used in the sense of "the very same, one and only," as in *está en el mero centro* (it's right in the middle of town). *Ya mero* means "almost," as in *ya mero me caigo* (I almost fell).

Syntactic Characteristics of Mexican American Spanish

Mexican American Spanish is beginning to diverge syntactically from mainstream dialects of Mexico, although this is primarily true of Mexican Americans who live away from Mexican immigrant communities (García 1977). One gradual shift is the increasing use of the indicative for the subjunctive in some constructions (Floyd 1978; Ocampo 1990; Silva-Corvalán 1997; Escamilla 1982). There are subtle changes in the use of some prepositions, as well as past tense forms (Chaston 1991; Floyd 1982). Occasional erosion of noun-adjective gender concord occurs among Spanish-recessive bilinguals,[1] as does convergence of *ser* and *estar* (Gutierrez 1990, 1992, 1994; Kirschner and Stephens 1988). Loan translations abound among Spanish-English bilinguals. Most escape the notice of all but the closest observers, and many are disputed as true Anglicisms even in Latin American countries. Combinations involving *para atrás* (*patrás*) to translate the English particle "back" are frequent, as in other varieties of Spanish in the United States: *llamar patrás* (to call back, return a call), *dar patrás* (to give back, return a borrowed item), *pagar patrás* (to pay back [a loan]), *pensar patrás* (to think back, reflect), and so forth. These expressions are treated in more detail in chapter 12. Found particularly in California and sometimes in New Mexico and Arizona are configurations like *hacer fix* (to fix) and *hacer improve* (to improve), which Reyes (1976a, 1976b) has analyzed as an example of code switching, but which are really more profound syntactic modifications. This construction is less frequent than the simple creation of new verbs, such as *taipiar* (to type), *espeliar* (to spell), *frizar* (to freeze), or *tochar* (to touch).

As the balance of bilingual abilities shifts towards English, syntactic patterns typical of English and less frequent or even inappropriate in monolingual varieties of Spanish begin to appear in Mexican American speech. One issue is noun-adjective order, in which the predominant placement of descriptive adjectives after the noun in Spanish (*la casa grande, el libro azul*) exhibits alternatives with preposed adjectives, in circumstances when the usual exceptions for preposed adjectives in Spanish do not apply (Denning 1986).

Silva-Corvalán (1982, 1983, 1986, 1988, 1990, 1991a, 1991b, 1993, 1994) has documented a number of features of second- and third-generation Mexican American bilinguals in Los Angeles that may be the result of reduced fluency in Spanish and/or syntactic convergence with English. These phenomena include use of the copula *estar* in contexts where *ser* would be preferred in monolingual varieties, use of redundant subject pronouns, a simplification of the verbal tense system, less flexibility in clitic placement, and a more rigid subject + verb word order, to the detriment of frequently postposed subjects and other alternative constructions found in fully fluent monolingual or bilingual varieties of Spanish.

Code switching, meaning the switching between Spanish and English within the confines of a single sentence or conversation, is common in Mexican American Spanish, as in other Spanish-speaking communities in the United States. This topic is treated in more detail in chapter 12. Mexican American Spanish has provided the greatest number of research studies of code switching, as well as a growing literary expression in which code-switched discourse is the primary language.[2] Code switching only takes place among fluent bilinguals, and a code-switched conversation will abruptly stabilize in a single language upon arrival of a monolingual speaker or one who is known to disapprove of code switching (e.g., a parent, older relative, or neighbor). This provides clear evidence that bilingual speakers are always aware of which language they are speaking, and that code switching is neither "confusion" nor a hopeless tangle of two languages, but rather a deliberately chosen strategy that may be suppressed at will. Code switching is therefore not an anomaly, but rather a natural result of fluent bilingualism.

Lexical Characteristics of Mexican Spanish

Mexican Spanish retains a number of archaisms that were once commonplace in Spain (Lope Blanch 1964). Few are exclusive to Mexico, although some are more prominent in that country. Most "Mexicanisms" are words of Nahuatl origin, although some patrimonial Spanish words receive a different meaning in Mexico. The majority of Mexicanisms are also found in Mexican American Spanish, except for the most regionalized or rustic words in Mexico. Common Mexicanisms include the following:

ándale (let's go, that's OK, I agree [in response to a suggestion],
    you're welcome [when being thanked])
bolillo (American, Caucasian foreigner [derog.])
camión (bus)
¿bueno? (said upon answering the telephone)
chamaco (small child)
charola (tray)
chingadera (unspecified object [vulg.])
chingar (to have sexual intercourse, to ruin, to bother)
escuincle (small child, brat [central Mexico])
gavacho ([Anglo-] American [derog.])
güero (blond, fair complexioned)
híjole/ jíjole (expression of surprise or awe)
huerco (small child [mostly northern Mexico])
¿mande? (said in requesting repetition of something not understood)
naco (crybaby, in bad taste, pretentious [central Mexico])
órale (come on, let's get going)
padre (very good, super)
pinche (cursed, damned) This word derives from a noun meaning "kitchen helper,"
    but is normally used in Mexico as a derogatory adjective: *no entiendo este pinche*
capítulo (I can't understand this cursed chapter).
popote (soda straw)
troca (truck, pickup truck)
úpale (said when lifting heavy objects)

The Mexican American Lexicon

Delimiting just what is the Mexican American or Chicano vocabulary is a controversial topic, because much of what has been attributed to this category are either English borrowings or vernacular Mexicanisms. The patrimonial Spanish component of the Mexican American lexicon is shared with Mexico, including words of Nahuatl origin and numerous archaisms among the rural population. As in any bilingual community, Anglicisms are freely created, and many are widely accepted. Most Anglicisms are based on the spoken form, resulting in written forms that frequently bear little resemblance to the English equivalent: *mira* (meter), *cuara* (quarter [25 cents]), *espica* (speaker), *juila* (wheeler), and so forth.

Such Anglicisms are often created spontaneously and do not necessarily represent core vocabulary as used by Mexican Americans; the transparent phonetic derivation of such items makes them easy to recognize even when they are spontaneous creations. Other Anglicisms (many of which are now in use in Latin America) have been more extensively modified to fit Spanish phonotactics: *troca/troque* (truck), *lonche* (lunch), *bonche* (bunch), *rufa* (roof), and so forth.

The most legitimately "Chicano" form of expression, rooted in Mexican Spanish but uniquely formed in the United States, is Pachuco or *caló* slang. The precise origins of this lexical subvariety are unclear. A widely held view is that this was once the jargon of thieves and prisoners, which like similar varieties in other cultures, was gradually adopted by youth as an in-group slang, and eventually penetrated the speech of the middle class, devoid of any sinister connotations (Barker 1950; Coltharp 1965; Webb 1976; Ornstein-Galicia 1987). This assertion remains to be definitively proven and may embody a simple rejection of rebellious youth by more traditional Mexican families and a negative attitude toward Hispanics by Anglo-Americans. Pachuco seems to have entered the United States in Texas, possibly in El Paso. Oral tradition posits as a possible etymology for Pachuco the deliberate distortion of [*El*] *Paso*, with a resident of the city being known as a *vato del Pachuco*. Pachuco speech spread to California in the 1920s and 1930s, and became associated with cultural patterns that at one time included zoot-suits and slick hairstyles, and whose contemporary reincarnation is the Low Rider. Pachuco or *caló* is and has traditionally been a male language, used by young men as an expression of individualism and independence, and only occasionally and semiseriously by older men. Women do not generally use this language form, except in abusive interchanges. More recently, female variants of *caló* have emerged, but this usage carries strong connotations of rebellion and defiance of linguistic norms (Galindo 1992, 1995). Many Mexican Americans resent that what may have once been an underworld slang is frequently identified with all of Mexican American culture, but the fact remains that Pachuco language and cultural patterns are a uniquely Mexican American phenomenon.

Linguistically, Pachuco uses a characteristic singsong intonation, as well as deliberate distortion or clipping of words, which partially obscures the meaning to noninitiates. Typical examples of "traditional" Pachuco vocabulary, now outmoded, are *simón* and *sirol* for *sí* (yes), *Los* for *Los Angeles* (e.g., *me tiro pa Los* for "I'm going to Los Angeles"), *Califa* (California), *Mejicle* (Mexico), and the universally known *La Migra* (*imigración*) for "U.S. Immigration and Naturalization Service," and its most common manifestation, the Border Patrol. The Pachuco vocabulary also includes numerous slang terms, some of which are used in general Spanish with another meaning. Like *lunfardo* of the Río Plata, Pachuco is in constant evolution—new words are coined and old words pass out of circulation. Some other protypically Pachuco words, recognized if not used by most Mexican Americans, include *ranfla* (car), *ruca* (girlfriend), *birlotear* (to dance), *refinar* (to eat), *chale* (no, shut up), *carnal/carnala* (close [Mexican American] friend, soul brother), *vato* (guy, dude), (*la*) *raza* (Mexican Americans; e.g., *ahí va pura raza* for "only Mexican Americans go there"), and *a(h)í te huacho/nos huachamos* (see you later).

Scholarship on Mexican American Spanish

The bibliography on Mexican American Spanish is vast, spanning more than a century of published research from all across the United States and representing more publications than all of the other U.S. Spanish varieties combined. It is impossible to do justice to this enormous quantity of scholarship within the confines of a single chapter. Many important studies are cited throughout this chapter, as well as in chapter 1. The following section will trace some of the historical research milestones, will mention some of the more contemporary lines of investigation, and will highlight some panoramic presentations. The selection is admittedly personal but is hopefully representative of work already done and suggestive of future research topics.

From the earliest studies of Mexican American or "Chicano" Spanish and continuing through the final decades of the twentieth century, attention focused almost exclusively on deviations from cosmopolitan Spanish usage, on rustic or archaic forms carried over from rural Mexican dialects, on English borrowings and loan-translations, and in some cases on objectively measurable losses of competence in Spanish as language shifts in the direction of English occur. This is not unexpected given that the aim of most traditional dialectological studies has been to highlight unique or noteworthy features of a particular variety, especially elements felt to be quaint, rustic, or archaic, rather than stressing the potentially much larger common ground shared by other dialects of the language. In the case of Mexican American Spanish, however, the combined impact of the published literature has often been taken to imply a Spanish dialect that is both (1) internally quite homogeneous and (2) characterized by a very high degree of archaic, rustic, nonstandard, and even ungrammatical elements. In reality, Mexican American Spanish is a continuum of idiolects and sociolects that span the entire spectrum from a weak second language of third-generation speakers to full fluency and expressive potential at the level of educated native speakers. Moreover, the proportion of archaic or nonstandard elements is often quite low, except for in particularly isolated communities or those resulting from previous homogeneous immigration from marginalized rural areas of Mexico. Finally, the earliest studies, dating from the first decades of this century, but only anthologized under the heading of "Chicano Spanish" beginning in the 1970s, do not systematically distinguish between traditional isolated nonimmigrant varieties of Spanish (e.g., in New Mexico, southern Colorado, and parts of Arizona), whose long-term isolation has indeed given them a rustic and archaic flavor, and the demographically more representative Spanish that results from twentieth-century immigration, in which the linguistic particulars are not so strongly at odds with prescribed usage.

Hernández-Chávez, Cohen, and Beltramo (1975) was a ground-breaking anthology of earlier, previously published articles that for the first time provided scholarly resources on Mexican American Spanish, past and present. The editors' introduction (v-xviii) gives a reasonable overview of the variety and diversity of Mexican American Spanish, including the mix of urban and rural dialect features, differing levels of influence of English, and domains of usage. However, nearly half the studies in the volume deal with archaic varieties of Mexican American Spanish in New Mexico, Colorado, Arizona, and Texas, and most cover only the first half of the twentieth century.[3]

Bowen and Ornstein (1976) was another seminal anthology, composed of studies written for that volume. Among the articles, Bills and Ornstein (1976) make a clear call for empirical dialect research on the subdivisions of southwestern (Mexican and Mexican American) Spanish, following the lead of Craddock (1973). Hensey (1976) offers a grammatical analysis of Mexican American Spanish, which concentrates on deviations from prescriptive Spanish usage. Craddock (1976) updates the study of the southwestern Spanish lexicon, stressing interference from English. Bowen (1976) highlights the large number of archaic and analogical forms in the verbal system of traditional New Mexican Spanish. Cohen (1976) studies bilingual usage among Mexican American children and documents many cases of bilateral interference. Finally, Vallejo (1976) correlates socioeconomic status with language mixture among Mexican American children.

Sánchez (1972) contributed a seminal article that did much to place the linguistic characteristics of Mexican American Spanish before linguists and sociologists. She asserts, *"podría hablarse del dialecto méxico-americano del sudoeste de EEUU. Conviene considerar que no sólo es un habla regional sino también una variedad social que identifica a una minoría étnica vista por los anglos y los otros hispanos en nuestro ambiente como un pueblo sin líderes, sin ambiciones, de escasos recursos, de poca educación y de un bajo nivel socio-económico."* (One can speak of a Mexican American dialect in the southwestern United States. It is important to mention that it is not only a regional dialect but also a social variety that identifies an ethnic minority seen by Anglos and other Latinos as a group without leaders, without ambition, with few resources, poorly educated, and of low socioeconomic status [Sanchez 1972, 47].)

Her article begins with some examples from Texas, including older women (*comadres*), a Pachuco (*vato loco*), a Chicano activist, and a teenage girl. Each of the examples shows some deviation from textbook Spanish, including English borrowings and loan translations, politically and socially charged slang, popular phonetic traits, code switching, and sociolinguistically neutral Mexican regional features. Sánchez then goes on to describe possible variation within the Mexican American community, in sociopolitical terms (1972, 49) based on the notion of diglossia, as found in Arabic-speaking countries. She asserts that there is a standard Mexican dialect found in the media and in some churches, but that vernacular speech is more varied. At the low end of the spectrum of variation are speakers who possess a limited lexical repertoire and a simplified syntax. As an illustration of her points, Sánchez presents a compendium of features found among thirty Mexican American students from various parts of Texas. Despite the obvious attempt to create an objective description of Mexican American Spanish in its true variety, many of Sánchez's examples dwell on rustic (i.e., rural, not just informal, popular, or uneducated) variants. The phonetic examples are all typical of rustic Spanish worldwide, with none of the examples being uniquely or even predominantly Mexican. Similarly, Sánchez gives many examples of verb forms created by analogy, extending diphthongs (*pierdemos*), regularizing accents (*cómamos*), and so forth. Yet her research, as one of the first comprehensive descriptions of Mexican American speech considered "Chicano Spanish" (i.e., the language of a socially disadvantaged group, subject to linguistic persecution) and written by an "insider," set the stage for much subsequent research.

Galván and Teschner (1975, 1977) provides the first widely available dictionary purported to describe Chicano Spanish that is neither a dictionary of Mexicanisms published in Mexico nor a glossary of forms found in a single Spanish-speaking community in the United States. In the preface to the first edition (v), the authors note that the volume in fact deals with the Spanish of Texas, while adding the caveat that "[this] is not a 'full-length' dictionary for the simple reason that it does not give items which form part of 'standard' Spanish as defined by the several canons of inclusion of those monolingual and bilingual dictionaries." In compiling the dictionary, the authors examined several descriptions of regional varieties of Spanish, in addition to consulting worldwide Spanish dictionaries and relying on the authors' personal knowledge of Spanish language usage in Texas.

The authors state that (vi) "we do *not* claim that the entries in our lexicon are 'peculiar to' the Spanish of this particular Spanish-speaking region and thus, by inference, unknown or else accepted solely as foreignisms 'elsewhere' throughout the Hispanic world." In the second edition (1976), the authors include data from California, Arizona, New Mexico, Colorado, and even Florida, thus making the dictionary, originally called the *Diccionario del español de Tejas,* into the *Diccionario del español chicano.* The *Diccionario del español chicano* is still a valuable reference tool, but because of the limitations in data collection and verification, the dictionary contains many items that are common to vernacular Spanish over a much wider area, as well as occasional oddities that are not truly representative of Mexican American Spanish as a whole. The authors include in their dictionary phonetic variants that typify (predominantly northern) Mexican Spanish or colloquial Spanish in general. These include *pa* < *para* (for), *calzoncío* < *calzoncillo* (underpants), *toavía* < *todavía* (yet), *tualla* < *toalla* (towel), and so forth. Such rapid-speech and regional phonetic variants are not found in provincial or national dictionaries of other varieties of Spanish, and their inclusion in the Chicano Spanish dictionary gives the impression that rather unremarkable phonetic reductions found throughout the Spanish-speaking world are somehow more exaggerated in this dialect. Another potential difficulty is the lack of indication of frequency of usage. The authors do acknowledge certain items as obsolete but include items such as *vide* for *vi* (I saw), *traiba* for *traía* (I/he/she used to bring), *truje* (I brought), which are typical only of the most isolated or rustic speakers of Texas and other Mexican American varieties of Spanish.

The issue of archaisms in Mexican American Spanish lies at the heart of the debate on the "standardness" or "correctness" of these varieties. Objectively, many truly archaic forms can be found in communities whose speakers label themselves Mexican American or Chicano. In a few cases (northern New Mexico, southern Colorado, the Sabine River isolate), the archaisms represent nonimmigrant varieties of Spanish that developed in what is now U.S. territory several centuries ago and were subsequently isolated from more recent innovations of Mexican Spanish. In other cases, such as along the U.S.-Mexican border, archaic forms derive in large measure from uneducated rural speakers, especially from areas of Mexico where public education is precarious at best, and contact with more prestigious sociolects is limited. Although the average socioeconomic level of Mexican immigrants to the United States is quite low by American standards, it is by no means the case that all or even most Mexican immigrants speak rural or uneducated varieties of Spanish. There are hundreds of thousands of Mexican Americans of modest means who never use such items as *asina* (thus); *vide, truje, muncho* (much); *traiba, mesmo* (same); or *agora* (now). Some Mexican American speakers appear to use both the archaic and the contemporary variants for stylistic effects (Green 1986a, 1986b).

Peñalosa (1980) was another milestone in the linguistic study of Mexican American Spanish as a phenomenon situated within the United States, and not simply as a collection of displaced Mexican variants. Written by a sociologist, the book brought together much of the earlier scholarship on "Chicano Spanish." Although Peñalosa relied heavily on Sánchez (1972) and other early linguistic studies, his portrayal of the variety and diversity of Mexican American Spanish is realistic, given the bibliography available at the time. More important, the book is not merely or even predominantly a study of linguistic particulars, but rather focuses on the social matrix in which both Spanish and English used by Chicanos are embedded. Code switching, public and private language domains, and language attitudes are treated as integral components of the Chicano language experience.

Advancing significantly beyond her earlier article, Sánchez (1983) represents an eloquent sociolinguistic and sociopolitical portrayal of Chicano language, viewed from the inside. Sánchez takes the stance that Chicano language and culture are under assault and views with pessimism the possibilities for significant linguistic and cultural retention in view of the heavy pressure to assimilate to Anglo-American society. Cast in a neo-Marxist framework, Sánchez (1983) examines the root causes for Chicano language behavior, rather than confining herself to simply describing the end product. Her description of Chicano Spanish is considerably more mature than her earlier work (Sánchez 1972), both in terms of descriptive detail and in encompassing the entirety of Mexican American language usage. She distinguishes among "standard Spanish," "popular urban Spanish," and "popular rural Spanish" in describing Mexican American speech and treats all Chicano language usage from a discourse perspective. Linguistic behavior is set in terms of domains of usage, integration into distinct strata of U.S. society, linguistic and cultural attitudes, and rural/urban origin. Sánchez definitely demonstrates that not all Mexican American Spanish is "archaic" or even "non-standard" and that despite the relative socioeconomic disadvantage with respect to the Anglo-American population, the Mexican American community contains a variety of styles and registers comparable to those used by monolingual native speakers of English.

Among morphological, syntactic, or lexical variants that separate rustic Mexican Spanish from its urban counterparts, the following are worthy of mention, because all have appeared at one time or another in undifferentiated descriptions of Chicano Spanish. Items listed as urban correspond to universal Spanish norms, whereas the rural/rustic items are not peculiar to Mexico or Mexican American Spanish, but are found in many rural Spanish dialects throughout the world.

Urban	Rural/Rustic	
abuelo/abuela	*agüelo/agüela*	(grandfather, grandmother)
aguja	*abuja*	(needle)
ahora	*agora/abora*	(now)
así	*asina, ansina, ajina*	(thus)
comprar	*mercar*	(to buy)
dijeron	*dijieron*	(they said)
donde	*onde*	(where)
fui, fue, etc.	*jui, jue,* etc.	(I went, was; he/she went, were)
hablastes	*hablates*	(you spoke)
he dicho	*ha dicho*	(I have said)
íbamos	*íbanos*	(we used to go)
maíz	*maiz*	(corn)
mamá/papá	*amá/apá*	(mother, father)
mismo	*mesmo*	(same)
mucho	*muncho*	(much)
nos vemos	*los vemos*	(so long, see you later)
somos	*semos*	(we are)
soy	*seigo*	(I am)
traía	*traiba*	(I/he/she used to bring)
traje/trajo	*truje/trujo*	(I/he/she brought)
vaya	*vaiga*	(go [imperative])
vi/vio	*vide/vido*	(I/he/she saw)
vuélvamos/volvamos	*vuélvanos*	(we return [subjunctive])

By the end of the 1980s, scholarship on Mexican American Spanish increasingly concentrated on contemporary speech and devoted much attention to issues of educational equity, language maintenance, bilingual and heritage language education, and sociolinguistic variation. Valdés (1988 and the updated 2000) offers an excellent contemporary perspective as well as a review of pertinent literature. Valdés and Geoffrion-Vinci (1998) describe issues of educational equity with regard to Chicano Spanish. Hidalgo (1987) offers an excellent guide to social and pedagogical issues surrounding the Chicano versus "standard Mexican" Spanish dichotomy. Hidalgo (2001) documents reverse language shift (i.e., greater use of Spanish) along the U.S.-Mexican border in southern California, extending observations of Hidalgo (1993, 1995). Galindo (1992, 1995), Mendoza-Denton (1994, 1996, 1997, 1999), and the works appearing in Galindo and Gonzales (1999) document the nuances of language as used by Mexican American women, particularly in urban settings. Potowski (2004) documents language shift among Mexican Americans in Chicago. Bayley and Pease-Álvarez (1997) contribute to the ongoing study of null and overt pronoun usage among Spanish-English bilinguals, in this case in the discourse of Mexican American children. Many of the articles in Colombi and Alarcón (1997), a volume of essays on the topic of teaching Spanish to native speakers in the United States, address pedagogical issues that impact the Mexican American community.

Notes

1. Lipski (1985a, 1986b, 1993a, 1996b); García (1998) finds little evidence of this phenomenon.
2. Barkin (1978), Gingras (1974), Jacobson (1977a, 1977b, 1978a, 1978b), Lance (1975a, 1975b), Lipski (1985a), Peñalosa (1980), Pfaff (1979), Reyes (1976a, 1976b), Redlinger (1976), Sánchez (1983), Timm (1975), Valdés-Fallis (1976a, 1976b, 1981).
3. These include Cárdenas (1975), Espinosa (1975), Espinosa, Jr. (1975), Ornstein (1975b), Rael (1939), Post (1931), Lance (1975a), Lastra de Suárez (1975), E. García (1975), Sawyer (1964), Bowen (1975), Beltramo and Porcel (1975), Barker (1975).

5

Cuban Spanish in the United States

Introduction

Cuban Americans are the third-largest Hispanophone group in the United States, with a population of more than 1 million, the majority of whom speak Spanish. The presence of a large Cuban community in the United States has prompted a number of detailed phonological, sociolinguistic, and lexical studies, nearly all focusing on the educated speech of Havana. No comprehensive monograph on the Spanish of Cuba has yet been written, although a linguistic atlas project is in the works.[1] Cuban Spanish is the variety most heard throughout Florida and is well represented in the greater New York City area as well as in other communities scattered across the country.

Cuba was visited by Columbus on his first voyage, and small settlements were established almost immediately. The first Cuban town to achieve recognition was Santiago de Cuba, at the eastern end of the island near the already prospering colony of Española. In the second half of the sixteenth century, Spain adopted the system of sending two fleets to the Americas annually, to carry passengers and trade goods and to return with treasure. One fleet sailed to Veracruz, and the other to Nombre de Dios (later to Porto-belo). Both fleets stopped at Havana (which had been relocated to the north coast from its original location on the southern coast) upon arrival from Spain and also on the way back out of the Caribbean. This brought enormous prosperity to western Cuba, whereas eastern Cuba entered a period of social and economic stagnation from which it was never to fully recover. The results of this geopolitical imbalance are noticeable in contemporary Cuban Spanish, where the speech of the *orientales* (known as *palestinos* in contemporary Cuban slang) shares a greater similarity with Dominican and Puerto Rican Spanish than with that of Havana.

The Cuban sugar industry received a boost with the Haitian Revolution in 1791, which destroyed the world's largest source of sugar production. Many Haitian planters escaped to Cuba, some even bringing their slaves, and the rapid increase in world sugar prices resulted in a frenzied conversion of all available land in Cuba to sugar cultivation. Some three-quarters of a million slaves were imported in less than a century (Pérez 1988, 85), and in the first quarter of the nineteenth century African slaves represented as much as 40% of the total Cuban population. If to this figure is added the large free black population, Africans and Afro Cubans made up well over half the Cuban population for much of the nineteenth century. The demographic distribution was not even; in the larger cities, the population was predominantly of Spanish origin, whereas in rural sugar-growing areas, the Afro-Hispanic population was very high. The linguistic effects of this demographic shift were considerable, and the full range of phenomena attributable to the African presence in Cuba has sparked a lively debate.

Also significant in nineteenth century Cuba was the influx of European immigration, primarily from Spain. Immigration from Galicia/Asturias and the Canary Islands was especially heavy in the second half of the nineteenth century. Canary immigration peaked in the first decades of the twentieth century, and was responsible for a considerable amount of linguistic transfer between the two territories. So concentrated was Spanish immigration that Cubans began to refer to all Spaniards from the Peninsula as *gallegos* (Galicians) and to the Canary Islanders as *isleños* (islanders). At the time of the Spanish-American War of 1898, almost half of Cuba's white population had been born in Spain.

Cuban Spanish in the United States: The Early Arrivals

The presence of Cubans in the United States long preceded the Spanish-American War; indeed, by the end of the nineteenth century an estimated 100,000 Cubans lived in the United States, mostly in Tampa, Key West, and New York (García and Otheguy 1988, 166). Beginning in the middle of the nineteenth century, Cuban nationalists—foremost among them José Martí—used the United States as a safe haven for launching revolutionary schemes and publishing nationalist broadsides. This early presence was composed entirely of Cuban intellectuals who, in the eyes of U.S. citizens, were as much Spaniards as Cubans. The Cuban revolutionaries were welcomed as the champions of independence for one of the last Spanish colonies in the Americas, a reception no doubt aided by the general sentiment in the United States that Cuba would sooner or later become part of its nation. The failure of the U.S. government to sufficiently quell Cuban revolutionary fervor met with the strong disapproval of Spain, but prior to the end of the nineteenth century, the Cuban presence in the United States went all but unnoticed by most Americans. One carryover of this early Cuban appearance in the United States was the Cuban colony of Key West, Florida (known in Spanish as *Cayo Hueso*). Prior to the Cuban Revolution, this small group of Cubans lived in relative isolation on the tiny island and preserved a variety of Spanish harking back to the final decades of the nineteenth century (Beardsley 1972). This community has since been completely overrun with post-1959 Cuban arrivals, and little or nothing remains of the traditional dialect.

With its excellent natural harbor and proximity to Havana (only 90 miles in an easy passage), Key West was a natural way station for voyages between Cuba and the United States. The first significant Cuban settlement in the United States was formed in Key West, where Cuban cigar makers established themselves as early as the 1830s (the first cigar factory was opened in 1831, by an American entrepreneur). During the independence movements led by Cuban nationalists against Spain, Key West was a safe haven for Cuban patriots who did not wish to live as far away from their homeland as those who sought refuge in continental American cities. Thousands of pro-independence Cubans took refuge in Key West, bringing with them the beginnings of the cigar industry (Alvarez Estévez 1986). Later in the century, José Martí, the author of Cuba's second independence movement (which never reached fruition as a result of the Spanish-American War) also visited Key West and Tampa. Although Martí was killed in an early skirmish in 1895, his revolutionary movement gained momentum, and the Spanish government's repression of nationalists increased steadily, bringing a further stream of Cuban refugees to Key West.

The largest permanent Cuban settlement in the United States prior to the Cuban Revolution was in Tampa, where the Cuban cigar industry flourished over the first half of the twentieth century. In 1886 the first Cuban cigar factory was established in Ybor City, a section of Tampa, by Cubans from New York, Key West, and Havana (Covington 1980). The enclave was named after a Spanish-born immigrant who had moved his cigar factory from Cuba to Key West in 1869. As a result of the increasing number of Cubans moving to Tampa, Ybor decided to set up a branch factory in that city; other Cuban entrepreneurs established themselves in Tampa at the same time, and by the end of the century Cubans in Tampa had their own schools, businesses, and a Spanish-language newspaper, the *Revista de la Florida.* By 1890 Ybor City had some 1,300 Cubans (Olson and Olson 1995, 24); by 1900 there were more than 3,500 Cubans in a city whose total population was 23,000. The Tampa Cuban colony numbered in the thousands and transplanted an entire Cuban lifestyle to this growing Florida city. To this day traditional Cuban clubs and organizations recall the flourishing cigar industry in Tampa, alongside a smaller number of recent Cuban arrivals. Canfield (1951a) is a linguistic study of Tampa-Cuban Spanish. Today this speech community is rapidly vanishing, although a good number of older speakers recall the heyday of Tampa Cubans.

The 1870 census found 5,300 individuals of Cuban origin living in the United States (Olson and Olson 1995, 20). By 1880 there were 7,000 Cubans officially in the United States, with 2,000 in Key West, and the rest scattered in Tampa, Mobile, Pensacola, New Orleans, Miami, New York, Philadelphia, and Baltimore. Only five years later Key West alone had 5,000 Cuban settlers. In 1900 there were 11,000 people of Cuban ancestry in the United States. By 1930, approximately 19,000 Cubans were living in the United States, most of them in Key West and Tampa. In 1959, on the eve of the Cuban Revolution, some 30,000 Cubans lived in the United States, although more than 100,000 Cubans had immigrated to the United States between 1900 and 1950. By 1960 this number had jumped to 79,000 Cuban-born individuals in the United States, out of an official total of 124,416 residents of Cuban origin, with many exiles having left during the first year of the Castro regime (Olson and Olson 1995, 40).

Cuban Spanish in the United States: The Machado and Batista Years

By far the greatest number of Cubans to settle in the United States arrived following the Cuban Revolution of 1959, but the events that led to the fall of Fulgencio Batista and the meteoric rise to power of Fidel Castro began in the final years of the nineteenth century. The Spanish-American War quickly came to an end thanks to the massive U.S. military intervention, but the American government expressly refused to allow the patriotic Cuban forces to participate, fearing that an overly nationalistic zeal might jeopardize U.S. investments in Cuba. Cuba remained a U.S. military protectorate until 1902, but the Platt Amendment, passed in 1901, gave the United States the permanent right to intervene in Cuba whenever U.S. interests were at stake and to review all treaties and loans between Cuba and third countries. It also required that Cuba lease or sell naval and coaling stations to the United States, one of which, at Guantánamo Bay (obtained in 1903), is still occupied by American forces. The Platt Amendment was a bitter pill for Cuban nationalism, and Cubans' worst fears were confirmed by several U.S. military interventions, including another military occupation from 1906 to 1909 following disputed elections. The events surrounding the Spanish-American War and the early U.S. occupations of Cuba resulted in some 56,000 Cubans being admitted to the United States between 1896 and 1910 (Pérez 1986).

Early Cuban governments struggled to impart a sense of identity to the new nation. The first presidents were largely U.S.-educated and strongly pro-U.S. intellectuals and businessmen, and it appeared that Cuba would emulate the United States to a greater extent than other Latin American countries. This perception came to an end with the government of Gerardo Machado (elected in 1925), whose first few years in office led to later comparisons with Franklin Roosevelt. His regime quickly slipped into authoritarian intolerance, and all dissidence was harshly suppressed; at the same time corruption began to reach levels characteristic of previous Cuban regimes.

In 1933 Machado was forced into exile, and Carlos Manuel de Céspedes was named as interim president. This provoked mass chaos, and in September a young army sergeant named Fulgencio Batista organized a military revolt against the officers. Quickly "promoted" to the rank of colonel, Batista supported the presidency of Ramón Grau San Martín (Céspedes had lasted only three weeks in office), who was regarded as dangerously left-leaning by the newly elected American president Franklin Roosevelt. The U.S. government refused to recognize Grau, and Batista maneuvered to have the pro-U.S. Colonel Carlos Mendieta named as president. This began a series of puppet governments clearly controlled by Batista, who as army chief of staff remained the power behind the throne until 1940, when he himself was elected president.

In the 1944 elections Batista expected his hand-picked successor Carlos Saládrigas to win, but in a surprise victory Ramón Grau San Martín was elected for a second time. Batista reluctantly accepted the results and left the country for retirement in Key Biscayne, Florida. In the 1952 elections Batista decided to run as a candidate, but before the elections could take place, sympathetic military officers staged a coup to return the now General Batista to power. Although some Cubans viewed with relief the end of a succession of corrupt civilian governments, for patriotic Cubans this was the last straw, and the nation seemed doomed to a perpetual succession of military dictators more typical of struggling "banana republics" than of the prosperous and well-educated Cuban populace.

On July 26, 1953, a young lawyer named Fidel Castro (whose party, the Ortodoxos, was robbed of almost certain victory in the 1952 elections by Batista's coup), together with other budding revolutionaries, led a Quixotic attack on the military barracks at Moncada in Santiago de Cuba. The attackers were quickly captured and imprisoned; while in prison Castro penned his first revolutionary manifestos. Castro and his comrades in arms were pardoned in 1955, and Castro left for self-imposed exile in Mexico, where he immediately began planning a return to Cuba. It was in Mexico that Castro met the idealistic young Argentine doctor Ernesto "Che" Guevara, who was to become one of the driving forces of the Cuban Revolution. In 1956 the ranch where Castro and his followers were staying was raided by Mexican police, and when the Cubans were finally released they planned an immediate return to Cuba. The tiny revolutionary "army" departed from the Mexican coastal town of Tuxpan and returned to Cuba in 1956. The group traveled in the motor launch *Granma,* purchased in Brownsville, Texas, whose name has been immortalized in the title of the Cuban Communist Party's newspaper, as well as in a renamed Cuban province.

Back in Cuba, Castro's small group seemed destined to fail again, but circumstances conspired to give them the upper hand, although they were by no means the only or even the most prominent group acting in opposition to Batista. In a series of guerilla operations Castro's operatives succeeded in spreading chaos and insecurity far out of proportion to their small numbers. In 1957 they even staged an unsuccessful attack on the presidential palace in Havana. Castro's struggle against Batista was compared in the media with the battle between David and Goliath; Castro was interviewed by U.S. media, including Herbert Matthews of the *New York Times,* and was presented to the American public as a courageous young leader determined to stamp out the corruption and excesses of Cuba's military and civilian governments. Despite much sound and fury, Castro's guerrilla band had inflicted comparatively little damage on the Batista government, and few were prepared for Batista's sudden abdication and flight from Cuba on January 1, 1959. During the second Batista regime (1951–58), some 63,000 Cubans had sought refuge in the United States.

Cuban Spanish in the United States: 1959 and Beyond

Once in control of Cuba, Castro rapidly dismantled all vestiges of the Batista government. The first changes were widely hailed as a long-overdue transition to a true democracy, but it soon became apparent that Castro intended to perform a vast socialist experiment that went far beyond the expectations of even the most left-leaning Cubans. The expropriation of foreign-owned firms was followed by nationalization of most forms of private property, including land, housing, and most private businesses, and the formation of the dominant Cuban Communist Party, closely aligned with the Soviet Union (and, until the falling-out between the two nations, China). The transition to a communist state was neither peaceful nor painless; hundreds of opponents were summarily tried and executed, thousands of others were imprisoned for varying periods of time, and all dissent was rapidly and violently suppressed. By early 1960 middle- and upper-class Cubans who had never entertained thoughts of leaving their country during the Batista regime were escaping from Cuba, under increasingly difficult conditions. As soon as the Castro government realized the potential for capital flight and a brain drain, permission to leave Cuba was strongly curtailed; families who sought to leave essentially had to go into exile, forfeiting any properties and assets in Cuba and frequently leaving the country with no more than a single change of clothes. Although these Cubans were forced to burn many bridges behind them, few expected that they would remain in the United States for more than a few months, a year at most. The United States was in the midst of the Cold War and surely would not tolerate a Communist government—a Soviet satellite state— only 90 miles from its shores. Even after the U.S. government unexpectedly backed away from open support of Cuban exiles seeking to return in the Bay of Pigs invasion of 1961, hope remained strong in the U.S. Cuban community that the United States would soon put an end to the Castro regime. In 1962 when the discovery of Soviet nuclear missiles in Cuba produced not the ouster of Castro but rather the U.S. promise never again to invade Cuba (in return for the Soviet removal of the missiles in question), the Cuban exile community finally realized that life in the United States was going to be more than a transitory stopover. Prior to this time, most Cubans in the United States (most of whom had remained in south Florida) firmly believed that their stay in that nation would be short, and their principal concern was preserving as much as possible of Cuban society and culture until their return to their homeland. Cubans set up Spanish-language schools and churches and recreated in southwest Miami much of the social and commercial structure of late 1950s Havana. Even after the Cuban Missile Crisis, Cuban Americans clung to the conviction that Castro would soon be overthrown and that they would return to a Cuban society that would quickly recover from the aberrations of the communist period and restore the civil structure of circa 1959.

Post-1959 Cuban immigration to the United States occurred in several well-defined waves, although between major events Cubans continued to arrive in smaller numbers. The real push began in 1960, roughly a year after the onset of the Castro regime, and after the true extent of the social, political, and economic changes promoted by the new government became apparent to the Cuban population. During the first year, emigrés were mostly those who had been directly implicated in maintaining the Batista government, but in 1960 Cuba's professional classes and upper middle classes began to seek refuge in the United States. Although much land had been expropriated through an Agrarian Reform law in 1959, 1960 brought the most sweeping changes to Cuba. Castro nationalized all private schools; expropriated foreign oil refineries, sugar mills, and all other companies based in the United States; established diplomatic and trade relations with the Soviet Union; organized the first of the block-by-block Comités de la Defensa de la Revolución; and began to overhaul (or overrun, depending upon one's point of view) the judicial system. The United States in turn halted the importation of Cuban sugar and began an embargo against U.S. exports to Cuba, which has continued ever since. The following year brought the termination of diplomatic relations between the United States and Cuba; the aborted Bay of Pigs invasion, spearheaded by Cuban exiles and supported—erratically—by the U.S. government; and Castro's declaration that he was and always had been a Marxist-Leninist. In 1962 the United States and the Soviet Union had a standoff over Soviet nuclear warheads that were to be installed in Cuba, bringing both nations to the brink of nuclear war. In return for a withdrawal of the Soviet missiles, the United States agreed not to invade Cuba in the future. During these years, Cubans who were not in synchrony with the Castro government found the environment increasingly hostile, and even requesting permission to immigrate to the United States put Cubans at risk.

Demographic figures demonstrate the proportions of this early Cuban exodus (Prohias and Casal 1980, 12–13). In the 1960 census, there were just over 124,000 Cubans in the United States, of which some 79,000 were born in Cuba. By 1970, there were more than 560,000 Cubans in the United States, of which 439,000 were of Cuban birth. The Cuban refugee center in Miami estimated that nearly 448,000 Cubans entered the United States during this decade. More specifically, during the period 1959–62 some 215,000 Cubans were officially admitted by the United States. During the interlude 1962–65 only 56,000 Cubans entered the United States, many arriving via third countries; approximately 7,000 clandestine arrivals and 6,000 released Bay of Pigs prisoners and their families round out this number. In September 1965 the Cuban government allowed Cubans in the United States to pick up relatives in Cuba; this resulted in 5,000 departures.

By 1973, an estimated 273,000 Cubans lived in the United States. In the second interlude, from April 1973 to April 1980, only 50,000 Cubans officially entered the United States (Boswell 1984). Between 1960 and 1980, more than 350,000 Cubans fled the island, with most ending up in the United States, often via circuitous routes involving third countries (Jamaica, Panama, Costa Rica, Mexico, Spain, etc.). The representative figures are approximately as follows; these figures do not take into account the full effects of the Mariel boatlift, since the 1980 figures end in September of that year (Portes and Bach 1985, 85):

Year	Cuban Immigration to the United States
1959	26,527
1960	60,224
1961	49,661
1962	78,611
1963	42,929
1964	15,616
1965	16,447
1966	46,688
1967	52,147
1968	55,945
1969	52,625
1970	49,545
1971	50,001
1972	23,977
1973	12,579
1974	13,670
1975	8,488
1976	4,515
1977	4,548
1978	4,108
1979	2,644
1980	122,061

The Mariel Boatlift and the *Balseros*

Cubans arriving in South Florida were uniformly treated as political refugees, and most received some resettlement assistance. The hard-working, well-trained, and determined Cuban American community grew and prospered in greater Miami and greater New York City, and the sociodemographic profile of this group came to define all Cubans, at least as far as other U.S. residents were concerned. In 1980, a chain of events that began with numerous hijackings of small boats by Cubans seeking to escape to the United States, by Castro's repeated threats to retaliate through unlimited immigration, and finally by the storming of the Peruvian embassy in Havana by a group of Cubans seeking political asylum and passage out of the country, eventually unleashed a migratory torrent that brought other elements of Cuban society to the United States. As the crisis in the Peruvian embassy spiraled out of control, the United States first offered to accept a few thousand Cubans as a humanitarian gesture, but once Castro announced that any Cuban American who arrived on the Cuban coast at the port of Mariel was free to pick up relatives, the U.S. government could not hold back the masses of south Florida Cubans who flooded the Cuban coast in all manner of small craft (e.g., Larzelere 1988).

When the boatlift "officially" ended six months later, more than 125,000 new Cubans had arrived in the United States, oversaturating all services in southern Florida. Unfortunately for the reputation of the Cuban American community, Castro had released many common criminals, misfits, and mentally ill people among the would-be refugees awaiting pickup by family members, and once in the United States, some of these same individuals quickly ran afoul of the law in several high-profile incidents. At the same time, the Mariel boatlift included a proportionately higher number of lower middle– and working-class Cubans, including many of African origin. Cubans who had arrived in the first immigration wave were overwhelming white (94%), older (average age 34), well-educated (average of 14 years of education), and prosperous. The second wave, lasting through the 1960s and early 1970s, was 80% white, less educated, and less prosperous. The Mariel arrivals were 60% white and considerably less educated and less affluent as a group than the previous arrivals (Llanes 1982). The distinctly middle-to-upper class established Cuban American community at times reacted with disdain to the *marielitos* (as the new arrivals were quickly dubbed), many of whom brought new forms of speech to the previously rather homogeneous Cuban groups in the United States. Found in the new mix were both sociolects slanted towards less educated working classes and forms from interior provinces that had previously been rare among the largely Havana-based Cuban immigrant population (Fernández and Narváez 1987, Portes and Stepick 1985, Boswell 1984, Boswell and Curtis 1983).

Time worked in favor of the Mariel emigrés, and most eventually became well-integrated members of Cuban American society. Fernández and Narváez (1987) suggest that educational level was not the main factor responsible for the initial marginalization of the Mariel boatlift refugees, claiming that the latter's average educational and skill levels were comparable to those of earlier Cuban arrivals, who had become more easily integrated into U.S. society. These authors point to the fact that the Mariel arrivals had spent more time under a communist/socialist regime and were more inclined to rebel against the capitalist society, to seek less refuge in traditional family structures, and to be somewhat more inclined to social protest. It is widely acknowledged that the state-controlled economy of Cuba did little to encourage individual initiatives and that many later Cuban arrivals found it difficult to acclimate to the up-by-the-bootstraps work ethic of earlier Cuban immigrants. Some became disgruntled after being dismissed from jobs for not exhibiting the level of productivity demanded in most U.S. jobs. They also discovered that certain social services that had been free and taken for granted in communist Cuba (e.g., health-care benefits, subsidized housing) carried a high price in the United States and were not within reach of those at the lower end of the wage scale.

In the past two and a half decades, following the attempted arrival of tens of thousands of *balseros* (raft people) to the United States, the U.S. government has been forced to rethink its open-arms immigration policy, which extended immediate resident status to any Cuban who managed to reach the United States by any possible means. A large wave of *balseros* was intercepted by the U.S. Coast Guard and Navy in 1994–95 and taken to the U.S. naval base at Guantánamo Bay, Cuba, where they shared facilities with a large number of intercepted Haitian "boat people." The initial U.S. gambit was to refuse entry to the United States to any Cuban who attempted to arrive illegally via boat or raft. A new agreement with the Cuban government allowed for an increased number of legal immigrants to the United States each year. This represented a major departure from previous U.S. policy, and after considerable political wrangling, the Guantánamo refugees were ultimately admitted to the United States. As of this writing, the United States is attempting to stave off massive sea arrivals by facilitating legal immigration through the United States Interests Section in Havana. This policy is reinforced by the broadcasts of Radio Martí, a special service of the Voice of America that broadcasts to Cuba twenty-four hours a day. Although these broadcasts were once the subject of intense jamming in Cuba, and people who listened to them ran the risk of political persecution, Cubans now openly listen to these broadcasts, and the Cuban government tacitly recognizes Radio Martí as a source of updated information on U.S. government views and policies.[2]

Current Profile of Cuban American Communities

As of the 1980 census, 58.5% of the Cubans in the United States lived in Florida, 10% in New Jersey, 9.6% in New York, 7.6% in California, 2.4% in Illinois, and 1.8% in Texas (Moore and Pachon 1985, 57). The 1990 census documented 1.05 million Cubans in the United States, of whom 298,000 were U.S.-born. The 2000 census registered 1.24 million Cubans in the United States (3.5% of the total Hispanic population). Most live in south Florida and the urban Northeast, but there are significant groups in other states, as follows:

Florida	833,100
New Jersey	77,300
California	72,300
New York	62,600
Texas	25,700
Puerto Rico	19,800
Illinois	18,400
Georgia	12,500
Nevada	11,500
Pennsylvania	10,400
Massachusetts	8,900
Louisiana	8,400
Virginia	8,300
North Carolina	7,400
Michigan	7,200
Connecticut	7,100

The largest Cuban American community resides in the greater Miami area. The U.S. government has always tried to resettle Cubans throughout the country, via sponsorships with churches and civic groups, but many displaced Cubans inevitably drift back to South Florida. As a result, Spanish has become the de facto lingua franca throughout South Florida, a situation that has not pleased many previous residents who have been forced to learn Spanish or face severe economic marginality. Miami Spanish is overwhelmingly Cuban, although the city also harbors large communities of Nicaraguans, Colombians, Puerto Ricans, Dominicans, and other Latin American groups. It is Cuban Spanish that shows through the ostensibly dialect-neutral speech of radio and television newscasters and Cuban Spanish that provides the regional spice to the largest Spanish-language newspaper, the *Nuevo Herald* (a Spanish-language version of the *Miami Herald*), and to the thousands of official signs and announcements throughout Dade County. Nearly all Spanish-language radio programs employ Cuban personnel, with the exception of occasional Nicaraguan programming. Among the most "Cuban" of the radio stations are those playing popular music and those that provide a forum for political commentary— invariably diatribes against the Castro government. In some cases, such as with the powerful Radio Mambí (once an illegal clandestine station, now legitimized as the most potent Spanish-language AM station in South Florida), it is clear that many of the broadcasts are, in fact, directed at audiences in Cuba.

Although it is common to speak of the Miami Cuban community as a monolithic whole, there are important linguistic and socioeconomic differences that permeate the area. Within Miami itself, the classic Cuban community is "Little Havana," centered on Southwest 8th Street on the edge of Coral Gables. In Spanish, *la Calle Ocho,* of the *Saugüesárea* (the Hispanized version of "Southwest Area"), are the usual designations. Although the majority of South Florida Cubans now live outside this area, the Southwest Area is still the most important commercial, gastronomical, and social center of the traditional community. Upwardly mobile Cubans and Cuban Americans who are not inclined to live in ethnically homogeneous neighborhoods do not publicly identify with *La Calle Ocho,* but most visit the area at least occasionally, and many have family members living there. After the Mariel boatlift of 1980, many of the recently arrived and less prosperous Cubans immediately moved to this area, which made it less desirable in the eyes of more established Cuban American families. This fact notwithstanding, Little Havana continues to typify the more Cuban-leaning lifestyle of South Florida's Cuban community. Spanish is virtually the only language throughout the area, and Spanish is spoken immediately to any individual one meets, regardless of physical appearance.

A number of Cubans have also migrated to Kendall, a residential community immediately south of Miami. When the first Cubans arrived, they found themselves in the midst of Anglo American suburbia, but in many parts of Kendall the Cuban population is now large and may be a majority in some neighborhoods. These are Cubans who have lived for a long time in the United States, and the younger community members were born in this country. Spanish is spoken at home, but less frequently in public shopping areas. It is certainly not axiomatic that everyone will speak Spanish in Kendall, with the result that English is more commonly used as a first gambit, unless an unfamiliar interlocutor shows unmistakable external signs of Latin American origin.

A much more "Cuban" community in the traditional sense is found in Hialeah, just north of Miami. Many Cubans in Hialeah represent the first generation of refugees from the Cuban Revolution, and there are extensive commercial areas where Spanish is the primary language. South Florida Cubans generally regard Hialeah as on a par with *La Calle Ocho*; Hialeah, however, is seen as predominantly a residential community, with a significant Anglo American component, whereas southwest Miami is indisputably a Cuban bastion.

There are several large Cuban communities outside of South Florida, with the largest being located in Union City and West New York, New Jersey (Rodríguez Herrera, Rogg, and Cooney 1980). Throughout the metropolitan New York City area the Cuban population is considerable and well organized (Bogen 1987, chapter 10), but except in Union City there are few predominantly Cuban neighborhoods. As a group, Cubans rank among the most prosperous Latin Americans in the New York area, and this fact, combined with a politically conservative stance, often places Cubans at odds with the largest Spanish-speaking groups of the region, the Puerto Rican and Dominican communities. Unlike in South Florida, Cuban Spanish does not define the area norms for "New York Spanish," although Cuban Spanish naturally shares many similarities with the neighboring Caribbean varieties.

Other large Cuban communities are located in New Orleans, Houston, Atlanta, Los Angeles, and other major cities, and in many places Cuban entrepreneurs have a significant impact in the mass media, as owners or publishers of Spanish-language newspapers, radio and television stations, and advertising services. For example, the publisher of a Spanish-language paper in Houston, Texas, with a predominantly Mexican and Mexican American readership, is Cuban, as are the publisher of a local news bulletin and the owner of a Spanish-language television station in Albuquerque, New Mexico.

Linguistic Features of Cuban Spanish

Cuba contains several distinct dialect zones and considerable sociolinguistic variation throughout the country. The following traits are general to most varieties of Cuban Spanish, unless otherwise indicated.

Phonetics and Phonology

Cuban Spanish shares phonetic characteristics with other Caribbean dialects.[3] Principal phonetic traits include the following:

- /j/ is strong and resists effacement; phrase-initially it is sometimes an affricate (almost like the *j* in English *Joe*), but the affricate pronunciation is not as frequent as in some other Caribbean dialects (Saciuk 1980).
- The *jota* /x/, as in *trabajo* (work) or *gente* (people), is a weak [h] and often disappears.
- Phrase-final and word-final prevocalic /n/ is routinely velarized to [ŋ], as in English *sing*.[4]
- Throughout Cuba, the trill /r/ as in *carro* is frequently devoiced, especially in the eastern portions of the island. This is sometimes described as "preaspiration" and transcribed as [hr]; what actually emerges is a sound that is trilled throughout its entire duration, but in which voicing is delayed or totally suppressed.
- Neutralization of word- and phrase-final /l/ and /r/ is characteristic of all Cuban varieties of Spanish, but the phonetic manifestations vary according to region and socio-cultural group. Loss of phrase-final /r/ is rather common in colloquial speech (e.g., *voy a trabajá* [I'm going to work]), but among lower classes, particularly from the central and eastern regions, pronunciation as [l] is the more common alternative (e.g., *pol favol* for *por favor* [please]). Among Cuban communities in the United States, the pronunciation of phrase-final /r/ is a major sociolinguistic differentiator between the first groups of immigrants, representing the professional classes of Havana, and those arriving during and after the Mariel boatlift of 1980, among which there was a heavy representation of

working class speakers and residents of rural central provinces. More recent emigration from Cuba includes an increasingly large proportion of natives of the easternmost provinces, where modification of syllable-final liquids is prominent in all social strata.

- Preconsonantal /l/ and /r/ also receive a varying pronunciation. Simple interchange of one sound for the other, /r/ > [l] and /l/ > [r] is the least common possibility. In Havana, retroflexion of the first element is quite common. In rural central provinces, gemination of the following consonant is more common: *puerta* > *puetta* (door), *algo* > *aggo* (something), and so forth.[5]
- Syllable- and word-final /s/ weakens to an aspiration [h], whereas prepausally complete elision is more common.[6] In the eastern provinces, the rate of total elision in all positions rises proportionately.

Morphological Characteristics

- Cuban Spanish uniformly uses *tú* for the familiar pronoun. In contemporary usage, this treatment is extended to first-time acquaintances in circumstances where *usted* would be more common in other Spanish dialects.
- Cuban Spanish, like the dialects of Colombia, Venezuela, and Costa Rica, prefers diminutives in -*ico* following a /t/ in the stem: *ratico* (short while), *momentico* (just a moment), *chiquitico* (very little [child]), and so forth.

Syntactic Characteristics

- Noninverted questions are the rule when the subject is a pronoun:

¿Qué tú quieres? (What do you want?)
¿Cómo usted se llama? (What is your name?)

For most Cubans, placing the subject pronoun in postverbal position gives a challenging or aggressive tone.

- *Más* precedes negative words in the combinations *más nunca* (never again), *más nada* (nothing else), *más nadie* (nobody else).
- Lexical subjects of infinitives are common in Cuban Spanish (Lipski 1991b) and in the case of *para* occur to the almost total exclusion of subjunctive constructions, in casual speech:

¿Qué tú me recomiendas para yo entender la lingüística? (What do you recommend for me to understand linguistics?)

Lexical Characteristics

Some words acknowledged by Cubans and external observers alike as typically Cuban are the following:[7]

(*arroz*) *congrí* (dish made of black beans and rice cooked together)

babalao (priest of Afro-Cuban cults)

bitongo (wealthy and spoiled)

biyaya (very intelligent)

botella, de (for free [*pedir botella* is "to hitch hike"])

cañona, dar (play a dirty trick; make a dangerous move in traffic)

chucho (light switch)

fajarse (to fight)

fotuto (automobile horn)

fruta bomba (papaya)

fuácata, estar en la (to be very poor, broke)

guajiro (peasant)

jimaguas (twins)

juyuyo (in great abundance)

lucirle a uno (to seem, appear)

máquina (automobile)

ñángara (communist)

picú(d)o (pretentious, gaudy)

pisicorre (small van, station wagon)

Differences between Cuban and Cuban American Spanish

Among Cuban-born residents of the United States, linguistic patterns are not likely to differ from speakers in Cuba, except for greater use of English, but younger generations of Cuban Americans are beginning the gradual shift to English as their primary language (M. Fernández 1987; C. Solé 1979, 1980, 1982). To date, few major differences between Cuban and Cuban American Spanish have been uncovered, except for the inevitable spread of Anglicisms among the latter communities.[8] One Cuban American described the impression of hearing the speech of newly arrived *marielitos* after years of living in the United States (Llanes 1982, 186): "The sound of fresh *Cubano* floated across to me . . . the sound of *Cubano* is unmistakable . . . it sounds like music to my ears. But the *Cubano* one usually hears in the United States is a bit stale. It is often spoken by someone . . . who left Cuba fifteen or twenty years ago. Since then the language has gotten mixed up with English and the Spanish of other Hispanics, and it doesn't sound quite like it used to." García and Otheguy (1988) mention that some uniquely Cuban expressions such as *máquina* (automobile) are giving way to more pan–Latin American words like *carro*.

The once homogeneous middle-class Havana speech of the first Cuban arrivals in the United States has been diversified by the introduction of regional and social varieties representing a broad cross-section of the Cuban population. As a result, young Cuban Americans born in the United States often acquire baseline traits not found in the speech of their parents and grandparents, especially if the latter represent middle-class Havana circa 1960. Younger Cuban Americans of all socioeconomic backgrounds tend to glottalize or geminate preconsonantal /r/ and /l/, not only in the pan-Cuban *porque* > *pocque* (because), but across the Spanish lexicon. The change of syllable-final /r/ to [l] (e.g., *puerta* > *puelta* [door]) is still relatively uncommon among Cuban Americans, but can be heard among young Cuban Americans with a frequency high enough to reveal the non-Havana origins of many immigrants of the last fifteen years. Those Cuban Americans with little formal education in Spanish may categorically eliminate syllable-final /s/, not restoring [s] in formal speech or writing.

Scholarship on Cuban Spanish in the United States

Cuban Spanish in the United States has not received scholarly attention in proportion to the demographic, social, and political importance of this group. However, the majority of research done (outside of Cuba) on "Cuban" Spanish since 1960 has in fact taken place among the exile community in the United States. Thus, Haden and Matluck (1973), Guitart (1976, 1978, 1980), Hammond (1976, 1978, 1979a, 1979b, 1980, 1986b), Uber (1986), Cuéllar (1971), Lamb (1968), Núñez Cedeño (1987a, 1988a), Terrell (1977, 1979), Vallejo-Claros (1970), and Clegg (1967) offer phonetic and phonological analyses of data obtained in the United States. Varela (1992) and García and Otheguy (1988) summarize work on Cuban American Spanish. Lipski (1996c) examines patterns of pronominal behavior among Cuban and Cuban American speakers.

Notes

1. García Riverón (1991). Partial studies of Cuban Spanish include Alzola (1965), Bachiller y Morales (1883), Isbǎșescu (1968), Montori (1916), Salcines (1957), and the articles in Alonso and Fernández (1977) and López Morales (1970). See also Lipski (1994a) for a general overview of Cuban Spanish.
2. The question of whether increased Cuban tolerance of Radio Martí as well as recent journalistic exchanges signal a real opening in Cuban policy remains hotly debated, but the Radio Martí programs are drawing together the Cuban and Cuban American communities in previously unavailable ways. Radio Martí's daily political discussion programs include the participation—via long-distance telephone—of dissident Cuban journalists, writers, and political activists. The voices of the exile community mix with the speech of those remaining within Cuba and are heard by both groups. Even more popular is the daily "Puente Familiar" program, in which Cubans living in the

United States call a toll-free Radio Martí telephone number to record brief greetings to friends and relatives in Cuba. The callers cover the entire spectrum of Cuban emigration but cluster around the most recent arrivals, typically from provincial towns and speaking varieties of Spanish that are qualitatively different from that of the Havana-born professional community that had previously set the tone for Cuban American Spanish.

3. General descriptions of Cuban pronunciation (which also carry over to Cuban American speech) include Almendros (1958), Costa Sánchez (1976–77), C. Espinosa (1935), Haden and Matluck (1973), Isbašescu (1965, 1968), Lamb (1968), Rodríguez Herrera (1977), Ruíz Hernández and Miyares Bermúdez (1984), Salcines (1957), Sosa (1974), Trista and Valdés (1978), and Vallejo-Claros (1970), among others. Hammond (1976, 1979a, 1979b, 1980) has specifically focused on Miami Cuban Spanish.

4. Hammond (1979b), Lipski (1986d), Terrell (1975), Uber (1984). Personally collected data (Lipski 1986f) representing the speech of the Havana area give the following figures:

Context	n## {phrase-final}			n#V {prevocalic}		
Allophone	[n]	[ŋ]	[Ø]	[n]	[ŋ]	[Ø]
% used	8	54	38	3	59	38

5. Costa Sánchez and Carrera Gómez (1980a, 1980b), García González (1980), Goodgall de Pruna (1970), J. Harris (1985), Ruíz Hernández and Miyares Bermúdez (1984), Terrell (1976), Uber (1986), Vallejo-Claros (1970).

6. Guitart (1976), Hammond (1979a, 1980), Lipski (1986f), Terrell (1979), Uber (1984). Personally collected data for the Havana region (Lipski 1986f) show the following range:

/s/C			/s/#C			/s/##			/s/#V			/s/#v		
[s]	[h]	[Ø]	[s]	[h]	[Ø]	[s]	[h]	[Ø]	[s]	[h]	[Ø]	[s]	[h]	[Ø]
3	97	0	2	75	23	61	13	26	48	28	25	10	53	27

C = consonant; V = tonic vowel; v = atonic vowel; # = word boundary; ## = phrase boundary

7. Basic sources of Cuban vocabulary include Dihigo (1928), Dubsky (1977), Entralgo (1941), Espina Pérez (1972), Macías (1885), Ortiz (1974), Paz Pérez (1988), Pichardo (1976), Ramos Huerta (1997), Rodríguez Herrera (1958–59), Sánchez-Boudy (1978), Santiesteban (1982), and Suárez (1921). Cruz (1996) gives an informal vocabulary of Cuban American Spanish.

8. For example, Cuéllar [Varela] (1974), García and Otheguy (1988), Valdés Bernal and Gregori Torada (2001), Varela (1992).

6

Puerto Rican Spanish in the United States

Introduction

Puerto Ricans represent the second-largest Latino group in the United States. In much of the Northeast, Puerto Rican is virtually synonymous with Latino, and popular notions of Latino culture are often confused with the harsh reality of urban ghettoization, which was the sad fate of the first generations of Puerto Ricans in the industrial northeastern United States.

Puerto Rico was visited by Columbus on his second voyage. In his descriptions, Columbus used the name preferred by the indigenous inhabitants, *Boriquén*. This word has been remade into the Spanish terms *boricua,* meaning "true Puerto Rican" in Puerto Rican Spanish, and the derived and more learned adjective *borinqueño*. When the Spaniards arrived in the Caribbean, the Taíno represented most of the indigenous population of Puerto Rico, but this group had all but disappeared within a century of European colonization. The adoption of the *flotilla* routes between Spain and Spanish America resulted in the complete marginalization of Puerto Rico, which lay well off the established paths. The Spaniards remaining in Puerto Rico turned to agriculture; sugar production was soon surpassed by coffee, ginger, tobacco, and cattle raising.

Puerto Rico was ceded to the United States in 1898, through the Treaty of Paris, which ended the Spanish-American War. Following the Spanish-American War of 1898, United States' attention focused on Cuba and the

Philippines, while Puerto Rico was neglected. Its residents were given no official status as either U.S. citizens or colonial subjects for more than a decade. From 1898–1900 Puerto Rico was under U.S. military rule; the military administration came to an end with the Foraker Act, which placed Puerto Rico directly under the control of the U.S. Congress, which had the power to set tariffs and establish trade policies. Puerto Ricans did not receive U.S. citizenship until 1917, through the Jones Act, which also provided for a territorial governor appointed by Congress and for a population election of both houses of the Puerto Rican legislature. Puerto Ricans were not given the opportunity to elect their own governor until 1947, and the first elected governor, Luis Muñoz Marín (who took office at the beginning of 1949) became a symbol of growing Puerto Rican identity. Muñoz Marín was instrumental in negotiating a new political status for Puerto Rico, known as the Associated Free State (informally known as the commonwealth), which created an ambiguous political situation for Puerto Rican residents. On one hand Puerto Ricans have no representatives in the U.S. Congress; on the other hand they are exempt from certain federal taxes. Despite a lack of representation in federal matters, Puerto Ricans were eligible for the draft, a circumstance that brought thousands of Puerto Ricans into military service in subsequent decades. The island also has a lower minimum wage than the United States, which has both attracted some mainland employers and also appears to have extended the depressed economic conditions on the island and the heavy dependence on federal assistance programs. In Puerto Rico political sentiments have usually been roughly evenly divided between those who wish to continue the Associate Free State, and those who wish for full statehood. A small but vocal minority consistently votes in favor of total independence and the formation of a sovereign nation.

Under the first U.S. administration, all education in grades 9–12 was mandated to be taught in English, but in the first eight grades English was an obligatory "special subject." By 1903 dissatisfaction was high among both Puerto Ricans and U.S. education officials, and the newly created school system was nearing collapse. In that year the U.S. education commissioner made English the sole language of instruction in all school grades, an event that triggered massive protests by Puerto Ricans and accusations of unpatriotic behavior by the United States. The effects of American administration inevitably pushed more Anglicisms into the Puerto Rican lexicon, while driving Spanish out of the classroom for several decades. The latter event retarded the establishment of an educated standard for Puerto Rican Spanish, because all varieties of Spanish were for a time treated as social outcasts. Eventually, Spanish was reinstated as the primary language of instruction in Puerto Rican schools, aided by the efforts of Luis

Muñoz Rivera, father of the first elected governor of Puerto Rico, Luis Muñoz Marín. Today, the results of earlier attempts at implanting English in Puerto Rico are far overshadowed by the effects of commercial advertising, television, and cinema, and Puerto Ricans with only a minimal knowledge of English use a large number of Anglicisms. This fact notwithstanding, Puerto Rico as a nation is not bilingual, although a considerable portion of the urban professional and middle classes command a useful variety of English. Claims of English penetration of the morphology and syntax of Puerto Rican Spanish (except perhaps for journalistic usage) have been overstated.[1] Regardless of objective linguistic considerations, the fear that an increasingly Anglicized Spanish will triumph is a significant political and social force in Puerto Rico, as reflected by a recent decision of the Puerto Rican legislature to declare Spanish as the sole official language of the territory.

Puerto Ricans in the Continental United States

The 1990 census found that nearly 2.7 million residents of the United States considered themselves to be Puerto Rican. By the 2000 census this number had jumped to more than 3.4 million or 9.6% of the Hispanics in the United States (not including the island of Puerto Rico). The largest concentrations continue to be found in the states of the Northeast and in Florida, but considerable populations are also found in some midwestern cities. The following are representative figures from the 2000 census:

New York	1,050,000
Florida	482,000
New Jersey	366,800
Pennsylvania	228,600
Massachusetts	199,200
Connecticut	194,400
Illinois	157,900
California	140,600
Texas	69,500
Ohio	66,200

Not all these individuals speak Spanish, but many people who might be objectively regarded as Puerto Rican or of Puerto Rican origin were not reported as such by the census. However, bilingual Puerto Ricans in the continental United States represent a considerable demographic and social force, as reflected by even the roughest census figures (Zentella 1988).

Puerto Rican immigration to the United States mainland has led to the formation of large Puerto Rican communities in the industrialized cities of the Northeast.[2] Return migration brings the *Nuyoricans* into contact with islanders. Mutual relations are not always smooth, but the end result is a much closer cultural and linguistic contact between Puerto Rico and the continental United States than would be suggested by their geographical location.

Historical Demographics of Puerto Ricans in the Continental United States

Beginning immediately after the Spanish-American War, Puerto Ricans left the island and settled in the United States in various areas and for several reasons. Among the first to leave in significant numbers were those who worked in sugar plantations in Louisiana and especially in (the then U.S.-governed territory of) Hawaii (Natal 1983). A smaller number of Puerto Ricans also worked in plantations in the Yucatán Peninsula of Mexico, an ironic switch from the ill-conceived importation of indigenous contract laborers from Yucatán to Cuba in the nineteenth century (Menéndez 1928, 1932). In Hawaii vestiges of this early Puerto Rican population survive to the present day, and Puerto Ricans contributed words and cultural items to Hawaiian life. The Puerto Ricans became known as *Pokoliko, Poto Riko,* or *Borinki,* and the Puerto Rican *arroz y gandules* (small green beans cooked with rice) became transmuted to *gandude rice.*

Although it is generally believed that Puerto Rican settlements in the industrialized cities of the northeastern United States began in the 1940s and 1950s, in reality Puerto Ricans began working in U.S. cities during the first decades of the twentieth century, principally in the cigar and garment industries (Urciuoli 1996, 51). By the 1920s large Puerto Rican neighborhoods could be found in New York's Lower East Side, East Harlem, and Green Point (Brooklyn). Following World War II, the Puerto Rican territorial government attempted to attract industry and stimulate economic development. Operation Bootstrap, or *Operación Fomento,* a plan that began in 1948, is credited with creating some 68,000 new jobs (and indirectly adding about the same number in service-related trades) between 1947 and 1970 (Fitzpatrick 1987, 34). With the new industries came all the accoutrements of modern society, including large numbers of automobiles, radio and television sets, cinemas, and a wide variety of consumer goods. Many Puerto Ricans viewed these changes with some ambivalence because Anglo American culture and values had flooded the island, often displacing traditional elements. The industrialization of the island also had the negative effect of driving many Puerto Ricans off the land, which became increasingly scarce and costly as large corporate holdings expanded. Unable to earn a living in Puerto Rican cities, these *jíbaros* moved to the United States. The outward migration was aided by business interests in the United States—for example, through highly subsidized or free one-way air passage from Puerto Rico to New York. There were also formalized programs of farmworker recruitment, similar to those that brought Mexican workers to the United States. This recruitment began informally around 1940, and in 1947 and 1948 laws were passed in Puerto Rico that attempted to regulate the increasingly exploitative contract labor trade.

Migration out of Puerto Rico began very early, although it was only after the initiation of Operation Bootstrap that the floodgates were opened. In 1900, the first group of sugar cane cutters went to Hawaii; the total numbers have yet to be determined. By 1920, there were more than 12,000 Puerto Ricans in the mainland United States. In 1930, there were some 53,000 Puerto Ricans on the mainland; by 1944, the number had risen to 90,000 (Moore and Pachon 1985, 33). Between 1940 and 1950 the mainland Puerto Rican population quadrupled; it tripled again between 1950 and 1960. These landless and homeless Puerto Ricans ended up in the cold, industrialized cities of the Northeast where they frequently suffered even worse conditions than those left behind in Puerto Rico. The plight of these displaced Puerto Ricans, who cannot be considered voluntary immigrants in the true sense of the word, is poignantly covered in many literary works, including the collection of stories *Spiks* by Pedro Juan Soto (1956), the play *La carreta* by René Marqués (1963), and the sociological study *La vida* by Oscar Lewis (1966). Forced by economic hardship and racial prejudice to live in ghettoes and tenements, and deprived of the opportunity to be educated in their home language, many Puerto Ricans dropped out of school and therefore returned to their neighborhoods, which in turn consolidated the retention of Spanish. These literary texts accurately depict the fact that the majority of Puerto Ricans who arrived in the continental United States in the 1950s and 1960s were from rural regions and had never lived in urban environments in Puerto Rico. Thus the shock experienced by these displaced individuals extended across several fronts: they were exposed to an unexpectedly harsh climate, a foreign language whose speakers exhibited little tolerance for those who could not speak it fluently, a decaying urban environment, racial prejudice, and nearly impenetrable racial and social barriers.

In the mainland United States, Puerto Rican communities have traditionally been concentrated in the industrial Northeast, with the largest concentrations being found in the greater New York City area (including cities in coastal New Jersey, such as Newark, New Brunswick, and Perth Amboy), Boston, and Philadelphia. Smaller groups are found in Detroit; Chicago; Cleveland; Lorraine, Ohio; and Bridgeport,

Connecticut. However, it is *El Barrio* of New York, including areas of Manhattan, Brooklyn, and Queens, that typifies the cultural heartland of the mainland Puerto Ricans. Some demographic figures show the basic trends of Puerto Rican migration to the mainland United States (Fitzpatrick 1987, 15–22). In 1910 there were approximately 1,500 Puerto Ricans in the United States, all island-born, of which approximately 550 lived in New York City. In 1930, almost 53,000 Puerto Ricans lived in the United States (figures for New York City are not available). By 1940 this number has risen to nearly 70,000 (with more than 61,000 living in New York City), but only a decade later, the 1950 census found 226,000 island-born Puerto Ricans in the United States, with more than 187,000 living in New York City. In 1960 the total was more than 615,000 (around 430,000 in NYC); in 1970 the figure was 810,000 (473,000 in NYC), whereas in 1980 approximately 1.1 million island-born Puerto Ricans lived in the United States, with 473,000 living in the greater New York City area. If mainland-born individuals of Puerto Rican origin are added to the mix, the 1950 figure rises to 301,000 (246,000 in NYC); in 1960 888,000 (613,000 in NYC); in 1970 nearly 1.4 million (860,000 in NYC), and in 1980 2 million (860,000 in NYC). These figures show that after 1960 Puerto Ricans increasingly moved to areas other than New York City, some after having spent some time in this city, others arriving directly from Puerto Rico to other U.S. destinations. Thus the total Puerto Rican population of New York City grew very little from 1960 to 1980. For example, the 1980 census, which listed 860,000 individuals of Puerto Rican origin in New York City, also counted more than 243,000 in New Jersey, more than 112,000 in Chicago, almost 95,000 in Florida, 93,000 in California, 92,000 in Pennsylvania (of which 47,000 lived in Philadelphia), 88,000 in Connecticut, 76,000 in Massachusetts, 32,000 in Ohio, almost 13,000 in Indiana, nearly 23,000 in Texas, and some 10,000 in Wisconsin.

From the outset the large Puerto Rican communities in New York and other industrial cities have lived at the margins of prosperous U.S. society, ghettoized because of language, culture, and race, and not enjoying the benefits of educational and social programs purportedly designed to serve all Americans. Beginning at the end of the 1950s, and particularly during the 1960s, Puerto Ricans in the United States began to take a more active role in community development and the struggle for self-realization. The Puerto Rican Forum, founded in 1950, focused attention on New York Puerto Rican problems from a community-based perspective. The organization ASPIRA (taking its name from the Spanish verb meaning "to aspire") was founded in 1961 and strove to maintain Puerto Rican culture among those living in urban mainland settings, while at the same time making advances in educational opportunities for young Puerto Ricans.[3] In the 1970s ASPIRA was instrumental in securing bilingual education programs in New York City. Other important community organizations include the Puerto Rican Community Development Project, the Puerto Rican Family Institute, and the Puerto Rican Legal Defense and Education Fund, all founded in the 1960s and 1970s. In 1980, the nationwide National Puerto Rican Coalition was formed, based in Washington, D.C. In the intervening years, Puerto Ricans in the United States have held posts as mayors of New York City boroughs, state senators and representatives, and U.S. representatives. Puerto Ricans in the New York City area have their own newspapers and radio programs and are increasingly integrated into the social, economic, and artistic fabric of the region. In other U.S. cities, matters are not always as hopeful. Chicago's Puerto Rican population continues to live below the city's norms on most measures of economic and educational achievement. Puerto Ricans in Philadelphia and northern New Jersey face a similar plight. The advent of bilingual education programs and the general raising of the social consciousness toward ethnic minorities in U.S. cities have yielded some positive results, and, taken nationwide, the situation of Puerto Ricans in the United States is not as depressed as in earlier decades.

A significant return migration of Puerto Ricans from the mainland United States to Puerto Rico began in the late 1960s. Such migration had always occurred on a smaller scale; many Puerto Ricans worked for a few years in the United States and then returned to the island with their savings. Some repeated this cycle several times during their working career (Hernández Alvarez 1967). In subsequent years economic conditions in the northeastern United States were often very unfavorable, although the island's economy had seen some periods of relative prosperity, which coincided with downturns in the continental United States. As a result, there have been years when the net migratory trend has been from the mainland to the island. The traditional return migrant comes from a rural area of the island. For example, data collected for return migrants in 1960 indicated that 54% were from rural regions, 25% were from San Juan, and the remainder was from the island's smaller cities and towns (Hernández Alvarez 1967, 29). Not all return migrants settled in the areas from which they had emigrated. Many took up residence in San Juan or other urban areas, and they often worked in the service sector. Not all return migration has been smooth; the first groups of return migrants tended to occupy the lower rungs of urban society in Puerto Rico, although more recent patterns show a greater socioeconomic spread.

Puerto Rican Spanish

Puerto Rican Spanish belongs to the Antillean/Caribbean zone, sharing many similarities with the Spanish of the Dominican Republic. Although Puerto Rico is politically dominated by the United States, Puerto Rican Spanish has not suffered massive Anglicizing or "transculturation," as is frequently asserted (e.g., by

Granda 1972; Lloréns 1971; Pérez Sala 1973; Castel 1974). At the time of the first major treatise on Puerto Rican Spanish (Navarro Tomás 1948, the field-work for which was carried out in 1928) there were still many socially and geographically isolated areas of the island, and a regionalized distribution of both phonetic and lexical variants was noteworthy. With the increasing urbanization of Puerto Rico; the movement from rural areas to the cities; and the improvement of roads, schools, and communication systems, much of the strictly regional variation in Puerto Rican Spanish has been smoothed out, particularly as regards pronunciation (some regional variation in vocabulary still remains), leaving the vertical sociolinguistic stratification as the most significant differentiator. López Morales (1979b, 1983a) and Vaquero (1991) offer modern studies of contemporary Puerto Rican Spanish, and Morales (1986a) provides many useful analyses. Morales and Vaquero (1990) contain the transcriptions of the Norma Culta interviews for San Juan.

Since 1898 the major linguistic influence on Puerto Rican Spanish has been U.S. English. Anglicisms have penetrated every aspect of the Puerto Rican lexicon, although a clear division still remains between the highly Americanized language of business, consumer products, advertising, and commerce, and the archaic Spanish of rural regions and domestic activities. The documented influence of English rarely goes beyond simple lexical borrowing. Some observers, based on the often poorly constructed language of newspaper headlines and advertising copy, have claimed deeper penetration of English grammatical constructions (e.g., Lloréns 1971; Pérez Sala 1973; Castel 1974), but most Puerto Ricans use the same grammatical constructions as their neighbors in other Caribbean countries. Impartial scrutiny reveals no "un-Hispanic" combinations.

Characteristics of Puerto Rican Spanish

Navarro Tomás (1948) remains the most complete study of Puerto Rican Spanish, although many of the rustic variants he described are no longer current. Matluck (1961) offers useful phonetic information. López Morales (1979a, 1979b, 1983a, 1983b) provides sociolinguistic data on Puerto Rican pronunciation, and Alvarez Nazario (1957, 1972, 1981, 1982, 1990, 1991) deals with historical development and provides a thorough bibliography. The following description is valid both for Spanish as spoken in Puerto Rico and for the Spanish of Puerto Ricans living in the continental United States. To the extent that objective linguistic differences exist between the two groups (other than the obvious increase in Anglicisms and code switching among Puerto Ricans residing on the U.S. mainland), popular and rural variants have traditionally been prominent in

U.S. Puerto Rican Spanish, given the historical conditions of migration. This does not hold for the growing Puerto Rican professional sector in the United States, but rather for the traditional urban working class, which did not enjoy the advantages of Spanish-language education.

Phonetic Characteristics

The principal phonetic traits of Puerto Rican Spanish are as follows:

- Syllable- and word-final /s/ in Puerto Rican Spanish is weakened to an aspiration [h] or deleted.[4]
- Puerto Rican Spanish is known for the frequent neutralization of syllable-final liquids, particularly the shift of /r/ to [l]: *puerto* > *puelto, comer* > *comel,* and so forth.[5] Although found throughout all of Puerto Rico, this pronunciation carries a sociolinguistic stigma, is more frequent among the lower social classes and among older speakers (although age-related differences in frequency are not substantial), and within each social group is more frequent among male speakers.
- Puerto Rican Spanish often exhibits a "velarized" trill /r/, similar or identical to Spanish *jota* but occasionally closer to the French uvular /R/ (Vaquero and Quilis 1989). This pronunciation alternates with the usual Spanish trill and its preaspirated (partially devoiced) variant. Although Puerto Ricans sometimes joke that *Ramón* (Raymond) and *jamón* (ham) become homophones, this rarely occurs (but cf. Dillard 1962). Currently, velarized /r/ is found throughout Puerto Rico, but is somewhat more frequent in the interior highlands and in the western portion of the island (Figueroa 1971; Hammond 1986b; Vaquero 1972). Although many Puerto Ricans feel that the sound is improper and should be avoided, others have adopted it as the most "Puerto Rican" of all sounds and use it constantly, even in the most formal discourse. The sociolinguistic distribution is characterized by ambivalence and bipolarity, as opposed to the other sociolinguistic markers in Puerto Rican Spanish, which show more nearly constant variation across social classes.[6]
- Phrase-final and word-final prevocalic /n/ is generally velarized to [ŋ].[7]
- /j/ is frequently given an affricate pronunciation word-/phrase-initially and does not weaken intervocalically (Saciuk 1977, 1980).
- Intervocalic /d/ is weak and sometimes disappears, particularly in the suffix -*ado.*[8]
- The affricate /tʃ/ (written *ch*) in Puerto Rican Spanish is sometimes given a fricative pronunciation [ʃ], as in English *ship.*[9]
- The posterior fricative /x/ (the Spanish *jota*) is a weak aspiration [h].

Syntactic Characteristics

- It is usually asserted that Puerto Rican Spanish retains subject pronouns, particularly *yo, tú* and *usted,* in instances where they would be redundant in other

Spanish dialects. Historically, this may be partially a result of the erosion of final consonants that signal verbal morphology (Hochberg 1986; López Morales 1983a, 63–66; Morales 1980, 1986a, 89–100; 1986b), and perhaps even a result of lingering traces of earlier contact with African and creole languages (e.g., Lipski 2001b). In contemporary Puerto Rican Spanish the choice of null or overt pronouns is not conditioned by phonological erosion, but it is correlated with a complex array of pragmatic and sociolinguistic factors.[10] In the New York City setting English influence has at times been implicated in the high rate of overt subject pronouns, but Flores-Ferrán (2004) provides data that dispute this assertion.

- Questions accompanied by subject pronouns are frequently not inverted in Puerto Rico:[11] *¿Qué tú quieres?* (What do you want?)
- Personal pronouns freely occur as preposed lexical subjects of infinitives (*para yo hacer eso* [for me to do that]; *antes de tú venir aquí* [before you came here]); as in other Spanish dialects, *para* is the most frequent trigger of this combination (Morales 1988, 1989; Lipski 1991b).
- The usage of the subjunctive in Puerto Rico and in Puerto Rican Spanish in the United States has been studied by Granda (1972), Torres (1990), and Vázquez (1986). There is some evidence that usage of the subjunctive is evolving, but not in favor of the erosion of the indicative-subjunctive distinction that some have claimed for Puerto Rican Spanish.
- Because of the obvious penetration of English in Puerto Rico, several observers have claimed wholesale syntactic calquing or loan translations. Pérez Sala (1973) and Lloréns (1971) have noted combinations such as

¿Cómo te gustó la playa? (How did you like the beach?) [*¿Te gustó/cómo lo pasaste?*]
El problema está siendo considerado (the problem is being considered) [*Se está estudiando el problema*]
Te llamo para atrás (I'll call you back) [*te vuelvo a llamar*]
El sabe cómo hablar inglés (He knows how to speak English) [*El sabe hablar inglés*]

- Lipski (1975) reanalyzes putative syntactic Anglicisms in Puerto Rico, many of which are not found in daily speech but only in obviously translated journalistic and advertising language. In some instances legitimate Spanish usage of other regions is reflected, but in other instances archaic survivals may be involved. A number of combinations, including the all-pervasive *para atrás* (*patrás*) constructions, are plausibly the result of at least some penetration of English (Lipski 1985e, 1987d). In all cases, however, only loan translation is involved, keeping within the grammatical bounds of already existing Spanish constructions. No rules of Spanish grammar are violated, and no case can be made using loan translations as a criterion for "convergence" (Pousada and Poplack 1982) or "creolization" (Lawton 1971).

Lexical Characteristics

Major studies of the Puerto Rican lexicon include Altieri de Barreto (1973), Gallo (1980), Hernández Aquino (1977), Malaret (1955), Maura (1984), and Rosario (1965). Lexical items considered typically Puerto Rican, at least with the meanings given, include the following:

aguinaldo (Christmas carol)
ay bendito (oh, goodness [common interjection])
bomba (form of traditional music with strong African influence)
chavos < ochavos (money [chavo = penny])
china (sweet orange)
chiringa (kite)
coquí (type of small frog—the cultural icon of Puerto Rico)
cuatro (small guitar with ten strings)
escrachao (ruined, broken)
guagua (bus)
habichuela (red bean)
mahones (blue jeans)
matrimonio (dish of red beans and rice)
pantallas (earrings)
pastel (meat pie made with crushed plantains)
petiyanqui (obsequious admirer of American ways)
plena (type of typical music with heavy percussion, including a large tambourine)
tapón (traffic jam)
zafacón (garbage can, waste basket)

All of these words are used in U.S. Puerto Rican communities, although some of the cultural referents have been attenuated. At the same time mainland U.S. Puerto Rican groups have introduced evolved vocabulary items unknown in Puerto Rico, mostly youth slang.

Puerto Rican Spanish in the United States

Known, often derisively, as Nuyoricans in Puerto Rico, Puerto Ricans born or raised in the United States exhibit both similarities and differences in Spanish usage with respect to their compatriots on the island. In the United States Puerto Rican Spanish is often spoken in relatively closed communities in which the full gamut of sociolinguistic variation may not be present. Although some radio and television programming is available, broadcast personnel may themselves be of U.S. origin and may speak forms of Spanish acquired in the United

States, which do not necessarily correspond to the linguistic standards for broadcasting in Puerto Rico. Similarly, in those few areas where Spanish-speaking teachers are available, they are usually chosen in order to facilitate integration into English-speaking society, and they rarely comment on linguistic usage in Spanish. Inward migration from Puerto Rico continues in many communities, but this does little to foster the type of all-purpose linguistic environment in which sociolinguistic differentiation can flourish. As a result Puerto Ricans in the United States with little literacy in Spanish have often extended originally variable rules (e.g., reduction of /s/ and lateralization of /ɹ/) to nearly categorical status. This may lead to phonological restructuring, so that the word *puerta* (door), for example, may be phonologically reinterpreted as /puelta/, and *pues* (well then) as /pue/. Some U.S. Puerto Ricans have also adopted a categorical velarized /r/. The cumulative auditory effect of this speech on listeners from the island may suggest a relatively low level of formal education, although the speakers may be highly trained in an English-language environment. It is this mismatch that is responsible for the mistaken notion that U.S. Puerto Rican Spanish represents only the lowest common denominators of island Spanish, when in fact other linguistic indicators, including grammatical structures and vocabulary, may belong properly to middle varieties of Spanish.

Overall, there are no significant syntactic differences between Puerto Rican Spanish as spoken by fluent native speakers in the United States and Puerto Rican Spanish as spoken by Puerto Ricans on the island, except those attributable to the increasing English-dominant bilingualism of Puerto Ricans born and raised away from large Spanish-speaking communities.[12] These include loan translations of English idiomatic expressions and some uncertainty as to the use of particular verb tenses and moods (Pousada and Poplack 1982; Reyes 1981). Similarly, the lexicon of Puerto Ricans in the United States contains words absorbed from English—sometimes phonologically adapted to Spanish and sometimes unassimilated—that reflect the surrounding environment.

Bilingual Code Switching among Puerto Ricans in the United States

The stable and long-lasting bilingualism of traditional Puerto Rican communities on the United States mainland has given rise to a full array of code-switching phenomena, much as in other bilingual groups. Puerto Rican code switching was the subject of seminal research by Poplack (1980c) and Zentella (1981a, 1981c, 1983, 1988, 1997). This work demonstrates that code switching in Puerto Rican Spanish in the United States is not a form of nonfluency, but rather represents a rule-governed linguistic register that is controllable by speakers and that does not break with fundamental structural rules in either language. Torres (1989, 1992, 1997, 2002) and Alvarez (1989) demonstrate that Puerto Rican code switching has evolved into an elaborate discourse strategy.

Scholarship on Puerto Rican Spanish in the United States

Research on Puerto Rican Spanish in the United States began with descriptive studies of individual speech communities, but it eventually encompassed a broad range of linguistic issues. In part as a result of the high concentration of research universities in the greater New York City and Philadelphia areas, Puerto Rican Spanish in the U.S. urban setting was incorporated into several research paradigms central to the development of contemporary sociolinguistics. Current research also includes topics of language education, social identity, and bilingual discourse, both in the traditional urban settings and in more recently formed suburban Puerto Rican communities.

Early descriptive studies of Puerto Rican Spanish in the United States include Porges (1949) for New York City; Decker (1952) for Lorraine, Ohio; Kreidler (1958) for Jersey City, New Jersey; and Beck (1970) for Bowling Green, Ohio. These initial studies set the stage for more ambitious projects. These began with the first large-scale account of a Spanish-speaking community in the United States, the Puerto Rican neighborhood of Jersey City, New Jersey. The studies are included in Fishman, Cooper, and Ma (1975), originally published as a research report in 1969 and based on research conducted mostly in 1966–67. In addition to numerous sociological, psychological, and historical accounts, the articles include demographic studies, sociological analyses, and the results of a house-to-house survey in chosen neighborhoods. The linguistically-oriented studies include Fishman and Herasimchuk (1975) on phonological variation, Fishman and Terry (1975) on census data in ethnolinguistic research, Fishman (1975a, 1975b) on sociodemographics and research methodology, Hoffman (1975) on ethnography, and Ma and Herasimchuk (1975) on large-scale bilingual communities. The researchers provide one of the earliest quantitative studies on phonetic realization in a Spanish dialect, providing information on the sociolinguistic stratification of syllable-final /s/ and /P/, as well as the possible relationship between retention versus loss of /s/ and the grammatical function performed by this sound. This pioneering work presages the outpouring of Spanish variational studies produced in the 1970s and 1980s.[13]

In one of the first major applications of quantitative variational methods in sociolinguistics, Poplack (1979a) offered a comprehensive variational study of phonological elements in Philadelphia Puerto Rican Spanish (see also Poplack 1979b, 1980a, 1980c, 1981). This was the first widely publicized application of the multivariate analysis program known as VARBRUL (and its current microcomputer-based descendent GOLDVARB).[14] One hypothesis put to the test in Poplack's work was the possible functional correlation between grammatical value of final /s/ and /n/ and effacement of these sounds. Flores, Myhill, and Tarallo (1983), Uber (1984), and Hochberg (1986) continued this line of research on U.S. Puerto Rican Spanish.

Attinasi (1978, 1979) provides early documentation of language attitudes among New York Puerto Ricans. Flores, Attinasi, and Pedraza (1981, 1987), and Milán (1982) offer additional perspectives on the linguistic ethnography of the New York Puerto Rican community. Casiano Montáñez (1975) found the same popular phonetic traits in New York Puerto Rican Spanish as are found within Puerto Rico. Significantly, all informants were born in Puerto Rico, with residence in New York ranging from a few years to more than 20 years. In a sense this study does not represent "New York Puerto Rican Spanish" because the informants all represent transplanted island varieties of the language, and only those who arrived in the United States at a very young age would be expected to significantly alter their pronunciation of Spanish. Code switching among Puerto Ricans in the United States was also incorporated into mainstream research on code switching and bilingual discourse. Coming shortly after the early study of Anisman (1975), Poplack (1980b, 1983) used New York Puerto Rican data in her theoretical model of bilingual code switching.

Among the most recent research, Zentella (1988) provides an overview of scholarship on Puerto Rican Spanish in the United States. Zentella (1997; also 1981b, 1983, 1985) examines the language of Puerto Rican children in New York, documenting the rich array of bilingual behavior exhibited by this population. Zentella (1988, 2000) provides an overview of Puerto Rican Spanish in the United States. Gutiérrez González (1993) is the first study devoted entirely to the lexicon of New York Puerto Rican Spanish. Torres (1997, 2002) offers a sociolinguistic profile of the Puerto Rican community in Brentwood, New York, a suburban area with characteristics that differ significantly from the inner-city Puerto Rican neighborhoods that formed the basis of earlier studies. Both monographs summarize previous work by the authors and give an overview of other research on U.S. Puerto Rican Spanish. Urciuoli (1996) discusses the racialization of Puerto Ricans and their language in the continental United States, showing how varieties of Spanish that objectively differ little if at all from more prestigious dialects are stigmatized both by island Puerto Ricans and by Anglo Americans (most of whom know no Spanish), simply because they are spoken by working class Puerto Ricans in the United States.

Notes

1. For example, Granda (1972), Pérez Sala (1973); for a more balanced approach, cf. López Morales (1971, 1974), Morales (1986a), also Lipski (1975).
2. Bogen (1987), Fitzpatrick (1987), Hernández Cruz (1994), J. Morales (1986).
3. ASPIRA continues to be a leading Puerto Rican association; www.aspira.org.
4. Terrell (1977) provided the first quantitative data for Puerto Rico. Poplack (1980a, 1980c, 1981) and Flores, Myhill, and Tarallo (1983) study the behavior of /s/ in the Philadelphia variety, whereas Ma and Herasimchuk (1975) describe the behavior of /s/ in Jersey City. Uber (1984) and Hochberg (1986) have analyzed the interaction between the grammatical status of final /s/ and the process of reduction. López Morales (1983a, 37–75) describes the situation in San Juan. While aspiration is found in all social classes and ages, elision of /s/ appears to have its origins in the capital, and to be spreading outward. The interlocking of sociolinguistic variables in San Juan is covered by several studies in López Morales (1979b), whereas Hammond (1982, 1991) provides data from some rural regions. Personally collected data for the San Juan region (Lipski 1986f) show the following range:

/s/C			/s/#C			/s/##			/s/#V			/s/#v		
[s]	[h]	[∅]	[s]	[h]	[∅]	[s]	[h]	[∅]	[s]	[h]	[∅]	[s]	[h]	[∅]
3	92	5	4	69	27	46	22	32	45	32	23	16	53	30

C = consonant; V = tonic vowel; v = atonic vowel; # = word boundary; ## = phrase boundary

5. Navarro Tomás (1948) observed considerable regional variation in this phenomenon, but currently the social differentiation is more noteworthy. López Morales (1983a, 77–103; 1983b, 1984) describes in detail the behavior of /r/ in San Juan.
6. López Morales (1979b, 1983a, 137–46) documents highly negative attitudes toward velarized /r/ in San Juan. However, fully a third of the interview subjects expressed a clearly positive attitude toward this sound, and the most frequently cited reason for approval was the "Puerto Rican" origin of this pronunciation. There is a preference for velarized /r/ among the lower social classes, among speakers of rural origin, and among male speakers.
7. Cf. Lipski (1986f), López Morales (1980, 1981, 1983a, 65–122). Poplack (1979a, 1979b), studying the Puerto Rican Spanish community of Philadelphia, demonstrated that elision of final /n/ occurred more frequently when the /n/ represented a verbal inflexion than when it formed part of a monomorphemic word such as *también* (also); the grammatical information ostensibly lost by the erosion of the verbal inflexion was signaled elsewhere in the sentence, for example in indicating noun and adjective plurality. These conclusions are somewhat different from

those of Ma and Herasimchuk (1975), on the Puerto Rican Spanish of Jersey City, New Jersey. Uber (1984) analyzed the velarization of /n/ in Puerto Rican Spanish in terms of overall phonological perceptibility. A cross-section of San Juan speakers of all social classes gives a figure of roughly 25% for the velarized variant, whereas figures from rural western regions provided by Hammond (1986b) show rates of velarization as high as 90%. Throughout the country, data presented by Vaquero (1972) suggest that the process is spreading, despite negative attitudes propagated by the educational system. Personally collected data (Lipski 1986f) representing the speech of the San Juan area give the following figures:

Context	n## {phrase-final}			n#V {prevocalic}		
Allophone	[n]	[ŋ]	[Ø]	[n]	[ŋ]	[Ø]
% used	22	69	9	8	79	13

8. López Morales (1983a, 123–35) gives precise data on the sociolinguistic distribution of /d/ in the speech of San Juan. As in other Spanish dialects, elision of intervocalic /d/ is most frequent in the verbal desinence -ado, reaches higher frequencies among the lower social classes, particularly in rural regions, and is more common among older speakers, exhibiting a partial reversal among younger generations. In San Juan, at least, reduction of /d/ is somewhat more common among women. Cameron (2005) provides data that partially contradict the assertion that /d/ is susceptible to elision; see also Medina-Rivera (1999) for some correlations between style and phonological variation.
9. Quilis and Vaquero (1973) and Vaquero (1978) find an increasing tendency for fricative realization of intervocalic /tʃ/. López Morales (1983a, 147–56) determined that the fricative pronunciation is relatively recent in San Juan, is preferred among women, and is being reversed in the youngest generations. The fricative pronunciation is more frequent in the lower social classes, but only in the urban environment.
10. Cameron (1993, 1996) provides additional data.
11. Lantolf (1978) has argued for a spontaneous development, based on child language acquisition strategies. In at least one Puerto Rican community in the United States, noninversion of subjects in questions has been extended to some full nouns (Lantolf 1980), as an innovation among the youngest speakers. Cf. Lipski (1977b) for some other views on this phenomenon in Caribbean Spanish. Lizardi (1993) provides additional syntactic and sociolinguistic considerations.
12. As with other Latino groups in the United States there are also considerable English-dominant Puerto Rican speakers, who are not fully fluent in Spanish, and whose Spanish usage is sometimes unfairly taken as "proof" of the linguistic impoverishment of all Puerto Ricans.
13. Spearheaded by Terrell (1977, 1979, 1980, 1981, 1982, 1983, 1986) and Poplack (1979a, 1979b, 1980a, 1980b, 1981).
14. In fact the FORTRAN code for the original VARBRUL program appears as an appendix to Poplack's dissertation.

7

Dominican Spanish in the United States

Introduction

From the early twentieth century until very recently, the largest Spanish-speaking group in the New York City urban area was Puerto Ricans—first those born on the island, and then those born and raised in the mainland United States. In the last decade or so, the Dominican Republic has replaced Puerto Rico as the source of the largest number of New York City's Spanish speakers (although individuals of Puerto Rican origin still outnumber Dominicans), and varieties of Dominican Spanish are increasingly becoming part of New York Spanish, as well as that of other urban areas of the Northeast.

Dominican Spanish shares similarities with the Spanish of its Antillean neighbors, particularly Puerto Rico. The linguistic development of the Dominican Republic is linked to the history of Santo Domingo, which was rapidly transformed from Spain's front door to the New World into a colonial backwater.[1] The island of Española was visited by Columbus on his first voyage, and he left a small settlement on the north coast. When he returned to La Navidad on his second voyage, all the inhabitants had perished. Columbus had brought nearly a thousand settlers on his second trip, and he founded the village of Isabela farther to the east, leaving his brother Bartolomeo in charge. Hostile attacks from native Taínos and internal dissent ravaged the colony, and Bartolomeo was led to found Nueva Isabela, later renamed Santo Domingo, on the island's south coast. As had been the case in Puerto Rico, the Dominican gold deposits were soon exhausted, and the discovery of fabulous wealth in Mexico and Peru enticed colonists away from the Antilles. As Spanish interest in Española declined, so did the colony's economic situation, and the competition of the French and the English for the western part of the island caused additional difficulties. During the course of the eighteenth century, Spain sent large numbers of settlers from the Canary Islands to hold the line against French incursions. The significant proportion of Canary Islanders in rural western regions and also in the capital city may in particular account for some of the features of Dominican Spanish. The French eventually prevailed at the western end of the island, establishing the wealthy colony of Saint Domingue, whose economy was exclusively based on sugar cultivation, and where African slaves represented as much as 90% of the total population.

African slavery was also important in Spanish Santo Domingo, although slaves were found in lesser numbers than in the French colony.[2] The sugar plantation boom that affected Cuba and Puerto Rico at the beginning of the nineteenth century was less important in Santo Domingo, because the effects of the Haitian revolt were too close at hand, and there was a natural reluctance to duplicate a system that had just been overthrown in the neighboring colony. Nor were these fears unfounded, for only a few years after the Haitian revolution, the Haitian general Toussaint L'Ouverture invaded and conquered the Spanish colony. Napoleon subsequently sent his own army, under Leclerc, to overcome the Haitians, but Santo Domingo remained under French control until 1809, when the French were driven out with British assistance. With the Dominican declaration of independence in 1821 came the aid of the Haitian president Jean-Pierre Boyer, but Haiti ended up occupying and controlling the future Dominican Republic from 1822 to 1844. The Dominican forces finally revolted in 1844, and after fierce fighting the Dominican Republic came into existence. Since that time, Haiti and the Dominican Republic have shared a history of invasions, counterinvasions, and mutual hostilities.[3]

Over the years, Dominican leaders tried to annex their nation to Spain and to the United States. De facto return to Spanish control was accomplished in 1861, and for four years the Dominican Republic was a protectorate of Spain, flooded with Spanish settlers and subject to the economic exigencies of the former colonial power. Yet another war was required to bring the second Spanish domination to a close, but even this did not end the problems. The Dominican Republic was under virtual U.S. control from 1899 to 1916 as the result of a disintegrating political and financial situation, and it was actually occupied by United States military forces from 1916 to 1924. Since that time, the Dominican economy has revolved around cash-crop agriculture, with sugar being the principal product. Cattle raising and coffee production are also important sources of foreign exchange but exacerbate the classical dilemma of cash-crop economies: small farmers and peasants are driven off their land or forced to grow cash crops instead of devoting the land to food production for internal consumption. Tourism is also an important factor in Dominican economic development; it has brought international acclaim not only to the capital city but also to the formerly isolated northern coast.

Dominicans in the United States

Dominicans have lived in the United States since the nineteenth century, but emigration from the Dominican Republic to the U.S. was never significant until the latter part of the 1960s.[4] During the Trujillo dictatorship (1930–1961), foreign travel emigration was severely curtailed, and even obtaining a passport was difficult for most Dominicans. Following Trujillo's death, the United States established a larger consulate, located on the outskirts of Santo Domingo, and began issuing large numbers of visas to Dominicans to enter the United States. In 1961, the year of Trujillo's death, 1,789 visas were issued. By 1963, this number had already jumped to 9,857 (Grasmuck and Pessar 1991, 33). In the same year, almost 11,000 Dominican immigrants were admitted to the United States, and more than 56,000 Dominican nonimmigrants (some of whom remained in the country as immigrants) were admitted (Grasmuck and Pessar 1991, 20–21). The numbers dropped in 1964 and 1965, reflecting the civil strife in the Dominican Republic, but since the restoration of a constitutional government, official Dominican emigration has continued to rise, with current figures approaching 30,000 per year. The number of Dominican "nonimmigrants" who entered the United States peaked in the 1970s, with some 149,000 arriving in 1975; 207,000 in 1976; 155,000 in 1977; 166,000 in 1978; and 134,000 in 1979. In the period 1982–89, nearly 116,000 Dominicans arrived in New York alone (García and Otheguy 1997, 158).

The demographics of the Dominican population in the United States are also much more restricted than those of many other Spanish-speaking populations. In 1980, almost 78% of all Dominicans in the United States lived in New York (most in the New York City area), more than 8% in New Jersey, and 4% in Florida; thus 91% of the population was found in three states, with New York being disproportionately represented.[5] As of the 1990 census, of the 520,000 Dominicans in the United States (of whom 153,000 were U.S. born), nearly 333,000 lived in New York, representing 18.7% of the New York Hispanic population; some 897,000 Puerto Ricans (50.3% of the Hispanic population) lived in New York, many of whom speak only English. The 2000 census found 765,000 Dominicans in the United States—2.2% of the total Hispanic population of the United States. They are concentrated in the following states:

New York	455,100
New Jersey	102,600
Florida	71,000
Puerto Rico	56,100
Massachusetts	49,900
Rhode Island	17,900
Pennsylvania	12,200
Connecticut	9,500
Maryland	5,600
California	5,000
Texas	4,300
Virginia	3,500
Georgia	3,200
Illinois	2,900

The Dominican population continues to be concentrated in the urban Northeast, particularly the greater New York City area, including parts of New Jersey, and greater Boston, carrying over into Rhode Island. Many Dominicans are moving into Pennsylvania, settling in medium-sized cities such as Reading and Scranton. A large Dominican population resides in south Florida, and a significant Dominican community is found in Atlanta.

The geographical origin of Dominican immigrants is similarly skewed, with an overwhelming number coming from rural areas. The Cibao province of Santiago represents more than 20% of immigrants, whereas the National District surrounding the capital is the home of more than 30% of the immigrants (Grasmuck and Pessar 1991, 24–25). As is the case with Puerto Rican immigrants to the United States, there is considerable return migration of Dominican immigrants, and some oscillate regularly between the island and the mainland. In U.S. settings, Dominicans have until now lived in ethnically homogeneous neighborhoods, duplicating the patterns of the early years of Puerto Rican immigration. Unlike the latter, Dominicans are not U.S. citizens, and those entering the country illegally (the majority in some neighborhoods) avoid the school system and social services, thus further marginalizing this group. Undocumented Dominican laborers tend to work with (37%) and for (32%) other Dominicans—much higher rates than those for legally admitted Dominicans (33% and 18%, respectively), often for lower than legally allowable wages and under difficult conditions (Grasmuck and Pessar 1991, 180–81).

Linguistic Characteristics of Dominican Spanish

The Spanish language exhibits considerable regional and social variation within the Dominican Republic. The following traits are representative of the entire country and Dominicans residing in the United States, unless otherwise indicated.

Phonetics And Phonology

The Dominican Republic can be divided into at least three dialect zones, based largely on the pronunciation of word-final consonants (Canfield 1981, 47, suggests four zones). The first is the northern Cibao region, whose residents' speech has been stereotyped in Dominican literature and folklore. The second is the region surrounding the capital city, Santo Domingo. Together, these two dialect zones represent the origins of the vast majority of Dominican immigrants to the United States. The third zone is the extreme eastern tip of the island, where slight phonetic and lexical differences distinguish this region from the capital.[6] Principal phonetic characteristics of Dominican Spanish include the following:

- The posterior fricative /x/ or *jota* is a weak aspiration [h]: *Jorge* [horhe].
- /j/ is strong and is often an affricate phrase-initially, as in *yo voy* (I'm going) (Jiménez Sabater 1975, 109; Jorge Morel 1974, 81).
- Intervocalic /d/ regularly falls in all sociolects and in all regions, especially in the suffix *-ado: hablado > hablao* (spoken).
- Phrase-final and word-final prevocalic /n/ is velarized or elided.[7]
- The trill /r/ as in *carro* (car) is partially or totally devoiced or "preaspirated."
- Syllable- and word-final /s/ in Dominican Spanish is aspirated or, more frequently, lost. Even among educated speakers, rates of loss of word- and phrase-final /s/ are so high as to be nearly categorical.[8] This has given rise to incipient phonological restructuring and an exceptionally high level of hypercorrection, exemplified by the mocking term *hablar fisno* (< *fino*) (to speak fancy), with hypercorrect inserted [s] (Bradley 2006; Núñez Cedeño 1986, 1988b; Terrell 1982, 1986).
- The pronunciation of syllable-final /l/ and /r/ is also subject to both sociolinguistic differentiation and regional variation in the Dominican Republic. At the vernacular level, some sort of neutralization usually occurs, but the phonetic results vary widely; /r/ is more frequently affected, but /l/ also weakens in many contexts.[9] In the Cibao region of the northwest, syllable-final liquids are "vocalized" to a glide [i]: *algo* [aiɣo] (something), *mujer* [muhei] (woman). At the vernacular level, the phenomenon is found in nearly the entire northern half of the Dominican Republic (Jiménez Sabater 1975, 90–91; Lipski 1994b). In the contemporary Dominican Republic, Cibaeño liquid vocalization is receding as a result of sociolinguistic stigmatization and is concentrated in rural regions.[10]

Morphological Characteristics

• In some parts of the Dominican Republic, plural nouns are formed by adding *se* rather than *s*: *casa-cásase* (house(s)), *mujer-mujérese* (woman/women), etc.[11] These plurals can occasionally be heard in the U.S. setting.

• Found in rural dialects of the interior is the replacement of indicative verb forms by subjunctive forms in main clauses, particularly in the first person plural. This usage is variable and occasional, even at the idiolectal level: *tenemos > tengamos* (we have), *venimos > vengamos* (we come), etc. (Henríquez Ureña 1940, 177; Jiménez Sabater 1975, 166; Megenney 1990).

Syntactic Characteristics

• Dominican Spanish makes frequent use of redundant subject pronouns (Benavides 1985; Jiménez Sabater 1975, 164–65; 1977, 1978): *Cuando tú acabe tú me avisa* (Let me know when you finish). At the vernacular level, Dominican Spanish even uses overt subject pronouns for *inanimate* nouns, something not found in other Spanish dialects: *Cómprela . . . que ella son bonita* (Buy them [= *las piñas* "the pineapples"], they are nice) (Jiménez Sabater 1978).

• Jiménez Sabater (1977, 1978) suggests that the extension of overt subject pronouns to inanimate cases is at the root of the uniquely Dominican use of *ello* instead of the normally subjectless constructions found in other varieties of Spanish:[12] *Ello hay maíz* (there is corn), *Ello hay que parar con eso* (That must be stopped), *Ello es fácil llegar* (It is easy to get there).

• Dominican Spanish retains noninverted word order for questions containing subject pronouns, such as *¿qué tú quieres?* (what do you want?) (Jiménez Sabater 1975, 68–69; Núñez Cedeño 1983).

• Preposed subjects of infinitives are common in Dominican Spanish (Henríquez Ureña 1940, 230; Jiménez Sabater 1975, 169): *antes de yo llegar* (before I arrived), *para tú tener una idea* (for you to get an idea). They involve long noun phrases and not merely subject pronouns.[13]

• Reduplicated *no* in postposed position (e.g., *nosotros no vamos no* [we aren't going]). Although occasionally found elsewhere in Latin America, this construction is frequent in vernacular Dominican Spanish.[14] Postposed emphatic *sí* is also frequent.

Lexical Characteristics

Dominicans share with Puerto Ricans the terms *china* (sweet orange), *guagua* (bus), and *habichuela* (red bean). Other typically Dominican words include the following:[15]

busú (bad luck)
cocoro/cocolo (black person, (English-speaking) native of the eastern Antilles)
fucú (evil spirit, bad luck)

guandú(*l*) (small green bean)
mangú (dish made with mashed plantains)
mangulina (type of folk music)
mañé (Haitian) (derog.)
mofongo (dish made with meat and mashed plantains) (also used in Puerto Rico)
tutumpote (rich, powerful individual), a term used by Trujillo in his early regime
(Díaz Díaz 1987, 41–51).

Dominican Spanish in the United States

Dominicans in the United States represent in large measure rural and working-class dialects, many of which have been little-studied even in the Dominican Republic. Once arriving in the United States, most frequently in the greater New York City area, Dominicans inevitably find themselves surrounded by other Spanish speakers, and despite the existence of large Dominican neighborhoods, dialect contact and leveling takes place almost immediately. Absorption of English words and phrases also occurs naturally, so that U.S. Dominican Spanish begins to develop characteristics that are qualitatively and quantitatively different from varieties spoken in the Dominican Republic. The generally low level of literacy of Spanish of Dominican immigrants, their predominantly rural background, and the lack of strong normative influences on Spanish in the U.S. setting, combine to accentuate variable phenomena found in Dominican Spanish and to skew the language in the direction of rural and regional variants unchecked by pressures to adhere to an educated standard speech.

In phonology, Dominican Spanish in the United States follows the same trends observable among Puerto Ricans: elimination of syllable-final /s/ and neutralization or loss of syllable-final /l/ and /r/ become nearly categorical, resulting in lexical restructuring, as reflected in the written language of many Dominicans. The Cibao pronunciation of syllable-final /l/ and /r/ as semivocalic [i] is also more frequent in the unconstrained sociolinguistic environment of the New York *barrios*. Lexically, Dominicans carry over many of their regional and colloquial forms, while at the same time absorbing Spanish and English items from neighboring groups. Among Dominican words common in the New York setting are the following (García and Otheguy 1997, 166–67):

carajito (small child)
chepa (chance coincidence)
chercha (party)
chin (small quantity)
cinco cheles (nickel, 5 cents)

cuartos (money, loose change)
diez cohetes, toletes (ten dollars)
funda (bag)
paquitos, muñequitos (cartoons [on television])
tiguerito (small child)
tipa (girl)
yerba (grass, lawn)

Scholarship on Dominican Spanish in the United States

With the recent upsurge of Dominican immigration to the United States, empirical research on Dominican Spanish in the United States is on the increase. García and Otheguy (1997) offer useful observations on New York Dominican Spanish. Toribio (2000b, 2001b, 2002) examines formal aspects of Dominican and Dominican-American syntax, whereas Toribio (2000a, 2003, 2006), Jensen et al. (2006), and Bullock and Toribio (2006) study issues of language loyalty and racial and ethnic attitudes among Dominicans in the United States. Building on earlier work in Bailey (2000), Bailey (2002) is a monographic study of Dominican American language and ethnic identity, particularly with respect to the interaction with the surrounding African American communities.

Notes

1. Henríquez Ureña (1940) and Jiménez Sabater (1975) are the most complete studies of Dominican Spanish, and several other monographs deal with pronunciation and vocabulary. Alba (1990a), Benavides (1985), and Megenney (1990) also cover broad aspects of Dominican dialectology. Lipski (1994a, 1994b) and Granda (1986) survey much of the available bibliography.
2. The African contribution to Dominican culture is the most significant extra-Hispanic influence. Unlike what happened in Cuba and to a lesser extent in Puerto Rico, the Dominican Republic did not see an upsurge in the importation of African slaves around the turn of the nineteenth century. The cultural and linguistic roots of most Afro Dominicans go much further back, and these groups have spoken Spanish for so long that only a few lexical Africanisms are found. Among the more prominent Afro Dominicanisms, some of which are also used in other Caribbean dialects, are *changa* and *congo* (types of dances), *fucú* (evil spirit, bad luck), *guandú(l)* (small green bean), *mandinga* (devil, bad luck), *busú* (bad luck), *baquiní* (funeral ceremony for a dead child), *mangulina* (type of folk music), *quimbamba* (far away), and place names such as Mandinga, Lemba, Samangola, and Zape (Megenney 1982, 1990; Deive 1978, 119–49).
3. The impact of Haitian Creole on Dominican Spanish is today largely confined to the rural border region and to life on the sugar plantations, or *bateyes*, where most

of the labor force is recruited from Haiti. Over time, Haitian creole has influenced rural varieties of Dominican Spanish in many subtle ways (Lipski 1994a, 2004c).

4. Báez Evertsz and D'Oleo Ramírez (1985), Bray (1984), Castro (1985), Chaney (1985), Del Castillo and Mitchell (1987), Duany (1990), Frank Canelo (1982), Garrison and Weiss (1979, 1987), Georges (1984, 1990), N. González (1970, 1976), Grasmuck and Pessar (1991), Hendricks (1974), Kayal (1978), Moya Pons (1981), Sassen-Koob (1987), Torres-Saillant (1989), Ugalde, Bean, and Cárdenas (1979).

5. These figures represent only legally sanctioned immigration. If undocumented Dominican workers are taken into account, the numbers are much higher. In official terms, the 1980 census reported nearly 269,000 legal Dominican immigrants, nearly 171,000 Americans of Dominican descent, and 19,000 undocumented Dominicans. Real numbers are undoubtedly much higher. For example, a 1985 study carried out by Fordham University estimated 300,000 undocumented Dominicans in the United States, and a report in *Time* magazine from the same year place the number of illegal Dominican residents at 350,000 (Báez Evertsz and Ramírez 1985, 13). An estimate in 1984 placed the total number of Dominicans possibly residing in the United States at some 880,000 individuals (Báez Evertsz and Ramírez 1985, 16).

6. Full-length descriptions of Dominican pronunciation are found in Alba (1990b), Benavides (1985), Henríquez Ureña (1940), Jiménez Sabater (1975), Jorge Morel (1974), and Núñez Cedeño (1980).

7. Velarization of /n/ is also common before nonvelar consonants (Jiménez Sabater 1975, 116–19, Jorge Morel 1974, 82–83, Hache de Yunén 1982; Núñez Cedeño 1980, 47–69). Personally collected data (Lipski 1986f) representing the speech of the Santo Domingo area give the following figures:

Context	n## {Phrase-final}			n#V {Prevocalic}		
Allophone	[n]	[ŋ]	[Ø]	[n]	[ŋ]	[Ø]
% used	4	74	22	7	80	13

8. Alba (1982), Núñez Cedeño (1980). Personally collected data for the Santo Domingo region (Lipski 1986f) show the following range:

/s/C			/s/#C			/s/##			/s/#V			/s/#v		
[s]	[h]	[Ø]	[s]	[h]	[Ø]	[s]	[h]	[Ø]	[s]	[h]	[Ø]	[s]	[h]	[Ø]
8	17	75	5	25	70	36	10	54	50	5	45	17	22	61

C = consonant; V = tonic vowel; v = atonic vowel; # = word boundary; ## = phrase boundary

9. In the capital, neutralization of preconsonantal /l/ and /r/ in favor of [l] is the most common manifestation, but only among the lower socioeconomic strata (Núñez Cedeño 1980, 25–45; Jorge Morel 1974, 78–81). Similar to Puerto Rican pronunciation, *puerta* "door" may emerge as *puelta*. González (1989) suggests that among younger generations of the capital city, loss of /r/ and /l/ is overtaking

lateralization. Other variants, attested throughout the Dominican Republic, include an aspiration [h], a nasalized aspiration sometimes transcribed as a velar nasal, particularly in the word *virgin*, and a variety of retroflex sounds that result from amalgamation with a following consonant (Jiménez Sabater 1975, 88–105).

10. Alba (1988), Coupal, Germosen, and Jiménez Sabater (1988), Jiménez Sabater (1986); cf. Pérez Guerra (1991) for a different perspective. Vocalization is being replaced by other manifestations of the neutralization of liquids, in particular [l] and geminated consonants. Additional phonological details are given in Alba (1979), Guitart (1981, 1988), J. Harris (1983, 47–50), Rojas (1982).

11. Jiménez Sabater (1975, 150–51). Phonological erosion of the singular sometimes results in a plural form that is substantially different from its etymological precursor: *barbudos* > *barbuse* "bearded men" (Harris 1980).

12. In answer to questions, *ello sí/ no* is commonly offered, a combination not unknown in other Spanish dialects. Uniquely Dominican, however, is the isolated *ello* in answer to questions, to indicate a degree of probability (Henríquez Ureña 1939, 225). Currently, this usage of *ello* in place of a pleonastic subject is confined to the northern region of the Dominican Republic (Jiménez Sabater 1975, 165–66).

13. Occasionally this usage even extends to gerunds and past participles (Henríquez Ureña 1940, 230):
Después de *tú ido* (After you were gone)
en *yo llegando* (while I was arriving)

14. Benavides (1985), Jiménez Sabater (1975, 170). A possible African or Haitian creole contribution may be at work here, as in Brazilian Portuguese and the Colombian Chocó (Megenney 1990, Schwegler 1996, Lipski 1996a).

15. Principal studies of the Dominican lexicon include Brito (1930), Deive (1986), González Grullón, Cabanes Vicedo, and Garcia Bethencourt (1982), Olivier (1967), Patín Maceo (1947), and Rodríguez Demorizi (1975, 1983). Dominican Spanish shares the Taíno/Arawak lexicon of the other Antilles; Tejera (1951) surveys indigenous elements in the Dominican lexicon, including scores of place names.

8

Central American Spanish in the United States

Introduction

Beginning in the 1980s immigration from Central America to the United States reached considerable proportions, and as of the 2000 census Central American communities in the United States represent some 5% of the total Latino population, outnumbering both Cubans and Dominicans. A combination of economic reasons and political pressures—the latter particularly acute during the Central American civil wars of the 1980s—has stimulated the northward migration of economically stable family units. Because there is no common border between Central America and the United States, and because many families arrive by air or by sea, there is a greater tendency to settle in geographically delimited population clusters, which then form centripetal nuclei attracting further immigration. It is common for Central American immigrants, like their fellow Latin Americans, to settle in cities with large Spanish-speaking populations; this follows both from the geographical location of such cities, which usually represent the southern border of the United States and/or major airline termini, and from the desire to live in a minimally foreign environment. Although the Central Americans who move to already-established colonies at first interact principally with their compatriots, it is not long before the inevitable contact with other Hispanic Americans and American-born Latinos takes place, leading to transculturation and the expansion of social horizons of all groups involved.

Regional and Social Variation in Central American Spanish

Central America is a region of great disparities in levels of personal wealth and education, both in urban and rural regions. This has noticeable effects on language variation, with considerable vertical stratification of sociolinguistic variables in all Central American countries. The main Central American migrations to the United States have involved people from rural regions with relatively low levels of formal education; as a consequence, linguistic traits common to rustic speech but shunned in formal academic settings are often prominent in Central American speech communities in the United States.

As a dialect zone Central America is the least well documented of all the major Latin American regions, and most of the core bibliography dates back half a century or more. Until the 1980s almost no linguistic studies of Central American Spanish were based on fieldwork (Canfield 1953, 1960 for El Salvador is a noteworthy exception), and the region remains underrepresented in linguistic studies to this day. In broad terms Central American Spanish can be divided into three major dialects: Guatemala, Costa Rica, and the triad of El Salvador–Honduras–Nicaragua. The main features that distinguish these dialects involve the pronunciation of key consonants, particularly final /s/ and the trill /r/; vocabulary items tend to be more evenly distributed across these five countries, and all Central American nations share the use of the subject pronoun *vos,* described in the following section.

The two flanking countries of the former Capitanía General de Guatemala, later the ill-fated Central American union, share a strong pronunciation of word-final /s/ that bears a great similarity with most of Mexico and the Andean zone. The three central countries aspirate word-final /s/ as [h] to a greater or lesser extent and, in general, have weaker consonantal articulations. Both Guatemala and Costa Rica exhibit some preference for a fricative /r/ (somewhat like the *s* in English *measure*) and the pronunciation of the group /tr/ as an affricate, approaching English *ch.* There are many regional differences among the Central American dialects, which share the following phonetic traits:

- Weak pronunciation of the posterior fricative /x/ (the *jota*) to a simple aspiration [h]. In words like *trabajo* (work) the /x/ is barely audible.
- Weak pronunciation of /j/ in contact with /i/ and /e/; the /j/ often disappears in words such as *gallina* (hen), *silla* (chair), *sello* (stamp).
- Word-final /n/ is velarized, as in English *sing.*

Central American Morphology: The *Voseo*

The five Spanish-speaking Central American republics exhibit a great amount of linguistic diversity among themselves, and yet there exist certain common characteristics that may be used to define the entire group as opposed to the Mexican area to the north and the Panamanian/Caribbean region to the east and south. Perhaps the most noteworthy feature of Central American Spanish is the all-pervasive use of the second person familiar pronoun *vos* instead of *tú,* which appears in Mexico, the Caribbean, Spain, and much of South America. Historically, these forms have always prevailed in Central America, and yet there has traditionally been a learned reaction against the *voseo,* which has been considered vulgar, plebian, anti-literary and a barrier to Central American aspirations to higher culture, principally because such forms had long since disappeared from Peninsular dialects.[1] One may find such condemnations in the works of grammarians, linguists, novelists, poets, journalists, and politicians.[2] Poetry and prose by Central American authors, even when set among the Central American proletariat or peasantry, has nearly always employed a *tuteo,* which is totally at odds with linguistic reality. Official announcements, as well as commercial advertisements, political slogans, religious announcements, and the like, have similarly standardized the *tuteo,* when not using *usted,* as have hymns, anthems, and prayers. The latter case is curious, since many Central Americans of humble origin, when formulating personal petitions and prayers, address God and the Virgin Mary as *vos,* while officially learned and recited prayers use either *tú* or *vosotros,* with the latter form also being used by many parish priests, whether or not they are of Central American origin (traditionally many have been from Spain or from other Latin American nations). The dichotomy between the official position and the everyday environment has created an insecurity or inferiority complex that Haugen (1968) has termed "schizoglossia," particularly evident when Central Americans speak with Spaniards or Latin Americans from other areas, even those who also employ some variant of the *voseo.* Typical comments include "we don't use the correct forms," or "we shouldn't use those words."

Recently, however, the popular attitude toward the *voseo* has been shifting in Central America, largely as a result of the efforts of writers and popular leaders representing nationalistic sentiments frequently aligned with leftist political tendencies. This is most noteworthy in the stories and novels written in the past three decades, among which may be mentioned the following: El Salvador: Roque Dalton (*Pobrecito poeta que era yo*), Salvador Cayetano Carpio (*Secuestro y capucha*), Manlio Argueta (*Caperucita en la zona roja*); Nicaragua: Sergio Ramírez (*¿Te dio miedo la sangre?*), Fernando Silva (*El vecindario*); Honduras: Ramón Amaya Amador

(*Cipotes*), Roberto Castillo (*Subida al cielo*), Horacio Castellanos Moya (*¿Qué signo es usted, niña Berta?*); Costa Rica: Carlos Luis Fallas (*Mamita Yunai*) and the novels of Fabián Dobles and Quince Duncan; Guatemala: Virgilio Rodríguez Macal (*Guayacán*).

On official levels, Central America still maintains the *tuteo*, together with the more common *usted*, with only Sandinista Nicaragua having adopted the *voseo* as a symbol of Central American individualism.[3] In post-Sandinista Nicaragua, official use of *vos* in documents and slogans is rare verging on vanishing, but neither has the non-Central American *tuteo* reemerged (Lipski 1997). Only Costa Ricans, with few major political upheavals to their record, seem most comfortable with the *voseo* among more cultured speakers, while at the same time employing *usted* with a greater frequency than is found in the other Central American republics.

Naturally enough, when Central Americans travel to other Latin American countries or interact with Mexicans, Cubans, and Puerto Ricans in the United States, one of the first points of linguistic culture shock is the *voseo*, for the situation is asymmetrical. While the Central Americans are familiar with the *tuteo*, if only passively, most other Latin Americans, especially those with little formal education, are thoroughly baffled by the *voseo* and find it alternately strange, humorous, or even offensive. The Central American, in turn, may react in a variety of ways, ranging from completely suppressing the *voseo* in order to more readily integrate into other Hispanic communities to aggressively maintaining the *vos* in order to symbolize individuality and the desire not to lose cultural identity. Whereas the speakers of Mexican or Caribbean dialects rarely suffer linguistic modifications upon coming into extensive contact with Central Americans, the same is not true of the numerically inferior latter group; the pronominal system experiences a number of pressures, resulting in a more complex hybrid system identical neither with the Central American nor with the Mexican/Caribbean standards of U.S. Latinos.

The Central American *voseo* patterns are as follows:

PRESENT INDICATIVE:	*hablás*	*comés*	*decís*
PRESENT SUBJUNCTIVE:	*hablés*	*comás*	*digás*
IMPERATIVE:	*hablá*	*comé*	*decí*
FUTURE:	*hablarás*	*comerás*	*dirás*
PRETERITE:	*hablastes*	*comistes*	*dijistes*

The indicative form of *ser* (to be) is *sos*, whereas the future forms maintain the suffix vowel *a*, except in a few marginal regions that maintain the archaic suffix *-és*. In rural regions, it is still possible to find (*ha*)*bís* instead of *has* in the present perfect, as well as other archaic or analogical verb formations.

Although the verb conjugations remain the same across Central America, choice of pronoun + verb varies from country to country and across sociolinguistic categories within each country. Thus, for example, Costa Ricans may use *usted* even in intimate family settings, between siblings or spouses, with *vos* being considered rustic and/or rude, whereas in neighboring Nicaragua almost everyone is treated to a spontaneous use of *vos,* a trait that gives the *nicas* the reputation of being *confianzudos* (overly familiar). In Guatemala, in contrast, field studies suggest that men use *voseo* constructions more frequently than women and avoid using them to women as a sign of respect (Pinkerton 1986). In the U.S. setting, where Central American varieties are usually in contact with dialects from Mexico and/or the Caribbean, additional nuances emerge. To cite a typical example, a survey conducted in the 1980s among Salvadorans (in Houston) and Hondurans (in New Orleans) in comparison with compatriots in participants' home countries, indicated that modifications to the traditional uses of *vos, tú,* and *usted* were already occurring (Lipski 1986a). An interesting situation was observed in the treatment of children by parents, because in most of Central America parents normally address children as *usted* in early years, until they are five to seven years of age, so that the children learn the respectful forms of address first. This usage is invariable in those families that demand the *usted* from their children, but even in families that eventually tolerate *vos* from children to parents, it is customary for the latter to use *usted* with smaller children. Naturally, the *usted* also reappears with older children when the need to reprimand is foremost. Among Central Americans who have spent considerable time in the United States, the custom of using *usted* with small children is on the decline, as is the use of *usted* from children to parents. Some familiar form is normally employed in both situations, the nature of which varies. A summary of the findings appears in table 8.1.

Baumel-Schreffler (1994) conducted surveys among working-class Salvadoran residents in Houston, Texas. Her results are comparable to those reported above, although with some differences. The male informants preferred *vos* (50%), *usted* (37.5%), and *tú* (12.5%), respectively, as a first gambit when speaking to another man, but opted for *vos* (44%), *usted* (33%), and *tú* (22%) when speaking to a woman. Female informants, on the other hand, overwhelmingly preferred *usted* as a first gambit in all situations. As for attitudes regarding the *voseo,* 71% of the informants felt that *tú* was more refined than *vos* (20% found no difference, and 10% felt that *vos* was more refined). On the other hand, 61% believed that *vos* was a friendlier form, as opposed to 20% who found it to be less friendly, and 20% who found no difference. Although based on a small number of informants, this survey is illustrative of the complexity surrounding pronominal usage in Central American dialects.[4]

Table 8.1 A Cross-section of Central American Pronominal Usage

Context	El Salvador	Salvadoran in the United States	Honduras	Honduran in the United States
Children to parents	U (V)	V	U (V)	V
Parents to children	U + V	V	U + V	V
Close friends	T/V	T/V	V	V (T)
Fellow students	T/V	T/V	V	V (T)
Professional colleagues	T/V (U)	T (V)/U	V (U)	V (T)/U
Insult	V	V (T)	V	V (T)
Lovemaking	V	V (T)	V/U	V (T)
Official usage	U/T	U/T	U/T	U/T
Love letters/poetry	T	T	T	T
Hispanic friend	T (V)	T	T (V)	T
Anglo friend	T	T	T (V)	T
Compatriot in United States		V (T)		V (T)
Compatriot in Central America	V		V	

T = *tú*; V = *vos*; U = *usted.* Forms in parenthesis indicate very limited use. Forms added by + indicate recent trends. Forms added after / indicate alternate usage, depending upon contextual variables.

The Central American Lexicon

The five Spanish-speaking nations of Central America embody a wide range of vocabulary, some derived from local indigenous languages, and some of Spanish origin but with modified meanings (Folse 1980). Few if any of these items are confined to the geographical boundaries of a single nation, as a result of the historical context in which the Spanish language evolved in individual Central American colonies. Some of the more regionalized words are listed in the chapters on individual Central American varieties in the United States; among the words commonly associated with Central America (at least with the four nations that have provided the majority of immigrants to the United States) are the following:

andar (to carry on one's person)
barrilete (kite)
bayunco (clumsy, worthless)
bolo (drunk)

chele (blond, fair-skinned)
chompipe (turkey)
chucho (dog)
cipote (small child)
guaro (liquor)
pisto (money)

Scholarship on Central American Spanish in the United States

The bibliography on Central American varieties of Spanish in the United States is quite small, and most of the available studies focus on a single dialect. Peñalosa (1984) is an early study on Salvadorans and Guatemalans in Los Angeles. There is a brief description of the Salvadoran and Guatemalan dialects but no mention of the use of these Spanish varieties in the multidialectal and multilingual Los Angeles setting. Lipski (1985d) compares the variable pronunciation of final /s/ in the Central American dialects, which can be largely extrapolated to transplanted Central Americans living in the United States. Lipski (1988a) briefly compares Central American and Chicano/Mexican American varieties in the U.S. setting. Saragoza (1995) studies the needs of Central American children in U.S. school classrooms, without explicit focus on Spanish language behavior. Varela (1998–99) describes Central American Spanish in Louisiana, particularly the Hondurans in New Orleans. Rivera-Mills (2000) gives a detailed sociolinguistic study of a multidialectal Latino community in northern California, in which Central Americans (from El Salvador and Guatemala) interact in Spanish with individuals from Mexico and some other Spanish American dialect zones. Lipski (2000b) offers an overview of the linguistic situation of Central Americans in the broader context of immigrant language communities.

Notes

1. For a general descriptive and historical presentation of the *voseo* in Latin America, albeit somewhat inaccurate in the case of Central America, see Páez Urdaneta (1981), Rona (1967), Chart (1954).
2. Cf. the following examples: Láscaris (1977, 168–88) is mildly critical. Agüero Chaves (1960a: 44–48; 1960b: 87f), Arroyo Soto (1971, 71–74) are also mildly critical but mainly descriptive. Mántica (1973, 55) is merely descriptive, whereas Membreño (1895, 204–5) is more critical and cites the criticisms of Bello (1903, 113). Another vocal critic of the *voseo* was Cuervo (1885), who amended the criticism to a descriptive note in subsequent editions of this work. Valle (1948) and Batres Jáuregui (1892) also adopt a critical attitude toward the *voseo*.

3. During the Sandinista period one could see billboards and slogans such as *Nicaragüense, cumplí con tu deber*, whereas some visas, stamped in passports, bear the slogan *Nicaragua espera por vos*, and letters sent out to *compañeros*, both Nicaraguan and foreign and on official stationary, routinely employed the *voseo*, whereas only *usted* would normally be appropriate following official protocol.

4. Comparable data for other Central American varieties are found in Baumel-Schreffler (1995) and Pinkerton (1986) [Guatemala]; Castro-Mitchell (1991) [Honduras]; Gaínza (1976), Vargas (1974), and Villegas (1965) [Costa Rica]; Rey (1994) [Honduras and Nicaragua].

9

Salvadoran Spanish in the United States

The Diaspora of Salvadoran Spanish

Salvadorans make up 2% of the U.S. Latino population, the same order of magnitude as the Dominican population reported in 2000 (although the rapid growth of the latter group will probably eclipse Salvadoran immigration in the future). Even before the civil turmoil in El Salvador that began in the late 1970s, Salvadorans immigrated in large numbers to neighboring Central American nations, as well as to the United States. El Salvador is the most densely populated nation in Central America, and its population density contrasts markedly with neighboring Honduras, as well as with Belize, Guatemala, Nicaragua, and southeastern Mexico. A peasant revolt in 1932, spearheaded by Communist Party leader Farabundo Martí, was brutally suppressed by the Salvadoran government in a harbinger of the violence of the 1980s (Anderson 1971). By the 1960s, the population density of El Salvador, combined with landholding practices in which most of the available land was held by a few large landowners who devoted production to cash-crop agriculture, forced thousands of Salvadoran peasants to seek opportunities elsewhere. Neighboring Honduras, whose population density was a fraction of that of El Salvador, was a natural destination, and by the late 1960s some 300,000 Salvadorans were squatting across the border in Honduras (Peterson 1986, 6). Thousands of other Salvadorans worked in the banana plantations of northern Honduras. In 1969 smoldering resentment of Salvadorans within Honduras came to a head after a bitterly disputed soccer match, and for a brief but bloody period the two nations went to war (Anderson 1981). The outside world ridiculed the "soccer war" between two "banana republics," but the real cause had more to do with displaced workers and an increasingly difficult labor situation within Honduras. As a result of this conflict, thousands of Salvadorans were forcibly repatriated or coerced into leaving Honduras. Guatemala—El Salvador's other neighbor— became the next major destination, as Salvadoran agricultural workers flooded into southwestern Guatemala to work on coffee, sugar, and cotton plantations. These jobs had traditionally been held by laborers from northern Guatemala, but the Salvadorans were willing to work for less money. It is estimated that as many as 300,000 Salvadorans migrated to Guatemala in the 1970s, nearly all illegally because Guatemala did not grant work permits to foreign workers.

Mexico was also a favorite destination of Salvadorans, particularly after the Salvadoran civil war broke out, but Salvadorans in Mexico were never regarded as anything more than transitory visitors on route to the United States. Despite the unfriendly, often brutal treatment afforded them by Mexican authorities, thousands of Salvadorans settled in Mexico; in 1985 it was estimated that about 116,000 undocumented Salvadorans lived in that country (Peterson 1986, 9). An estimate made the preceding year placed the number closer to 120,000 (Montes 1986, 56), whereas as early as 1982, as many as 140,000 Salvadorans had been estimated to be living in Mexico (Torres Rivas 1986, 10). Of these, approximately 40,000 lived in the greater Mexico City area, with others found in Guadalajara, Monterrey, and towns along Mexico's northern and southern borders.

By the end of the 1970s, social conditions for El Salvador's largely rural, poverty-stricken population had become intolerable, and various armed movements had arisen in opposition to the increasingly brutal attacks by the Salvadoran armed forces. A military coup in 1972 annulled the national elections, and another— supposedly reformist—coup in 1979 further undermined confidence in the democratic process. In 1980 five of the leading insurgent groups banded together to form the Frente Farabundo Martí para la Liberación Nacional (FMLN), which was to become the strongest guerrilla army in the history of Latin America. A number of right-wing paramilitary groups arose as a result, complete with death squads and close links to the Salvadoran military apparatus and landed oligarchy. Following the 1979 Sandinista victory in Nicaragua the United States became actively involved in El Salvador, in an attempt to prevent a leftist takeover of this nation all the while holding off right-wing takeover threats (Byrne 1996; Gettleman et al. 1987; Lungo Uclés 1990). In the rapidly deteriorating situation the FMLN launched its first major offensive in 1981, and the civil war continued unabated for nearly a decade thereafter. In 1984 president José Napoleón Duarte was democratically elected, bringing momentary hope to some observers of the civil war, but Duarte proved unable to rein in the paramilitary groups, and the Reagan administration in the United States kept up the pressure to achieve a military victory over the insurgents. In 1988 the far-right ARENA party scored decisive victories in legislative elections, and in late 1989 the FMLN carried out another major offensive, right in the middle of the nation's capital, San Salvador. By this time more than 70,000 lives had been lost in the civil war, and millions of Salvadorans had fled to other countries. During 1990 and 1991 intense negotiations finally brought an uneasy peace to El Salvador. The nation has avoided a return to civil war since that time, but a devastated economy and lingering concerns about political stability have prevented many expatriate Salvadorans from returning. The long self-exile of large segments of the Salvadoran population has also brought problems for returning refugees, many of whom have been unable to readapt to life in their former homeland. Young Salvadorans born or raised in the United States in urban ghettoes have bequeathed the bitter gifts of gang violence (by the *maras* or youth gangs) and rejection of the traditional family-centered Salvadoran society.

Demographics of Salvadorans in the United States

Salvadoran migration to the United States was already significant before the outbreak of civil war, considering its small size and relative distance from the United States. Some 73,000 Salvadorans appeared in the 1980 U.S. census (a small fraction of the total number residing in the United States), nearly all of whom had migrated during the 1970s. However, it was not until the outbreak of civil conflict in the late 1970s that Salvadoran emigration reached staggering proportions. In 1980, the total population of El Salvador was approximately 5 million inhabitants; in 1980–81 alone, more than 300,000 Salvadorans, or 6% of the total population, left the country. The trends were similar for most of the 1980s, such that by the end of the period, a third or more of all Salvadorans were living outside the country.

The large-scale political turmoil in Central America that dominated the 1980s and extended into the beginning of the 1990s brought new waves of immigration to the United States, not only from the privileged classes, but also, in increasing numbers, from members of the lower-middle and lower-working classes, including the peasantry, who by whatever means escaped the violence, destruction, and instability of their homelands and sought a haven in the United States. During the worst of the violence, wealthy Salvadorans fled the likely possibility of death or injury and loss of their property; middle-class citizens fled to reestablish small businesses in other nations rather than risk certain ruin in El Salvador. Left-leaning intellectuals and professionals fled to avoid falling into the hands of the police intelligence system, aided by a program of anonymous denunciations and "death squads," which cast a pall of uncertainty and fear over large segments of the citizenry. Peasants fled the country following destruction of their villages by American–Vietnam War–style scorched earth tactics, after having had home and family destroyed by confrontations between military forces and guerrillas, or after having failed to find a safe haven in neighboring areas of Honduras and Guatemala. Tens of thousands of these Salvadorans ended up in the United States. Although some Salvadorans have returned to their home country, or have been deported, since the end of the political violence, the majority of those who arrived in the United States during the 1980s still reside there. As a result, the cross-section of Salvadoran émigrés is very broad, as is the political spectrum, ranging from fierce right wing to revolutionary left wing, passing through a neutralist/isolationist desire for peace at any price.

By the end of the 1980s, as many as 1 million Central Americans lived in the United States, the majority of them undocumented refugees living in diffi-cult conditions. Today, emigration from Central America has slowed consider-ably, but Central Americans in the United States are still caught up in a tangle of conflicting perspectives on immigration reform and repatriation of former refugees. Because of the difficult conditions under which they arrived and lived, the language and culture of Central Americans in the United States has not received an acknowledgment proportional to the numerical strength of this population.

The demographics of the Salvadoran population within the United States have changed considerably since 1979, with the number of Salvadorans reaching a peak in the late 1980s and declining somewhat in the early 1990s, as relatively peaceful conditions return to the country for the first time in many decades. By the middle of the 1980s, some 500,000 Salvadorans had been internally dis-placed, and as many as 750,000 had fled the country (Ferris 1987, 22); this rep-resents well over 20% of the national population. Several hundred thousand took refuge in Guatemala (100,000), Nicaragua (21,000), Honduras (30,000), Costa Rica (23,500), Belize (2,000) and especially Mexico (150,000–250,000), while still others made the longer trek to the United States (Ferris 1987, 35; Montes 1986, 56–57; Morel 1991). By the middle of the 1980s, as many as 850,000 Salvadorans were living in the United States (Ferris 1987, 121; Aguayo and Weiss Fagen 1988, 58). The emigration pattern can be broken down roughly as follows,

using the time period 1941–87 as representative of Salvadoran immigration to
the United States (Montes Mozo and García Vásquez 1988, 9; Cabib 1985):

Time Period	Percentage of Immigrants
1941–1976	16.7
1977–1978	6.0
1979–1981	28.5
1982–1987	48.8

In the period 1941–81, about 34% of the Salvadoran immigrants had entered
the country legally, 46% were undocumented, and 20% were attempting to obtain
legal immigrant status. In the period 1982–87, only 16% entered the country
legally; 66% were undocumented, and 18% were applying for legal residence.
Some representative figures of Salvadorans in the United States for 1984 showed
the following concentrations (Universidad para la Paz 1987, 177):

Greater Los Angeles	300,000
Houston/South Texas	120,000
Washington, DC, area	100,000
New York City area	100,000
San Francisco area	85,000
New Orleans	60,000
Chicago	30,000
Boston	10,000

For most of the regions, the above figures are probably too low because they
only include immigrants who were identified by the U.S. government, through census counts, use of social services, and so forth. Although some illegal immigrants
are included in these figures, the true numbers have always been considerably
greater, especially in major centripetal areas such as Houston and Los Angeles.

Analyses vary as to the relative proportion of urban and rural immigrants to the
United States, among voluntary immigrants and displaced persons. Montes (1987,
56), who carried out a study in El Salvador among families of immigrants to the
United States, discovered that 47% were from urban areas, including provincial
capitals or *cabeceras* (several of which have only a few thousand residents); the
number was 53% among voluntary immigrants, but only 20% among displaced
persons. A study carried out among Salvadoran immigrants in the United States
gave similar results. Peasant farmers represented 12% of the reported immigrant

population (9% among voluntary immigrants and 20% among displaced persons). The remaining breakdown of occupations (according to family members remaining in El Salvador) was as follows (Montes 1987, 84):

Profession	Voluntary %	Displaced %
Professional	3.2	2.6
Laborer	9.7	9.8
Subordinate	25.5	9.4
Small business owner	13.1	8.5
Mechanical trade worker	15.9	12.7
Domestic laborer	18.6	28.7
Farm laborer	9.4	19.9
Other	6.4	8.5

The figures were highly skewed according to gender. For example, domestic laborers represented 1.3% of the male immigrants, but 35% of the female immigrants. Among laborers, 40.1% were male and 17.6% female. Educational levels varied widely, from illiterate rural residents to urban residents with the equivalent of a high school education. Taken as a group, the educational level of displaced Salvadorans was in the 6–8 years range.

A private study conducted in 1985 gave the following maximum estimates for the Salvadoran population in the following cities (Montes 1987, 86–87):

Los Angeles	350,000
Washington, DC	150,000
Houston/South Texas	100,000
New York City	100,000
San Francisco	100,000
New Orleans	40,000
Chicago	40,000
Miami	15,000
Phoenix/Tucson	8,000

More recent census figures for the Salvadoran population in the United States suggest that the numbers have decreased following recent peace initiatives in El Salvador and the remainder of Central America, but given the undocumented status of most Salvadorans in the United States, the new numbers must be regarded cautiously. The 1990 U.S. Census found 565,000 Salvadorans in the United States, of whom 106,000 were U.S.-born. That census showed the following breakdown of the 464,798 known Salvadoran immigrants by state (including some but not all those who entered the country illegally) (Funkhouser 1995, 29):

California	281,100
Texas	46,500
New York	38,400
Virginia	21,300
Maryland	13,600
Florida	10,000
District of Columbia:	9,600
Massachusetts	7,000
Illinois	5,200

Cities with large concentrations of Salvadorans as of 1990 include the following:

Los Angeles	211,400
Washington, DC	43,700
Houston	30,800
San Francisco	27,900
New York	21,700
Nassau, Long Island	15,800
Anaheim	10,900
Dallas	9,900
Oakland	7,600
Boston	6,500
Riverside	6,100
Jersey City	5,600
Chicago	4,600
San Jose	4,950
Newark	4,400

Of the total reported Salvadoran population between the ages of 18 and 65 in the 1990 census, the immigration patterns are broken down as follows:

1985–89	118,853
1980–84	151,674
1975–79	59,625
1970–74	26,720
Before 1970	19,979

The 2000 census registered some 655,000 Salvadorans living in the United States, although the true number is probably higher. Much of this increase comes from natural growth within the Salvadoran community already residing in the United States. Some of the states with the highest concentration of Salvadorans are the following:

California	273,000
Texas	79,200
New York	72,700
Virginia	43,700
Maryland	34,400
New Jersey	25,200
Florida	20,700
Massachusetts	15,900
Washington, DC	11,700
Nevada	9,400
North Carolina	8,700
Georgia	8,500
Colorado	3,400
Illinois	7,100
Washington	4,000

Even taking into account underreporting and return migration, the effects of the Salvadoran civil war, which began around 1979 and produced a mass exodus during the 1980s, can be clearly seen from these figures.

Characteristics of Salvadoran Spanish

There is little regional variation in the Spanish of El Salvador. The principal differentiating factors are the rural-urban distinction and the level of education. The following features are representative of all Salvadorans unless otherwise indicated.

Phonetic Traits

There are few available studies of Salvadoran Spanish phonetics.[1] There is little geographical variation in pronunciation; the major differentiating factor is level of education. Principal defining characteristics include the following:

- One characteristic of the Salvadoran dialect, as compared with the relatively conservative northern and central Mexican dialects, is the weakening of several consonantal articulations, and the consonant most readily associated with these processes is /s/. El Salvador ranks toward the middle of the scale with regard to the erosion of /s/, above the Caribbean nations, Panama, and Nicaragua, but the contrasts with

Mexico are nonetheless strong. Salvadoran Spanish more closely approximates the Caribbean dialects with regard to the pronunciation of /s/; during fieldwork conducted among Salvadorans in Houston (Lipski 1986a), when asked which of the Spanish dialects commonly heard in Houston came closest to their own in terms of pronunciation, most Salvadorans indicated Cuban, despite the fact that they felt greater cultural (and lexical) ties with Mexico.

- An additional feature of Salvadoran (and Honduran) Spanish that separates this dialect from Mexican Spanish is the frequent aspiration of word-initial and word-internal intervocalic /s/ (*la semana* (the week) [lahemana], *el presidente* (the president) [elprehiðente]). This phenomenon occasionally occurs elsewhere in Latin America but does not reach systematic proportions outside of this Central American region (Lipski 1985d, 1986d, 1987b, 2000a). Similar aspiration of word-initial /s/ occurs in traditional New Mexican Spanish, but this dialect is confined to small communities in relatively remote areas, while Salvadoran Spanish can be heard in many large cities in the United States. Many speakers of other varieties of Spanish are startled by the frequent pronunciation of word-initial /s/ in Salvadoran Spanish as [h], and in rapid speech this may even affect understanding.
- Also characteristic of Salvadoran and other Central American dialects of Spanish is the velarization of word-final /n/ (the sound of final -*ng* in English *sing*), sometimes resulting in the nasalization of the preceding vowel and loss of the final nasal consonant (Canfield 1981; Lipski 1986f, 1987b).
- Intervocalic /j/ is weak and frequently disappears in contact with /i/ (*silla* [chair] sounds like *sía, gallina* [hen] as *gaína*) or following /e/ (*sello* [stamp] sounds like *seo*). Hypercorrect insertion of a hiatus-breaking [j] is quite frequent in Salvadoran speech (e.g. *día* [day] > *diya*), but this phenomenon is largely limited to rural uneducated speech.
- (The posterior fricative /x/ (written as *j* as in *trabajo* [work] or *g* as in *gente* [people]) is a weak aspiration [h], and in conjunction with back vowels (e.g., *trabajo*) is at times barely audible.

Morphological Traits

The principal distinguishing morphological trait of Salvadoran Spanish is the use of the familiar pronoun *vos* and the corresponding verb forms. This usage is common to all of Central America and is covered in the preceding chapter. Many urban educated Salvadorans also use *tú* with other Salvadorans (a term usually reserved only when speaking to non-Central Americans), signaling the incipient creation of a three-way distinction. *Vos* remains the pronoun of maximum familiarity and solidarity, while *usted* expresses distance and respect. *Tú*, when used, corresponds to an intermediate level, expressing familiarity but not *confianza* or deep trust (Lipski 1986a). Rural and working class Salvadorans do not make this distinction, using *vos* and more frequently *usted* in all circumstances.

Syntactic Characteristics

- A frequent Salvadoran (and Guatemalan) construction, not often found in other dialects, is the pleonastic use of *vos* and *usted* to punctuate a conversation (Lipski 1994b, 2000a). This trait is frequently represented in Salvadoran literature:

  estos son muy buenos, usted (these are very good [sir/madam, etc.])
  está rica esta babosada, vos (this stuff is really good) (Argueta 1981, 98)
  ¿vamos a trer las bestias, vos? (are we going to bring the mules?)
     (Peralta Lagos 1961, 26)
  encendé la fogata, vos (light the fire) (Rodríguez Ruíz 1961, 89)
  ¿nos habrá reconocido, vos? (do you suppose he recognized us?)
     (Rivas Bonilla 1958)
  qué friyo, vos (it's really cold) (Salarrué 1970, 1: 291)
  de veras, vos, *qué bonito* (that's really pretty) (Salarrué 1970, 1: 424)
  de juro ques el mar, vos (it's really the sea) (Salarrué 1970, 1: 426)
  ¿por qué, vos? (why?) (Salarrué 1970, 1: 337)
  vamonós, vos (let's get going) (Salarrué 1970, 1: 330)
  ¿te dolió, vos? (did it hurt you?) (Salarrué 1970, 1: 326)

- Salvadoran Spanish exhibits a construction also found at times in Guatemala, the combination indefinite article + possessive adjective + noun: *una mi amiga* (a friend of mine) (normal *mi amiga/una amiga mía*). Such combinations are invariably singular, and the posssessives most frequently used are *mi* and *su*: *una su pareja de cipotes* (his two children), *una mi bailadita* ([I like to have a] dance). A partitive (one out of many) reference is often implied, but in a case such as *un mi pecadito* (my little sin), *un su sueño* (his nap), and so forth, the implication is of an action or event that occurs only occasionally (Rodríguez Ruíz 1968, 210, 295). In still other instances, there is no apparent reason for the pleonastic article + possessive, as exemplified by the following examples from Salarrué (1970, 2: 22, 32, 40, 71, 105, 122):[2]

  un su *cipotío chelito* (her blond child) [p. 22]
  tenía unos sus *2 años* (he was 2 years old) [p. 32]
  hijo de un su *papá* (son of his father) [p. 40]
  tenía un su *hambre* (he was hungry) [p. 71]
  un su *palito de lata* (his little metal stick) [p. 105]
  una su *herida* (her wound) [p. 122]

- Combinations with *hasta* are used to signal the beginning of an event: *¿Hasta cuándo viene el jefe?* (When will the boss arrive?)

Lexical Traits

Few words are unique to the Salvadoran lexicon; words like the following are considered typically "Salvadoran," although some are found in neighboring countries:[3]

andén (sidewalk)

bicho (small child)

caite (rustic sandal)

canche (red-haired, having a ruddy complexion) [means "blond" in Guatemala]

caneche (friend)

chero (friend)

chibola (carbonated soft drink)

chimbolo (tadpole, minnow)

chimpe (youngest child in a family)

cotón (t-shirt)

cuilio (soldier or policemen)

cuto (maimed, missing a limb)

majoncho (type of banana; the Salvadoran National Guard)

mara (youth gang)

muchá (*muchachada*) (guys, fellows)

peche (thin, an orphaned child)

piscucha (kite)

pupusa (dish made with two corn tortillas filled with cheese or pork rinds)

tiste (mixture of cocoa, cinnamon, and sugar used to make a beverage)

Accommodation to U.S. Varieties of Spanish

The linguistic behavior of Salvadorans in the United States has evolved considerably over the past three decades. In the 1980s, when the majority of Salvadorans had entered the country illegally, there was pressure to blend in with legally established Hispanic communities. Salvadorans faced an ambivalent situation with regard to their linguistic and cultural identity. On one hand, their natural pride as Central Americans led them to affirm this identity, to retain Salvadoran social and cultural organizations, and to openly congregate at Salvadoran-owned businesses and organizations. On the other hand, their often precarious immigration status made it desirable to blend in with surrounding Hispanic populations, most frequently those of Mexican origin. This at times led to avoidance of typically Salvadoran linguistic features, particularly use of *vos* and certain key words, as well as of explicit denial of Salvadoran origin, hoping in this fashion to be bypassed by zealous immigration officials, for whom the Mexican presence is so familiar as to go unnoticed.

In the ensuing quarter century, the Salvadoran community has become established in various cities, and a generation of U.S.-born Salvadorans has altered the language mix of this rapidly evolving group. Not only is the use of English and contact with other dialects of Spanish imprinting the patrimonial Salvadoran speech forms, but innovative combinations are emerging, to set this speech community apart from other Spanish-speaking Americans.

Among Salvadoran immigrants to the United States in the 1980s, largely representing the lower working classes and peasantry, there was a correlation between a strong identification as Salvadorans and a receptivity toward leftist positions with regard to the political future of El Salvador. Not all recent arrivals actively sympathized with the guerrilla movements, but most harbored negative feelings toward the privileged classes, and the government's counterinsurgency policies. When asserting Salvadoran identity, at meetings, during politically motivated speeches, or in discussions touching the Salvadoran civil conflict, many Salvadorans appeared to accentuate phonetic patterns that characterize this dialect (Lipski 1986a, 1989c). Naturally, not all speakers were able to effect major changes in their speech habits, nor did all feel a need to do so. Nonetheless, the ability and willingness to modify phonetic patterns in accordance with circumstances and audience was found especially among more educated speakers, intellectuals whose awareness of other dialect traits is correspondingly higher. Interestingly enough, the opposite patterns were observed in conservative (professional class) Salvadorans, who generally supported the right-wing regimes; when discussing in public the political situation in El Salvador, particularly when acting in a quasiofficial capacity, a more formal, precise diction was heard, whereas in more general discussions in which strong political emotions were not aroused, less precise diction was more often in evidence. The vast majority of Salvadorans living in the United States in the 1980s came from the poorest rural regions of El Salvador. Many were illiterate, and virtually none knew English before arriving in the United States (Nackerud 1993, 211). Precariously finding employment in work sites staffed by other undocumented Spanish speakers, and excluded through fear or by law from access to adult education programs, few Salvadoran adults moved beyond the pale of Spanish-speaking neighborhoods. Most acquired the rudiments of English that allowed them to conduct basic transactions in English, but at work and at home, the Salvadoran community continued to be overwhelmingly Spanish-speaking. With the coming of amnesty programs, a greater number of Salvadoran children began to attend school, usually in bilingual education programs. As Salvadorans discovered that most school systems accepted children without documentation of immigration status, larger numbers of Salvadoran children entered the U.S. school system (Saragoza 1995). These numbers increased even more after the amnesty of 1986, and even though many Salvadorans were excluded from amnesty or political asylum, today most young Salvadorans in this country are receiving public education. Since the originally arriving Salvadorans spoke little or no English, the children were normally placed in transitional bilingual education classes, often surrounded by a cohort of Mexican children.

Salvadoran children were at a disadvantage for several reasons. First, their predominantly rural upbringing in contrast to the increasingly urban origin of recent Mexican immigrants meant that they were less familiar with any sort of formal schooling; many were behind the grade level of their Mexican classmates. Furthermore, available bilingual education materials focused primarily on Mexican (or occasionally Caribbean) dialects of Spanish, particularly in vocabulary. Salvadoran children were at times alienated by these materials, while at other times they simply could not understand the items in question. Few bilingual teachers were familiar with Central American dialects, and not all reacted favorably to the unexpected words and pronunciations. Although there is little hard evidence of specific educational deficits occasioned by culture and dialect clash, anecdotal accounts suggest that matters were not always easy. To this day there are no comprehensive accounts of Spanish dialect differences appropriate for bilingual education teachers, but as the number of non–English-speaking Salvadorans entering the American school system diminishes, group-specific educational problems are also on the decline. Finally, and perhaps most importantly for school achievement, many Salvadoran children arriving in the 1980s had personally witnessed political terror, torture, and murder in their homeland, and had been traumatized to the point where academic success was an unattainable goal (Arroyo and Eth 1985). A number of students had been forced to leave school in El Salvador because of fear of violence and death, an experience which further hindered their entry into the U.S. school system. Currently, the number of Salvadoran children in U.S. schools who have personally experienced political violence is very small, and their situation is falling into line with that of economic immigrants who have not lived under the shadow of terror in their homeland.

The problem of assimilating and accommodating a group which by and large has had no extensive prior contact with the United States is rendered acute by the large number of Salvadorans who continue to immigrate to this country. In addition to the inevitable culture shock, many have experienced a linguistic shock that results from immersion in a predominantly Mexican (or Cuban or Puerto Rican) community, and the large number of unfamiliar English and even Spanish terms needed to survive in the United States. The overall impact of Central Americans in the United States will be in direct proportion to the number of immigrants, but all available facts point to the need to recognize the existence of Central

Americans, particularly Salvadorans, as a distinct subset of the Hispanic community in the United States, a subset which has a different background and different needs, and which at the same time will make new contributions to the formation of linguistic patterns of U.S. Spanish.

Currently, young Salvadorans born in the United States who have never lived in El Salvador rarely use *voseo* verb forms or other markedly Salvadoran morphosyntactic traits. However, many add the tag *vos* to questions and affirmations, much as is done in Central America, as an explicit affirmation of their Salvadoran identity. They may also use *vos* in conjunction with verb forms corresponding to *tú*. This occurs more frequently when speaking with other Salvadoran Americans, and less frequently when using Spanish with members of other ethnic groups:[4]

> *George tiene mi dinero,* vos (George has my money)
>
> Vos, *¿por qué no te compras unos zápatos nuevos?*
>   (Why don't you buy some new shoes?)
>
> Vos *vienes a la fiesta conmigo* (You're coming to the party with me)
>
> *¿Puedes ver la televisión* vos*?* (Can you see the television?)
>
> Vos *no te olvides de la fiesta* (Don't forget the party)
>
> *Sí/no* vos (Yes/no)
>
> Vos *mira, eso es cierto* (Look, that's right)
>
> *¿Vienes mañana,* vos*?* (Are you coming tomorrow?)

Scholarship on Salvadoran Spanish in the United States

As a group, Central American Spanish dialects are among the least-studied in terms of serious linguistic inquiry, and El Salvador has been the recipient of very little research. Salvadoran Spanish in the United States has received even less attention, and scholarship on this important dialect has yet to assume proportions commensurate with the demographic strength of this group. Peñalosa (1984) described the social and political situations of Salvadorans in Los Angeles. Lipski (1985d) described the pronunciation of /s/ in Central American Spanish. The sociolinguistic situation of Salvadorans in the United States is explored by Lipski (1986a, 1989c, 1992, 2000a, 2000b). Baumel-Schreffler (1989, 1994, 1995) examined use of *vos* and competing variants among Salvadorans and Guatemalans in the United States. Rivera-Mills (unpublished manuscripts) offers important observations on emerging "neo-Salvadoran" speech among young Salvadorans born and raised in the United States. Hernández (2002, 2007) describes recent accommodations between Salvadorans and Mexicans in Houston, including use of *vos* and accompanying verb forms, and the transitive use of *andar* (as in *no ando pisto* [I don't have any money on me]). Hoffman (2004) describes the sociolinguistics of Salvadoran

Spanish in Toronto, Canada, a scenario offering many parallels with Salvadoran Spanish in the United States.

Notes

1. The early work by Canfield (1953, 1960) is quite accurate. Geoffroy Rivas (1975, 1978) contains some rudimentary observations on pronunciation. More recently, quantitative aspects of Salvadoran pronunciation have been studied by Lipski (1985d, 1986a, 2000a).
2. Martin (1978, 1985) analyzes a similar construction in Guatemalan Spanish as a syntactic calque (loan translation) from Mayan.
3. The most complete study of the Salvadoran lexicon is by Geoffroy Rivas (1978). Other sources include Geoffroy Rivas (1975), the early and normative studies of Salazar García (1910), the limited lexical studies of Schneider (1961, 1962, 1963) and Tovar (1945, 1946), the study of the Quiché/Maya element by Barberena (1920), and glossaries found in several literary works (González Rodas 1963; Rodríguez Ruíz 1960, 1968; Salarrué 1970).
4. Rivera-Mills (unpublished manuscripts). Rivera-Mills notes the similarity of the tag *vos* with the use of the tag vocative *dude* in English (also used by many of the same third-generation Salvadorans when speaking in English).

10

Nicaraguan Spanish in the United States

The Nicaraguan Diaspora

Nicaraguan Spanish is the third largest Central American variety of Spanish represented in the United States (after Salvadoran and Guatemalan), but in areas where Nicaraguans are a majority, it is naturally the prevailing variety. The largest single Nicaraguan community in the United States is found in Miami, especially in the Sweetwater-Fountainbleu area, at the extreme west end of the city. In this zone, entire shopping centers, apartment complexes, and schools are owned, inhabited, or frequented exclusively by Nicaraguans. Another large Nicaraguan settlement is found in Los Angeles. Considerable numbers of Nicaraguans are found in Houston, Chicago, New Orleans, New York, and other large urban areas, but without the coherence of ethnically unique neighborhoods. Groups from Nicaragua's Atlantic (Caribbean) coast—traditionally speaking West Indian Creole English and/or Miskito—generally live in other areas. Some Miskito fishermen have taken up residence around Port Arthur, Texas, while a considerable number of black, English-speaking Atlantic coast residents live just to the north of Miami, especially in Opa-Locka.

On July 17, 1979, Anastasio Somoza Debayle, the beleaguered president of Nicaragua, gave up struggling against rebels trying to topple a nearly forty-year-old dynastic dictatorship and fled the country. Political power was immediately seized by the spearhead organization of the armed resistance, the Frente Sandinista de Liberación Nacional

(FSLN), a group that took its name from Augusto César Sandino, a Nicaraguan nationalist hero who had fought against the U.S. military intervention in Nicaragua in the 1930s and who—after having been tricked into a peace accord—was murdered by order of Anastasio Somoza García, the first member of the Somoza family dictatorship. For the next eleven years, the Sandinista movement would totally dominate Nicaragua, taking over the economic, political, social, military, cultural, and educational structures of the country. Among the most interesting aspects of the Nicaraguan political transitions—from Somoza to the Sandinistas to the post-Sandinista regime—are the changes in public language usage, both gradual and abrupt (Lipski 1997). A few political terms that arose during the Sandinista regime have made their way into Nicaraguan popular culture, and even Nicaraguan sports language has been influenced by the regime (Ycaza Tigerino 1992). The presence of Cuban advisors in Nicaragua may also have left more than passing memories. A more recent examination of Nicaraguan popular Spanish usage (Peña Hernández 1992, 73) uncovered instances of non-inverted questions such as ¿Qué tú dices? (What do you say?), a typically Cuban construction previously unknown in Nicaragua, instead of the more usual universal Spanish format ¿Qué dices tú? or the Central American ¿Qué decís [vos]?

Members of the FSLN had seized power with the departure of Somoza, and although they enjoyed broad popular support at the beginning, they were in effect only the armed vanguard of an ideologically more heterogeneous and considerably less left-leaning Nicaraguan population. As the Sandinistas' Marxist-Leninist ideology became apparent, as ties with Cuba and the Soviet Union broadened, as hostile relations with the United States became the order of the day, and as increasingly totalitarian control of the population sank in, rejection of the Sandinistas as heir to political power became widespread. In 1984 Nicaragua held presidential elections under the supervision of United Nations observers. The Sandinista candidate, Daniel Ortega, won a decisive victory. Although international observers reported the elections to be generally fair and free, the United States rejected the results and intensified political and military pressure on the Sandinista government. In 1990 Nicaragua once more held elections, this time under preconditions and at a level of scrutiny that even the United States government found acceptable. Although it was widely believed that Daniel Ortega would easily be reelected, the Nicaraguan people opted instead for Violeta Barrios de Chamorro, widow of a charismatic newspaper publisher who had been assassinated for his opposition to the Somoza regime. Chamorro was supported by a broad coalition of opposition groups, ranging from ex–National Guard members who had supported Somoza to more moderate business leaders and even former Sandinista combatants.

Violeta Chamorro was widely viewed as the candidate of the reactionary former Somoza supporters—given the high profile of the former Somoza National Guard and family business structure among the opposition groups—despite the fact that her husband had presumably been killed under Somoza's orders. Observers on all points of the political spectrum assumed that the clock would quickly be turned back on the social, economic, and political changes introduced by the Sandinistas—in particular, a rapid abandonment of Marxist-Leninist ideology and of a state-controlled economy as well as a return to unabated capitalism were the assumed outcomes. It therefore came as something of a surprise when Chamorro retained Sandinista military leader Humberto Ortega (brother of the former president) as head of the Nicaraguan armed forces, and when she did not undertake the expected purge of Sandinista officials in the new government of "national reconciliation." In many ways, Chamorro's policies pleased no one. Pro-Sandinista groups resented Chamorro's redistribution of confiscated land that had been handed over to peasants during the Sandinista regime, while ultraconservative groups longed for a more decisive return to the privileges of the past. Armed rebellion—by former anti-Sandinista guerrillas and disgruntled Sandinista supporters—broke out on both sides, and during the early 1990s it seemed that Nicaragua would sink back into the same self-destructive civil war that had marked the second half of the 1980s. A succession of post-Sandinista governments has done little to improve the lot of Nicaraguans, and as of this writing (shortly after Daniel Ortega had once again been elected to the presidency, on a post-Sandinista but still leftist platform), the political situation can be best characterized as an uneasy truce amid continued economic stagnation, sniping from both political extremes, and little foreign investment.

Sandinista ideology quickly penetrated the area of public education, in particular with a reevaluation of rural culture, the beginnings of a literacy campaign, and the formation of revolutionary organizations such as the block-by-block defense committees, as well as Sandinista organizations of women, peasants, city workers, and youth. In retrospect, the Sandinistas overestimated the average Nicaraguan's appetite for revolutionary rhetoric as opposed to a simple return to an untroubled life and a freedom from political persecution. From the outset, conservative radio stations (including those associated with the Catholic Church and those representing large business owners) took a dim view of the Sandinista clamor, and they began calling for moderation in both language and content. Comparative studies of the language used in Sandinista and private (almost by definition more conservative) stations during the early Sandinista period show an increasing polarization of language, not only in terms of revolutionary vocabulary and slogans but even in the style of delivery, not to mention the overall program content. In 1980 the

Sandinistas undertook a five-month nationwide literacy campaign with the aim of reducing the illiteracy rate, which was among the highest in Latin America. In an attempt to help the young Nicaraguan literacy brigade workers, volunteer teachers from Cuba, the United States, Canada, and European countries joined in the crash program, which after six months resulted in a claimed illiteracy rate of only 12% nationwide, down from 55%. These figures must be taken cautiously; although the pre-Sandinista figures are believable, the growth in literacy that can result from a stopgap campaign such as the one carried out by the 1980 brigades is quite limited. Most of the new *alfabetizados* could barely read revolutionary slogans and billboards (in effect, the immediate goal of the Sandinista literacy campaign was to ensure the ability to read revolutionary broadsides and pronouncements). Despite the short-term success of the literacy campaign, anti-Sandinista sentiments rapidly grew among large sectors of the Nicaraguan population, nowhere more so than on the Atlantic coast, where the Somoza government had left the black creole and indigenous populations alone. Coastal residents were resentful of Sandinista forced military service, of obligatory vigilance, and—because they had not participated actively in the struggle against Somoza and harbored no historical anti-Yankee sentiments—of an ideology that seemed distant and artificial.

Nicaraguan Spanish in the United States

Nicaraguans have always been present in the United States in small numbers, but no large groups of Nicaraguans were to be found until the Sandinista insurrection against the Somoza regime began. Four decades of dictatorial Somoza rule—including the father (Anastasio), two sons (Luis and Anastasio Jr.), a grandson in training (Anastasio III), and interim puppet presidents—had created the inevitable exile population, but most relocated in Mexico or neighboring Central American countries. When the Sandinista armed insurrection began to gather force in 1978, the increasing death toll, the political repression, the guerrilla warfare in both urban and rural areas, the shortages and blackouts, and the general climate of insecurity prompted many Nicaraguans with the means at their disposal to temporarily leave the country or, at least, send their children abroad. The United States was a favored safe haven for those who could afford it because other Central American countries had problems of their own. Honduras openly supported the Somoza government, but Costa Rica increasingly favored the Sandinistas, and El Salvador and Guatemala were rapidly sliding down the path to civil war.

With the abdication of Somoza and the triumph of the Sandinista Revolution in July 1979, political violence temporarily stopped. However, the rapid social changes that accompanied the Sandinistas' rise to power provoked an almost immediate exodus of the wealthiest elements of Nicaraguan society—some of whom had actively contributed to the prosperity of the Somoza regimes—and of those who were regarded with suspicion and hostility by revolutionary supporters simply because of their elevated socioeconomic status in this poor nation. Almost immediately after the Sandinista takeover, a counterrevolutionary movement was formed, spearheaded by former members of the Somoza National Guard and supported financially by Nicaraguans whose fortunes had diminished by the transition from Somocismo to Sandinismo. The United States government also provided crucial economic and logistical support to the *contras*, through both public and clandestine channels.

The *contras* began an active military campaign against the Sandinista regime, which in practice affected virtually all residents of the country. The largest *contra* group, and the one most closely associated with the Somoza National Guard, was based in Honduras and operated the principal rebel radio station—Radio 15 de Septiembre—whose transmitter was always located in or around Tegucigalpa. A southern front was also formed under the leadership of a disaffected former Sandinista, Edén Pastora. Pastora, who had fought the Somoza forces, at first distanced himself from the northern *contras*, but both he and the Costa Rican government hosting him ultimately accepted aid from the U.S. government and from pro-Somoza groups. For a time, Pastora's group operated La Voz de Sandino, a clandestine shortwave broadcast station based in Costa Rica. Finally, Miskito and other Atlantic coast residents— who felt that active Sandinista intervention was more harmful than the neglect and marginality bestowed by the Somoza governments—formed the Misurata (from MIskito, SUmo, RAma) front. The principal leader of the Misurata was Steadman Fagoth, the half-Miskito son of a German immigrant, who received considerable support from the U.S. intelligence community. This group operated Radio Miskut from the Miskito coast of Honduras. This station transmitted in Miskito, Sumu, and Spanish. Radio Monimbó, another rebel station, delivered much smoother and less inflammatory programming. This station, whose location was never disclosed (it may have been operating from South Florida), was apparently funded by more moderate elements of the Nicaraguan opposition (Lipski 1991a).

As a result of the intensified *contra* activity and of increasing Sandinista interference in all aspects of Nicaraguans' lives, the Nicaraguan exodus grew from a trickle to a torrent. Large numbers moved to the United States, especially Miami and Los Angeles, where they established small businesses or found other employment. Although those who left assumed at first that their return to Nicaragua would be imminent, the reality of exile soon became apparent, as matters in Nicaragua went from bad to worse. Stable Nicaraguan communities with an internal structure that duplicated patterns found in the home country took shape in the United States. Particularly in Miami, the climate was favorable for educated middle-class refugees fleeing a leftist revolutionary government, one that further-more was openly embracing communist Cuban support. This is not to suggest that all exiled Cubans in Miami welcomed Nicaraguans with open arms, as both groups were often placed in competition for scarce resources. But the fact that these two groups had a common enemy served to smooth over many differences.

The Nicaraguan community in exile was jubilant over Chamorro's election, but—perhaps predictably—this event did not spur a large-scale permanent return of expatriates. Many Nicaraguans had now lived in the United States for many years, had established successful businesses, were living in comfortable and safe neighborhoods, had children in American schools, and were little inclined to return to a chaotic post–civil war environment in which economic fragility and political uncertainty were the order of the day. Reverse migration was slow, and to this day Nicaragua has failed to attract back the torrent of returning exiles one would expect given the number of displaced persons during the Sandinista period (Ortega 1991). Within the country, the return of displaced persons to their orig-inal homes has been extensive, as has the repatriation of Nicaraguans from the neighboring countries of Honduras and Costa Rica. By 1984, approximately 25,000 Nicaraguans were known to have taken refuge in neighboring Honduras (including at least 14,000 Miskitos), and at least 4,000 in Costa Rica (Montes 1986, 57; Farías Caro and Garita Salas 1985, 43–59). Some estimates place the total number of Nicaraguans in the two neighboring countries at more than 40,000 during the first years of the 1980s (Torres Rivas 1986, 11). By 1986 more than 30,000 Nicaraguans were living across the border in Costa Rica.

Immigration of Nicaraguans to the United States during the Sandinista period is better documented than emigration of refugees from other Central American countries in the same time period, as a result of the preferential treatment afforded the former group by the U.S. government. During the insurrection against Somoza, some 100,000–200,000 Nicaraguans left the country as refugees; another 800,000 were internally displaced (the total population of the country at the time was perhaps 2.5 million). In the first year of the Sandinista triumph (1979), many Nicaraguans took refuge in the United States, most of whom had been directly implicated in the Somoza government or the Nicaraguan military. It was estimated that by 1984 some 30,000 lived in the Miami area alone, with smaller numbers in Los Angeles, New York City, and New Orleans (Universidad para la Paz 1987, 178). By 1985 some 50,000 Nicaraguans were estimated to live in the United States, undoubtedly a figure much lower than the true population (Ferris 1987, 35). The 1990 census found some 203,000 Nicaraguans in the United States, of which 38,000 were native. In the 2000 census some 178,000 Nicaraguans were counted, indicating that some of the previous residents had returned to Central America. Nearly two-thirds of all Nicaraguans live in Florida or California. The states with the largest Nicaraguan population are as follows:

Florida	79,600
California	51,300
New York	8,000
Texas	7,500
New Jersey	4,400
Maryland	3,400
Virginia	3,200
Louisiana	2,800
Nevada	1,600
North Carolina	1,450

Linguistic Features of Nicaraguan Spanish

Few comprehensive linguistic studies of Nicaraguan Spanish have been published, and even fewer are based on systematic fieldwork.[1] Nicaragua is currently the Central American nation with the smallest research bibliography with regard to linguistic behavior.

Phonetics and Phonology

Few published studies describe the pronunciation of Nicaraguan Spanish (Lacayo 1954, 1962; Lipski 1989b; Ycaza Tigerino 1980). There is little sociolinguistic variation in pronunciation, and even regional phonetic variation is very slight. General phonetic traits are as follows:

- Intervocalic /d/ readily disappears in a variety of contexts, especially in the ubiquitous ending -ado (e.g., hablao for hablado [spoken]).
- As in the rest of Central America, the posterior fricative /x/ or jota is normally pronounced as a weak aspiration [h], and this sound frequently disappears intervocalically, particularly between nonfront vowels: trabajo > [traβao] (work).
- In common with other Central American dialects, intervocalic /j/ is pronounced with little or no friction and is often dropped when one of the vowels is /i/ or /e/, providing that the first vowel is not /o/ or /u/ (Lipski 1990a): gallina > gaína (hen), sello > seo (seal), calle > cae (street). Nicaraguans routinely insert a hypercorrect [j] in hiatus combinations beginning with /i/, thus converting María to Mariya and Darío to Dariyo. Rural speakers also insert [j] in hiatus groups beginning with /e/ as in vea > veya (see, [imp.]) (Lacayo 1962, 10).

- Earlier accounts of Nicaraguan Spanish (Lacayo 1954, 1962, 10; Canfield 1981, 65–66) claim an occlusive pronunciation of /b/, /d/, and /g/ after nonnasal consonants, as in *algo* (something), *alba* (dawn) and *arde* (it burns). This pronunciation is quite infrequent in contemporary Nicaraguan Spanish.
- Word-final /n/ is uniformly velarized as *-ng* in English *sing*, both phrase-finally (*muy bien* [very well]) and when followed by a word-initial vowel (*bien hecho* [well done]). A common alternative in phrase-final position is nasalization of the preceding vowel, combined with elision of the nasal consonant.[2] There is little social stigma associated with velarization of /n/; however, data from radio broadcasting suggest some reluctance to display velarization to a wide audience (Lipski 1983a).
- Aspiration to [h] or elimination of syllable- and word-final /s/ occurs to a greater extent in Nicaraguan Spanish than in any other Central American variety, with frequencies comparable to Caribbean dialects. This elimination of final /s/ has given rise to the nickname *muco,* a term originally referring to a cow missing one or both horns and applied to Nicaraguans by neighbors in Honduras. In Nicaraguan Spanish, retention of phrase-final [h] is more frequent than in Caribbean Spanish, and preconsonantal /s/ rarely disappears, giving Nicaraguan speech a breathier quality—in words such as *pues > pueh* (well) and *entonces > entonceh* (then)—not found in other Caribbean dialects in which loss of preconsonantal and phrase-final /s/ is the rule. Syllable-final /s/ is pronounced as [s] only in carefully monitored speech.[3]

The phonetic features just described are valid not only for most of the Nicaraguan territory but also for the Nicoya/Guanacaste region of Costa Rica. The only area where the preceding description does not hold in its entirety is the Caribbean coast of Nicaragua, among residents for whom Spanish is not a first language. One of the most common phonetic discrepancies often noted in the Spanish of Nicaragua's Caribbean coast is the pronunciation of the trill /r/ as a single flap [ɾ], or the pronunciation of both /ɾ/ and /r/ as a retroflex glide (that is, similar to the English *r*). Occlusive pronunciation of intervocalic /d/ is also common, and in rapid speech the resulting sound approaches [ɾ], as in *toro* for *todo* (all).

Morphological Characteristics

Nicaraguan Spanish uses only *vos* as the familiar pronoun, with the corresponding *voseo* verb paradigms (Thiemer 1989). Among Central Americans, Nicaraguans are noted for the great ease with which they use this familiar form of address, even with complete strangers. This usage stands in sharp contrast with neighboring Costa Rica, where use of formal *usted* may even extend to interaction between siblings or spouses (Rey 1994; Gaínza 1976; Vargas 1974; Villegas 1965). Neighboring Hondurans are also considerably more reluctant to use the familiar *vos* with strangers or outsiders (Castro-Mitchell 1991; Rey 1994). Nicaraguans had traditionally enjoyed the dubious reputation of being *confianzudos* (overly familiar), but Sandinista policies pushed this propensity for familiar address to extremes not previously found in Nicaragua. Official documents—including correspondence between government ministries—used *vos* instead of the universally mandatory *usted*. Billboards exhorting public support for the government, which in pre-Sandinista days would have used *usted* (or occasionally the artificial, non–Central American *tú*) bristled with *voseos* (e.g., *Nicaragüense, cumplí con tu deber* [Nicaraguan, do your duty]). This writer has a passport stamped with a Nicaraguan visa that reads *Nicaragua espera por vos* (Nicaragua awaits you), a remarkable deviation from the usual diplomatic protocol.

Syntactic Characteristics

- Nicaraguan Spanish shares with the rest of Central America the use of *hasta* to indicate the beginning of an event: *el jefe viene hasta las nueve* (the boss is coming at 9:00).
- Some rural speakers use a pleonastic clitic *lo*, both in sentences indicating the existence of something (*lo hay una mata de lirios* [there is a lily plant]) and in contexts where no direct object is called for (*lo temo que se muera* (I'm afraid that he will die), *por cierto que lo sois rico* (you're rich for sure) (Ycaza Tigerino 1980, 6). This usage is archaic and seldom heard in contemporary Nicaraguan Spanish or in the Spanish of Nicaraguan emigrants.

Lexical Characteristics

Most of the Nicaraguan Spanish lexicon is composed of commonly used Spanish elements, or words derived from Nahuatl used throughout Mexico and Central America. Only a handful of items may truly be called Nicaraguan. Of the regional words, most are derived from Native American languages once spoken in Nicaragua. These words usually refer to local flora, fauna, and domestic activities, and they are known only to older rural dwellers. Many words used in Nicaragua are used elsewhere in Latin America, but with partially or totally different meanings. A brief selection of words that Nicaraguans themselves most often regard as distinctively *nica* includes the following:[4]

bajo/ baho (a meat dish)
chachaguas (twins)
chavalo (child)
chele (blond, fair-skinned—used also in Honduras and El Salvador)

chigüín (small child)

chiltoma (bell pepper)

chimar (to bruise, scrape)

chocho (expression of surprise)

chunche (unnamed object, thing of no value—used also in neighboring countries)

cipote (small child—used also in Honduras and El Salvador)

cuaches (twins)

cumiche (youngest child of the family)

gallo pinto (dish of red beans and rice—used also in Costa Rica)

idiay (greeting, expression of surprise)

jodido (friendly greeting, expression of surprise—this is an obscene word in most other Spanish dialects)

maje (guy, individual)

pinol (drink made of toasted corn)

pinolillo (drink made of toasted corn and cacao)

pipante (native canoe)

reales (money)

vigorón (dish made of yucca and pork rinds [*chicharrón*])

Accommodation to Other U.S. Varieties of Spanish

Nicaraguans in exile, like their Cuban neighbors, have resolutely refused to carry over the revolutionary forms of address, avoiding the use of *compa* even among friends who might have used this term in pre-Sandinista days.[5] On the other hand, the usual Nicaraguan *voseo* has not been diminished. Perhaps one of the most tangible linguistic effects of the Sandinista revolution was to bring vernacular speech elements—including vocabulary items, use of *vos,* and a relaxed, consonant-weak pronunciation—into all spheres of public life. High government officials publicly addressed one another as *vos* on radio and television, as did government radio announcers and publications. Thus *vos*—a form of address that had traditionally been regarded as substandard, overly colloquial, and simply incorrect (although used routinely by all Nicaraguans)—gained official recognition as a legitimate aspect of Nicaraguan national culture.

In Miami, Nicaraguan Spanish comes into contact with Cuban Spanish on a daily basis. Cuban Spanish—representing a variety of registers, generations, and degrees of bilingualism with English—is the norm in Miami when it comes to Spanish-language broadcasting and journalism, and it is the de facto lingua franca in most parts of the city. It is nearly impossible for a Spanish speaker in Miami, particularly one who relies on Spanish more heavily than on English, to avoid contact with Cuban Spanish, regardless of individual attitudes toward Cubans and their language. Less frequently, depending on personal circumstances, Nicaraguans in South Florida encounter other Spanish dialects, with Salvadoran, Colombian (of several regions), and Puerto Rican being perhaps the most common.

Virtually all Nicaraguans living in the greater Miami area have definite opinions and attitudes regarding Cuban Spanish, Nicaraguan Spanish, and the interface between the two. Those Cubans who are familiar with Nicaraguans and their speech have equally well-defined opinions. In a survey conducted by the present writer in the 1990s among middle-class Nicaraguans in Miami, a majority of those over the age of about 20 expressed at least some negative sentiments towards Cuban Spanish. Frequently, these feelings were vague and not associated with particular linguistic characteristics; rather, they reflected cultural differences and perhaps concealed some resentment at the obviously dominant position enjoyed by Cubans in South Florida. One such nonspecific negative sentiment (by no means characteristic of the entire Nicaraguan community) is reflected in the remark that Cubans speak "too loud," "too fast," "too nasty," and so forth. These are precisely the same unsubstantiated criticisms that neighboring Central American countries level against Nicaraguans, and they are typical of xenophobic attitudes worldwide. As with all stereotypes, the comments made by Nicaraguans about Cuban Spanish have a kernel of truth: compared with the baseline Central American varieties of Spanish, Cuban Spanish in the more emotionally charged registers is objectively marked by greater intonational swings, often perceived as absolute differences in volume. In animated conversations, Cubans (particularly Cuban men) tend to prefer simultaneous participation—with each intervention taking place at a successively higher volume level—to a greater emphasis on turn-taking, which prevails throughout Central America. To the ear unaccustomed to such energetic exchanges, a Cuban conversation can seem impossibly rapid, deafeningly loud, and incredibly rude.[6]

On a more specific basis, many Nicaraguans residing in the United States criticize Cubans living there for an excessive use of Anglicisms, particularly loan translations and slightly adapted borrowings. The most commonly cited loan translation is the use of *pa(ra) atrás* as a literal translation of the English verbal particle *back*, as in *te llamo patrás* (I'll call you back), *me pagó patrás* (he/she paid me back). This combination is indeed common among younger generations of increasingly English-dominant Cuban bilingual speakers. The use of noninverted questions—such as *¿Qué tú quieres?* and *¿Dónde usted vive?*—is also regarded as unacceptable by Nicaraguans in the United States, many of whom suspect English interference in such questions. At the time of the survey, the members of the Nicaraguan community in Miami had not resided in a bilingual environment long enough for this type of subtle syntactic Anglicism to penetrate their vernacular speech. Nicaraguan adolescents picked up these combinations naturally, both through contact with Cuban friends and by simply living in the Hispanophone environment in Miami. Older Nicaraguans are predictably dismayed when their children begin using constructions from other groups, particularly when, in the parents' eyes, the combinations are socially unacceptable.

Nicaraguans less frequently commented on Cubans' pronunciation of Spanish, except to note neutralization of preconsonantal /l/ and /r/, giving rise to forms such as *pocque* < *porque* (because) and *calta* < *carta* (letter). Objectively, though, Cuban Spanish does not often change /r/ > [l]; in fact, such change is much more frequent in Puerto Rican and even Dominican dialects. In Cuba this neutralization is characteristic of the lower classes in the central and eastern provinces, and it was not widely found in the Cuban exile community until after the Mariel boatlift of 1980, in which large numbers of less educated working-class or rural Cubans arrived in the United States. Neutralization of liquids was always stigmatized among educated Cubans, but it is becoming increasingly common—and, correspondingly, less objectionable—as the demographic profile of the South Florida Cuban community evolves, and as young Cuban Americans receive less sociolinguistic feedback regarding their pronunciation in Spanish. Glottalization of syllable-final liquids, combined with gemination of consecutive consonants, is found throughout Cuba, including Havana, and it is also characteristic of the speech of members of the lower social classes. Certain words—such as *pocque* < *porque* (because),—routinely undergo gemination even when they are produced by educated Cubans, but variants such as *puetta* < *puerta* (door) and *aggo* < *algo* (something) have become common in Florida Cuban Spanish only in the last decade. Such deviations from standard Spanish phonology strike Nicaraguans as unacceptable.

Relatively few Cubans in Miami have close enough contact with Nicaraguans to have formed clear opinions regarding Nicaraguan Spanish. Among those Cubans who do mention specific features, the use of *vos* stands out as the most striking difference. The adjectives used by Cubans to describe this distinctly non–Caribbean phenomenon range from "strange" to "incorrect." A few Cubans comment on Nicaraguans' weak pronunciation of intervocalic /j/, especially in contact with /i/ and /e/, which can make *gallina* (hen) sound like *gaína* and *sello* (stamp) emerge as *seo*. Cubans also comment on the frequency with which Nicaraguans punctuate their speech with *pues* [pueh] (well then), a trait of which Nicaraguans themselves are also aware. Among the most shocking differences between Cuban and Nicaraguan Spanish is the use of *jodido* as a casual greeting among Nicaraguans of both sexes. To Cubans, use of this word as anything other than an insult is unthinkable.

In the context of Latin American Spanish, it is unfortunately not uncommon for Central Americans to have a low opinion of Central American dialects, regarding them as excessively laden with archaic and vulgar elements. Historical comments by prestigious grammarians—such as Andrés Bello and Rufino José Cuervo—as well as by well-known Central American writers have done little to improve the situation. The relative poverty and instability of the region is another contributing factor, as is the fact that national literatures invariably both reflect the speech patterns of an intellectual elite (usually educated abroad) and attribute Central American linguistic traits only to marginalized characters such as peons and the urban proletariat. In recent decades, a more positive attitude has been emerging, as populist authors and university communities insist on legitimizing homegrown varieties of Spanish and on diminishing the mindless admiration of foreign patterns. Nicaraguans are not exempt from feelings of linguistic insecurity, but the Nicaraguan community in the United States is less afflicted by such sentiments than are other Central American groups. A high level of education and a more comfortable socioeconomic status are probably the main contributing factors, aided by a certain smugness from being the bearers of a form of Spanish as yet unaffected by the overwhelming influence of English. Few Nicaraguans consciously alter their language when speaking to Cubans, and even fewer willingly adopt Cubanisms into their own speech. With regard to the characteristically Central American use of *vos,* a majority of Nicaraguans stated that they use such forms to address Cubans with whom they had attained a level of *confianza* that warrants such usage. A few confessed to employing *tú* so as to not shock or offend Cubans.

Scholarship on Nicaraguan Spanish in the United States

To date there has been very little published scholarship on Nicaraguan Spanish in the United States. Lipski (1997) peripherally mentions the U.S. Nicaraguan community, as does Peñalosa (1984). Lipski (2000b) covers the U.S. Nicaraguan community in somewhat greater detail.

Notes

1. Arellano (1980, 1992) contains a partial bibliography as well as several shorter essays by various authors. Mántica (1989) is the only major monograph, whereas Ycaza Tigerino (1980) is a shorter compilation. Valle (1976) contains many useful observations.
2. Lipski (1986d). Some personally collected quantitative data representing a cross-section of Nicaraguan speakers are as follows (Lipski 1986f, 1988b):

Context	n## {Phrase-final}			n#V {Prevocalic}		
Allophone	[n]	[ŋ]	[Ø]	[n]	[ŋ]	[Ø]
% used	7	55	38	10	81	9

3. Some basic quantitative data representing a cross-section of Nicaraguan Spanish are as follows (Lipski 1989b):

/s/C			/s/#C			/s/##			/s/#V			/s/#v		
[s]	[h]	[Ø]	[s]	[h]	[Ø]	[s]	[h]	[Ø]	[s]	[h]	[Ø]	[s]	[h]	[Ø]
13	84	4	2	86	12	35	59	6	28	70	2	7	90	3

C = consonant; V = tonic vowel; v = atonic vowel; # = word boundary; ## = phrase boundary

4. The Nicaraguan lexicon has been studied by Barreto (1893), Berendt (1874), Buitrago Morales (1940), Castellón (1939), Castrillo Gámez (1966), Mántica (1989), Matus Lazo (1982), Rabella and Palais (1994), Ramírez Fajardo (1993), and Valle (1972, 1976).

5. During the initial insurrection against Somoza, Sandinista combatants were known as *compas*, a colloquial Nicaraguan term of address (derived from *compadre* or perhaps *compañero* [comrade]), whose meaning was narrowed to include only rebel fighters. After the Sandinista takeover, use of *compa* among all Nicaraguans became de rigueur as a sign of revolutionary solidarity; the use of traditional *señor, señora, don/doña*, and so forth was taken as an anachronistic and even unpatriotic acknowledgement of former class hierarchies. The situation is completely parallel to that of revolutionary Cuba, where use of *compañero/compañera* has almost completely supplanted *señor/señora*, at least in public conversations. The extent of direct Cuban influence on revolutionary Nicaraguan terms of address is debatable. Given the similar circumstances—in both countries rebel groups gained power through armed struggle—the carryover of military camaraderie to the civilian sector is not unexpected.

6. Claims of vulgar talk normally involve certain key lexical items that are inoffensive and common in one dialect, while carrying a heavy negative connotation in the other. Cuban Spanish is noted for the very frequent use of *coño*, an obscene epithet still very common in Spain but rarely heard in Latin America outside of the Caribbean. Nicaraguans are aware that *coño* is a "bad" word, although the word is not normally used in Nicaragua, and they are sometimes surprised at the ease with which well-bred Cubans, including women and children, employ this term. Even more shocking to the Nicaraguan ear is the uninhibited use of *comemierda*, which Cubans employ as meaning simply *fool* or *gullible person*. Cubans in turn find the free and easy Nicaraguan use of *jodido* as a friendly greeting (including by many women) astoundingly vulgar, as this term in Cuba could only be an insult.

11

Guatemalan and Honduran Spanish in the United States

Guatemalans

Guatemalans represent the second largest Central American group in the United States, after Salvadorans. In some areas significant groups of Guatemalans are concentrated in one locality, and there are pockets of Guatemalan Spanish in the United States. Most of these communities are formed of indigenous Guatemalans speaking a variety of Mayan languages, and in some instances these languages take precedence over Spanish, even in the U.S. setting (e.g., Hagan 1994).

In Central America the Spanish presence was strongly felt in Guatemala, the eventual seat of the Captaincy General of Guatemala. In theory this colony was subordinate to the larger Viceroyalty of New Spain, whose capital was Mexico City, but in practice the captaincy generals were independent entities, responding directly to Spain and having little political contact with distant viceroyalties. In the case of the Captaincy General of Guatemala, the location of the capital at one geographical extreme of the territory resulted in a diminishing cultural, political, and linguistic influence as a function of distance from the capital city. During most of the colonial period, the only city of importance was Guatemala City, which enjoyed the benefits of a university and other contacts with the administrative and cultural centers of Spain. Although Spain maintained an administrative presence in Guatemala with close ties to Mexico, the Caribbean, and Spain, the indigenous population was large and diverse and precluded large-scale Hispanization. The implantation of the

Spanish language in rural Guatemala was less effective than anywhere else in Central America, being limited, during the colonial period, to a handful of urban nuclei. Even today, it is estimated that at least half the population of Guatemala does not speak Spanish, or speaks it only as a recessive second language. These monolingual populations are scattered away from the urbanized central and southwestern regions. A visitor to Guatemala City may receive the impression that Guatemala is fundamentally a Spanish-speaking nation, but an observer of life in a small village or in the remote northern jungles would find little Spanish in use anywhere.

The Captaincy General of Guatemala was important to the Spanish imperial effort, although its mineral wealth was outranked by the treasure pouring in from Mexico and Peru. On the Caribbean side, commerce with Spain and the West Indies was carried out through Puerto Caballos (modern Puerto Cortés) in Honduras. More contact was maintained via overland routes from Mexico, along Guatemala's western lowlands. No major Pacific ports were developed partially as a result of the lack of natural harbors (the nearest port being Acajutla in El Salvador), and therefore Guatemala was ignored both by pirates and by the Spanish government. This created the paradoxical situation wherein the language variety representing a nominal administrative seat could develop in isolation, showing many of the same archaisms and signs of linguistic aban-donment and drift as territories such as Costa Rica, which was marginalized from the outset.

Spain established the *encomienda* system of indigenous labor/tribute in Guatemala, but it did not work as smoothly as it had in some other colonies. A number of export crops were attempted, including indigo and sarsaparilla, but colonial Guatemala never enjoyed economic prosperity. Following independence, coffee became the main cash crop, later to be augmented by bananas, grown under the auspices of American fruit companies. During peaceful interludes, tourism is a major source of income in Guatemala, with Antigua, the markets of Guatemala City, and the spectacular Mayan ruins of Tikal being among the principal attractions. Religious fervor brings thousands to venerate the Black Christ statue at the town of Esquipulas, near the Honduran border.

During the twentieth century Guatemala suffered numerous political convulsions and military coups. In 1944 the military dictator Jorge Ubico was overthrown, and there followed ten years of liberal democracy, under the presidencies of Juan José Arévalo and Jacobo Arbenz. The latter instituted an agrarian reform in a nation that had long been dominated by a small and powerful landowning elite. His actions were viewed with alarm by political and business leaders in the United States, and in 1954 a military coup largely engineered by the U.S. Central Intelligence Agency toppled Arbenz and returned Guatemala to despotic military rule (with a brief civilian interlude from 1966–70), which continued for more than three decades (Schlesinger and Kinzer 1982). Insurgency against the Guatemalan military began in the 1960s, but the first movements were handed a bloody defeat in 1968 by counterinsurgency Colonel Carlos Arana Osorio, who went on to assume Guatemala's presidency in 1970. The next two decades were marked by increasingly violent armed conflict between largely Mayan-based insurgent groups and the Guatemalan military and paramilitary death squads, apparently in the pay of the large landowners. The events in neighboring El Salvador—spearheaded by the flamboyant Frente Farabundo Martí para la Liberación Nacional (FMLN)—eclipsed the growing bloodshed in Guatemala, and Guatemalans inmigrated illegally to Mexico and the United States.[1]

The beginning of the significant Guatemalan presence in the United States can be traced to the CIA-engineered coup against elected president Jacobo Arbenz in 1954. However, the real exodus began in the 1970s when the counterinsurgency campaigns increased their intensity. Guatemala, like neighboring El Salvador, suffered a low-intensity civil war pitting armed insurgents against military governments and paramilitary death squads (Delli Sante 1996; Jonas 2000; North and Simmons 1999; Schirmer 1998; Wilkinson 2002). The insurgency reached its peak around 1981 when as many as half a million armed guerrilla combatants and active supporters could be counted within Guatemala. A new Guatemalan constitution was written in 1985, and following the 1985 presidential elections the military began to disengage from its bloody counterinsurgency activities. Armed resistance and military and paramilitary reprisals continued, however, well beyond the 1990 presidential elections, and it was not until December of 1996 that formal peace accords were finally signed, bringing an end to more than three decades of civil war. Since that time the economic and human rights profile of Guatemala has improved considerably, but many Guatemalans living abroad in the United States and elsewhere have chosen not to return in the immediate future.

Demographics of Guatemalans in the United States

The largest Guatemalan community is located in Los Angeles (Hamilton and Stoltz Chinchilla 2001; Kohpahl 1998). A smaller and locally almost unknown group lives in rural southern Florida, where community members work in agriculture alongside immigrants from Mexico and the Caribbean. Smaller groups of Guatemalans are found in Houston, Chicago, Boston, Washington, DC, and other cities. There are also significant numbers of Guatemalans in rural areas, including the Pacific Northwest and the Midwest. In assessing Guatemalan Spanish in the United States, it is necessary to focus on bilingual indigenous communities, whose use of Spanish is often little-studied, and which receives little prestige either in Guatemala or abroad.

By the mid-1980s, there were some 80,000 Guatemalans in Los Angeles, with smaller groups in San Francisco, Chicago, Washington, DC, and Houston (Universidad para la Paz 1987, 178). Some 100,000 lived in Mexico as well (Ferris 1987, 35; Montes 1986, 56). Some 3,000 Guatemalan refugees lived in neighboring Belize, and at least 1,000 in Honduras. Internally, at least 400,000 Guatemalans were displaced during the first half of the 1980s (Montes 1986, 56). By 1988, there were at least 200,000 Guatemalans living in the United States (Aguayo and Weiss Fagen 1988, 23) and as many as 150,000 living in Mexico (Aguayo and Weiss Fagen 1988, 58). The 1990 census reported 269,000 Guatemalans in the United States, of which 53,000 were U.S.-born. In the 2000 census some 372,500 Guatemalans were reported, which equals 1.1% of the total Hispanic population in the United States. They are concentrated in the following states:

California	143,500
New York	29,000
Florida	28,650
Illinois	19,800
Texas	18,500
New Jersey	17,000
Massachusetts	11,400
Georgia	10,700
Virginia	10,000
Rhode Island	8,950
Maryland	8,300
North Carolina	6,000
Connecticut	5,300
Arizona	4,350
Nevada	4,100
Oregon	3,500

Characteristics of Guatemalan Spanish

In Guatemala Nahuatl-derived cultures and languages were not the primary indigenous force, although some Nahuatl and Pipil groups occupied the southwestern coastal regions. The principal indigenous groups belong to the Maya-Quiché family, and given the cultural ascendancy of these groups even after the decline of the Maya empire, Mayan languages were never displaced by Nahuatl as occurred in El Salvador and Honduras. Among the languages still spoken in Guatemala are some four members of the Quiché group, six members of the Mam group, four members of the Pocomam group, two members of the Chol group, and a tiny contingent of Pipil.[2] As a group the Mayan languages have not contributed to Guatemalan Spanish in proportion to their numbers, but some lexical items of indigenous languages are in common use.

The study of Guatemalan Spanish suffers from the lack of regional studies of any dialect and from the fact that in much of the country Spanish is not the home language. Accessible studies of Guatemalan Spanish pronunciation include Alvar (1980), Canfield (1951a), Lentzner (1938), and Predmore (1945). A nationwide phonetic description has yet to be undertaken. What is normally described as "Guatemalan Spanish" represents the middle and upper class, monolingual Spanish speech of Guatemala City and the surrounding highland regions. "Popular Guatemalan Spanish" usually represents southwestern regions near the Honduran and Salvadoran borders, where monolingual Spanish usage prevails. Among Guatemalans speaking Spanish as a first language or as a fluent second language, there is some regional variation in pronunciation, but not as noteworthy as, for example, the regional variations in pronunciation present in Mexico or Honduras.

Sociolinguistic stratification within regions is much more significant, and the correlation between sociolinguistic variation and ethnicity is very high, with much popular Guatemalan Spanish reflecting the influence of Native American languages or imperfect learning of Spanish. The most striking regional variation is found along border areas, particularly the border with El Salvador and Honduras, where some of the consonantal weakening tendencies of the latter countries are found. To the northwest, Guatemalan Spanish shades smoothly into the variety spoken in the Mexican state of Chiapas, which was originally part of the Captaincy General of Guatemala. The remote northern Petén territory is primarily Maya-speaking, but the Spanish found in that region is a continuation of the Mexican Yucatán zone.

Phonetics and Phonology

Among the principal phonetic traits of Guatemalan Spanish are the following:

- In common with other Central American dialects, the posterior fricative /x/ or *jota* is a weak [h], dropping frequently: *trabajo* (work) [traβáho]/[traβáo].
- As another pan–Central American trait, intervocalic /j/ drops in contact with /i/ or /e/ (e.g., *sello* [stamp] > *seo*, *silla* [chair] > *sía*), but hiatus-breaking [j] (as in *día* [day] > *diya*, *sea* > [be] (subj.) *seya*) is sociolinguistically stigmatized.

- Common in central Guatemala is the alveolar and affricated pronunciation of /tr/ almost reaching [ʃ], particularly in postconsonantal position as in *entre* (between). The emerging sound is somewhere between the sounds represented by Spanish *ch* and (American) English *tr*. This pronunciation is not as frequent as in Costa Rica and the Andean dialects of South America, and it appears to be receding among younger generations, particularly in urban areas.
- Syllable-final /r/ is assibilated (and sounds much like [s] or [z]) in much of central Guatemala. This pronunciation is less frequent among younger, urban speakers.
- The trill /r/ is given a fricative pronunciation [ʒ], such as the realization of /j/ in Buenos Aires, or the s of English *measure*.
- Word-final /n/ is velarized in Guatemala, as in the *–ng* of English *ring*, although retention of alveolar [n] in prevocalic position is more frequent than in other Central American dialects.[3]
- Syllable- and word-final /s/ resists erosion more so than any other Central American dialect. Rates of retention of a sibilant [s] are comparable to those of central Mexico, and only along the border with El Salvador, along the Pacific coast and near the border with Belize is a slight weakening of preconsonantal /s/ to be found.[4]

Morphological Characteristics

Use of *vos* and accompanying verb forms is the rule in Guatemalan Spanish. The *voseo* verb forms are identical to those used elsewhere in Central America. Pinkerton (1986) suggests that among Guatemalan *ladinos* (those identifying with Hispanic rather than indigenous culture and language), *tú* carries a higher social value, especially among women. In his comparative studies Baumel-Schreffler (1989, 1995) found considerable complexity in the choice of familiar pronouns among Guatemalans in the United States.

Syntactic Characteristics

Few syntactic structures are peculiar to Guatemala. Combinations of the sort *una mi amiga* (a friend of mine), also found in El Salvador, are frequent in vernacular Guatemalan Spanish. Martin (1978, 1985) has suggested a Mayan influence, but archaic carryover may also have occurred, because similar constructions were prevalent in old Spanish.

Lexical Characteristics

Guatemalan Spanish has fewer Nahuatl elements than Mexican and other Central American dialects, but it still has more words of Mayan origin than Mexican and other Central American dialects. However, the latter are surprisingly few in number and bear witness to the fact that the Hispanization of Guatemala's indigenous population was never more than partial, occurring on the periphery of large Spanish settlements. Among lexical items largely or totally confined to Guatemala are the following:[5]

canche (blond, fair-complexioned)
chapín (Guatemalan)
chirís (small child)
chirmol (tomato sauce)
chojín (a type of salad)
mesho (fair-haired)
patojo (small child)
trobo (drunk, intoxicated)
zafada (excuse)

Scholarship on Guatemalan Spanish in the United States

Little research has been done on the linguistic peculiarities of the Guatemalan population in the United States. With the exception of a few sociological studies (e.g., Peñalosa 1984), there is little accurate information on any aspect of the Guatemalan community within the United States. Baumel-Schreffler (1989, 1994, 1995) examines the sociolinguistics of *voseo* usage among Guatemalans in the United States. The majority of Guatemalans are undocumented political or economic refugees, usually from rural regions, and almost invariably from an indigenous background. Some speak little or no Spanish, and those who speak Spanish most often do so with the linguistic characteristics of second-language speakers.

Hondurans

Although the most prominent Central American dialects in the United States are those of El Salvador, Guatemala, and Nicaragua, in descending order of number of speakers, there are large Honduran communities in several cities. The longest-standing is found in New Orleans, where the Honduran community first arose as part of the banana industry, which linked the northern Honduran ports of Tela and La Ceiba via maritime routes with the port of New Orleans. Another large group of Hondurans, mostly from the central part of the country, is found in New York City, where they do not enjoy the same sense of community identity as in New Orleans. In nearby Yonkers, New York, an even larger group of Hondurans, all recent immigrants, have formed an ethnically identifiable enclave. Yet another group of Hondurans, this time living together with Salvadorans and other Spanish speakers, is found in the many towns of western and central Long Island, where the Latino community now makes up well over 10% of the Long Island population (up from 6.3% in 1990 and 3.9% in 1980). Miami is also home to many Hondurans, as are Los Angeles and Washington, DC. The 1990 census found 131,000 Hondurans in the United States, of whom 30,000 were U.S.-born. By the 2000 census this number had jumped to nearly 218,000, and this number continues to grow. The most significant population clusters are distributed as follows:

Florida	41,200
New York	35,100
California	30,400
Texas	24,200
New Jersey	15,400
Louisiana	8,800
North Carolina	8,300
Virginia	7,800
Illinois	6,000
Georgia	5,200
Massachusetts	5,100
Maryland	4,000
Connecticut	2,000

A brief glimpse at Honduran Spanish is therefore a useful addition to the study of United States Spanish. The tiny Central American nation of Honduras contains within its borders a complex mosaic of ethnolinguistic variation, archaisms, and the results of linguistic drift. Situated squarely in the middle of Central America, Honduras does not properly contain any major dialect zone; regional features of Honduran Spanish spill over into Guatemala, El Salvador, and Nicaragua. Honduran Spanish has been little studied. Herranz (1990) provides a thorough bibliography. Herranz contains an anthology of studies on Honduran Spanish, together with a bibliographical update.

Honduras is extremely mountainous, and in most of the interior communication is limited to footpaths or precarious trails that can be traversed by sturdy vehicles only during the dry season. Geography was not the original factor that motivated the isolation of Honduras. Following an early period of prominence, Honduras declined in importance. The postcolonial governments were left with few resources upon which to build, and Honduras drifted into the sphere of interest of U.S. fruit growers. These foreign interests were intensely active along the northern coast, while also exerting a strong influence over the national government in Tegucigalpa.

In postcolonial times Honduran Spanish is largely the product of the geographical isolation of interior regions and a traditionally high rate of illiteracy, estimated at 60–70% nationwide and reaching 90% or higher in many rural areas. The majority of Hondurans are not in contact with normative linguistic influences, and even where schools exist, the speech of teachers is likely to represent the same rural tendencies. An extensive network of private and government-sponsored radio stations covers the entire nation. The linguistic usage of radio announcers, few of whom have had formal broadcast training, is potentially the single most important centripetal factor in shaping Honduras's Spanish, because even in the most remote regions, battery-powered radios are avidly listened to in every community.

Phonetics and Phonology

The study of Honduran Spanish pronunciation has languished until recently. Canfield (1981, 58–59) offers personal impressions resulting from a brief visit to Tegucigalpa. Subsequently, more researchers have been attracted to the study of Honduran Spanish, including Amastae (1989), Herranz (1990), Lipski (1983b, 1986d, 1987b), López Scott (1983), and Medina-Rivera (1999). Major features of Honduran pronunciation include the following:

- Postconsonantal /b/, /d/, and /g/ normally receive an occlusive pronunciation as in English, rather than the fricatives found in most other Spanish dialects, even after semivowels, as in *Ceiba, verde* (green), *algo* (something) (Amastae 1989).
- Intervocalic /j/ is weak and falls in contact with /i/ and /e/ as elsewhere in Central America, but the tendency to insert hypercorrect [j] as a hiatus-breaker is limited to marginal rural varieties.
- The posterior fricative /x/ or *jota* is pronounced weakly as [h] and disappears frequently in intervocalic position.
- Word-final /n/ is usually velarized as in English *sing,* with little sociolinguistic stratification or regional variation (Lipski 1986f).
- In contrast to neighboring Guatemala but in line with El Salvador and Nicaragua, /s/ before consonants is weakened to [h] except in a few regions along the Guatemalan border. Phrase-final and word-final prevocalic /s/ is also reduced to [h], but with greater geographical and sociolinguistic variability. The northern coast, as well as the southeastern departments near Nicaragua (particularly Choluteca and Paraíso), reduce /s/ proportionately more, with rates similar to those found in Nicaragua. These are the regions that have yielded the greatest number of immigrants to the United States, so that Honduran Spanish as heard in the United States typically has a weak final /s/. The interior departments of the country

show much variation. The Lenca-dominated, isolated, and entirely rural depart-ments of La Paz, Intibucá, and Lempira show relatively strong /s/ (Lipski 1983b, 1986d).

- As in El Salvador, in most of Honduras word-initial /s/ is often pronounced as [h], when occurring intervocalically in connected speech: *la semana* [lahemana] (the week.) To a lesser extent, word-internal intervocalic /s/ is also weakened in words such as *presidente* [prehiðente] (president) and *licenciado* [lihensiaðo] (attorney). This is a phenomenon of casual speech, completely absent in monitored or self-conscious speech, reading, and public speaking. It is also strongly correlated with socioeco-nomic class, being very prevalent among the lower working classes and rural inhab-itants, and infrequent in even the most colloquial speech of educated Hondurans. There is some regional variation, but initial /s/-reduction appears to more closely reflect sociolinguistic marginality. Among the most common words whose initial /s/ is realized as [h] in postvocalic contexts are *centavo(s)* (cents), *semana* (week), the clitic pronoun *se* (e.g., *no se puede* [it can't be done]), and the numbers *seis* (six), *cincuenta* (fifty), *sesenta* (sixty), and so forth. For many speakers these words have become effec-tively lexicalized with initial [h], so that *un centavo* may be pronounced with word-initial [h].

Morphological Characteristics

Honduran Spanish uses *vos* exclusively instead of *tú,* with the same verbal mor-phology found in the other Central American countries. It is possible to find future forms in *-és* rather than *-ás,* although this usage is disappearing. Among the working classes and rural dwellers, use of *usted* predominates. Children of these groups are referred to as *usted* when they are young, so that the respectful form of address will be learned first. Van Wijk (1969) gives other observations, although based entirely on literary examples.

Syntactic Characteristics

- Honduran Spanish employs *hasta* to refer to the beginning of an event (*el bus viene hasta las cinco* [the bus will arrive at 5:00]).
- In some rural areas, pleonastic use of the clitic *lo* is found: *te lo fuistes de mí* (you left me), *se lo fue de viaje* (he left on a trip), *me lo pegastes* (you hit me), and so forth. (van Wijk 1969).
- Among uneducated speakers, double possessives are occasionally used: *mi casa mía* (my house).
- Combinations with pleonastic article + possessive, such as *una mi amiga* (my friend), are heard at times, but are not as frequent as in Guatemala and El Salvador, despite suggestions to the contrary by van Wijk (1969).

Lexical Characteristics

Few accurate lexical studies of Honduran Spanish are to be found. Membreño (1895) continues to be the major published source; other recent additions include *Gran Diccionario Académico* (1984), Nieto (1986), and Walz (1964). Aguilar Paz (1981) provides a representative sample of popular sayings, many of which incorporate regionalisms. The Honduran Spanish lexicon contains a heavy proportion of elements of Nahuatl origin, shared with the rest of Central America (Aguilar Paz 1970; Membreño 1901, 1907). Very few Mayan words are in use. The Lenca contribution is substantial, but mostly limited to the departments where Lenca was once spoken; the majority of Lenca words are not in use elsewhere in Honduras. Lexical borrowings from other indigenous languages are virtually nonexistent, whereas borrowings from English are concentrated along the Caribbean coast, where American banana companies have exercised a strong cultural and economic influence. Few lexical items are strictly limited to Honduras; most words felt to be "Honduranisms" are also found in neighboring countries or throughout Central America. Among the most commonly used words that are most closely associated with Honduras are the following:

búfalo (10 lempira coin = 5 U.S. cents)
catracho (colloquial term for Honduran)
chafa (military person)
cipote (small child—also used in El Salvador and parts of Nicaragua)
daime (20 lempira coin = 10 U.S. cents)
guaro (cheap rum—used elsewhere in Central America)
papada (worthless item)
suelto (loose change)
tinguro (tadpole)

Notes

1. The film *El Norte* (Navas and Thomas 1984) dramatizes the plight of Guatemalans crossing Mexico to reach the United States during these troubled times and offers a fictionalized but realistic indication of the linguistic strategies used by Guatemalans in their attempt to pass for Mexicans.
2. Barberena (1920), Castañeda Paganini (1959), Martin (1978, 1985), Monteforte Toledo (1959), Stoll and Goubaud Carrera (1958), and Whetten (1961, 55–57).
3. Personally collected data (Lipski 1986f) representing the speech of the Guatemala City area give the following figures:

Context	n## {Phrase-final}			n#V {Prevocalic}		
Allophone	[n]	[ŋ]	[Ø]	[n]	[ŋ]	[Ø]
% used	4	80	16	23	69	8

4. Personally collected data for the Guatemala City region (Lipski 1985d, 1986f) show the following range:

/s/C			/s/#C			/s/##			/s/#V			/s/#v		
[s]	[h]	[Ø]	[s]	[h]	[Ø]	[s]	[h]	[Ø]	[s]	[h]	[Ø]	[s]	[h]	[Ø]
93	7	0	69	30	1	93	9	4	100	0	0	100	0	0

C = consonant; V = tonic vowel; v = atonic vowel; # = word boundary; ## = phrase boundary

5. The main sources for the Guatemalan lexicon are Armas (1971), Batres Jáuregui (1892), Bueno (1978), Morales Hidalgo (1978), Rubio (1982), and Sandoval (1941–42).

12

Traditional Varieties: New Mexico and Louisiana

Introduction

In addition to the Spanish-speaking communities described in the preceding chapters, all of which have resulted either from immigration or from the territorial expansion of the United States over the past 150 years, there exist several varieties of Spanish that stem from much different circumstances. These are linguistic enclaves of older dialects of Spanish that because of sociohistorical circumstances have not been absorbed by the modern forms of Spanish currently found in the United States. The speech communities in question are found in New Mexico, southern Colorado, and Louisiana. In the case of New Mexico/Colorado, the Spanish-speaking community is relatively large and, in New Mexico at least, linguistically prominent across a wide expanse of territory. The Louisiana groups are small, isolated, vestigial, and all but unknown outside of the immediate vicinity where they are spoken. Taken as a group they provide a window into earlier stages of the Spanish language that have long since disappeared from contemporary dialects. They also round out the panorama of the Spanish language in the United States, giving testimony to linguistic and cultural contacts that go far beyond the most commonly presented scenarios.

The Traditional Spanish of New Mexico and Southern Colorado

According to the 2000 U.S. census, New Mexico has the highest Latino population of any state: more than 765,000, or 42% of the total population. By some estimates the Hispanic population is more than 50%, which would make New Mexico the only majority Latino state. Taking into account the considerable Native American population, New Mexico is one of two "majority minority" states, the other being Hawaii. New Mexico is also the only state in which Latinos have the option of declaring themselves as *Hispanos,* a term not related to any country of origin. Indeed this idiosyncrasy reflects the historical origins of the traditional Spanish-speaking population of New Mexico, always a frontier outpost at the far edge of Spain's northernmost viceroyalty and never part of Mexico. The 2000 census found 330,000 New Mexican residents (43%) that consider themselves Mexican, only a few thousand Cubans and Puerto Ricans, and more than 428,000 (56%) "other Hispanic or Latino." Interestingly, some 74,000 New Mexicans wrote in "Spanish" despite the fact that probably no more than a few dozen Spaniards are to be found in the entire state. A visit to the Albuquerque city council chamber reveals the coats of arms of many prominent Spanish families, all of which have descendents living in northern New Mexico; there is a flourishing Hispanic genealogy society, an impressive Hispanic Cultural Center, and one of the few Cervantes Institutes in the country, funded by the government of Spain. The southern part of the state contains a large population of more recent Mexican origin, and cultural ties to Mexico are strong. The varieties of Spanish found in southern New Mexico are in large measure a continuation of those of rural Chihuahua in Mexico, although some vestiges of more traditional speech are still found. Central and northern New Mexico are home to a Hispanic population that dates its origin to the Juan de Oñate expedition of 1598, and who regard themselves as direct descendents of Spaniards. When speaking Spanish, such individuals frequently refer to themselves as *españoles,* although the language itself is often called *mexicano.* The only large city in the state, Albuquerque, combines both the traditional dialect and the results of recent immigration from Mexico because it offers economic opportunities not found in the sparsely populated rural areas of the state.

The data from Colorado reflect both the traditional presence of colonial Spanish that migrated northward from New Mexico and contemporary immigration from Mexico. The 2000 census found almost 736,000 Latinos (17% of the total population), of which 451,000 (61%) declared themselves to be Mexicans, as compared with 268,000 (36.5%) "other Hispanic."

The traditional Spanish dialect of New Mexico is arguably the oldest continually spoken variety of Spanish anywhere in the Americas that has not been updated by more recent immigration from Spain or neighboring countries. It is indisputably the oldest community speaking any European language in the United States. A more detailed look at Spanish in New Mexico is therefore of considerable relevance to the linguistic history of North America.

The Historical Origins of New Mexico's Spanish-Speaking Population

The area that is now the state of New Mexico once belonged to the northern fringe of Spanish, then Mexican, provinces in North America.[1] During the Spanish rule, the area encompassing New Mexico was known as Nuevo México, an area that began roughly at El Paso del Norte (today El Paso, Texas) and extended indefinitely northward. Immediately to the south was Nueva Viscaya, an early colonial division approximately corresponding to the present Mexican states of Durango, Chihuahua, and much of Coahuila. Until 1734 the modern Mexican states of Sonora and Sinaloa also belonged to Nueva Viscaya. The capital of Nueva Viscaya was Durango, but Chihuahua gradually grew in importance, eventually equaling or even surpassing Durango. To the south was the important mining region of Zacatecas, belonging to the province of Nueva Galicia. From Zacatecas to Mexico City, Spanish settlement was nearly continuous, and communication was good. To the north, hostile Indian groups, wide expanses of forbidding terrain, and scattered nuclei of Spanish population made the area a series of colonial outposts rather than a truly settled province.

During the sixteenth century, Durango was the largest city of Nueva Viscaya. By the seventeenth century, silver discoveries in Parral made that town into the leading growth area, and by the eighteenth century Chihuahua was coming into its own as the most important city in northern Nueva España. These mining settlements were important in the development of New Mexico because many settlers arrived in New Mexico from Parral and Chihuahua. During the nineteenth century, the Santa Fe–Chihuahua trade route, coupled with the annual trade fairs at Chihuahua, provided a commercial, cultural, and linguistic lifeline between the northern areas of New Mexico and Nueva Viscaya.

Nueva Viscaya was primarily a mining region, and such agriculture as was practiced served the needs of mining communities. Landholdings were large, and the overall population was sparse except in the *villas* and towns. The original expeditions sent to New Mexico were searching for mineral wealth, seeking to duplicate

the loose web of mining towns and ranches found in Nueva Viscaya. The territory of New Mexico was first visited by Spaniards during the Coronado expedition of 1540. Coronado had made contact with many of the Pueblo Indians of
New Mexico, and his actions and those of his men had so antagonized the Indians
that later expeditions were to suffer the results. Subsequent visitors included the
friar Agustín Rodríguez with the military escort of Francisco Sánchez Chamuscado.
The Chamuscado expedition returned at last to Santa Barbara after several of the
missionaries had been killed by Indians. Antonio de Espejo set out (too late, as it
turned out) in 1582 to rescue the remaining friars, and his expedition visited
pueblos along the Río Grande and further afield. The first official colonization
expedition was that of Juan de Oñate, who took some 600–700 settlers, cattle,
horses, and seeds, and set forth from Zacatecas in 1598. Oñate was a native of
Zacatecas and a member of a Basque family that had amassed considerable wealth
in the silver mines of that province. The Oñate expedition moved along the Río
Grande, visiting many of the Indian pueblos, and finally reached the present Santo
Domingo Pueblo. In July of 1598, Oñate founded San Juan de los Caballeros at
the junction of the Río Grande and the Río Chama. The community was subsequently moved to the site of a Tewa village and named San Gabriel de los
Españoles. Santa Fe was founded in 1610 by Oñate's successor, Pedro de Peralta,
and given the status of *villa,* attracting many of the inhabitants of San Gabriel.
Because none of the expeditions sent to New Mexico had found mineral wealth
or other desirable attributes, the initial Spanish reaction was to abandon this land
indefinitely. The missionary friars prevailed and the Spanish government authorized permanent settlements in New Mexico. The missions constituted the most
important Spanish presence in New Mexico for much of its colonial history.
Until the Pueblo Indian revolt of 1680, Santa Fe was the only major Spanish
settlement in New Mexico, although several small missions were scattered
throughout the territory. The Spanish population of New Mexico was roughly
2,900 in 1680.

In 1680 the smoldering resentment of the various Pueblo Indian groups
came to a head in a well-organized conspiracy, in which several villages arose
simultaneously against the Spanish colonists, killing many and causing the
remainder to flee to the south. As a result of the Pueblo revolt, the approximately 2,000 survivors regrouped in El Paso del Norte. Some of these refugees
stayed in El Paso, but others migrated back into Nueva Viscaya. By the time that
Diego de Vargas began the Spanish reconquest of New Mexico, only about a
thousand settlers were living around El Paso. The next *villa,* Santa Cruz (La
Cañada), was founded in 1695, and the fourth, Albuquerque, was founded in
1706. During the remainder of the colonial period, New Mexico had only four

villas, although small villages or *placitas* sprung up throughout the territory. The original Spanish settlements in New Mexico were clustered around El Paso del Norte and Santa Fe. By the eighteenth century, increasing pacification of the Indians resulted in expansion of Spanish settlement, away from the Río Grande and the original *presidios* and *villas.* Despite the violence of the Pueblo Revolt of 1680, and subsequent uprisings of lesser magnitude, the ongoing relationship between Spanish settlers and Pueblo Indians was not hostile. Pueblo Indians were often allied with Spaniards, especially when Apache and Comanche hostilities so required (Jones 1966).

The original Spanish settlements in New Mexico were made in the northern mountain valleys (Gonzales 1969), in an approximately 50-mile radius centered on Santa Fe. To the north, settlement eventually spread into the San Luis Valley of Colorado, whereas to the south the population was strung out in small communities all the way to Albuquerque. Settlement of southern New Mexico and areas to the east and west of the Río Grande came much later. For example, the Estancia Valley was not settled until the 1820s, Atrisco was settled in 1880, Socorro in 1816, Mora in 1835, and the Mesilla Valley in the 1840s. The town of Las Vegas was founded in 1835–36 by a group of settlers from San Miguel del Bado, which is a little to the southwest of present-day Las Vegas. The town reached its apogee towards the end of the nineteenth century with the Santa Fe Trail and the arrival of the Santa Fe Railroad. It later declined in importance. However, the Spanish language was maintained there as a primary vehicle of expression well into the twentieth century. The Spanish of this area must be considered essentially traditional New Mexican Spanish, despite the recent date of founding, because immigration from Mexico or elsewhere outside the northern New Mexico area was practically nonexistent (Perrigo 1982). Despite these relatively late settlement dates, most of the settlers came from other established Spanish communities within New Mexico; few represent subsequent immigration. As a consequence, the linguistic features of areas such as Las Vegas and Mora are similar or identical to that of long-established northern villages.

Southern New Mexico was not settled by Spanish speakers until the Mexican period, from 1821–46. Most arrivals came directly from Mexico, and Mexican nationals continued to arrive well into the twentieth century, spurred by the Mexican Revolution of 1910 and by later oil and mining booms. Linguistically and culturally, this region bears the greatest resemblance to modern Mexico; indeed, the language is often identical to that of northern Mexico, except for a higher proportion of Anglicisms. The Mesilla Valley was first occupied during the Mexican period. The building of the Elephant Butte Reservoir in 1915 resulted in a rapidly expanding agricultural basis for the region, and many Mexican farmworkers immigrated to the Mesilla Valley. Their descendents constitute the principal Spanish-speaking community at the present time.

The life of Spanish settlers in New Mexico was crucially shaped by several circumstances, which were not all shared with the remainder of New Spain. Given the minimal amount of readily exploitable mineral wealth, combined with the arid land, Spanish New Mexicans principally devoted themselves to small-scale agriculture, including the cultivation of corn, beans, and chilis, and to livestock ranching, particularly sheep. Accumulation of great wealth was a rare occurrence, and possession of cash was even less common. Barter trade was the usual means of exchange, and many residents had to improvise or do without, lacking the means of acquiring manufactured products and implements. This fostered a natural sense of self-reliance, a pride in self-sufficiency, and a spirit of inventiveness and independence. At the same time, knowledge of lifestyles in Spanish America's more prosperous regions was very limited. Such lack of knowledge extended to linguistic innovations occurring in Spanish-speaking metropolitan areas, thus providing one explanation of the archaic nature of New Mexican Spanish.

The administrative structure of New Mexico and its insertion into the Viceroyalty of New Spain changed considerably over the colonial period. At the beginning, following the Oñate expedition, New Mexico was regarded primarily as a mission field. Indian attacks and a hostile climate and terrain almost caused permanent abandonment of this region, but the friars prevailed, and the Spanish government reluctantly agreed to subsidize missions in a territory that would never provide a profit for the crown. For more than a century, all official traffic and commerce into and out of New Mexico was dictated by the needs of the missions. By the later decades of the seventeenth century, the civilian population of New Mexico was significant, and the protection afforded by the isolated *presidios* was not sufficient to encompass the widely scattered rural population (Moorhead 1975), as the Pueblo Revolt of 1680 was to demonstrate. Even following the Spanish reoccupation of New Mexico and the nominal peace accords reached with the Pueblo Indians, attacks by hostile nomadic Indians continued to plague the Spanish settlements, which kept immigration to a minimum.

During the eighteenth century, the Spanish government became increasingly concerned by French, British, and finally American encroachment on the vast but vaguely defined territory of Spanish North America. Spanish outposts at Los Adaes and Nacogdoches were established in the 1730s to keep the French in check within the Louisiana territory, giving rise to the "Sabine River" Spanish-speaking communities, which will be described in later sections of this chapter. When the Louisiana territory was ceded to Spain in 1762, the pressure to maintain a far-flung outpost was relieved somewhat, but the tenacious defense of the northernmost provinces of New Spain caused the Spanish government severe pre-occupation. In 1766 the Marqués de Rubí was charged with making a thorough visit of the northern provinces and offering recommendations for improving military, economic, and social conditions. Rubí's report described a situation bordering on chaos, with venial government officials, poorly trained and demoralized soldiers who were often pressed into private service to escort the Santa Fe–Chihuahua trade caravans, and a rural population that was scattered so widely as to make Spanish forts and *presidios* essentially useless. Another official visitor, General José de Gálvez, observed many of the same problems and recommended the creation of a separate military district (*comandancia general*) to cover the entire frontier region, which stretched from California to Texas. The military leaders were responsible directly to the King of Spain and were merely required to inform the Viceroy of New Spain of events along the frontier, without seeking approval or authorization.

In 1772 Provincial Governor Mendinueta noted the dispersion of the settlers and the vulnerability to Indian attacks, a warning that was subsequently repeated by Antonio de Bonilla (Simmons 1968, 75–76). In the 1780s Fray Agustín de Morfi deplored the poor defensive configurations of New Mexico's settlements, focusing especially on Albuquerque, whose population was so sprawled along the banks of the Río Grande as to be nearly helpless in the case of Indian attacks.

By 1776 the Provincias Internas became recognized as a separate and "special" region of New Spain, including the provinces of Alta and Baja California, Sonora, Sinaloa, New Mexico, Nueva Viscaya, Nuevo León, Nuevo Santander, Texas, and Coahuila (Bannon 1974). Later, the Provincias Internas were restricted to Sonora, Nueva Viscaya, New Mexico, Coahuila, and Texas (Simmons 1968). The military headquarters was first established at Arizpe, Sonora, but it was eventually moved to the city of Chihuahua, thus making this city doubly prominent. The new military administrators did effect some changes in New Mexico, succeeding in partially regrouping the populations of Santa Fe, Albuquerque, and Santa Cruz de la Cañada.

Demographic Input to New Mexican Spanish

Little information is available concerning the geographical origins of immigrants to New Mexico, except for the earliest expeditions. Among the 129 families that accompanied Juan de Oñate, fifty-four *vecinos* (heads of household) came from different areas of Spain with no single region being favored. One can assume that most of the remaining household members were also from Spain. Thirty-nine heads of household came from New Spain, of which fourteen were from Mexico City, eight from Zacatecas, and so forth. The remaining settlers were a motley bunch, coming from various parts of Latin America, the Canary Islands, Portugal, and so forth. Hammond (1927, 187–210) provides detailed data on the geographical origins of the members of Oñate's original expedition as well as settlers who traveled to New Mexico in 1600. Nothing in the demographics of the early expeditions suggests that any single region of Spain contributed a high proportion of settlers, thus placing in jeopardy any theory that ascribes to the first settlers the definitive linguistic characteristics that eventually developed in Latin American communities. Less is known about the settlers who took part in Vargas's reconquest of New Mexico, but it is likely that most were either New Mexican–born refugees from the Pueblo revolt or natives of northern New Spain (Mexico).

Once the Spanish presence was established at Santa Fe, a regular supply system from Mexico was established (Moorhead 1958). Loosely organized wagon caravans traveled from Mexico City to Santa Fe, ostensibly to supply the missions, but in fact making contact with any Spaniards residing in the distant territory. Officially, one wagon train was supposed to make the trek every three years. In each journey, six months were allotted for the trip to Santa Fe, another six months to distribute the cargo, and a further six months for the return trip. In practice the caravans were less frequent, paralleling the situation with the Spanish fleet system that was supposed to send a fleet from Spain to the West Indies every six months, but which often followed a much more irregular schedule. Because of the precarious nature of the supply trains, Spanish settlers in New Mexico soon developed the self-reliance and improvisational skills that were to characterize this population thereafter. On its return trip the supply train often carried goods produced in New Mexico.

The original Camino Real lead from Mexico City to Santa Fe, a long distance even by current standards of transportation, and prohibitive during the colonial period. With the settling of northern Nueva Viscaya, in particular the founding of Chihuahua, the supply route was shortened, and a mechanism was created whereby New Mexicans could enjoy somewhat more frequent contact with the remainder of Nueva España. Chihuahua began with a Spanish mission named Nombre de Dios, founded in 1697. The population of the area grew, and in 1718 the chartered city of San Felipe el Real de Chihuahua came into existence. The city was sustained by local silver mining, and it quickly grew to become the major city in northern Nueva Viscaya. By 1807, on the eve of colonial independence, Chihuahua had some 7,000 residents.

When Chihuahua was first founded, the supplying of New Mexico was still in the hands of the religious community, but by the middle of the eighteenth century, Chihuahua merchants gained control over a significant proportion of the trade. Once the supply caravans could use Chihuahua as a base, the journeys became more nearly stabilized around an annual schedule. New Mexican merchants first traveled to the annual fair in Taos, held in late summer, trading with Comanches and other Indian groups. Grant (1934) gives an account of the later years of the Taos fair, which became doubly important because of the trade that arrived via the Santa Fe Trail. The southbound caravan usually left Santa Fe for Chihuahua in December for a trip that averaged forty days. The average size of the caravans, known as *conductas,* is impossible to determine with certainty, but some approximate ideas may be given (Hallenbeck 1950). Normally, at least 500 adult men accompanied each caravan. Women and children frequently accompanied the men, both to break the monotony of isolated rural life and because hostile Indian raids could take advantage of households where armed males were absent. This makes for caravans of at least 1,500–2,000 people, whose size swelled as additional voyages joined the southward march. Some accounts state that at least half the total (Spanish) population of New Mexico made the annual trek to Chihuahua, but this is surely exaggerated. Even with caravans averaging a few thousand people, however, a sizeable proportion of the northern New Mexican population sustained the economic, cultural, and linguistic contact with Chihuahua.

Once in Chihuahua, New Mexicans attended the January trade fair, which lasted about two weeks. Because as many as 30,000 travelers from all over northern New Spain poured into Chihuahua during the fair period, lodging was scarce, and most visitors stayed in tents or in their wagons. Given that women and children were a major portion of each New Mexican contingent, two weeks of visiting with people from all over Nueva Viscaya, as well as residents of Chihuahua proper, was able to take place in a sustained fashion. Two weeks of intense linguistic contact with speakers of a somewhat different regional dialect is capable of temporarily or even permanently affecting the speech of visitors. Colonial New Mexican Spanish was probably never very different than the vernacular speech of Chihuahua, but more than a century of intense trade and the profound linguistic effect that the annual Chihuahua trade caravans had on New Mexico helped ensure that the dialects would never drift completely apart.

Although the Chihuahua route was the most regular and extensive, New Mexicans participated in other trade routes, particularly in the late eighteenth and early nineteenth centuries. Trade with Sonora was especially intense, although the available documentation is insufficient to attempt a quantitative account. Linguistic contacts with Sonora are important because Sonora is one of the few regions of Mexico's interior where word-final and even word-initial /s/ is regularly aspirated. Rural Sonora speech is also characterized by a strong nasality and a tendency to pronounce /s/ as a dental or interdental fricative [θ] as in the English word *thick*. All the aforementioned tendencies characterize rural New Mexican Spanish. Whereas nothing suggests that these traits were imported from Sonora (because they are also found, in attenuated fashion, in rural Chihuahua), trade contacts with Sonora would reinforce these tendencies among New Mexican Spanish speakers, who at the same time were geographically and politically isolated from the urban prestige norms that were developing in Mexico proper. These developing prestige norms would eventually push vernacular forms resembling those of New Mexico back into isolated rural redoubts. Following the discontinuation of the Chihuahua trade fair, around 1805, New Mexican merchants and traders spread their activities across wider stretches of the states of Chihuahua and Sonora.

Development of the Spanish Language in New Mexico

In assessing the development of New Mexican Spanish, a distinction must be made between geographical remoteness—combined with lack of large-scale inward migration—and linguistic isolation. It has often been claimed that New Mexican Spanish is an archaic isolate, containing linguistic structures that have scarcely changed since the early seventeenth century. In favor of such a view are the demographic facts regarding the development of New Mexican speech communities. Following the repopulation of New Mexico by Vargas at the end of the seventeenth century, the largest proportion of population increase was the result of natural reproduction of New Mexican–born residents rather than of inward migration. The latter was always a constant at the periphery of the colony, but there was little to attract new settlers except hard work, difficult climatic and geographical conditions, and the ever-present threat of Indian raids. Among established residents, on the other hand, the battle against natural and human forces hardened their resolve to remain, a sentiment that is essential in the formation of the New Mexican character. The aforementioned factors of high illiteracy, precarious and intermittent mail service, and official restrictions on movement exacerbated the tremendous distances that had to be traveled in order to bring New Mexicans into contact with compatriots in the heart of New Spain. However, with the establishment of the Santa Fe–Chihuahua trade route in the eighteenth century and the intensification of traffic between New Mexico and Nueva Viscaya in the nineteenth century, the geographical isolation was diminished.

An unusual circumstance of the extreme northern frontier of New Spain was the prohibition by Spanish authorities for colonists to freely travel from one region to another without an official permission, a passport, or a letter of authorization. The logic behind such a policy was not always fully revealed, but one motive was to keep the Spanish population strategically spread across the territory, combating the natural tendency to cluster together as a reaction against Indian raids. It is difficult to determine the extent to which this control of individual movement was ever enforced, but at the very least the official position encouraged settlers to stay put, increasing their isolation and forcing them to turn inward both linguistically and socially.

Another factor that shaped the Spanish language of New Mexico was the lack of a well-established prestige dialect reinforced by schools, churches, and government agencies. Spanish New Mexico fared dismally with regard to education, both public and private. Until well past Mexican independence, no public schools were found in the entire territory, and even following annexation to the United States after the Mexican-American War, the establishment of an effective compulsory education system lagged far behind the rest of the nation. Anglo American disdain for a poor, rural, Spanish-speaking population was not without effect. That this cannot be the only reason for the slow pace of school creation in New Mexico is demonstrated by the much more effective educational system implanted by the United States during its occupation of the Philippines, despite a condescending and often oppressive attitude toward the "little brown brothers." Even during the Spanish period, illiteracy was the common property of nearly the entire New Mexican population, including many government officials and clergy. One linguistic consequence of widespread illiteracy is the gradual fading from collective memory of literary language, ranging from poetry and narrative to the stylized formulae of religious, bureaucratic, and military documents.

One immediate consequence of the isolation, illiteracy, relatively low standard of living, and the interdependence of nearly all community members, was a breakdown in social class and caste barriers that rigidly partitioned more "mainstream" Spanish-American societies. Available documentation demonstrates frequent marriage across social groups, and in most of New Mexico there was no opportunity for an elite class to develop. Few New Mexicans could afford servants, and even fewer owned slaves. Most of the settlers worked their own land or engaged in small businesses. Peninsular-born Spaniards were few and far between, and after the initial settlements, direct immigration from Spain to New Mexico was nearly nonexistent. This meant that the usual two-tiered system of European-born *españoles* and American-born *criollos* was not reproduced in New Mexico, and Peninsular Spanish dialects were not held forth as the speech of a special class. Indeed it is unlikely that most New Mexicans had ever come face to face with the *norma culta* (educated speech norm), either of Mexico City or of any part of Spain.

The totality of the circumstances just enumerated resulted in the severe isolation of New Mexican Spanish from linguistic currents developing elsewhere in the Spanish-speaking world. This isolation increased under U.S. domination because the use of Spanish for anything other than strictly personal affairs was no longer regarded as normal. The only renovating influences on New Mexican Spanish occurred through immigration from Mexico, a phenomenon that always existed, but that became significant in the early decades of the twentieth century. However, by this time the displacement of New Mexican Spanish by English had already begun, as had another phenomenon that was to have an equally profound effect on New Mexican Spanish: the identification as "Spanish American" rather than "Mexican American," and the consequent rejection of many linguistic and cultural attributes regarded as "Mexican."[2]

By well into the twentieth century, many New Mexicans had begun to take Spanish classes in high school; up until recently, the majority of the Spanish teachers were from outside New Mexico, being either Anglo Americans who had learned some amount of Spanish, or occasionally Spaniards or Latin Americans. As occurred with other rural vernacular language varieties in the United States (including black, Appalachian, and Ozark English; Gullah; and immigrant varieties of other European languages), Spanish teachers in New Mexico were rarely sympathetic to the rustic and unlettered speech of their students. Rather than acknowledging that these students, for whom Spanish was the first and stronger language, had a functional competence in the "foreign" language that far exceeded that of even the highest achieving Anglo American pupils, teachers more often belittled nonstandard lexical and grammatical variants. The natural reaction of most New Mexicans was to regard their own speech as inferior—not *español* but only *mexicano*. A few fiercely resisted the inferiority complex, rejecting instead the *escuelao* (school-taught) speech of their teachers and textbooks. The net result in both cases was the complete insulation of authentic New Mexican Spanish from any influence by school-taught varieties.

When the United States took over New Mexico in the middle of the nineteenth century, Anglo Americans regarded this territory as a wilderness of hostile Indians and poor "Mexicans." Following the immigration of Anglo Americans from other areas of the United States, Spanish-speaking New Mexicans were gradually drawn into American cultural and social patterns. At some point as the possibility of New Mexican statehood was contemplated on a larger scale, Spanish-speaking New Mexicans became fully aware of the American disdain for "Mexicans" and of the unlikelihood that a territory widely regarded as "Mexican" would be admitted as a state. Perhaps because of this growing awareness and perhaps as a continuation of the aloofness from the rest of Mexico that had characterized New Mexico even during colonial times, Spanish-speaking New Mexicans as a group have tenaciously identified themselves as "Spanish" and "Spanish Americans." As national and regional resentment of undocumented Mexican migrant laborers increased, New Mexican Spanish came to adopt the term *mojao* (wet [back]) for anyone born in Mexico, the equivalent of English *wetback* (ironically disregarding the fact that to pass from Mexico into New Mexico, no river need be crossed).

Given the often hostile reception that Anglo Americans gave to Spanish-speaking New Mexicans, it is sometimes assumed axiomatically that all schooling under the new American government was conducted entirely in English. There is no doubt that such was the official intent of American educators, but the reality was often far different. Indeed, until 1871 there were no public schools in the entire territory. An 1876 report (Gonzales 1969, 17; Rideling 1876, 19) stated that there were 133 schools with 5,625 pupils. Of these schools, 10 were English-only, 12 used both English and Spanish, and the remaining 111 were Spanish-only schools. By 1928 the report of Bohannan (1928, 2) showed little change: "the teachers in these public schools are Spanish-Americans and practically all of the instruction in the school is carried on in the Spanish language." In 1915 the first jury trial in Socorro without an interpreter was considered a historical event. Children leaving the rural villages and coming to cities like Albuquerque often suffered from little or no knowledge of English. In the 1930s community leaders, such as state senator Dennis Chávez, insisted that more English be taught in schools and used in public life. Regardless of the educational success of Spanish-only versus English-only schools (legitimate bilingual programs were very late in coming), it is not possible to claim that Spanish was rapidly displaced in New Mexico primarily through the school system's exclusive use of English. Although later generations of Hispanic New Mexicans found fewer opportunities to use and refine their Spanish language in schools, prior to the 1940s Spanish was a viable school language in many northern communities.

Linguistic Features of New Mexican Spanish

Traditional New Mexican Spanish shares many key characteristics with northern Mexican Spanish and with many Mexican American varieties of Spanish, but the differences are equally significant. Perhaps the most striking aspect of traditional New Mexican Spanish is the extremely high variation from one community to the next and the considerable idiolectal variation within the same community and even the same family. Long-standing isolation and limited communication among rural enclaves is at the root of much of this variation. In the twentieth century, language shift away from Spanish in the direction of English has resulted in decreased attention being paid to Spanish language usage. As a consequence, younger Spanish speakers may acquire a form of the language that differs in important ways from the speech of older community members. Sociolinguistic pressure from a wider Spanish-community has diminished; younger learners may spend relatively little of their time engaged in conversations with other Spanish speakers. The erosion of the traditional dialect, in favor of English and, more recently, of contemporary varieties of Spanish, is documented in Bills (1997a) and Bills and Vigil (1999).

Phonetic and Phonological Features

- Intervocalic /j/ is very weak, receiving a semivocalic articulation at best. No audible friction accompanies any realization of /j/, and this consonant drops in contact with /e/ or /i/. Using data from Mexican American Spanish, Ross (1980) defines two partially overlapping environments: contact with a preceding or following /i/ and contact with a preceding /e/: *silla* [sía] (chair); *billete* [biéte] (bill, as in money); *sello* [séo] (seal). In New Mexican Spanish, Espinosa (1930, 197–99) described loss of /j/ in all the environments described by Ross, plus in /eje/, /aje/ (e.g., *calle* [street]) and less frequently /oje/ (e.g., *oyendo* [hearing]). In Colorado Spanish, Espinosa even found loss of /j/ between two nonfront vowels, providing neither was /u/, such as *caballo* > *cabao* (horse).[3] In contemporary New Mexican Spanish, loss of /j/ in contact with nonfront vowels does not occur, except idiosyncratically (Lipski 1990a). In contact with /e/ and /i/, however, /j/ routinely disappears, a pronunciation that has been taken over into Anglicized pronunciation of Spanish words in New Mexico. For example the artisan town of *Cerillos* is pronounced [səɹíəs] in English, and *Tierra Amarilla* (a northern village) is [tʰiɛɹəaməɹíə].
- Word-final /n/ is uniformly alveolar. Velarization or loss of final /n/ never takes place.
- The trill /r/ at times receives a groove fricative pronunciation (e.g., similar to that found in Costa Rica, Guatemala, and the Andean region). At times, a partially retroflex fricative closely approximating English *r* also alternates with the usual trill [r]. Because the retroflex pronunciation is more frequent among younger speakers, carryover from English is implicated.
- The combination /tr/ is frequently given an alveolar pronunciation, and the /r/ may resemble or be identical to English retroflex /ɹ/. The same pronunciation of /r/ also extends to the groups /pr/, /kr/, /gr/, /br/, and so forth.
- Intervocalic /d/ is weak; it routinely falls in intervocalic contexts, with most instances of -*ado* being effectively relexified to -*ao*. Thus *colorao* is universally used to mean "red"; [koloraðo], for most speakers, could only refer to the state of Colorado. Word-final /d/ is usually not pronounced at all.
- The posterior fricative /x/ normally receives a velar fricative pronunciation in New Mexico, particularly in the northern regions. Occasionally, a uvular fricative, reminiscent of the /x/ heard in Castile, is found. The weak [h], which characterizes the Caribbean and parts of northern Mexico, is found only in southern New Mexico, probably a carryover from more recent contacts with northern Mexico.

- The consonant /b/ is frequently realized as labiodental [v] in contexts where a fricative realization emerges (most instances except phrase-initially and following a nasal). English influence may lie behind the extension of [v] over bilabial [β], but given that the same alternation is found in other Spanish-speaking areas where no English influence exists undermines the direct impact of English on New Mexican Spanish [v].
- Perhaps the most striking phonetic feature of most traditional varieties of NMS, which sets this dialect zone apart from other "Mexican American" varieties found in the Southwest, is the pronunciation of /s/. In the majority of U.S. Spanish dialects placed under the rubric of "Mexican American" or "Chicano," syllable- and word-final /s/ is normally retained as a sibilant [s]. This reflects prevailing pronunciation patterns in most of contemporary Mexico; in particular, the regions from which Mexican American dialects have emerged.

In traditional New Mexican Spanish, syllable- and word-final /s/ is frequently aspirated to [h]; complete loss is less common except phrase-finally in rapid speech (Gutiérrez 1981). This aspiration extends to word-final prevocalic contexts, such as *los amigos* [lohamíɣo(h)] (the friends). Finally, word-initial /s/ is frequently aspirated when found in phrase-internal intervocalic contexts (Brown 2004, 2005a, 2005b; Brown and Torres Cacoullos 2002, 2003; also García and Tallon 1995). This aspiration is more common before unstressed vowels as in *no se puede* [nohepuéðe] (it can't be done), but for some speakers it also extends to environments before a stressed vowel: *no sé* [nohé] (I don't know).

- Traditional New Mexican Spanish, both past and present, exhibits a number of syllabic consonants (Lipski 1993b; Piñeros 2005). Most of the phonetic variants described by early observers such as Espinosa (1909, 1925, 1946) and Hills (1906) for the Spanish dialect of northern New Mexico and southern Colorado are still to be found today, despite the fact that this variety of Spanish is rapidly being replaced by English and by the Spanish of immigrants from northern Mexico and southern New Mexico. The syllabic consonants described by Espinosa (1925), however, have all but disappeared, being found only sporadically among the oldest speakers whose lives overlap with the informants studied by Espinosa. This fact notwithstanding, Espinosa's observations are sufficiently explicit, and are not contradicted by current observations, to allow for a systematic analysis of this phenomenon. Syllabic [M] arises when the indefinite article *un* precedes a word beginning with a labial consonant (*un beso* [a kiss] [Mbeso]). This process occurs in other Spanish dialects and is very frequent in Brazilian Portuguese, as well as in many Italian dialects (Alonso 1930, 431–39). Syllabic [M] also appears frequently in the possessive *mi*, coming before a word-initial labial consonant: *mi papá* (my father). For many New Mexican speakers, this configuration, usually written and sometimes pronounced as *em papá*, has become quasilexicalized as an alternate realization of *mi papá* (my dad).

The most consistent cases of syllabic resonants observed by Espinosa occur before the diminutive endings *-ito* and *-ita*. Three "long" syllabic consonants are also described. The first, long syllabic [M], generally arises preceding the stressed vowel /i/, as in the diminutive ending *-ito/-ita* (e.g., *lomita* [loMta]) (little hill). Syllabic [N] arises before the diminutive endings *-ito/-ita* (*Anita* [aNta]). Occasionally, according to Espinosa, syllabic [N] arises when the article *un* comes before a nonlabial consonant (*un dedal* [Ndeðal]) (a thimble). Finally, long syllabic [L] occurs before the diminutive suffixes *-ito/-ita* (*bolita* [boLta]) (little ball).

- Also found sporadically throughout the northern New Mexico/southern Colorado area is a paragogic final *-e*, most frequently heard at the end of verbal infinitives and other words ending in a stressed vowel plus consonant. All regular and most irregular verbal infinitives in Latin ended in /-re/, giving rise to the three Old Spanish/Old Portuguese conjugations in *-are, -ere,* and *-ire.* Loss of inflectional consonants created numerous other words ending in *-Vre, -Vle, -Vne,* and so forth. In the medieval period, apocope of final /-e/ became widespread, and Spanish and Portuguese infinitives lost the final /-e/, as did such words as *papel* (paper), *paladar* (palate), *razón* (reason), and so forth. However, among isolated dialects of Spanish, Portuguese, and Galician, it is possible to find what appear to be remnants of the former /-e/, sometimes as a fleeting partially devoiced vocalic offglide and sometimes as a fully articulated final [e]. The few existing descriptions of such phenomena generally assume an archaic retention of original final vowels, although the possibility for a later paragogic vowel has never been systematically excluded, particularly because /e/ is the Spanish default vowel, which arises whenever prosodically motivated syllabic adjustments must be made. In New Mexico Spanish, paragogic vowels are found only word-finally, except for some lexicalized cases such as *tíguere* < *tigre* (mountain lion). Moreover, two conditions are virtually essential for the appearance of a paragogic final [e]: (1) the final syllable must be stressed, thus accounting for the very frequent appearance of paragogic [e] in verbal infinitives (one case of *cárcele* < *cárcel* [jail] has been noted); (2) paragogic vowels nearly always appear phrase-finally. When occurring in what appears to be phrase-medial position, at least some slight pause is usually detectable before the following segment.[4]
- Frequent throughout New Mexico is the fricative pronunciation [ʃ] of the affricate /tʃ/ (Jaramillo and Bills 1982; Jaramillo 1986). This is particularly noticeable in words such as *chile* [ʃile] (chile pepper) and *mucho* [muʃo] (much).

Morphological Features

Traditional New Mexican Spanish shares many of the morphological traits found in isolated, archaic, and rustic varieties of Spanish in other countries. Some of the characteristics are carryovers from earlier stages of the language, others are the result of analogical change or simplification, others are innovations not found in other Spanish dialects, and still others are best attributed to linguistic drift in traditionally isolated communities. There are no morphological traits that are exclusive to northern New Mexican/southern Colorado Spanish, nor are the phenomena to be described below used by all speakers. However, all of the following features are readily identifiable in traditional New Mexican Spanish, and few speakers of this variety do not use all or most of the combinations at least occasionally.

- Use of the first person plural verbal ending -*nos* instead of -*mos*, in those forms with antepenultimate stress (*fuéramos* > *fuéranos* [we went (subj.)], *teníamos* > *teníanos* [we had], etc.).
- The normally invariant combination *un poco* (*de*) (a little of) exhibits agreement with a following feminine singular noun phrase: *una poca de arena* (a little bit of sand), and so forth.
- The normally invariant adverb *medio* (half) exhibits agreement with a following adjective: *medio tonto* (half foolish), *medios tontos, media loca* (half crazy), *medias locas,* and so forth.

In dual clitic object combinations where both clitics are third person (in which case the first—indirect object—clitic is always *se*), the second (direct object) clitic agrees in number with the indirect object, although agreeing in gender with the direct object. *A los hombres les vendí la vaca* (I sold the cow to the men) > *se las vendí.*

The second person singular preterite always ends in /-s/; moreover, the preceding etymological /s/ often disappears: *fuiste* > *fuites* (you went), *comiste* > *comites* (you ate), and so forth. Analogical final /s/ is found in many other Spanish dialects, so that in New Mexican Spanish the loss of the /s/ in /-ste/ may be a result of the general weakening of syllable-final /s/ in the latter dialect. However, intermediate forms with aspirated /-s/ are not usually heard, which makes metathesis a more likely choice.

Lexical Characteristics

Although many Mexicanisms (usually of Nahuatl origin) are found in all varieties of New Mexican Spanish, most if not all appear to be early borrowings that entered New Mexico with the original settlers. There are many lexical items that are completely different in New Mexican Spanish and contemporary Mexican Spanish. New Mexicans who have had contact with Mexican-born Spanish speakers may use "Mexican" words, but they do so while being conscious of incorporating elements from another dialect and usually do so only to facilitate communication with other Spanish speakers assumed to be from Mexico. Thus, whereas English continues to make deep inroads into the lexicon (and grammar) of modern New Mexican Spanish, as well as rapidly displacing Spanish as a viable community and family language, modern Mexican Spanish has little or no effect on the Spanish spoken by native New Mexicans.[5]

The lexicon of New Mexican and southern Colorado Spanish is varied, and few of the items are not found in other Spanish dialects. There is some regional variation, but few of the items described below are not at least passively known to most speakers of this dialect. Unlike more recent immigrant varieties of Spanish in the United States, traditional New Mexican Spanish does exhibit a relatively more homogeneous vocabulary, unlike the mosaic of provincial Mexican items typical of many southwestern Mexican American communities. The following words are particularly noteworthy:

ánsara (goose—predominantly used in areas where *ganso* is used for turkey)
calzón (pants)
chuparrosa (hummingbird)
chupilote/ chopilote (buzzard—from Mexican Spanish *zopilote*)
cócono/ cócano (turkey)
cunques (sediment at the bottom of a cup of beverage; crumbs, leftovers)
estafeta (post office)
ganso (turkey)
guajolote (water salamander)
guíjalo (turkey)
jojolote (ear of corn; corn cob)
melaza (syrup)
miel virgin (honey)
miel (syrup)
ochá (a medicinal plant, used as a cough suppressant)
plaza/ placita (small town or village)
puela (frying pan, skillet)
ratón coludo (squirrel)
ratón volador (bat)
sopaipilla (type of fritter)
tripa (de agua) (garden hose)
túnico (woman's dress)

Additional Resources

The Spanish language of New Mexico and southern Colorado was the subject of an intensive dialect atlas project, supported by the National Endowment for the Humanities, and directed by Garland Bills and Neddy Vigil of the University of New Mexico in Albuquerque. As part of the data-collection phase, some 350 informants of all ages were interviewed, with each interview lasting several hours.

All the interviews were taped and will eventually be made available to researchers, thus representing the largest database of any variety of Spanish in the United States.

A number of New Mexican authors have incorporated local language usage into their writings. In addition, many stories and narratives incorporate realistic specimens of New Mexico Spanish (e.g., N. García 1987, 1992).

Scholarship on New Mexican Spanish

The traditional Spanish of New Mexico and southern Colorado has received considerable attention from linguists, although much work remains to be done on this variety. The pioneering works of Aurelio Espinosa (1909, 1911, 1925, 1946) are still the most complete descriptions of this dialect, despite the fact that New Mexican Spanish has evolved considerably since the early years of the twentieth century when Espinosa made his observations. Hills (1906) is another early study upon which subsequent research has built its foundations. Bowen (1976), de la Puente-Schubeck (1991), and Floyd (1976) described the verbal system; Boggs (1954), Cobos (1983), Durán (1965), Espinosa Jr. (1975), García (1939), Gross (1935), Kercheville (1934), Murphy (1972), Ornstein (1975b), Rael (1939), and Trager and Valdez (1937) provide lexical data, including the influence of English. Bowen (1952), Domínguez (1974), Hardman (1956), Lope Blanch (1990c), McSpadden (1934), Ortiz (1975, 1981), Parks (1989), Rael (1937), Ross (1975), Shoban and Singer (1970), Trujillo (1982), and Vigil (1990, 1993) give information on regional dialects. Bergen (1986), Bills (1997a, 1997b), Bills, Hernández-Chávez, and Hudson (1995), Hernández-Chávez, Bills, and Hudson (1996), and Hudson, Hernández-Chávez, and Bills (1992, 1995) examine language retention and language shift in New Mexican and other Southwest Spanish dialects. Brisk (1972), Fernández (1980, 1990), Jaramillo (1986, 1990, 1995), and Kravitz (1985) offer sociolinguistic and grammatical perspectives on New Mexican Spanish. Travis (2004) comments on subject pronoun usage in New Mexico. Brown (2004, 2005a, 2005b), Brown and Torres Cacoullos (2002, 2003), and García and Tallon (1995) are studies of contemporary pronunciation. Bills and Vigil (in press) is a complete linguistic atlas of the traditional Spanish of New Mexico and southern Colorado, based on hundreds of hours of field data collected throughout this region.

Spanish in Louisiana: The Isleños of St. Bernard Parish

Many Spanish dialects throughout the world contain archaic elements that reflect language usage of earlier centuries and that have generally disappeared in the contemporary Spanish-speaking world. These dialects are frequently spoken in isolated rural areas that have not been in constant contact with dynamic urban linguistic norms and that have consequently not absorbed the totality of evolutionary patterns that have affected the Spanish language. Among the isolated varieties of Spanish spoken in the United States, perhaps the most curious is the Isleño dialect of St. Bernard Parish, Louisiana, now reduced to a few hundred speakers after having survived more than 200 years in the swamps of eastern Louisiana. The area, which now includes the state of Louisiana, once belonged to Spain, and at the end of the eighteenth century, shortly before this territory passed into French hands, Spain encouraged colonization of strategic areas to the southeast of New Orleans in the swampy region known as Tierra de los Bueyes, modern St. Bernard Parish. The majority of the settlers in the latter region came from the Canary Islands, which is an area that has traditionally furnished a large number of immigrants to Spanish America. Despite having undergone French rule and later annexation to the United States, elements of Spanish heritage remained in a few of the more isolated regions of Louisiana, although in most of the state the descendants of Spanish settlers were absorbed into mainstream culture, losing their ancestral language and their cultural practices (Guillotte 1982; Montero de Pedro 1979). The first wave of Isleños was followed by sporadic arrivals from other areas of Spain, particularly in the last decades of the nineteenth century and the early years of the twentieth century, and as yet unverified but apparently significant number of natives of Andalusia, Galicia, Asturias, Valencia, and other parts of Spain moved into the Isleño communities and cast their lot with the descendants of Canary Islanders. The term *isleños* (islanders) refers as much to the heartland of this group, Delacroix "Island," (in reality an inland area surrounded by bayous) as to the insular origin of the Spanish settlers.

The St. Bernard region constitutes a nearly unique example of the preservation, over more than 200 years, of a markedly Spanish microcosm within the United States. Up until the second half of the twentieth century, this region had no good roads and was virtually unknown to and ignored by state and federal government authorities. As a result of the geographical and cultural isolation of the Isleños, from the turn of the nineteenth century until the 1940s, most members of the community were monolingual Spanish speakers, although some creole French crept into the Isleño lexicon over the years. Only with the opening of the first schools in St. Bernard Parish, well into the twentieth century, did Isleños learn English as a group. As of the end of the twentieth century, the oldest members of the Isleño community had learned Spanish as a first language and had suffered linguistic and social problems upon first attending school, in which then as now, classes were conducted entirely in

English. Many older Isleños were raised thinking that they were in Spain and that the entire nation where they lived spoke Spanish. This was how complete the cultural isolation was, even from the nearby *villa* of New Orleans.

In the twentieth century, several factors combined to affect a complete linguistic shift from Spanish to English as the predominant language among the Isleños. The educational system was foremost among the conditioning factors, as the St. Bernard area was gradually penetrated by schools and other government institutions. A severe hurricane in 1915 completely destroyed the Delacroix settlement and nearby communities, causing the Isleños to temporarily reside in New Orleans. Subsequent hurricanes, most recently Betsy in 1965, had the same effect, and in the latter case many Isleños left the region never to return permanently. World War II brought many male Isleños into military service, thus augmenting the incipient cosmopolitanism of this region. The building of roads through the swamps, the opening of ship channels, and the construction of electrical power and telephone lines into lower St. Bernard Parish brought the Isleños into easy and direct contact with the rest of Louisiana and the nation. Today, many Isleños residing in the towns of St. Bernard Parish still follow the traditional professions of fishing and fur trapping, but most of the younger residents have turned to jobs in nearby petrochemical complexes. Few Isleños under the age of 60 speak any Spanish at all, although some younger community members understand the language. The formation of the Spanish Cultural and Heritage Society in 1976 partially formalized the attempt at cultural preservation, although no structured attempt is being made in favor of retention of Spanish because this would be virtually impossible given the linguistic shift of the past two generations. This group currently maintains a website as well as the Isleño museum and visitor center.[6] Annual folk festivals reinforce the unique cultural traditions of the Isleño community and teach young people about a lifestyle that has long since disappeared from daily existence in St. Bernard Parish.

The Brule Spanish Speakers from the Canary Islands

The same Canary Island immigration to Louisiana in the late eighteenth century brought settlers to central Louisiana, around Donaldsonville. This group, whose Spanish dialect survived in vestigial form until nearly the end of the twentieth century, became known as the Brulis or Brules, from the French *terre brulée* (scorched earth) referring to the clearing of this area for farming. MacCurdy (1959) and Armistead (n.d.) describe this dialect, whose linguistic characteristics were essentially the same as the Isleños of St. Bernard Parish. Holloway (1997) gives a dramatic account of reviving the linguistic memories of the last remaining vestigial speakers.

Phonetics and Phonology of Isleño Spanish

- In the phonological dimension, Isleño Spanish is markedly similar to Andalusian and Canary Island dialects of Spanish in terms of consonantal reductions. Syllable- and word-final /s/ is normally aspirated to [h] or dropped altogether: *los isleños* [loh ihleño], *los patos* [loh pato] (the ducks).
- Intervocalic and word-final /d/ normally disappears: *entodavía* [entuaβía] (yet), *todito* [toíto] (everything).
- Syllable-final /l/ and /r/ are generally neutralized, resulting in [l], [r], or [h], apparently without regular application of specific phonological rules of neutralization; phrase-final /r/ and sometimes /l/ are normally lost: *vuelta* [vuerta] (turn, occasion); *puerta* [puelta] (door); *gobierno* [goβiehno] (government; English-speaking outsider), *trabajar* [traβaxá] (to work), and so forth. These features are common in Andalusian and Canary Island Spanish, and are attested in these areas, as well as in Latin America well before the eighteenth century, so that the Isleño data are consistent with empirical dialectal evidence. Currently in the Canary Islands, there are a few enclaves of more conservative pronunciation, particularly on the islands of El Hierro and La Gomera, but also in small interior villages of Tenerife and Gran Canaria, where consonants are less subject to reduction and neutralization. Although most Isleños have no accurate information on the exact geographical origins of their ancestors, those possessing adequate information indicate Tenerife and Gran Canaria as the most common areas of emigration. It is still not possible to determine whether the advanced state of consonantal reduction in the Isleño dialect is a direct reflection of the original Spanish dialects brought to St. Bernard or the result of posterior evolution, unchecked by normative influences that have prevailed in urban areas of the Canary Islands and Spain. In any event, the behavior of /s/, /l/, /r/, and /d/ in Isleño Spanish fits in among the dialects of the Canary Islands, being more advanced than some regions.
- In Isleño Spanish, phrase-final /n/ is not normally velarized, despite assertions by MacCurdy (1950, 38) to the effect that velarization is commonly "preceded by a back vowel." MacCurdy also indicates that following other vowels, phrase-final /n/ is often lost, leaving a nasalized vowel; however, the data collected for the present study indicate that this phenomenon is highly variable and that alveolar [n] occurs in a significant number of cases. Of greater importance is the behavior of word-final prevocalic /n/ in Isleño Spanish, for the alveolar variant [n] is almost universal, with a nasalized hiatus running a distant second, and a velar [ŋ] being almost nonexistent. This distribution is unlike any Caribbean dialect of Spanish and in fact is not characteristic of any variety of Latin American Spanish, although

it is occasionally found in rural areas of Mexico and the Southern Cone nations. Only in some rural regions of the Canary Islands does word-final prevocalic /n/ exhibit similar behavior, nasalizing the preceding vowel and eliding, without passing through the intermediate stage of velarization. Because the Isleños arrived from all parts of the Canary Islands, including those that even today evince scarce velarization of /n/, a degree of uncertainty remains, but given that the majority of the Isleños appear to be descended from immigrants born on Gran Canaria and Tenerife, where velarization of /n/ is commonplace today, the lack of velarization in Isleño Spanish is a telling bit of evidence. The almost total lack of velarization of word-final prevocalic /n/ in Isleño speech, as compared to the slight degree of velarization of word-final prevocalic /n/ in most contemporary dialects of the Canary Islands suggests that in the latter regions the extension is of relatively recent origin.

Morphological Characteristics

- Isleño Spanish frequently uses the clitic pronoun *los* instead of *nos* for first-person plural reference: *los vamos* (let's go). It is also frequent for pluperfect subjunctive and imperfect forms in the first person plural to end in *–nos* instead of *–mos: fuéranos* (we went [subj.]), *estábanos* (we were).
- There are many archaic and analogical verb forms: *di* < *ir* (to go); *vide* (I saw); *truje* (I brought); *habiera* (I had [subj.]) < *hubiera* through the influence of *haber*, and so forth.
- Many nouns that take the masculine gender in modern Spanish are grammatically feminine in the Isleño dialect: *la mar* (sea), *la calor* (heat), *la color* (color), *la azucra/ azúcara* (sugar).

Syntactic Characteristics

- Like rural Canary Island dialects, Isleño Spanish frequently employs noninverted questions with subject pronouns, much as is found in Cuban, Puerto Rican, and Dominican Spanish: *¿Cómo tú dice que era mejó anteh?* (How can you say that things were better before?); *¿Po qué tu no vinihte pa trah?* (Why didn't you come back?); *¿Cómo tú va sabé la gente del nolte y del sur?* (How can you tell northern people from southern people?); *¿Qué uhté llama un bandío?* (What do you mean by a bandit?)
- Isleño Spanish frequently uses the infinitive with preverbal subjects, as in the Caribbean and vestigially in the Canary Islands: *Pa un niño nacé, tenían partera* (For a child to be born, they had midwifes); *Eso no é pa loh pato poné loh huevo* (That isn't so the ducks can lay eggs); *Era duro pa yo meterme con esoh niño inglese* (It was hard for me to get along with those English-speaking kids).
- Apparently through the influence of English, some infinitives after the preposition *para* (for) take *mí* and *ti* in subject position instead of the expected *yo* and *tú: Eso é*

pa mí lonchá (That's for me to eat [for] lunch); *tú tieneh que ser sosedano [ciudadano] americano pa ti tené un bote* (You have to be an American citizen to have a boat).

Lexical Characteristics

The Isleño lexicon contains many archaic and analogical elements found in other rural Spanish dialects; these include *asina* (thus), *naide* (nobody), *probe* (poor), *entuavía* (still), and *endenantes* (beforehand). There are also many words of French origin, including *bayul* (bayou), *fruí* < French *fourbir* (to scrub a floor), *lacre* (inland lake), and *tanta* (aunt). There are also many Anglicisms, including *guachimán* (watchman), *marqueta* (market), *grosería* (grocery), *troleá* (to trawl), and *farmero* (farmer). The term *guagua* refers to a bus or small truck, as in the Canary Islands and the Spanish Antilles. *Gofio* is a Canary Island term still recalled by some Isleños to refer to a mixture of toasted grains. *Faca,* also found in the Canary Islands and ultimately of Galician-Portuguese origin, is a large knife. MacCurdy (1950) and Lipski (1990c) provide more extensive lexical lists.

Scholarship on Isleño Spanish

The first known scholarly mention of the St. Bernard or Isleño variety of Spanish comes in Fortier (1894, 197–210). Claudel (1945) published some folktales from this dialect, and MacCurdy (1950) is the seminal monograph that set the scene for serious investigation of Isleño Spanish. MacCurdy (1947, 1948, 1949, 1952, 1959, 1975) provides additional data on Louisiana Spanish folklore, as does Armistead (1978, 1979, 1981a, 1981b, 1982, 1983a, 1983b, 1985, 1992). Lipski (1990c) is a monograph based on fieldwork conducted more than two generations after MacCurdy's studies, which analyzes the gradual erosion of Isleño Spanish. Lipski (1984c, 1985c, 1986e, 1987c, 1990c) and Varela (1978, 1979) provide additional data. Coles (1999) provides a grammar of Isleño Spanish, continuing work from Coles (1991a, 1991b, 1993). Lestrade (1999) expands the knowledge of the Isleño lexicon and also includes more recent sociolinguistic surveys.

The Spanish Dialect of Los Adaes/Sabine River

Northwest Louisiana (Sabine and Natchitoches Parishes) is home to another very different Spanish dialect, which extends to a few areas on the other side of the Sabine River in East Texas (Nacogdoches County). The majority of the Spanish speakers in question are found in northwestern Louisiana, around the towns of Zwolle and Noble (Sabine Parish) and in the Spanish Lake community near

Robeline (Nachitoches Parish), and in Texas, in the Moral community just to the west of Nacogdoches. Even more than with the Isleños, the Spanish language has nearly died out along the Sabine River; the total number of individuals with significant active competence in Spanish was estimated in the 1980s to be no greater than fifty on each side of the state border, with perhaps only half being truly fluent. A generation later these numbers are even smaller, with a larger number of the community's oldest residents having a passive competence in the traditional Spanish dialect, recognizing words and phrases but being unable to sustain a conversation.[7] As with the Isleños, the Spanish language died out along the Sabine River in the course of little more than a single generation, largely for the same reasons.

Curiously, the Sabine River Spanish communities have no lexical items (such as, the term *isleño* as used in St. Bernard Parish) that identify the ethnic Spanish-speaking group, although the term *Adaeseño* (a derivative of the traditional *adae-sano*) has been applied by Armistead (1992, n.d.) and Armistead and Gregory (1986) to the Spanish Lake dialect, derived from the Spanish settlement of Los Adaes, which was located nearby. In my own research on this dialect (Lipski 1987a, 1988c, 1990b) I have used the term "Sabine River Spanish" to indicate the fact that the dialect extends to both sides of the Sabine River. Currently the creation of the artificial Toledo Bend Reservoir has separated the two communities, but historically they stem from a single settlement. Despite incontrovertible linguistic and ethnographic evidence to the contrary, Louisiana residents reject the designation *Mexican/mexicano* and do not identify themselves as descendents of arrivals from Mexican territory. In Moral, on the other hand, the term *mexicano* is freely used, and even the local Spanish dialect is frequently referred to as *mexicano* rather than *español*.

Little accurate information is available to trace the formation of the Sabine River Spanish communities, but such evidence as exists indicates that immigration occurred in several stages for more than half a century. Spain made several attempts to settle eastern Texas and adjoining areas of Louisiana, but it was not until 1716 that missions and then permanent communities were established at Los Aes (San Agustine), Nacogdoches, and subsequently at Los Adaes, near present-day Robeline, Louisiana. These communities prospered, despite general disinterest by the Spanish government and occasional raids by hostile Indians, and by the second half of the eighteenth century the settlements were well established and were indisputably home to all residents. Spain had intended to settle eastern Texas to create a buffer zone against incursions from French Louisiana, particularly the outpost at Natchitoches, but when the Louisiana territory was ceded to Spain in 1762 such a front line was no longer needed, and the Spanish government decided to withdraw all settlers from the troublesome border region. In 1773 the order arrived in East Texas to abandon the settlements at Nacogdoches, Los Aes, and Los Adaes within five days, for immediate resettlement in Béxar (San Antonio). Despite bitter protests, most residents were forced to abandon homes and crops and make an onerous journey of more than three months to the principal Spanish settlement in Texas. Upon arrival, the newcomers were treated poorly, given inferior land, and left to languish. Immediately they began planning for a return to the only place they knew as home. Finally in 1779, and with only reluctant approval by the Spanish authorities, many settlers moved back to eastern Texas, led by Antonio Gil Ybarbo, who founded the town of Nacogdoches in 1779 at the site of the old mission of Nuestra Señora de Guadalupe. It appears in fact that many of the original residents, including members of Ybarbo's immediate family (brother, mother, and sister-in-law), never left the region with the 1773 evacuation order. Instead they remained in the area surrounding Los Adaes, at Ybarbo's ranch near Los Aes and in other outlying regions, and thus some sort of continuous Spanish occupation can be postulated for this region. When the Louisiana territory once again came under French sovereignty in 1800, the Spanish settlers remained, and with the Louisiana Purchase by the United States government in 1808, immigration of English-speaking Americans became a significant factor.

Linguistically, Sabine River Spanish shares no similarities with the Isleño dialect, but is an offspring of rural Mexican Spanish. The number of subsequent direct arrivals from Spain among the Sabine River Spanish communities was evidently minimal, if there were any at all, and such dialect mixing as did occur consisted of successive overlays of Mexican Spanish from a variety of regions, social strata, and time periods. If this historical reconstruction is accurate, then the vestigial Spanish found among the Louisiana Sabine River Spanish speakers is a direct continuation of eighteenth century Mexican vernacular, whereas the dialect spoken in the Moral community may reflect some aspects of Mexican Spanish from the first decades of the nineteenth century. Both speech communities, then, represent the survival of some of the earliest varieties of Spanish still found in the United States.

Racially, the Sabine River Spanish speakers present a varied panorama, but, particularly in Louisiana, a significant number are of Native American extraction. The residents of the Ebarb community near Zwolle, Louisiana, (the name being an Anglicized version of Ybarbo) have largely identified with the Choctaw nation, but historical and linguistic evidence suggests that many descend from natives of Mexican territory. For example, the Aguayo expedition that founded the mission at Los Adaes in 1721 consisted of 117 conscripts, of whom only 44 were Spaniards, the rest being of mixed race. In the Moral community, there is less evidence of racial mixture, and although residents freely acknowledge that many are *trigueños* (dark complexioned) there is no identification with or even awareness of Native American culture.

Phonological Characteristics

Being a derivative of central and particularly northern Mexican Spanish (because the original settlers came from Coahuila and west/central Texas, with a few perhaps being from as far away as Mexico City), Sabine River Spanish is phonologically rather conservative. This is manifest in the general retention of consonants and the lack of neutralizations found in other dialects. At the same time, the rural/popular origins of Sabine River Spanish result in numerous phonological misidentifications and analogical creations. Detailed features include the following:

- Syllable-final and word-final /s/ is normally retained as [s], with a much lower proportion of cases of aspiration [h]. Certain cases of the change /s/ > [h] are pan-Hispanic, such as the popular pronunciation of *nosotros* (we) as *nojotros* (*lojotros* is more common in Sabine River Spanish).
- Phrase-final and word-final prevocalic /n/ is uniformly alveolar [n].
- The opposition between the single flap /r/ and the multiple trill /r/ is partially neutralized, with the majority of cases of the latter phoneme realized as [r]. Syllable-final and word-final /r/ is normally realized as [r], but in phrase-final position, elision of /r/ is relatively frequent, particularly in verbal infinitives.
- The phoneme /j/ is weak and frequently falls in contact with /i/ (*gallina* > [gaína] (hen), *silla* > [sía] (chair)) and after /e/ (*sello* > [seo] (stamp)).
- The opposition between intervocalic /d/ and /r/ is partially neutralized in favor of [r] (e.g., *cada* > [kara] (each)); this pronunciation is not consistent among Sabine River Spanish speakers, and probably results from English interference, because the same variation is found among other vestigial Spanish-English bilinguals.
- The phoneme /t/ is occasionally given an alveolar realization and may emerge as a voiceless flap; as in the preceding case, this is evidently a transfer from English.
- Sabine River Spanish speakers normally reduce unstressed vowels, giving them a centralized realization as schwa [ə].
- As in Isleño and other vestigial or isolated Spanish dialects, Sabine River Spanish exhibits many cases of phonological misidentification, both sporadic and unstable variations, and total relexification. Common examples include: *buja* < *aguja* (needle);

rabilán < *gavilán* (hawk); *bujero* < *agujero* (hole); *jalote* < *guajolote* (turkey); *amaricano* < *americano* (American).

Morphosyntactic Features

Sabine River Spanish is characterized by a high concentration of archaisms, forms typical of rural and popular Spanish, and analogical formations, as well as syntactic transference from English among the last generation of Spanish speakers. Among the salient morphosyntactic traits are the following:

- Archaic forms, including *trujo/truje* (he/she, I brought); *vido/vide* (he/she, I saw); *mesmo* (same); *muncho* (much); *asina/ansina* (thus).
- Numerous analogical verb forms, largely resulting in verbal paradigms with a single canonical root: *cierramos* < *cerramos* (we close); *dijieron* < *dijeron* (they said); *cocinear* < *cocinar* (to cook); *tenimos* < *tuvimos* (we had), and so forth.
- Use of *mero* instead of general Spanish *mismo* in the sense of "same, one and only": *aquí mero* (right here); *éste mero* (this very one). *Mero* also appears in the expression *ya mero* (almost); this use of *mero* is current in Mexican Spanish but is not normal in other dialects, which highlights the Mexican origin of Sabine River Spanish.
- The combination *de nosotros* completely supplants *nuestro/nuestra* (our) in the Sabine River area, as in some forms of popular Mexican and Caribbean Spanish.
- Expressions with *no más* (only, precisely) are used as in Mexican Spanish, to the complete exclusion of *sólo/sólamente*: *no más quería platicar contigo* (I only wanted to talk to you).
- Among Sabine River Spanish speakers there is consistent use of the copulative verb *estar* in cases where other Spanish dialects, including those of Mexico, employ *ser*, particularly with predicate nouns. This may be a function of vestigial usage, but nearly all Spanish speakers interviewed in both communities exhibit some nonstandard use of *estar*, leading to the supposition that this verb gradually evolved away from general and Mexican Spanish patterns at an earlier date. Examples include the following:

toa la gente que ta aquí ta blanco (all the people around here are white)
los Peñas están trigueños (the Peñas are dark skinned)
el tacuache no ta malo (possums aren't bad)
una coquena ta medio amarillo (a Guinea hen is sort of yellow)
si 'taban novios por mucho tiempo (if they were engaged for a long time)

- As in Mexican Spanish, the Sabine River dialects use questions with *¿qué tanto?/¿qué tan?* (how many, how much) nearly exclusively, instead of *¿cuánto?*; thus *¿qué tanto ganas?* (how much do you earn?) *¿qué tan vieja es esta casa?* (how old is this house?)

- As with other varieties of Spanish in contact with English, the Sabine River dialect employs expressions with *para atrás (patrás)* in combinations where English uses the verbal particle *back:*

habla patrás en español (answer in Spanish)
venga patrás mañana (come back tomorrow)
unos vinieron patrás con él (some came back with him)

Lexical Characteristics

The Sabine River Spanish lexicon is a combination of Mexican, archaic, and rural/popular Spanish items, with an admixture of French loans in the Louisiana community, and a handful of indigenous elements.

- MEXICANISMS. These are most abundant in Sabine River Spanish and definitively prove the Mexican provenance of this dialect. Common items include *atole* (thin sweet gruel); *guajolote* (turkey); *tecolote* (owl); *zopilote* (buzzard); *cacahuate* (peanut); *zacate* (grass, weed); *camote* (sweet potato, yam); *comal* (griddle for cooking tortillas); *nixtamal* (hominy); *metate* (grinding stone); *molcajete* (mortar for grinding herbs and chiles); *petate* (mat); *mecate* (rope); *cuate* (twin); *tacuache* (possum); *tejón* (raccoon); *güero* (blond, light complexioned); *elote* (tender cob of corn); *ejote* (snap bean); *charola* (tray); *labor* (division of land [approx. 177 acres]); *blanquillo* (egg); *tuza* (mole [rodent]); *ándale* (let's go, OK); *pinche* (damned, cursed); and the universal Mexican expletive *chingar* and its derivatives, originally referring to the sexual act, but now merely vulgar expressions.
- ARCHAIC/RUSTIC ITEMS. These include *mercar/marcar* (to buy); *calzón/calzones* (pants); *túnico* (ladies' dress); *calesa* (horse-drawn buggy); *la provisión* (supplies, provisions); *noria* (water well); *truja/troja* (barn); *encino* (oak tree); *peje* (fish); *fierro* (iron, tool); *lumbre* (fire); *prieto* (black)
- OTHER ITEMS. Additional lexical items found in the Sabine River dialect include *huaguín* (*waguín*) (farm wagon); *payaso* (bat) (alternating with the popular *murcégalo* < *murciélago*); the Caribbean *maní* (peanut), which alternates (in Louisiana) with English *goober* and the normal Mexican *cacahuate; ojo negro* (black-eyed pea); *pan de molino* (corn bread); and *cusca/cushca* (buzzard) of unknown etymology, which alternates with the Mexican *zopilote.*

Scholarship on Sabine River/Adaeseño Spanish

Stark (1980) offered the first linguistic description of the Louisiana component of the Sabine River dialect. Additional studies include Armistead (1992, n.d.), Armistead and Gregory (1986), and Lipski (1987a, 1988c, 1990b). Pratt (2004) and

Shoemaker (1988) offer an in-depth study of the Ebarb dialect. A website descriptive of Los Adaes and its culture is http://www.crt.state.la.us/siteexplorer/_html/3_02_00.htm.

Notes

1. Most of the facts regarding the history of New Mexico and its Spanish-speaking population are uncontroversial and easily accessible. In preparing this encapsulated history, I have drawn liberally on the following sources, in addition to those cited in the text: Bancroft (1889), Davis (1857), Gregg (1933), Jones (1979), and Magoffin (1926).

2. Among speakers of traditional New Mexican Spanish, the term *mexicano* is more common than *español* to refer to the Spanish language. *Castellano* is rarely used (except by those who learned the word in school). Although some New Mexicans use *español* and *mexicano* synonymously, others reserve the former term for the formal, usually Peninsular-oriented written language learned in school. New Mexicans of Spanish descent often refer to themselves as *Hispanos*, both in Spanish and in English. *Raza* also designates members of the New Mexico Hispanic community. The term *Latino* is not used (except by Spanish-speaking immigrants from other regions), and the word *Chicano* is a relative newcomer to New Mexico, used more in the context of political and social activism than as an all-encompassing ethnic identifier.

3. Henríquez Ureña (1938, 352–53) described similar behavior for parts of Mexico and Guatemala, whereas Oroz (1966, 135–36) found the same patterns of elision in southern Chile.

4. Of Hills's examples, only *pa consiguire la cosa* (to get the thing) contains an apparent example of paragogic [e] in nonphrase final position. In addition, paragogic [e] occurs only after coronal consonants, but this is not necessarily significant, because patrimonial Spanish consonant-final words (except for such exceptional forms as *reloj* [clock], typically pronounced without the final consonant) all end in coronal consonants. Paragogic final [e] occurs most frequently after final /r/, a figure inflated as a result of the high representation of verbal infinitives. The other conso-nant favoring paragogic vowels is /l/; paragogic vowels are rarely found after /n/, and virtually never after /s/ or /d/ (Espinosa 1909, 138, claims not to have heard such sounds in southern Colorado or northern New Mexico, but quotes Hills (1906, 724) as observing *maldade* < *maldad* (evil); *botone* < *botón* (button); *cuale* < *cual* (which), and so forth. For Espinosa, this change is possibly the result of "Galician or Western Gallego-Portuguese" (1909, 137). However, Hills (1906, 16) gives examples after /r/, /n/, and /l/, including *pa consiguire la cosa, tú serás el vencedore* (you will be the winner); *sa carne ole male* (that meat smells bad); and *l'ehpañol eh máh fácil qu'el alemane* (Spanish is easier than German). Hills speculates that because many Italians moved to southeastern Colorado, an Italian influence may be present. He also notes, although without establishing a connection, that Lisbon Portuguese adds a final -e in similar circumstances. McSpadden (1934, 95) describes the epenthetic vowel in Chilili as occurring after /l/, /n/, and /r/. This suggests that liquid con-sonants (or possibly sonorants) provide the most favorable environments. Rael

(1937) gives examples such as *baúle* < *baúl* (trunk); *bueye* < *buey* (ox); *Juani* < *Juan*, *cuali* < *cual*, *Manueli* < *Manuel*, and so forth. In the most complete study, Hernández-Chávez and Pérez (1991) find that paragogic [e] appears most frequently after /r/, followed by /l/, then /n/, and only occasionally /s/. They note that final /-d/ and /-x/ have effectively disappeared from New Mexico Spanish, and that final /-s/ is often a weak aspiration that is not conducive to the presence of a paragogic vowel. These authors discovered no clear grammatical conditioning (although verbal infinitives represent the most frequent cases), and give examples such as *sole* < *sol* (sun); *educacione* < *educación* (education); *despuese* < *después* (after); *adiosi* < *adios* (good bye); *dose* < *dos* (two); *magasine* < *magasín* (magazine); *inglese* < *inglés* (English); *Salazare* < *Salazar*, *Mondragone* < *Mondragón*, *Belene* < *Belén*, and so forth. After considering the historical development of final /-e/ in old Spanish, the authors conclude that most if not all cases of paragogic -[e] in New Mexican Spanish must be the result of innovation, and are not historical relics.

5. A partial exception to the trend of not emulating Mexican linguistic patterns is found among the several Spanish-language radio stations, which play popular music from both Mexico and New Mexico (and occasionally from the Caribbean and South America), and whose audience obviously includes a significant portion of Spanish speakers born outside of New Mexico. Given that radio broadcasting in Spanish postdates English-language broadcasting in New Mexico, native New Mexican Spanish speakers never had the opportunity to develop a distinctively New Mexican format for radio programs. As Spanish-language programming has arisen, and particularly when entire stations are devoted to broadcasting in Spanish, both Anglo American and Mexican models have served to mold the stations' format. Radio stations aimed more at young listeners, and/or located in central and northern New Mexico away from the proximity of Mexico, tend to use more English in both advertising and program language. A freely code-switched style characterizes many of the broadcasts, with the best example being Albuquerque's KABQ, which proudly proclaims itself to be "your official Mex-Tex station," employing intrasentential code switching throughout its musical announcements, news and weather, editorials and community announcements, and in much of its paid advertising. Music by New Mexican artists is also aired on public broadcast stations, sometimes in conjunction with regional varieties of Spanish. The polarization between "Mexican" and "New Mexican" Spanish on the radio is most noticeable in news broadcasting, both of national and world events and of regional/local coverage. Some announcers strive for a pan-Hispanic vocabulary, avoiding Anglicisms and using a language that many New Mexican Hispanics may find impenetrable. The presumed audience of such programs includes Spanish-speaking immigrants. Other announcers make greater use of Anglicisms, but almost never is true New Mexico vernacular Spanish heard on the air, replete with morphological and phonetic deviations from "world" Spanish. Whereas some speakers of traditional New Mexican Spanish do listen to Spanish-language radio (and to Mexican soap operas on television), most do so only out of nostalgia, or to add a bit of variety; few find broadcast language close enough to their own speech to provide reinforcement.

6. www.losisleños.org/.

7. Special thanks are due to the following individuals without whose help no material progress could have been made: Prof. Hiram Gregory of Northwestern State University in Natchitoches, Louisiana; Prof. James Corbin of Stephen F. Austin State University in Nacogdoches, Texas; Prof. Samuel Armistead of the University of California, Davis; Ms. Mary Van Rheenen of Louisiana State University, Baton Rouge; Mr. Sam Montes of the Moral Community, Nacogdoches, Texas.

13

Language Mixing and Code Switching

Introduction

The Spanish language in the United States is in constant contact with English. Many Latinos living here use English more frequently than Spanish, almost all have more formal education in English than in Spanish, and an undetermined but likely large segment of the Latino population is demonstrably more proficient in English than in Spanish. When two languages come together for sustained periods of time—in various parts of the world and in a wide range of circumstances—fluent bilinguals inevitably engage in three contact-induced speech phenomena. The first—which requires only a minimal amount of fluency in the second language—is borrowing of words, with or without modification, to fit the phonetics of the borrowing language. The second phenomenon requires a higher level of bilingual proficiency, and it consists of transfer of translated idiomatic expressions (calques) as well as tilting word order patterns in a fashion as to make patterns in both languages more convergent—usually by expanding or contracting already available options in one or both languages, and rarely by violating grammatical rules in either language. Finally, fluent bilingual speakers often switch between languages within the confines of a single conversation. This is expected when conversational participants, topics, and settings change (e.g., between home- and work-related domains). It is when speakers freely switch back and forth between languages—often within a single sentence and with no obvious external shifts of focus or participants—that nonbilinguals experience the greatest linguistic shock. As seen in chapter 2, in the context of English-Spanish bilingualism, all three phenomena have at times been referred to as Spanglish, although each is found in some form or another in every bilingual community in the world, past and present. However, the first two types of language mixing are found even in the speech of casual language learners, students, and tourists, whereas fluid code switching is confined to a subset of fluent bilingual and bicultural individuals.

Lexical Borrowing

Throughout its history, Spanish has borrowed freely from languages and cultures in contact with Spanish-speaking peoples. Prior to its expansion beyond the Iberian Peninsula, Spanish borrowed scores of words from Arabic, Greek, Italian, French, and German. In Latin America numerous indigenous words have entered regional dialects of Spanish, and some of the earliest borrowings from Nahuatl, Quechua, Carib, Arawak, and even Guaraní—such as *tomate* (tomato); *chocolate; huracán* (hurricane); *canoa* (canoe); *barbacoa* (barbecue); *tiburón* (shark); *poncho; cóndor;* and *ñandú* (rhea)—have become part of the worldwide Spanish lexicon. Over the past century, dialects of Spanish that are geographically, politically, and historically far removed from the United States have adopted numerous Anglicisms, including many variants of the verb *park* (as in *to park a car*)—such as *parcar, parquear, aparcar, parqueo, aparcamiento,* and *parcadero. Jungla* (jungle) entered Spanish through translations of Kipling's stories; *mítin* (meeting)—and probably *líder* (leader) and *lideranza, liderazgo* (leadership)—appeared during the self-proclaimed populist regime of Juan Perón in Argentina. English *lunch*—a concept far removed from the traditional Spanish *almuerzo* or *comida*—has given rise to *lonche* and *lonchera* (student lunch box), terms extensively used in Latin America. *Sandwich,* at its turn, has produced offspring in nearly every Spanish dialect, as have *cocktail, whiskey, sport, ski,* and *check* (as in medical checkup or airport check-in). Throughout the Caribbean, Central America, and part of South America, car mufflers are referred to by some derivative of the English word (such as *mufla, mofla,* and *mofle*), shock absorbers are *choques,* a clutch is a *cloche,* and wheels or rims are *rines.* International tourism, business, and technology have prompted the entry of enough Anglicisms into worldwide Spanish as to warrant the publication of many large dictionaries devoted exclusively to borrowings. Computer technology and Internet communication have spawned hundreds of new Anglicisms, and they have also led to the creation of cyber-Spanglish, much to the consternation of many Spanish speakers. Contrary to popular belief, though, proximity to the United States and suffocation under an avalanche of U.S. popular culture are not the determining factors underlying the transfer of most English terms into Spanish. Supporting this claim is the fact that stop signs in Spain read *STOP*, whereas in Mexico they say *ALTO* (halt), and in Puerto Rico and most other Latin American countries they read *PARE* (stop).

Within the United States, the tendency to use both English words and English borrowings while speaking Spanish is naturally stronger than in regions far removed from English-speaking communities. Although there is no single U.S. dialect of Spanish, most U.S. Latino Spanish varieties can be distinguished from the Spanish dialects from which they derive (that is, from the Spanish dialects as spoken in their countries of origin) principally through the greater frequency of Anglicisms in the speech of Latinos raised or living for extended periods of time in the United States. Although few objective observers would reject the notion that borrowings from other languages into Spanish have enriched the language over the centuries, the issue of current borrowings from English is so intertwined with highly charged emotions—ranging from dreams of opportunities and upward mobility to repudiation of Yankee imperialism and big-stick diplomacy— that matters cannot be resolved through scientific inquiry. Suffice it to say that English words continue to permeate Spanish in the United States in clusters of items that reflect particular circumstances. The adoption of *güelfer* < *welfare, yánitor* < *janitor,* and *sobgüey* < *subway* reflects migration to urban working-class neighborhoods; *aplicar para un trabajo* (to apply for a job) and the related *aplicación* (application form) are inevitable products of a paper-dependent bureaucracy, as is the use of *forma* (form to be filled out). Parents sending children to school or attending school or college themselves have introduced *registrar* (to register for a course), *principal* (school principal), and *grados* (school grades), in each case turning a false or partial cognate into a refashioned Spanish word. The words just mentioned are typically used in stable speech communities and may exist for several generations. Other Anglicisms do not show such clear pedigrees, respond to no obvious change in circumstances, and crop up spontaneously in the speech of Latinos who usually have little formal education in Spanish. The use of *tochar* (to touch), *puchar* (to push), or *liquiar* (to leak), among others, fill no gaps in the Spanish language; rather, they are likely to represent spontaneous crossovers between languages with similar patterns of word formation. The questions of whether to use Anglicisms when speaking Spanish, which Anglicisms to use, and how often to employ them find no objective answers within linguistics; rather, they must be settled by the speech communities themselves, individually and collectively. The balancing act between an artificially sterilized Spanish deprived of even the most widely used Anglicisms and an impenetrable tapestry of English words inserted to the point of limiting communication outside of small groups is a challenge that all bilingual societies face. And though linguists may point to the inevitable nature of borrowing during language contact, not all borrowings are equally accepted.

Loan Translations and Calques

In stable bilingual communities whose members speak languages with similar grammatical structures, borrowing often extends beyond individual words to embrace idiomatic expressions, which, taken in the widest sense, are combinations of words whose meaning cannot be deduced as the simple sum of the individual components. Thus the English expression "that goes without saying" is calqued from French *ça va sans dire,* whereas Spanish expressions such as *si Dios quiere* and *vaya con Dios* are loan translations from Arabic, and *no hay de qué* reveals the imprint of French *il n'y a pas de quoi*. In every contact situation involving contemporary Spanish, loan translations occur—sometimes passing unnoticed, sometimes considered only as quaint regionalisms. And particularly when coupled with an emotionally charged political environment, loan translations are the subject of harsh criticism. For example, when Catalan speakers produce utterances such as *el dormitorio está atacado [al lado de] a la cocina* (the bedroom is next to the kitchen) or *voy a colgar [acostar] a los niños* (I'm going to put the children to bed), other Spaniards may only smile, because Catalan language and culture are well-established and respected in Spain. However, in the Andean region of South America loan translations from Quechua and Aymara such as *de Juan su mamá* (Juan's mother) and *dame cerrando la puerta [cierra la puerta]* (close the door) are avoided by fluent Spanish speakers and stigmatized as pertaining to the speech of uncultured indigenous citizens.

Within the United States, loan translations are commonplace among bilingual Spanish-English speakers, and many are so subtle as to pass unnoticed, especially when they represent subtle departures from worldwide Spanish patterns: *soñar de* instead of *soñar con* (to dream of) or even *tomar una clase* instead of *seguir un curso* (to take a class). Others, such as *tochar* and *puchar,* arise spontaneously in bilingual conversations but have not become consolidated in U.S. varieties of Spanish. By far the most commonly cited—and most often criticized—loan translation found in all bilingual Spanish-English communities in the United States is the use of *para atrás* (usually pronounced *patrás*) as a translation of the English verbal particle *back,* as in *to call back, to pay back, to talk back, to give back*. In the Spanish of various bilingual Latino groups in the United States, *patrás* combines with the Spanish verbs that have the same meanings as the English verb + *back* constructions. Examples include the following:

> *llamar patrás* (to call back)
> *dar patrás* (to give back)
> *venir patrás* (to come back)
> *hablar patrás* (to talk back)
> *pagar patrás* (to pay back)
> *mover(se) patrás* (to move back)

Constructions based on *patrás* have been documented for all Spanish-speaking communities in the United States and, occasionally, within Puerto Rico as well. The use of *patrás* is particularly well known among Mexican American/Chicano, Puerto Rican, Dominican, and Cuban Spanish speakers born or raised in the United States (Lipski 1985e, 1987c; Sánchez 1983; Pérez Sala 1973, 67; Varela 1974), and it has made its way into popular U.S. Latino literature in works such as the novel *La vida es un special* by the Cuban American Roberto Fernández (1981); on page 74 in this novel, one reads "Llámame pa tra cuando tenga un tiempito" (Call me back when you have a moment). The same usage is found among more recent Central American immigrants as well as among the Isleños of St. Bernard Parish, Louisiana, who have been removed from contact with other varieties of Spanish for more than two centuries, which demonstrates the spontaneity with which *patrás* constructions can arise in the absence of imitation of more established bilingual varieties (Lipski 1987b):

> *Ven pa trah mañana* (Come back tomorrow)
> *Dió quiera que eso tiempoh nunca vengan pa tra* (May God will that those times never come back)
> *Te ponían el pie pa tra* (They put your foot back)
> *Tuve que dárselo pa tra* (I had to give it back to him)
> *Cuando se acaba la pehca, se va pa trah pal trabajo* (When the fishing season is over, he goes back to his job)

An even more striking demonstration of the pervasiveness of *patrás* constructions in all Spanish-English contact situations comes from a little-known bilingual region, Gibraltar. Although Gibraltar is nominally an English-speaking crown colony of Great Britain, the vast majority of its native-born residents speak Spanish as a first language, because they are descended from mixed marriages between Spaniards—who had possession of Gibraltar until the eighteenth century—and Britons. Spanish has no place in the official life of Gibraltar, but it is the predominant language for informal communication, except for those residents raised speaking English in the United Kingdom. Given the low prestige of nonstandard Gibraltarian Spanish (which in essence is a variant of popular Andalusian Spanish as spoken in nearby Algeciras), the influence of English has been enormous, even when one considers the relatively deficient English spoken by a large number of Gibraltarians. The English used in Gibraltar is based on educated British English, but syntactically it is very similar to U.S. English. The Spanish-English interface of Gibraltar bears an uncanny resemblance to the bilingual Hispanic communities of the United States in terms of specific lexical Anglicisms, especially in the area of calques, code switching, and syntactic interference (Lipski 1986d; Moyer 1992). Spanish-speaking Gibraltarians make frequent use of constructions with *patrás* in ways that parallel exactly U.S. Latino usage, as indicated by the following examples, which come from data collected by this author in Gibraltar:

> *Vengo pa trah mañana* (I'm coming back tomorrow)
> *Por favor, póngalo pa trah* (Please put it back)
> *Cuando quiera, te lo doy pa trah* (I'll give it back whenever you want)

Direct influence of U.S. Spanish dialects is out of the question in Gibraltar, and yet *patrás* is nearly as frequent there as it is in the United States; moreover, it is used in precisely the same environments. In combinations such as those listed above—which are also found in Dutch and in a somewhat similar fashion in German—*back* is not acting as a preposition or adverb but rather as a particle associated with the verb. *Back* follows the verb obligatorily if the object following it is a pronoun, and optionally if it is a full noun phrase: *I'll pay you back; Give me back the box; I put the book back on the shelf.* In the aforementioned combinations, *patrás* normally adopts the postposed position to the verb in Spanish, unless the direct object is expressed with a clitic, which obligatorily occurs before the verb:

> *Pagué el préstamo pa tras*/**Pagué pa tras el préstamo* (I paid back the loan)
> *Di el libro pa tras*/**Di pa tras el libro* (I gave the book back)

Although the expression *patrás* seems a clear-cut case of syntactic transference from English to Spanish, it is unique in (fluent) U.S. Spanish as a calque of an English verbal particle. Verbal combinations such as *knock over, sit down, figure out,* and *come through*—that is, formed with particles other than *back*—are virtually never calqued into Spanish, despite the fact that their Spanish equivalents are neither more common nor morphologically less difficult than *volver, regresar, devolver* and the like, all of which underlie *patrás* constructions.

Irrespective of one's personal views on the appropriateness of combinations using *para atrás* in U.S. varieties of Spanish, the fact remains that they are fully consistent with Spanish grammatical usage, and they do not differ structurally in any way from other *modismos* and idiomatic expressions found throughout the language, being no more "un-Spanish" than *de nada, no hay de qué* (you're welcome) or *por Dios* (for God's sake). Otheguy (1993) argues that *patrás* constructions are not the result of the direct influence of English grammar, despite the obvious similarities. But in order to account for the fact that *patrás* constructions of the sort mentioned above are found *only* in contact with English—and we might add that they occur in *all* stable Spanish-English contact environments—he acknowledges that the semantic notions conveyed by the English particle *back* could well have been carried over to Spanish:

> Speakers of Spanish in the U.S. could very well have gotten the idea from speakers of English that the concept of "behindness" in space could be applied metaphorically to the temporal notion of repetition. But they then deployed the resources of their language in a manner that . . . is syntactically and semantically different from that of English, and that, furthermore, appears to involve no alteration of any systematic area of Spanish lexis or grammar (Otheguy 1993, 35).

The combinations with *para atrás* are the most frequently repeated shibboleth, criticized both by visitors to the United States and by many U.S. Spanish speakers. Other frequently heard loan translations are *correr para* (to run for a political office), *aplicar para* (to apply for [a job, admission to a school, etc.]), and *¿Cómo te gusta . . . ?* (How do you like . . . ?). All such loan translations fully obey Spanish grammatical rules; many are based on partial or false cognate relationships between Spanish and English words, all arise spontaneously whenever Spanish and English are spoken in bilingual communities, and all are readily understood by Spanish-English bilinguals. Although it may be useful to direct attention to and even to teach avoidance of such Anglicisms—for example, when teaching the language of international business and journalism—it seems futile and counterproductive to wage campaigns against words and expressions that are natural consequences of bilingual encounters.

Code Switching among U.S. Spanish Speakers

Perhaps the most striking feature found among Spanish-English bilingual speakers in the United States is the phenomenon known as code switching—that is, switching between two languages within the same discourse involving the same

individuals. Everyone accepts the concept of changing languages to accommo-
date the arrival of monolingual speakers, but the interchange of languages without apparent external triggers causes not only consternation among observers
who are not familiar with this practice but also considerable criticism even from
within the bilingual speech communities, whose more prescriptive members
insist that speakers should stick with one language or the other. Code switching
reaches its highest level of bilingual interweaving—which is at once of great
interest to linguists and the source of the most vehement criticism—when both
languages are combined within the space of a single sentence, as typified by the
title of Poplack's (1980c) seminal article "Sometimes I'll start a sentence in English y termino en español." This type of intrasentential code switching provides
linguists with a proving ground for theories of language dominance and the representation of language in the cognitive apparatus of bilingual speakers. The
same examples serve as fodder for emotion-ridden arguments about the confusion and even "alingualism" produced when bilingualism runs amok. Given the
prevalence of code switching in U.S. Latino speech and literature, a further discussion is warranted.

When two languages come into contact in a situation of stable bilingualism,
both borrowing and code switching are normal events. Many observers have
claimed that borrowing during language contact is constrained by a quasi-
universal hierarchy of elements, with content words such as nouns being the most
frequently borrowed, whereas functional words such as conjunctions, prepositions, and complementizers (e.g., English *that* and Spanish *que*) are situated at the
opposite end of the spectrum.[1] More recent research has revealed that a priori
hierarchies or typologies of grammatical elements susceptible to borrowing are so
riddled with exceptions as to be meaningless in a global sense, although recurring
patterns emerge within individual language families.[2] The relationship between
grammatical structure, comparative typological hierarchies, and sociolinguistic
factors is nowhere better exemplified than in intrasentential code switching
among fluent bilinguals. Although some form of code switching occurs in all
bilingual societies, the fluent interweaving of languages within the confines of a
single sentence occurs with less frequency. This is principally the result of two
factors. The first is typological similarity: code switching within the same sentence
is facilitated when the languages in contact share the same basic syntactic
patterns—such as the order of subject, verb, and direct object; the use of prepositions or postpositions; the presence or absence of definite and indefinite articles;
the formation of questions and negative sentences, and so forth. These grammatical similarities can be studied in a straightforward fashion, and they have given
rise to an enormous and continually expanding research bibliography. The second

factor governing the extent to which language mixing within individual sentences occurs is less tangible and can be approached only through approximate comparisons; involved are notions of linguistic and cultural identity present both in individual speakers and across entire speech communities. Thus it is, for example, that intrasentential code switching is frequent among most U.S. Spanish bilingual communities (and also in Gibraltar), but it is quite infrequent among French-English bilinguals in Canada, despite the fact that English and French are as grammatically similar as English and Spanish. Presumably the social values attached to each language, official recognition or lack thereof, presence in school curricula, and the historical facts surrounding the arrival and formation of bilingual communities in Canada are responsible for the qualitative differences in language switching in that neighboring country.

Grammatical Constraints on Spanish-English Language Switching

Code switching, at least of the fluent intrasentential variety, is governed by a complex set of syntactic and pragmatic restrictions. The literature on the syntactic constraints that govern code switching is vast and still growing. Among the studies relating specifically to Spanish are Belazi, Rubin, and Toribio (1994); Dussias (2003); Gingras (1974); Jacobson (1977a, 1977b, 1978a, 1978b); Lipski (1977a, 1982, 1984a, 1985b); McMenamin (1973); Pfaff (1979); Poplack (1980c); Sankoff and Poplack (1981); Sobin (1984); Timm (1975); Toribio (2001a, 2001b); Woolford (1983); and Valdés-Fallis (1975, 1976a, 1976b, 1978, 1979). Among the syntactic factors, the most compelling ones are that (1) no grammatical rule in either language be violated and (2) the point of transition be smooth—in the sense that the material from the second language is in some way as likely a combination as a continuation in the first language. Fluent code switching may therefore produce combinations in which a switch occurs between article and noun, between a complementizer and a subordinate clause, between a conjunction and one of the conjuncts, and so forth.[3] Although there are many exceptions, some general observations will illustrate findings specific to Spanish-English code switching. Spontaneous code switches not accompanied by hesitations, pauses, or interruptions are normally unacceptable in the following environments (all examples listed as acceptable are actually occurring spontaneous speech of bilingual Latinos in the United States; these examples were collected by others for their research as well as by myself for my own studies). Sentences marked with an asterisk (*) are generally regarded as unacceptable.

- Between a pronominal subject and a predicate:

*_Él_ is coming tomorrow.
*He _viene mañana._

- Between a pronominal clitic and a verb:

*_Juan lo_ said. / *_Juan quiere decir_ it.
*_John wants to say_ lo.

- Between a sentence-initial interrogative word and the remainder of the sentence:

*_¿Cuándo_ will you come?
*_¿When vas a hacerlo?_

- Between an auxiliary verb (especially _haber_) and the main verb:

*_María ha_ finished the job.
*We had _acabado de comer._

Code switches are occasionally possible between the auxiliary verbs _"estar"_ and "be," and the gerund:

María está checking her answers.
Mary is _revisando su informe._
Porque ella está going to have a baby.

The gerund can appear in the English portion of the sentence even when a gerund would be unacceptable in the homologous Spanish sentence. Similarly, the Spanish gerund in a code-switched combination may retain the nominal force it can have in English (which is usually disallowed in monolingual Spanish):

Estoy por lowering the standard.
I'm talking about _conociéndonos._

- Adverbs of negation are normally in the same language as the verbs they modify:

*_El médico no_ wants that.
*The doctor does not _quiere eso._

In most cases the restrictions reflect the need to respect the grammatical rules of each language, following the linear order of major sentence constituents both in English and in Spanish. For example, the disallowed combination *el médico no wants that* contains a single negative adverb before the English verb, but negative sentences in the simple present tense normally require the support of a preceding "do"/"does." Leaving out "do"/"does" in this sentence creates a linear violation. In other cases, more subtle issues of syntactic governance come into play.

What does it mean to state that the aforementioned combinations are unacceptable? This is not the same as to say they are ungrammatical—as are configurations such as *I gone have store the* in English or *el niña vivimos aquí* in Spanish, both of which (1) violate rules of the respective languages for which there are no exceptions, (2) are not found in any regional or social varieties or even in second-language speech, and (3) are categorically rejected by all native speakers. Code switching, on the other hand, belongs to spontaneous, colloquial speech, and it is often unconscious when occurring in the middle of a sentence. When queried after the fact, speakers who have just performed an intrasentential code switch may be unaware of having done so or unsure about precisely at what point in the sentence the crossover occurred. Moreover, when pauses, hesitations, slips, or course changes occur during speech, virtually any syntactically bracketed code switch is possible (i.e., the material set off by pauses is treated as a self-contained "island"); the restrictions mentioned above apply only to speech without hesitations. Deviations from the proposed syntactic restrictions also occur in literary texts employing code switching, as the desired effect is often not the mimicking of true spontaneous speech, but rather the creation of a poetic effect through the juxtaposition of elements not normally occurring in close succession.

Obtaining grammaticality judgments from native speakers is next to impossible; some reject all switches out of hand, whereas others give confusing responses as a result of not having pondered on this form of speech. Most bilingual speakers can be coaxed into offering opinions on different types of switches, and those that most flagrantly violate the previously mentioned syntactic restrictions usually produce more negative reactions, but not in a fashion that can be scientifically replicated. Though limited to written language—hardly a representative measure of spontaneous speech (Dussias 2003)—psycholinguistic research based on eye movement during reading has provided some insights into actual processing and acceptance of code-switched utterances. (Ongoing work with real-time measurements of brain activity offers much eventual promise.) At the present time, it is best to speak not of cause and effect during language switching, but rather of patterns of speech that favor or disfavor slipping between Spanish and English whenever external pragmatic conditions are consistent with the possibility of bilingual discourse.

There are also circumstances that favor code switching among fluent bilinguals. They fall into two broad categories. The first is the unconscious anticipation of words or phrases intimately linked to the second language that are about to occur in the conversation. The second involves complex or compound sentences in which code switches occur between the individual clauses because, in effect, each full sentence is produced in a single language.

- The anticipated presence of a proper noun in the other language can trigger a switch prior to the actual insertion of the L2 proper noun, as shown in these recorded examples, representing Mexican American discourse in Houston, Texas:

Allá en el parque there's a little place called Sonny's.
Va a haber un benefit at the Starlight Ballroom.
Mucha gente no sabe where Manchester is.
. . . *todas las palomillas* that work at American Hospital Supply.
Escucharon a Lisa López's latest album, *una canción titulada* . . .
Mezcal va a tocar this coming Friday.
Corrí twelve miles for a Marathon.
Not only *en el estado de Texas pero en todo Aztlán.*
I'm a *Jiménez, todos los demás son Torres.*

- Switches are especially common between a main clause and a subordinate clause introduced by a relative pronoun or a complementizer such as *que, porque,* and so forth. Despite the vigorous theoretical debate concerning the governing properties of the complementizer—according to which the subordinate clause must appear in the same language as the complementizer—observed Spanish-English code switches occur frequently with the complementizer in the language of the main clause, suggesting that complementizers act as a linguistic fulcrum for switches rather than being inextricably linked to the subordinate clause. The following examples (from the same corpus and from previously cited studies) illustrate these possibilities:

There are many families on the block *que tienen chamaquitos.*
No sé porque I never used it.
She told me to make a special dedication to her son, *que le dicen el Pachuco de Rosenberg.*
It's the first shag *que se me hace que* looks good on a girl.
. . . *todas las palomillas* that work at American Hospital Supply.
No podemos hacer nada porque we don't have the power.
Me tiene envidia because I'm better lookin' than he is.
Escucharon a un señor que has been around for a long time.
There was this guy *que era un vato de México* . . .
I'm not sayin' that *son chuecos.*

- The presence of a coordinating conjunction (*y, pero,* etc.) is another fulcrum point that allows switches:

They're still meeting at Ripley house every Thursday night *y la gente se está juntando ahí.*

Si compran tickets en Saint Josephs you don't have to go to purgatory.

Sometimes *te pones serio* and you know that, you make good points.

Es que Pat was dry.

One more time Ruth, *pa que la gente se cuente y* they can call you at . . .

The Insertion of "So" as a Special Case of Language Mixing

Fluent Spanish-English code switching of the sort described in the preceding section is the almost exclusive purview of bilingual Latino speakers raised in the United States. An accepted axiom of Spanish-English code switching is that there are clear quantitative and qualitative differences between the language switches performed by (1) fluent bilinguals, (2) Spanish-speaking immigrants who learned English in adolescence or adulthood, and (3) native speakers of English who have acquired Spanish as a second language. The first group is most noted for intrasentential code switching and for the use of language switches to achieve pragmatic ends such as foregrounding, ethnic solidarity, persuasion, and the like. Calques of idiomatic expressions in English are frequent when speaking Spanish, with fewer cases of Spanish calques in English discourse, and numerous loans from English are present. Spanish-speaking immigrants typically switch only at major discourse boundaries such as sentences and paragraphs, usually in response to shifting domains of discourse. Calques from English are rare and English lexical items are usually inserted in nonassimilated fashion. English-speaking students of Spanish switch to English primarily when the demands of a particular communicative task exceed their abilities in Spanish, and they often show less sensitivity to the linguistic abilities and preferences of their interlocutors. Calques from English are common, including combinations that violate Spanish syntactic rules, and unassimilated English words may be freely inserted whenever the Spanish word is unknown. Seldom does a single type of language shifting span all three groups of nominally bilingual speakers. The reasons for these qualitative differences constitute a major research question, as does the related issue of what the bilingual grammars of all three groups of speakers have in common.

There is one bilingual language phenomenon that cuts across the entire spectrum of Spanish-English bilingualism in the United States, namely the insertion of "so" into otherwise all-Spanish discourse (other commonly inserted items include *but, anyway, you know, I mean,* with somewhat different pragmatic distributions). This phenomenon occurs in the speech of a wide variety of Spanish-English bilinguals in the United States—from Spanish-dominant speakers to balanced bilinguals to highly English-dominant semi-speakers of Spanish—and it is found in the speech of many individuals who disavow any conscious use of Anglicisms. It has also been observed in the speech of Spanish speakers born and raised outside of the United States who became bilingual upon learning English in the United States. Of the bilingual speakers who introduce "so" into Spanish discourse, some freely engage in various forms of code switching when speaking informally to other bilingual interlocutors, whereas others seldom or never do so.

"So"-insertion is found in the speech of native speakers of English who are acquiring Spanish as a second language and whose abilities in Spanish range from rudimentary to quite fluent. Typically, second-language speakers of Spanish, regardless of the level of fluency in Spanish, do not engage in code switching of the sort observed among true bilinguals, and those instances of language switching that do occur among second-language speakers are qualitatively different from patterns found among fluent bilinguals. "So"-insertion is one of the few bilingual switching phenomena to occur in both bilingual and second-language speech.[4] It also occurs in other bilingual contact environments, for example in Louisianian French and Canadian French (Roy 1979) and in Japanese-English (Nishimura 1986). I have also observed this phenomenon in the speech of Haitian-English bilinguals, and I have heard anecdotal accounts of "so"-insertion among Basque-English bilinguals in Nevada.

The examples below typify the use of "so" among bilingual Spanish-English speakers of widely varying backgrounds. Most of the examples come from my personal collection of recordings, comprising nearly 1,000 tapes of the Spanish and English usage of bilingual speakers throughout the United States. There are also examples taken from published sources, which coincide qualitatively with the recorded texts.[5] The level of fluency in Spanish and English varies widely among the speakers included in the sample: some are completely fluent in both languages, nearly balanced bilinguals; others speak little English, and still others are Spanish-recessive bilinguals. Some of the speakers are known to frequently engage in code switching, whereas others seldom or never do so. A wide variety of attitudes toward Spanish and English is also represented in the sample, but even speakers with a markedly negative attitude toward English may engage in "so"-insertion. The nonnative speakers of Spanish included in the sample are all native speakers of English, and all learned Spanish after adolescence, in a variety of circumstances that include formal instruction, foreign travel, volunteer and work experience, and marriage. Fluency in Spanish ranges from halting speech to total mastery.

So *él sabrá si se cambia su mente.* (Silva-Corvalán 1994, 173).

Es un poco difícil encontrar trabajo en Los Ángeles y papá no pudo establecerse, so *nos fuimos entonces para México.* (Teschner 1972, 896)

Compramos una casa cerca de la [calle] 45, ¿te dije antes? So *[sou] antes teníamos una pader entera, y mi esposa quería . . .* (Teschner 1972, 896)

So *[sou] este año le dieron cuando . . . le da un scholarship . . .* (Teschner 1972, 896)

Pero los niños creen que la madre es lo único que lo va a ayudar o curar, so *mi mamá estuvo allí aguantándome la mano.* (Mendieta 1999, 144–45)

The following examples derive from my own collection, and the abbreviations indicate ethnic group and speaker code designation:

Había gente que Fidel soltó de la cárcel. So *había de todo.* (Cub-Am. A-50)

. . . la gente de Colombia domina, so, *los coqueros . . .* (Colombia A-5)

Aquí tienen más tecnología, so *un pequeño pueblo . . .* (Costa Rica A-26)

O me das tu caltera o me das tu hima. So *soltó la caltera.* (Puerto Rico A-12)

Mi acento es como los del sur. So *yo tengo otras palabras.* (New Mex. A-22)

Hicia flood *todas las casas,* so *. . . a mí me da mucho miedo.* (New Mex. A-22)

No sé qué va pasar ahorita, so *. . . me pusieron en la cama.* (Anglo A-77)

Pa él su herencia es muy importante so *ende que era pequeño, él me enseñó hablar español.* (New Mex. A-1)

El domingo no trabajas, so *¿vas a descansar el domingo?* (Mex-Am. 41)

Él no jabía ler, so *nos volvimos pa tras.* (Colorado 60-1)

Estaban muy pobres, so *se casaron . . . una boda en la casa.* (Cuba A-4)

Siempre me ha gustado estudiar, so *creo que eso me va a ayudar.* (Puerto Rico A-12)

Inglés es loco, so *yo creo es más fácil aprender español.* (Anglo A-72)

What is the status of "so" in these sentences? Some consider it to be a simple borrowing, although it is not typical to borrow short function words, especially during early stages of language acquisition. In a survey of Anglicisms in U.S. varieties of Spanish, Mendieta (1999, 144–45) considers *so* to be a *"préstamo no adaptado"* (unassimilated loanword). Mendieta (1999, 105, 113) and Teschner (1972, 262–63) consider "anyway" and "but" to also be unassimilated loanwords, and they provide the following examples:

No sé, para proteger la, quizá, la gente, para que no pase más de allí o quizá pasan anyway, so *. . .* (Perth Amboy, NJ)

Se sienten que no quieren ir a la escuela pero [quieren] ir, anyway. (Perth Amboy, NJ)

El muchacho pequeño está enfrente, no, está al frente de la mesa, but . . . (San Antonio)

Es bueno pa un soltero, but *no me pesó tanto pa que . . .* (Teschner 1972, 263)

Pues de la policía no he tenido quejas. Anyway, *yo no he necesitado de ellos todavía.*
    (Teschner 1972, 157)

Anyway, *como en el inglés, hay muchas palabras del pachuco en inglés que se usa.* (Teschner
    1972, 157)

Teschner (1972, 896) indicates that "so" was frequent in his Chicago corpus (collected in the 1960s) and that it was pronounced with Spanish phonetic patterns in unstressed position and with English phonetics in stressed positions. This would suggest that speakers who used this word in stressed contexts recognized it as an English word. Silva-Corvalán (1994, 171), commenting on the use of "so" in the Spanish spoken in Los Angeles, states briefly that it is "a loan that replaces the Spanish conjunction *así que* even in the speech of Group I [Mexican-born] speakers. It is a stable, widespread loan in LA Spanish." Silva-Corvalán does not pursue this matter further, and her study gives no other case where a conjunction or other functional item has been borrowed from English into Spanish, even among highly Spanish-dominant bilinguals.

Unlike code switching between typologically different languages, Spanish-English "so"-insertion makes use of identical syntactic configurations; for this reason, structural integration cannot be used as a criterion to determine the status of "so." Those speakers explicitly queried about the use of "so"—many of whom were not previously aware of introducing this word—were unanimous in asserting that the word is English, and not an established Anglicism such as *lonche, troca,* or *sute.* This self-appraisal, although not sufficient in itself, is a key bit of evidence in determining the status of "so." However, it runs against the notion that frequently repeated L2 items embedded in L1 discourse cease to be code switches and attain the status of borrowings. The matter is put succinctly by Meyers-Scotton (1992, 36): "It is not that a B [borrowed] form *must* recur, it is that a CS [code-switched] form must *not* recur in order to be a CS form" [emphasis in original]. This contradiction between speakers' intuitions and general linguistic practice, combined with the frequently unconscious nature of "so"-insertion, motivates the claim that more than simple code switching is at stake.

If "so" is still behaving as an English word, then its relative high frequency as well as its status as a function word rather than a lexical content item rules it out as a nonce borrowing in the sense of Poplack, Sankoff, and Miller (1988, 1989) and Sankoff, Poplack, and Vanniarajan (1990). The fact that "so"-insertion often occurs in discourse with no other English elements and that "so" is used by individuals who do not normally engage in intrasentential code switching leaves little doubt that the sentences are produced in Spanish with English "so" embedded at appropriate points. In fact, Meyers-Scotton (1992, 22) regards relative frequency as the most important single factor in assigning a matrix language. Similarly, Poplack (1988, 220) ranks frequency and phonological integration as the major factors for distinguishing borrowings from code switches. She also notes that fluent code switching such as that observed in the New York Puerto Rican community is characterized by "an apparent 'unawareness' of the particular alternations between languages (despite a general awareness of using both codes in the discourse), insofar as the switched item is not accompanied by metalinguistic commentary, does not constitute a repetition of an adjacent segment . . . and is used for purposes other than that of conveying untranslatable or ethnically bound items." By these criteria, "so"-insertion could be regarded as momentary code switching. In a detailed study of the insertion of "so" and similar items, I have suggested (Lipski 2005) that Spanish sentences containing English "so" are metalinguistically bracketed by English. "So" "pops through" into Spanish discourse not as the usual nonce borrowing—which temporarily fills a lexical gap—nor as the usual fulcrum for code switching—which signals the transition to the other language. Rather, it reflects the fact that the speaker's bilingual monitoring mechanism—whether activated by a "switch" (e.g., Grosjean 1982; Macnamara and Kushnir 1971; and Paradis 1980) or by some other mechanism of language-tagging (e.g., Sridhar and Sridhar 1980)—is circumscribed by a meta-level based on key English-discourse delimiters such as "so."

This rather lengthy exposition on the use of "so"—which also applies to "you know," "I mean," and other momentary insertions from English—serves as a demonstration that language mixing in a complex bilingual environment such as that found in U.S. Latino communities goes beyond simple classifications and cannot be reduced to simple issues of right or wrong.

Why Do Spanish-English Bilinguals Code-Switch within Sentences?

In bilingual societies, borrowings and loan translations are universal occurrences, as is switching languages as conversational partners or topics shift. Switching languages within the confines of individual sentences—even when the two languages are typologically quite similar—is not as universally observed in bilingual speech communities, as demonstrated by the relative scarcity of intrasentential French-English shifting in Canada. Why, then, do Spanish-English bilinguals in the United States switch languages midsentence so frequently? The simplest answer is, of course, because they can, an answer that provides much of the rationale for code-switched literature and popular music.

More is at stake, however, than the simple demonstration of bilingual prowess, which in most daily circumstances is not called for. Muysken (2000) develops a three-way typology of bilingual language switching: (1) insertion of material from one language into the base structure of another language; (2) alternation between structures of each language; (3) congruent lexicalization of lexical items from each language into shared grammatical structures. In terms of sociolinguistic correlates, Muysken (2000, 8–9) asserts that alternation "is particularly frequent in stable bilingual communities with a tradition of language separation." Insertion "is frequent in colonial settings and recent migrant communities, where there is a considerable asymmetry in speakers' proficiency in the two languages."

Congruent lexicalization "may be particularly associated with second generation migrant groups, dialect/standard and postcreole continua, and bilingual speakers of closely related languages with roughly equal prestige and no tradition of overt language separation." Spanish-English bilinguals in the United States typically form stable bilingual communities, and the tradition of language separation is enforced both by the pragmatics of survival in an English-dominant country and also by statute, particularly in schools and many work environments.

To Muysken, correlates for frequent language alternation—in the U.S. setting, the traditional asymmetry of power, prestige, and acceptance—must be added to the list. Spanish has never been on an equal footing with English in the United States, and in the immigrant communities where sentence-level code switching has been most frequently studied, Spanish has definitely been under siege by the dominant society. Often feeling estranged from their countries of origin—and stigmatized in these same countries by terms such as *pocho* and *nuyorican*—Latinos in the United States have struggled to forge a new identity beyond "life on the hyphen," as Pérez Firmat (1994) has put it.

Interwoven language switching appears to be one manifestation of this identity, a fact viewed with alarm by some observers and with pride by others, as noted by Zentella (1997, 82), who writes that "more NYPRs are referring to 'Spanglish' as a positive way of identifying their switching," and by Ed Morales's (2002, 3) comment that "there is no better metaphor for what a mixed-race culture means than a hybrid language, an informal code . . . Spanglish is what we speak, but it is also who we Latinos are, and how we act, and how we perceive the world." More than any of the individual phenomena discussed in this book, fluent code switching provides the best possible definition of U.S. Spanish in the sense of a broad bilingual community that spans the entire nation.

Notes

1. Whitney (1881) is among the first attempts to systematically define a hierarchy of borrowing types. Further considerations on the typology of borrowing were made by Haugen (1950, 1956), Weinreich (1953), and more recently Romick (1984).

2. For example, Thomason and Kaufman (1988, 14) affirm, basing their claim on numerous examples that "as far as the strictly linguistic possibilities go, any linguistic feature can be transferred from any language to any other language; and implicational universals that depend solely on linguistic properties are similarly valid." They also declare (1988, 35) that "it is the sociolinguistic history of the speakers, and not the structure of their language, that is the primary determinant of the linguistic outcome of language contact. Purely linguistic considerations are relevant but strictly secondary overall."

3. Among the numerous relevant studies dealing with syntactic constraints in other code switching situations are Bautista (1991); Belazi (1991); Bentahila and Davies (1983); Berk-Seligson (1986); Bokamba (1987, 1988, 1989); Brown (1986); Choi (1991); DiSciullo, Muysken, and Singh (1986); Doron (1981); Eliasson (1989, 1991); Ewing (1984); Gibbons (1987); Grosjean and Soares (1986); Joshi (1985); Kamwangamalu (1987); MacSwan (1999); Marasigan (1983); Meyers-Scotton (1992); Muysken (2000); Nartey (1982); Nishimura (1986); Nortier (1990); Pandit (1987); Park (1990); Sankoff, Poplack, and Vanniarajan (1990); Scotton and Okeju (1973); Singh (1981, 1985); Sridhar and Sridhar (1980); and Treffers-Daller (1991).

4. Aaron (2004) also documents this phenomenon for New Mexican Spanish and demonstrates that this item acts as a trigger for code switching. Torres (2002) gives examples from Puerto Rican bilingual discourse.

5. Perhaps two-thirds of the recordings were made by me personally, and the remainder by students working under my supervision. All the data were collected as part of earlier research efforts or as class projects, in either case prior to the decision to study "so"-insertion. Therefore none of the interviews were affected by preestablished expectations as to the data to be elicited. The recorded interviews were chosen randomly from the larger data collection.

References

Aaron, J. 2004. "*So* respetamos un tradición del uno al otro": *So* and *entonces* in New Mexican bilingual discourse. *Spanish in Context* 1(2):161–79.

Academia Norteamericana de la Lengua Española. 1976. Noticias. *Boletín de la Academia Norteamericana de la Lengua Española* 1:95–106.

Acosta-Belén, E. 1975. Spanglish: A case of languages in contact. In *New directions in second language learning, teaching and bilingual education,* ed. M. Burt and H. Dulay, 151–58. Washington, DC: TESOL.

Aguayo, S., and P. W. Fagen. 1988. *Central Americans in Mexico and the United States.* Washington, DC: Hemispheric Migration Project, Center for Immigration Policy and Refugee Assistance, Georgetown University.

Agüero Chaves, A. 1960a. *El español en América.* San José: Universidad de Costa Rica.

————. 1960b. *El español en Costa Rica.* San José: Universidad de Costa Rica.

Aguilar Paz, J. 1970. *Topónimos y regionalismos indígenas.* Tegucigalpa: n.p.

————. 1981. *El refranero hondureño.* Tegucigalpa: Guaymuras.

Aguirre, A. 1978. *An experimental sociolinguistic analysis of Chicano bilingualism.* San Francisco: R & E Associates.

————. 1981. Toward an index of acceptability for code alternation: An experimental analysis. *Aztlán* 11:297–322.

————, ed. 1985. Language in the Chicano speech community. *International Journal of the Sociology of Language,* 53 [special issue].

Ajubita, M. L. 1943. Language in social relations with special references to the Mexican-American problem. MA thesis, Tulane University.

Alba, O. 1979. Análisis fonológico de /r/ y /l/ implosivas en un dialecto rural dominicano. *Boletín de la Academia Puertorriqueña de la Lengua Española* 7:1–18.

————. 1982. Función del acento en el proceso de elisión de la /s/ en la República Dominicana. In, *El español del Caribe,* ed. O. Alba, 15–26. Santiago de los Caballeros: Universidad Católica Madre y Maestra.

————, ed. 1982. *El español del Caribe.* Santiago de los Caballeros: Universidad Católica Madre y Maestra.

————. 1988. Estudio sociolingüístico de la variación de las líquidas finales de palabra en el español cibaeño. In *Studies in Caribbean Spanish dialectology,* ed. R. Hammond and M. Resnick, 1–12. Washington, DC: Georgetown University Press.

————. 1990a. *Estudios sobre el español dominicano.* Santiago de los Caballeros: Universidad Católica Madre y Maestra.

————. 1990b. *Variación fonética y diversidad social en el español dominicano de Santiago.* Santiago de los Caballeros: Universidad Católica Madre y Maestra.

Almendros, N. 1958. Estudio fonético del español en Cuba: región occidental. *Boletín de la Academia Cubana de la Lengua* 7:138–76.

Alonso, A. 1930. Problemas de dialectología hispanoamericana. *Biblioteca de Dialectología Hispanoamericana* I:315–469.

Alonso, G., and A. L. Fernández, eds. 1977. *Antología de lingüística cubana.* Havana: Editorial de Ciencias Sociales.

Alonso-Lyrintzis, D. 1996. *Entre mundos: an integrated approach for the native speaker.* Upper Saddle River, NJ: Prentice-Hall.

Altieri de Barreto, C. 1973. *El léxico de la delincuencia en Puerto Rico.* Río Piedras: Editorial Universitaria.

Alvar, M. 1980. Encuestas fonéticas en el suroccidente de Guatemala. *Lingüística Española Actual* 2:245–87.

Alvar, M., ed. 1981. *I simposio internacional de lengua española* (1978). Las Palmas: Excmo. Cabildo Insular.

————. 1996. *Manual de dialectología hispánica: el español de América.* Barcelona: Ariel.

Alvarez, C. 1989. Code-switching in narrative performance: A Puerto Rican speech community in New York. In *English across cultures, cultures across English,* ed. O. García and R. Otheguy, 373–86. Berlin: Mouton de Gruyter.

Alvarez Estévez, R. 1986. *La emigración cubana en Estados Unidos 1868–1878.* Havana: Editorial de Ciencias Sociales.

Alvarez Nazario, M. 1957. *El arcaísmo vulgar en el español de Puerto Rico.* Mayagüez: Ed. del autor.

————. 1972. *La herencia lingüística de Canarias en Puerto Rico.* San Juan: Instituto de Cultura Puertorriqueña.

————. 1981. Relaciones histórico-dialectales entre Puerto Rico y Canarias. Ed. Alvar, 289–310.

————. 1982. *Orígenes y desarrollo del español en Puerto Rico (siglos XVI y XVII).* Río Piedras: Editorial Universitaria.

————. 1990. *El habla campesina del país.* Río Piedras: Editorial de la Universidad de Puerto Rico.

————. 1991. *Historia de la lengua española en Puerto Rico.* San Juan: Academia Puertorriqueña de la Lengua Española.

Alzola, C. T. 1965. Hablar popular cubana. *Revista de Dialectología y Tradiciones Populares* 23:358–69.

Amastae, J. 1989. The intersection of *s*-aspiration/deletion and spirantization in Honduran Spanish. *Language Variation and Change* 1:169–83.

Amastae, J., and L. Elías-Olivares, eds. 1982. *Spanish in the United States: Sociolinguistic aspects.* Cambridge: Cambridge University Press.

American Association of Teachers of Spanish and Portuguese (AATSP). 1970. *Teaching Spanish in school and college to native speakers of Spanish.* Wichita, KS: AATSP.

Anderson, T. 1971. *Matanza: El Salvador's communist revolt of 1932.* Lincoln: University of Nebraska Press.

————. 1981. *The war of the dispossessed: Honduras and El Salvador, 1969.* Lincoln: University of Nebraska Press.

Anisman, P. 1975. Some aspects of code-switching in New York Puerto Rican English. *Bilingual Review* 2:56–85.

Arellano, J. E. 1980. *El español en Nicaragua: Bibliografía fundamental y análitica (1837–1980).* Managua: Universidad Nacional Autónoma de Nicaragua, Departamento de Español.

Arellano, J. E., ed. 1992. *El español de Nicaragua.* Managua: Instituto Nicaraguense de Cultura Popular.

Argueta, M. 1981. *Caperucita en la zona roja.* San José: Editorial Costa Rica.

Armas, D. 1971. *Diccionario de la expresión popular guatemalteca.* Guatemala City: Tipografía Nacional. 2nd ed. in 1982: Editorial Piedra Santa, Guatemala.

Armistead, S. 1978. Romances tradicionales entre los hispanohablantes del estado de Luisiana. *Nueva Revista de Filología Hispánica* 27:39–56.

————. 1979. Hispanic traditional poetry in Louisiana. In *El romancero hoy: nuevas fronteras,* ed. A. Sánchez Romeralo, 147–58. Madrid: Cátedra Seminario Menéndez Pidal.

————. 1981a. Hispanic folk literature among the *isleños.* In *Perspectives on ethnicity in New Orleans,* ed. J. Cooke and M. Blanton, 21–31. New Orleans: University of New Orleans.

————. 1981b. Spanish language and folklore in Louisiana. *La Corónica* 9(2):187–89.

————. 1982. Un corrido de la muerte de Madero cantado en Luisiana. *Anuario de Letras* 20:379–87.

————. 1983a. Más romances de Luisiana. *Nueva Revista de Filología Hispánica* 32:41–54.

————. 1983b. Spanish riddles from St. Bernard Parish. *Louisiana Folklore Miscellany* 5(3):1–8.

————. 1985. Adivinanzas españolas de Luisiana. In *Homenaje a Alvaro Galmés de Fuentes,* ed. D. Alonso, D. García, and R. Lapesa, t. II:251–62. Madrid: Gredos.

————. 1992. *The Spanish tradition in Louisiana I: Isleño folkliterature.* Newark, Delaware: Juan de la Cuesta.

————. n.d. *Three Spanish dialects in Louisiana.* University of California, Davis: n.p.

Armistead, S., and H. Gregory. 1986. French loan words in the Spanish dialect of Sabine and Natchitoches Parishes. *Louisiana Folklife* 10:21–30.

Arroyo, W., and S. Eth. 1985. Children traumatized by Central American warfare. In *Posttraumatic stress disorder in children,* ed. S. Eth and R. Pynoos, 103–20. Washington, DC: American Psychiatric Press.

Arroyo S., and V. Manuel. 1971. *El habla popular en la literatura costarricense.* San José: Universidad de Costa Rica.

Attinasi, J. 1978. Language policy and the Puerto Rican community. *Bilingual Review/Revista Bilingüe* 5(1–2):1–40.

_____. 1979. Language attitudes in New York Puerto Rican community. In *Ethnoperspectives in bilingual education research,* ed. R. Padilla, 408–61. Ypsilanti: Bilingual Review Press.

Avera, H. 2001. *Spanglish: a course in communication celebrating similarity/un curso de comunicación celebrando similaridad.* Raleigh, NC: Spanglish Unlimited, Inc.

Bachiller y Morales, A. 1883. Desfiguración a que está expuesto el idioma castellano al contacto y mezcla de razas. *Revista de Cuba* 14:97–104.

Báez Evertsz, F., and F. D'Oleo Ramírez. 1985. *La emigración de dominicanos a Estados Unidos: determinantes socio-económicos y consecuencias.* Santo Domingo: Fundación Friedrich Ebert.

Bailey, B. 2000. Language and negotiation of racial/ethnic identity among Dominican Americans. *Language in Society* 29:555–82.

_____. 2002. *Language, Race, and Negotiation of Identity: A Study of Dominican Americans.* New York: LFB Scholarly Publishing.

Baker, P. 1953. *Español para los hispanos.* Dallas: B. Upshaw. Subsequent printings by National Textbook Company, Skokie, IL.

Bakker, P. 1996. *"A Language of Our Own": The Genesis of Michif—the Mixed Cree-French language of the Canadian Métis.* Oxford: Oxford University Press.

Bancroft, H. H. 1889. *History of Arizona and New Mexico.* Albuquerque: Horn and Wallace, facsimile edition, 1962.

Bannon, J. F. 1974. *The Spanish borderlands frontier 1513–1821.* Albuquerque: University of New Mexico Press.

Barberena, S. 1920. *Quicheísmos.* San Salvador: Tipografía "La Luz."

Barker, G. 1975. Pachuco: an American-Spanish argot and its social function in Tucson, Arizona. Ed. Hernández-Chávez et al., 183–201. Originally published in the *University of Arizona Social Sciences Bulletin* 18 (1950), 1–38.

Barker, M. 1966. *Español para el bilingüe.* Skokie, IL: National Textbook Company.

Barkin, F. 1976. Language switching in Chicano Spanish: linguistic norm awareness. *LEKTOS: interdisciplinary working papers in language sciences,* special issue, 46–64.

_____. 1978a. Language switching in Chicano Spanish: a multifaceted phenomenon. *SWALLOW VI,* ed. H. Key, G. McCullough, and J. Sawyer, 1–10. Long Beach: California State University.

_____. 1978b. Loanshifts: an example of multilevel interference. *SWALLOW VII,* ed. Anthony Lozano, 1–10. Boulder: University of Colorado.

Barnach-Calbó, E. 1980. *La lengua española en Estados Unidos.* Madrid: Oficina de Educación Iberoamericana.

Barreto, M. 1893. *Vicios de nuestro lenguaje.* León, Nicaragua: Tipografía "J. Hernández."

Barrett, R. 2006. Language ideology and racial inequality: competing functions of Spanish in an Anglo-owned Mexican restaurant. *Language in Society* 35:163–204.

Batres Jáuregui, A. 1892. *Vicios del lenguaje y provincialismos de Guatemala.* Guatemala: Encuadernación y Tipografía Nacional.

Baugh, L. 1933. A study of pre-school vocabulary of Spanish-speaking children. MA thesis, University of Texas.

Baumel-Schreffler, S. 1989. Una perspectiva del voseo: una comparación de dos naciones voseantes, Guatemala y El Salvador. MA thesis, University of Houston.

_____. 1994. Second-person singular pronoun options in the speech of Salvadorans in Houston, Texas. *Southwest Journal of Linguistics* 13:101–19 [pub. 1998].

_____. 1995. The *voseo:* second person singular pronouns in Guatemalan speech. *Language Quarterly* 33(1–2):33–44.

Bautista, M. L. 1991. Code-switching studies in the Philippines. *International Journal of the Sociology of Language* 88:19–32.

Bayley, R., and L. Pease-Álvarez. 1997. Null pronoun variation in Mexican-descent children's narrative discourse. *Language Variation and Change* 9:349–71.

Beardsley, T., Jr. 1972. Influencias angloamericanas en el español de Cayo Hueso. *Exilio* 6:87–100.

_____. 1976. Bibliografía preliminar de estudios sobre el español en los Estados Unidos. *Boletín de la Academia Norteamericana de la Lengua Española* 1:49–73.

Beck, M. 1970. The English influence on the Spanish spoken in Bowling Green, Ohio. MA thesis, Bowling Green State University.

Belazi, H. 1991. Multilingualism in Tunisia and French/Arabic code switching among educated Tunisian bilinguals. PhD dissertation, Cornell University.

Belazi, H., E. Rubin, and A. J. Toribio. 1994. Code switching and X-bar theory: the Functional Head Constraint. *Linguistic Inquiry* 25:221–37.

Bello, A. 1903. *Gramática de la lengua castellana.* Paris: R. Roger y F. Chervoviz.

Beltramo, A., and A. de Porcel. 1975. Some lexical characteristics of San Jose Spanish. Ed. Hernández-Chávez et al., 122–37.

Benavides, C. 1985. El dialecto español de Samaná. *Anuario de la Academia de Ciencias de la República Dominicana* 9:297–342.

Bentahila, A., and E. Davies. 1983. The syntax of Arabic-French code-switching. *Lingua* 59:301–30.

Berendt, K. 1874. *Palabras y modismos de la lengua castellana según se habla en Nicaragua.* Managua: n.p.

Bergen, J. 1986. Spanish language shift and maintenance among Albuquerque police officers. In *Mexican-American language: usage, attitudes, maintenance, instruction, and policy.* Brownsville, Texas: Pan American University at Brownsville, Rio Grande Series in Language and Linguistics No. 1, ed. G. Green and J. Ornstein-Galicia, 71–90.

Bergen, J., ed. 1990. *Spanish in the United States: sociolinguistic issues.* Washington, DC: Georgetown University Press.

Berk-Seligson, S. 1986. Linguistic constraints on intra-sentential code-switching: A study of Spanish/Hebrew bilingualism. *Language in Society* 15:313–48.

Betanzos Palacios, O. 2001. El español en Estados Unidos: problemas y logros. Presented at the II Congreso de la Lengua Española, Valladolid, Spain.

Bills, G. 1989. The U.S. Census of 1980 and Spanish in the Southwest. *International Journal of the Sociology of Language* 79:11–28.

_____. 1997a. New Mexico Spanish: demise of the earliest European variety in the United States. *American Speech* 72:154–71.

_____. 1997b. Language shift, linguistic variation, and teaching Spanish to native speakers in the United States. Ed. Colombi and Alarcón, 262–82.

Bills, G., ed. 1974. *Southwest areal linguistics.* San Diego, CA: Institute for Cultural Pluralism, San Diego State University.

Bills, G., E. Hernández-Chávez, and A. Hudson. 1995. The geography of language shift: Distance from the Mexican border and Spanish language claiming in the southwestern United States. *International Journal of the Sociology of Language* 114:9–27.

———. 2000. Spanish home language use and English proficiency as differential measures of language maintenance and shift. *Southwest Journal of Linguistics* 19:11–27.

Bills, G., and J. Ornstein. 1976. Linguistic diversity in Southwest Spanish. Ed. Bowen and Ornstein, 4–16.

Bills, G., and N. Vigil. 1999. Ashes to ashes: the historical basis for dialect variation in New Mexican Spanish. *Romance Philology* 53:43–67.

———. In press. *The Spanish language in New Mexico and southern Colorado: a linguistic atlas.* Albuquerque, NM: University of New Mexico Press.

Bixler-Márquez, D., G. Green, and J. Ornstein, eds. 1989. *Mexican-American Spanish in its societal and cultural contexts.* Brownsville, TX: University of Texas Pan American at Brownsville.

Blackman, R. 1940. The language handicap of Spanish-American children. MA thesis, University of Arizona.

Blansitt, E., and R. Teschner, eds. 1980. *Festschrift for Jacob Ornstein.* Rowley, MA: Newbury House.

Bogen, E. 1987. *Immigration in New York.* New York: Praeger.

Boggs, R. 1954. Phonetics of words borrowed from English by New Mexico Spanish. *Homenaje a Fritz Krüger,* vol. 2, pp. 305–12. Mendoza: Universidad Nacional de Cuyo.

Bohannan, C. D. 1928. *Report on survy of Chacon, New Mexico community.* Prepared under the auspices of the Presbyterian Church in the U.S.A.

Bokamba, E. 1987. Are there syntactic constraints on code-mixing? In *Variation in language: NWAV-XV at Stanford,* ed. K. Denning et al., 35–51. Stanford: Linguistics Department, Stanford University.

———. 1988. Code-mixing, language variation, and linguistic theory. *Lingua* 76:21–62.

———. 1989. Are there syntactic constraints on code-mixing? *World Englishes* 8:277–93.

Boswell, T. 1984. The migration and distribution of Cubans and Puerto Ricans living in the United States. *Journal of Geography* 83(2):65–72.

Boswell, T., and J. Curtis. 1983. *The Cuban-American experience: culture, images and perspectives.* New Jersey: Rowman and Allanheld.

Bourke, J. 1896. Notes on the language and folk usage of the Rio Grande Valley. *Journal of American Folklore* 9:81–116.

Bowen, J. D. 1952. The Spanish of San Antonito, New Mexico. PhD dissertation, University of New Mexico.

———. 1975. Adaptation of English borrowing. Ed. Hernández-Chávez et al., 115–21.

———. 1976. Structural analysis of the verb system in New Mexican Spanish. In *Studies in Southwest Spanish.* Rowley, MA: Newbury House, ed. J. Bowen and J. Ornstein, 93–124.

Bowen, J. D., and J. Ornstein, eds. 1976. *Studies in Southwest Spanish.* Rowley, MA: Newbury House.

Braddy, H. 1953. Narcotic argot along the Mexican border. *American Speech* 30: 84–90.

———. 1956. Smugglers argot in the Southwest. *American Speech* 21:96–101.

———. 1965. The Pachucos and their argot. *Southern Folklore Quarterly* 24:255–71.

Bradley, T. 2006. Spanish rhotics and Dominican hypercorrect /s/. *Probus* 18(1):1–33.

Bray, D. 1984. Economic development: the middle class and international migration in the Dominican Republic. *International Migration Review* 18(2):217–36.

Brisk, M. E. 1972. The Spanish syntax of the pre-school Spanish American: the case of New Mexico five-year-old children. PhD dissertation, University of New Mexico.

Brito, R. 1930. *Diccionario de criollismos.* San Francisco de Macorís: Imprenta "ABC."

Brown, B. 1986. Cajun/English code-switching: a test of formal models. In *Diversity and diachrony,* ed. D. Sankoff, 399–406. Amsterdam: John Benjamins.

Brown, D. 1989. El habla juvenil de Sonora, México: la fonética de 32 jóvenes. *Nueva Revista de Filología Hispánica* 37:43–82.

Brown, E. 2004. The Reduction of Syllable-Initial /s/ in the Spanish of New Mexico and Southern Colorado: A Usage-Based Approach. PhD Dissertation, University of New Mexico.

———. 2005a. New Mexican Spanish: insight into the variable reduction of "le ehe inicial" (/s-/). *Hispania* 88:813–24.

———. 2005b. Syllable-initial /s/ in traditional New Mexican Spanish: linguistic factors favoring reduction *ahina. Southwest Journal of Linguistics* 24:1–18.

Brown, E. L., and R. Torres Cacoullos. 2002. ¿Qué le vamo(h) a(h)er?: Taking the syllable out of Spanish /s/ reduction. In *University of Pennsylvania Working Papers in Linguistics: Papers from NWAV 30,* ed. D. Johnson and T. Sanchez, 17–32. Philadelphia: University of Pennsylvania Press.

———. 2003. Spanish /s/: A different story from beginning (initial) to end (final). *A Romance perspective in language knowledge and use.* In *Selected papers from the 31st linguistic symposium of Romance languages (LSRL),* ed. R. Núñez-Cedeño, L. López, and R. Cameron. Amsterdam: John Benjamins.

Bueno, R. 1978. *Cambios semánticos en la expresión guatemalteca.* Guatemala: Universidad de San Carlos, Facultad de Humanidades.

Buitrago Morales, F. 1940. Vocabulario de pinolerismos. *Lo que he visto al pasar,* 383–486. León: Impr. Hospicio.

Bullock, B., and A. J. Toribio. 2006. Dominican Spanish in the United States: The language and its speakers. In *Increasing language diversity in linguistic courses: practical approaches and materials,* ed. M. DiPaolo and A. Spears. Columbus: Ohio State University.

Burunat, S., and E. Starcevic. 1983. *El español y su estructura: lectura y escritura para bilingües.* Fort Worth: Harcourt, Brace, Jovanovich.

Byrne, H. 1996. *El Salvador's civil war: a study of revolution.* Boulder, CO and London: Lynne Rienner Publishers.

Cabib, C. 1985. Salvadorans in the United States: A challenge to immigration and refugee policy. MA thesis, University of Florida.

Callicut, L. 1934. Word difficulties of Mexican and non-Mexican children. MA thesis, University of Texas.

Cameron, R. 1993. Ambiguous agreement, functional compensation, and nonspecific *tú* in the Spanish of San Juan, Puerto Rico and Madrid, Spain. *Language Variation and Change* 5:305–34.

———. 1996. A community-based test of a linguistic hypothesis. *Language in Society* 25:61–111.

———. 2005. Aging and gendering. *Language in Society* 34:23–61.

Canfield, D. L. 1951a. Guatemalan *rr* and *s:* a recapitulation of Old Spanish sibilant gradation. *Florida State University Studies in Modern Languages and Literatures* 3:49–51.

———. 1951b. Tampa Spanish: three characters in search of a pronunciation. *Modern Language Journal* 35:42–44.

———. 1953. Andalucismos en la pronunciación salvadoreña. *Hispania* 36:32–33.

———. 1960. Observaciones sobre el español salvadoreño. *Filología* 6:29–76.

———. 1976. Rasgos fonológicos del castellano en los Estados Unidos. *Boletín de la Academia Norteamericana de la Lengua Española* 1:17–23.

———. 1981. *Spanish pronunciation in the Americas.* Chicago: University of Chicago Press.

Cárdenas, D. 1970. *Dominant Spanish dialects spoken in the United States.* Washington, DC: ERIC Clearinghouse for Linguistics/Center for Applied Linguistics.

———. 1975. Mexican Spanish. Ed. Hernández-Chávez et al., 1–5.

Casiano Montañez, L. 1975. *La pronunciación de los puertorriqueños en Nueva York.* Bogotá: Ediciones Tercer Mundo.

Castañeda Paganini, R. 1959. *La cultura tolteca-pipil de Guatemala.* Guatemala: Editorial del Ministerio de Educación Pública "José de Pineda Ibarra."

Castel, A. 1974. L'effritement de la langue et de la culture espagnoles à Porto Rico. PhD dissertation, Université de Paris-Sorbonne.

Castellanos, Sister Mary C. 1968. English lexical and phonological influences in the Spanish of Cuban refugees in the Washington metropolitan area. MA thesis, Georgetown University.

Castellón, H. A. 1939. *Diccionario de nicaraguanismos.* Managua: Talleres Nacionales.

Castrillo Gámez, M. 1966. *Vocabulario de voces nicaragüenses y artículos históricos.* Managua: Imprenta Nacional.

Castro, M. 1985. Dominican journey: patterns, context, and consequences of migration from the Dominican Republic to the United States. PhD dissertation, University of North Carolina.

Castro-Mitchell, A. 1991. Usted porque no lo conozco o porque lo quiero mucho? The semantic functions of *usted* in Honduran Spanish. PhD dissertation, University of Pittsburgh.

Castro, X. 1996. El espanglish en Internet y en la computación/informática. Presented at the Internet Congress organized by Novell (Madrid, June 12–14 de junio, 1996).

Chaney, E. 1985. *Migration from the Caribbean region: determinants and effects of current movement.* Washington, DC: Occasional Paper Series, Georgetown University and the Intergovernmental Committee for Migration.

Chang-Rodríguez, E. 1976. Palabras del director del *Boletín. Boletín de la Academia Norteamericana de la Lengua Española* 1:5–6.

Chart, I. 1954. The *voseo* and *tuteo* in America. *Modern Language Forum* 28:17–24.

Chaston, J. 1991. Imperfect progressive usage patterns in the speech of Mexican American bilinguals from Texas. *Sociolinguistics of the Spanish-speaking world,* ed. C. Klee and L. Ramos-García, 299–311. Tempe: Bilingual Review Press.

Chávez, E. 1988. Sex differences in language shift. *Southwest Journal of Linguistics* 8:3–14.

_____. 1993. Gender differentiation in minority language loss among Hispanic children in northern New Mexico. *Southwest Journal of Linguistics* 12:39–53.

Cherry, A. 1966. *Tampa Spanish slang with English translation.* Tampa: Lamplight Press.

Choi, J. O. 1991. Korean-English code-switching: Switch-alpha and linguistic contraints. *Linguistics* 29:877–902.

Christian, C., Jr. 1971. Introduction to *Español para el bilingüe* by Marie Esman Barker. Skokie: National Textbook Company.

Christian, J. and C. Christian, Jr. 1966. Spanish language and culture in the Southwest. *Language loyalty in the United States,* ed. J. Fishman, 280–317. The Hague: Mouton.

Claudel, C. 1945. Spanish folktales from Delacroix, Louisiana. *Journal of American Folklore* 58:209–24.

Clegg, H. 1967. Análisis espectrográfico de los fonemas /a e o/ en un idiolecto de La Habana. MA thesis, University of Texas.

Coan, M. 1927. The language difficulty in measuring the intelligence of Spanish-American students. MA thesis, University of New Mexico.

Cobos, R. 1983. *A dictionary of New Mexico and Southern Colorado Spanish.* Santa Fe: Museum of New Mexico Press.

Cohen, A. 1976. The English and Spanish grammar of Chicano primary school students. Ed. Bowen and Ornstein, 125–64.

Coles, F. 1991a. Social and linguistic correlates to language death: research from the *Isleño* dialect of Spanish. PhD dissertation, University of Texas, Austin.

_____. 1991b. The *isleño* dialect of Spanish: language maintenance strategies. In *Sociolinguistics of the Spanish-speaking world: Iberia, Latin America, United States,* ed. C. Klee and L. Ramos-García, 312–28. Tempe: Bilingual Press/Editorial Bilingüe.

_____. 1993. Language maintenance institutions of the *isleño* dialect. In *Spanish in the United States: linguistic contact and diversity,* ed. A. Roca and J. Lipski, 121–33. Berlin: Mouton de Gruyter.

_____. 1999. *Isleño Spanish.* Munich: LINCOM Europa.

Colombi, M. C., and F. X. Alarcón, eds. 1997. *La enseñanza del español a hispanohablantes: praxis y teoría.* Boston and New York: Houghton Mifflin.

Coltharp, L. 1965. *The tongue of the tirilones: a linguistic study of a criminal argot.* University, AL: University of Alabama Press.

Conway, T. F. 1942. The bilingual problem in the schools of New Mexico. *Alianza* 36 (Feb.):13, 17.

Corpus Christi Independent School District. 1975. *Speaking Spanish for native speaker: teaching guide.* Corpus Christi, TX: CCISD.

Costa Sánchez, M. 1976–77. Descripción de particularidades acústico-articulatorias de algunos sonidos consonánticos del español hablado en Cuba. *Islas* 55–56, 3–42.

Costa Sánchez, M., and S. Carrera Gómez. 1980a. La vibrante simple. La vocal anaptíctica. *Islas* 65:15–42.

———. 1980b. Algunas características acústico-articulatorias de la vibrante múltiple en el español de Cuba. *Islas* 65:99–114.

Cotton, E., and J. Sharp. 1988. *Spanish in the Americas.* Washington, DC: Georgetown University Press.

Coulmas, F., ed. 1990. Spanish in the USA: New quandries and prospects. *International Journal of the Sociology of Language,* 84 [special issue].

Coupal, L., P. I. Germosen, and M. Jiménez Sabater. 1988. La /-r/ y la /-l/ en la costa norte dominicana: nuevos aportes para la delimitación del subdialecto cibaeño. *Anuario de Lingüística Hispánica* (Valladolid) 4:43–79.

Covington, J. 1980. Ybor City: A Cuban enclave in Tampa. Ed. Cortés, 85–90.

Craddock, Jerry. 1973. Spanish in North America. *Current trends in linguistics* v. 10, ed. Thomas Sebeok, 305–39, 467–501. The Hague: Mouton.

———. 1976. Lexical analysis of southwest Spanish. Ed. Bowen and Ornstein, 45–70.

Cruz, B. 1996. *Cubanamericanisms.* Miami Beach: s.n.

Cruz, B., and Teck, B. 1998. *The official Spanglish dictionary.* New York: Fireside.

Cuéllar [Varela], B. 1971. Observaciones sobre la "rr" velar y la "y" africada en Cuba. *Español Actual* 20:18–20.

———. 1974. La influencia del inglés en los cubanos de Miami y Nueva Orleans. *Español Actual* 26:16–25.

Cuervo, R. J. 1885. *Apuntaciones críticas sobre el lenguaje bogotano.* 4th ed. Chartres: Imprenta de Durand.

Davis, W. W. H. 1857. *El Gringo: New Mexico and her people.* New York: Harper.

Dearholt, D., and G. Valdés-Fallis. 1978. Toward a probablistic automata model of some aspects of code-switching. *Language in Society* 7:411–19.

Decker, B. 1952. Phonology of the Puerto Rican Spanish of Lorain, Ohio: a study in the environmental displacement of a dialect. MA thesis, Ohio State University.

Deive, C. E. 1978. *El indio, el negro y la vida tradicional dominicana.* Santo Domingo: Museo del Hombre Dominicano.

———. 1986. *Diccionario de dominicanismos.* 2nd ed. Santo Domingo: Politecnia.

Del Castillo, J., and C. Mitchell, eds. 1987. *La inmigración dominicana en los Estados Unidos.* Santo Domingo: CENAPEC.

De la Portilla, M., and B. Varela. 1979. *Mejora tu español: lectura y redacción para bilingües.* New York: Regents Publishing Company.

De la Puente-Schubeck, E. 1991. La pérdida del modo subjuntivo en el español chicano de Nuevo México. PhD dissertation, University of New Mexico.

DeLeon, F. 1993. *Español: material para el hispano.* New York: McGraw Hill.

Delli Sante, A. 1996. *Nightmare or reality: Guatemala in the 1980s.* Amsterdam: Thela.

Denning, G. 1986. Meaning and placement of standard and Kansas Spanish adjectives. Ed. G. Green and J. Ornstein-Galicia, 43–53.

Díaz Díaz, B. 1987. *Latinismo y español dominicano.* Santo Domingo: Editora Universitaria.

Díaz, R. 1942. A vocabulary of California Spanish words of English origin used by first generation Spaniards of California. PhD dissertation, Stanford University.

Dihigo, J. 1928. *Léxico cubano.* Havana: Imprenta "El Siglo XX."

Dillard, J. L. 1962. Sobre algunos fonemas puertorriqueños. *Nueva Revista de Filología Hispánica* 16:422–24.

DiPietro, R. 1978. Code-switching as a verbal strategy among bilinguals. Ed. Paradis, 275–82.

DiSciullo, A., P. Muysken, and R. Singh. 1986. Government and code-mixing. *Journal of Linguistics* 22:1–24.

Domínguez, D. 1974. A theoretical model for classifying dialectal variations of oral New Mexico Spanish. PhD dissertation, University of New Mexico.

Dorian, N. 1977. The problem of the semi-speaker in language death. *International Journal of the Sociology of Language* 12:23–32.

———. 1981. *Language death: the life cycle of a Scottish Gaelic dialect.* Philadelphia: University of Pennsylvania.

Doron, E. 1981. On a formal model of code-switching. *Texas Linguistic Forum* 22:35–59.

Duany, J., ed. 1990. *Los dominicanos en Puerto Rico: migración en la semi-periferia.* Río Piedras: Ediciones Huracán.

Dubsky, J. 1977. *Observaciones sobre el léxico santiaguero.* Prague: Univerzita Karlova.

Durán, F. 1965. A compilation of Anglicisms in the Peñasco area. MA thesis, New Mexico Highlands University.

Durán, R., ed. 1981. *Latino Language and communicative behavior.* Norwood, NJ: ABLEX.

Dussias, P. 2003. Spanish-English code mixing at the Auxiliary Phrase: evidence from eye-movement data. *Revista Internacional de Lingüística Iberoamericana* 1(2):7–34.

Elías-Olivares, L., ed. 1983. *Spanish in the U.S. setting: beyond the southwest.* Rosslyn, VA: National Clearinghouse for Bilingual Education.

Elías-Olivares, L., E. Leone, R. Cisneros, and J. Gutiérrez, eds. 1985. *Spanish language use and public life in the USA.* The Hague: Mouton.

Eliasson, S. 1989. English-Maori language contact: code-switching and the free morpheme constraint. *Reports from Uppsala University Department of Linguistics* 18:1–28.

———. 1991. Models and constraints in code-switching theory. *Papers for the workshop on constraints, conditions and models,* 17–50. Strasbourg: European Science Foundation.

Entralgo, El. 1941. *Apuntes caracteriológicos sobre el léxico cubano.* Havana: Molina y Compañía.

Escamilla, P. 1982. A sociolinguistic study of modal selection among Mexican-American college students in Texas. PhD dissertation, University of Texas at Austin.

Espina Pérez, D. 1972. *Diccionario de cubanismos.* Barcelona: Imp. M. Pareja.

Espinosa, A. 1909. Studies in New Mexico Spanish, part 1: phonology. *Bulletin of the University of New Mexico* 1:47–162. Translated and printed as "Estudios sobre el español de Nuevo Méjico" in the *Biblioteca de Dialectología Hispanoamericana* 1 (1930): 19–313.

———. 1911. *The Spanish language in New Mexico and southern Colorado.* Santa Fe: New Mexican Publishing Company.

———. 1911–12. Studies in New Mexican Spanish part 2: morphology. *Revue de Dialectologie Romane* 3:241–56; 4:251–86; 5:142–72.

———. 1913. Nombres de bautismo nuevomejicanos. *Revue de Dialectologie Romane* 5:356–76.

———. 1914–15. Studies in New Mexican Spanish part 3: the English elements. *Revue de Dialectologie Romane* 6:241–317.

———. 1917. Speech mixture in New Mexico: the influence of the English language on New Mexican Spanish. *The Pacific Ocean in history,* ed. H. M. Stephens and H. Bolton, 408–28. New York: Macmillan. Also in, ed. Hernández-Chávez et al., 99–114.

———. 1925. Syllabic consonants in New Mexican Spanish. *Language* 1:109–18.

———. 1927–8. The language of the cuentos populares españoles. *Language* 3:188–98; 4:18–27, 111–19.

———. 1930. *Estudios sobre el español de Nuevo Méjico; parte I: fonética.* Trans. Amado Alonso and Angel Rosenblat. Buenos Aires: Biblioteca de Dialectología Hispanoamericana 1:19–313.

———. 1934. El desarrollo fonético de las dos palabras "todo" "y" en la frase "con todo y" + sustantivo en el español de Nuevo México. *Investigaciones Lingüísticas* 2:195–99.

———. 1946. *Estudios sobre el español de Nuevo Méjico, parte II: morfología.* Biblioteca de Dialectología Hispanoamericana 2:1–102.

———. 1975. Speech mixture in New Mexico: the influence of the English language on New Mexican Spanish. Ed. Hernández-Chávez et al., 99–114.

Espinosa, A., Jr. 1975. Problemas lexicográficos del español del sudoeste. Ed. Hernández-Chávez et al., 13–16.

Espinosa, C. 1935. *La evolución fonética de la lengua castellana en Cuba.* Havana: Imp. Oscar Echevarría.

Ewing, A. 1984. Polish-English code-switching: a clue to constituent structure and processing mechanisms. *CLS* (Proceedings of the Chicago Linguistics Society) 20:52–64.

Fairclough, M. 2003. El (denominado) *Spanglish* en los Estados Unidos. *Revista Internacional de Lingüística Iberoamericana* 1(2):185–204.

Farías Caro, O., and A. T. Garita Salas. 1985. *Características demográficas, económicas y sociales de los inmigrantes centroamericanos por país de origen.* Washington, DC: Georgetown University, Hemispheric Migration Project.

Fernández, G., and L. Narváez. 1987. Social and political marginality among Mariel Cubans. Ed. Fernández et al., 102–23.

Fernández, M. 1987. Spanish language use among Cuban Americans of the first and second generation in West New York. MS thesis, City College of New York, School of Education.

Fernández, R. 1981. *La vida es un special.* Miami: Ediciones Universal.

Fernández, R. 1980. Some social constraints in the code-switching patterns in the speech of Mexican-Americans in New Mexico. PhD dissertation, University of New Mexico.

_____. 1990. Actitudes hacia los cambios de códigos en Nuevo México: reacciones de un sujeto a ejemplos de su habla. Ed. Bergen, 49–58.

Ferris, E. 1987. *The Central American refugees.* New York: Praeger.

Fickinger, P. 1930. A study of certain phases of the language problem of Spanish-American children. MA thesis, University of New Mexico.

Figueroa, E. 1971. Habla y folklore en Ponce. *Revista de Estudios Hispánicos* 1:53–74.

Fishman, J. 1975a. A sociolinguistic census of a bilingual neighborhood. Ed. Fishman et al., 157–76.

_____. 1975b. Bilingual attitudes and behaviors. Ed. Fishman et al., 105–53.

Fishman, J., R. Cooper, and R. Ma, eds. 1975. *Bilingualism in the barrio.* Bloomington: Indiana University, 2nd ed.

Fishman, J., and E. Herasimchuk. 1975. The multiple prediction of phonological variables in a bilingual speech community. Ed. Fishman et al., 465–79.

Fishman, J., and G. Keller, eds. 1982. *Bilingual Education for Hispanic students in the United States.* New York: Columbia University, Teacher's College.

Fishman, J., and C. Terry. 1975. The contrastive validity of census data on bilingualism in a Puerto Rican neighborhood. Ed. Fishman et al., 177–97.

Fitzpatrick, J. 1987. *Puerto Rican Americans: the meaning of migration to the mainland.* Englewood Cliffs, New Jersey: Prentice Hall. 2nd ed.

Flores-Ferrán, N. 2004. Spanish subject personal pronoun use in New York City Puerto Ricans: can we rest the case of English contact? *Language Variation and Change* 16: 49–73.

Flores, J., J. Attinasi, and P. Pedraza. 1981. La carreta made a U-turn: Puerto Rican language and culture in the United States. *Daedalus* 110:193–217.

_____. 1987. Puerto Rican language and culture in New York City. Ed. Sutton and Chaney, 221–34.

Flores, L., J. Myhill, and F. Tarallo. 1983. Competing plural markers in Puerto Rican Spanish. *Linguistics* 21:897–907.

Flores, Z. 1926. The relation of language difficulty to intelligence and school retardation in a group of Spanish-speaking children. MA thesis, University of Chicago.

Floyd, M. B. 1976. Verb usage and linguistic variation in Colorado Spanish. PhD dissertation, University of Colorado.

_____. 1978. Verb usage in Southwest Spanish: a review. *Bilingual Review* 5:86–90.

_____. 1982. Aspectual distinction in past reference: preterite and imperfect in southwest Spanish. *Journal of the Linguistic Association of the Southwest* 5:36–41.

Folse, K. 1980. An atlas of selected Spanish lexical items exhibited in the native speech of Honduras, Nicaragua, and El Salvador. MA thesis, University of Southern Mississippi.

Fontanella de Weinberg, M. B. 1992. *El español de América.* Madrid: Colección MAPFRE.

Fortier, A. 1894. *Louisiana Studies.* New Orleans: F. F. Hansell & Bro.

Foster, D. W. 1976. The phonology of Southwest Spanish. Ed. Bowen and Ornstein, 17–28.

Frank Canelo, J. 1982. *Dónde, por qué, de qué, y cómo viven los dominicanos en el extranjero: un informe sociológico sobre le e/inmigración dominicana 1961–62.* Santo Domingo: Alfa y Omega.

Friedman, L. 1950. Minorcan dialect words in St. Augustine, Florida. *American Dialect Society* 14:81.

Funkhouser, E. 1995. *A profile of Salvadoran emigration.* Santa Barbara: University of California, Santa Barbara, Department of Economics, Working Paper in Economics #4–95.

Gaínza, G. 1976. El español de Costa Rica: breve consideración acerca de su estudio. *Revista de Filología y Lingüística de la Universidad de Costa Rica* 2(4):79–84.

Galindo, L. 1992. Dispelling the male-only myth: Chicanas and caló. *Bilingual Review/Revista Bilingüe* 17:3–35.

———. 1995. Language attitudes towards Spanish and English varieties: a Chicano perspective. *Hispanic Journal of Behavioral Sciences* 17:77–99.

Galindo, L., and M. D. Gonzales, eds. 1999. *Speaking Chicana: voice, power and identity.* Tucson: University of Arizona Press.

Gallo, C. 1980. *Language of the Puerto Rican street.* Santurce: Book Service of Puerto Rico.

Galván, R. 1955. El dialecto español de San Antonio, Texas. PhD dissertation, Tulane University.

Galván, R., and R. Teschner. 1977. *El diccionario del español chicano.* 2nd ed. Silver Spring, Maryland: Institute of Modern Languages.

García, E. 1975. Chicano Spanish dialects and education. Ed. Hernández-Chávez et al., 70–76.

García, M. 1977. Chicano Spanish/Latin American Spanish: some differences in linguistic norms. *Bilingual Review/Revista Bilingüe* 4:200–207.

———. 1998. Gender marking in a dialect of Southwest Spanish. *Southwest Journal of Linguistics* 17(1):49–58.

García, M. E., and M. Tallon. 1995. Postnuclear /s/ in San Antonio Spanish: Nojotros no aspiramos. *Georgetown Journal of Languages & Linguistics* 3:2–4, 139–62.

García, N. 1987. *Recuerdos de los viejitos.* Albuquerque: University of New Mexico Press.

———. 1992. *Abuelitos: stories of the Rio Puerco Valley.* Albuquerque: University of New Mexico Press.

García, O., and M. Cuevas. 1995. Spanish ability and use among second-generation Nuyoricans. In *Spanish in four continents: Studies in language contact and bilingualism,* ed., C. Silva-Corvalán, 184–195. Washington, DC: Georgetown University Press.

García, O., and R. Otheguy. 1988. The language situation of Cuban Americans. Ed. McKay and Wong, 166–92.

———. 1997. No sólo de estándar vive el aula: lo que nos enseñó la educación bilingüe sobre el español de Nueva York. Ed. Colombi and Alarcón, 156–74.

García, T. 1939. A vocabulary of New Mexican Spanish words of English origin from southwestern New Mexico. MA thesis, Stanford University.

García González, J. 1980. Acerca de la pronunciación de R y L implosivas en el español de Cuba: variantes e influencias. *Islas* 65:115–27.

García Riverón, R. 1991. El Atlas Lingüístico de Cuba. *Lingüística Española Actual* 13:199–221.

García Rojas, M. A., and D. J. Molesworth. 1996. *Unravelling Spanglish: a practical guide to language interference*. Tunja: Universidad Pedagógica y Tecnológica de Colombia.

Garrison, V., and C. Weiss. 1979. Dominican family networks and U.S. immigration policy: a case study. *International Migration Review* 12:264–83.

———. 1987. Dominican family networks and United States immigration policy. Ed. Sutton and Chaney, 234–54.

Geoffroy Rivas, P. 1975. *El español que hablamos en El Salvador*. San Salvador: Ministerio de Educación.

———. 1978. *La lengua salvadoreña*. San Salvador: Ministerio de Educación.

Georges, E. 1984. *New immigrants and the political process: Dominicans in New York*. Occasional Paper 45, Center for Latin American and Caribbean Studies, New York University.

———. 1990. *The Making of a Transnational Community: Migration, Development, and Cultural Change in the Dominican Republic*. New York: Columbia University Press.

Gettleman, M., P. Lacefield, L. Menashe, and D. Mermelstein, eds. 1987. *El Salvador: Central America in the New Cold War*. New York: Grove Press.

Gibbons, J. 1987. *Code-mixing and code choice: a Hong Kong case study*. Clevedon: Multilingual Matters.

Gingras, R. 1974. Problems in the description of Spanish-English code-switching. Ed. Bills, 167–74.

Gonzales, N. 1969. *The Spanish-Americans of New Mexico: a heritage of pride*. 2nd ed. Albuquerque: University of New Mexico Press.

González, Carlisle. 1989. Neutralización de los fonemas /r/ y /l/ implosivas en el dialecto hablado en Santo Domingo. En *Actas del VII Congreso de la ALFAL*, v. II, 19–33. Santo Domingo: Asociación de Lingüística y Filología de América Latina.

González-Echeverría, R. 1997. Is "Spanglish" a language? *New York Times,* March 28, 1997, A29.

González Grullón, A., S. Cabanes Vicedo, and F. García Bethencourt. 1982. *Léxico básico de la lengua escrita en la República Dominicana*. Santo Domingo: Universidad Nacional Pedro Henríquez Ureña.

González, N. 1970. Peasants' progress: Dominicans in New York. *Caribbean Studies* 10(3):154–71.

———. 1976. Multiple migratory experiences of Dominicans in New York. *Anthropological Quarterly* 49(1):36–43.

González, R. J. 1967. Pachuco: the birth of a creole. *Arizona Quarterly* 23:343–56.

González Rodas, P. 1963. Jaraguá, una novela salvadoreña: estudio fonológico. San Salvador: Editorial Universitaria.

Gonzo, S., and M. Saltarelli. 1979. Monitoring, pidginization and immigrant languages. In *The acquisition and use of Spanish and English as first and second Languages,* ed. R. Andersen, 153–63. Washington, DC: TESOL.

Goodgall de Pruna, R. 1970. La pronunciación del idioma español en el centro de Cuba. *Islas* 37:155–60.

Granda, G. de. 1972. *Transculturación e interferencia lingüística en el Puerto Rico contemporáneo.* Río Piedras: Editorial Edil.

———. 1986. Sobre dialectología e historia lingüística dominicanas. *Anuario de Lingüística Hispánica* (Valladolid) 2:57–76.

Gran Diccionario Académico Honduras. 1984. Santo Domingo: Editorial Alfa y Omega.

Grant, B. 1934. *When Old Trails Were New: The Story of Taos.* New York: The Press of the Pioneers, Inc.

Grasmuck, S., and P. Pessar. 1991. *Between Two Islands: Dominican International Migration.* Berkeley and Los Angeles: University of California Press.

Gray, E. 1912. The Spanish language in New Mexico: a national resource. *University of New Mexico Bulletin Sociological Series* 1(2):37–52.

Green, G. 1986a. Archaic forms with a parallel ponderative function in the Spanish of the lower Rio Grande valley. Ed. Green and Ornstein-Galicia, 25–33.

———. 1986b. Parallel ponderative forms in the Spanish of the lower Rio Grande valley and the general Spanish system of nuancing infixes. Ed. Green and Ornstein-Galicia, 35–41.

Green, G., and J. Ornstein-Galicia, eds. 1986. *Mexican-American language: usage, attitudes, maintenance, instruction, and policy.* Brownsville, Texas: Pan American University at Brownsville, Rio Grande Series in Language and Linguistics No. 1.

Gregg, J. 1933. *Commerce of the prairies.* Dallas: Southwest Press [1st ed. 1844].

Griffith, B. 1947. The pachuco patois. *Common Ground* 7:77–84.

Grosjean, F. 1982. *Life with two languages.* Cambridge: Harvard University Press.

Grosjean, F., and C. Soares. 1986. Processing mixed languages: some preliminary findings. In *Language processing in bilinguals: psycholinguistic and neuropsychological perspectives,* ed. Jyotsna Vaid, 145–79. Hillsdale, N.J.: Lawrence Erlbaum Associates.

Gross, S. 1935. A vocabulary of New Mexico Spanish. MA thesis, Stanford University.

Guillotte, J. 1982. *Masters of the marsh: an introduction to the ethnography of lower St. Bernard Parish.* New Orleans: University of New Orleans, Dept. of Anthropology and Geology.

Guitart, J. 1976. *Markedness and a Cuban dialect of Spanish.* Washington, DC: Georgetown University Press.

———. 1978. Aspectos del consonantismo habanero: reexamen descriptivo. *Boletín de la Academia Puertorriqueña de la Lengua Española* 6:95–114.

———. 1980. Aspectos del consonantismo habanero: reexamen descriptivo. In *Dialectología hispanoamericana, estudios actuales,* ed. Gary Scavnicky, 32–47. Washington, DC: Georgetown University Press.

———. 1981. On the true environment for weakening and deletion in consonant-weak Spanish dialects. In *Issues in Language, Studies in Honor of Robert J. Di Pietro,* ed. Marcel Danesi, 17–25. Columbia, SC: Jupiter Press.

———. 1988. The case for a syntax-dependent post lexical module in Spanish phonology. In *Advances in Romance Linguistics,* ed. J.-P. Montreuil and D. Birdsong, 89–96. Dordrecht: Foris.

Gumperz, J., and E. Hernández-Chávez. 1975. Cognitive aspects of bilingual communication. Ed. Hernández-Chávez et al., 154–63.

Gutiérrez, J. 1981. An analysis of the phoneme /s/ in New Mexico Spanish. In *Proceedings of the 9th Annual Southwestern Areal Language and Linguistics Workshop,* ed., Charles Elerick, 234–39. El Paso: Department of Linguistics, University of Texas El Paso.

Gutiérrez, M. 1990. Sobre el mantenimiento de las cláusulas subordinadas en el español de Los Angeles. Ed Bergen, 31–38.

———. 1992. The extension of *estar. Hispanic Linguistics* 5:109–41.

———. 1994. Simplification, transference and convergence in Chicano Spanish. *Bilingual Review* 19:111–21.

Gutiérrez González, H. 1993. *El español en El Barrio de Nueva York: estudio léxico.* New York: Academia Norteamericana de la Lengua Española.

Hache de Yunén, A. 1982. La /n/ final de sílaba en el español de Santiago de los Caballeros. Ed. Alba, 143–54.

Haden, E., and J. Matluck. 1973. El habla culta de La Habana: análisis fonológico preliminar. *Anuario de Letras* 11:5–33.

Hagan, J. M.. 1994. *Deciding to be legal: a Maya community in Houston.* Philadelphia: Temple University Press.

Hallenbeck, C. 1950. *Land of the Conquistadores.* Caldwell, ID: The Caxton Printers, Ltd.

Hamilton, N., and N. Stoltz Chinchilla. 2001. *Seeking community: Guatemalans and Salvadorans in Los Angeles.* Philadelphia: Temple University Press.

Hammond, G. 1927. *Don Juan de Oñate and the founding of New Mexico.* Santa Fe: El Palacio Press. Historical Society of New Mexico, Publications in History vol. II.

Hammond, R. 1976. Some theoretical implications from rapid speech phenomena in Miami-Cuban Spanish. PhD dissertation, University of Florida.

———. 1978. An experimental verification of the phonemic status of open and closed vowels in Caribbean Spanish. In *Corrientes actuales en la dialectología del Caribe hispánico,* ed., Humberto López Morales, 93–143. Río Piedras: Editorial Universitaria.

———. 1979a. Restricciones sintácticas y/o semánticas en la elisión de /s/ en el español cubano. *Boletín de la Academia Puertorriqueña de la Lengua Española* 7:41–57.

———. 1979b. The velar nasal in rapid Cuban Spanish. In *Colloquium on Spanish and Luso-Brazilian linguistics,* ed. J. Lantolf, F. Frank, and J. Guitart, 19–36. Washington, DC: Georgetown University Press.

———. 1980. Las realizaciones fonéticas del fonema /s/ en el español cubano rápido de Miami. In *Dialectología hispanoamericana, estudios actuales,* ed. Gary Scavnicky, 8–15. Washington, DC: Georgetown University Press.

———. 1982. El fonema /s/ en el español jíbaro. Cuestiones teóricas. Ed. Alba, 155–69.

———. 1986a. En torno a una regla global en la fonología del español de Cuba. In *Estudios sobre la fonología del español del Caribe,* ed. R. Núñez Cedeño, I. Páez Urdaneta, J. Guitart, 31–39. Caracas: La Casa de Bello.

———. 1986b. La estratificación social de la R múltiple en Puerto Rico. *Actas del II Congreso Internacional sobre el Español de América,* ed. J. Moreno de Alba, 307–15. Mexico: Universidad Nacional Autónoma de México.

————. 1991. La /s/ posnuclear en el español jíbaro de Puerto Rico. In *Paragoge en el español de Nuevo México,* t. II, 1007–17, ed. E. Hernández-Chávez and G. Pérez. Presented at the XI Conference on Spanish in the United States, Los Angeles, November 1991.

Hanson, E. 1931. A study of intelligence test results for Mexican children based on English and Mexican test forms. MA thesis, University of Southern California.

Hardman, M. 1956. The phonology of the Spanish of El Prado, New Mexico. MA thesis, University of New Mexico.

Harris, J. 1974. Morphologization of phonological rules: an example from Chicano Spanish. In *Linguistic symposium on Romance languages,* ed., J. Campbell and M. Goldin, 8–27. Washington, DC: Georgetown University Press.

————. 1980. Nonconcatenative morphology and Spanish plurals. *Journal of Linguistic Research* 1:15–31.

————. 1983. *Syllable structure and stress in Spanish: a nonlinear analysis.* Cambridge: MIT Press.

————. 1985. Autosegmental phonology and liquid assimilation in Havana Spanish. Selected papers from the *XIIIth Linguistic Symposium on Romance Languages,* ed., Larry King and Catherine Maley, 127–148. Amsterdam: John Benjamins.

Hart-González, L., and M. Feingold. 1990. Retention of Spanish in the home. *International Journal of the Sociology of Language* 84:5–34.

Haugen, E. 1950. The analysis of linguistic borrowing. *Language* 26:210–31.

————. 1956. *Bilingualism in the Americas.* Publication no. 26 of the American Dialect Society, published by University of Alabama Press.

————. 1968. Schizoglossia and the linguistic norm. *Georgetown University Round Table, selected papers in linguistics 1961–1965,* 203–10. Washington, DC: Georgetown University Press.

Haught, B. F. 1931. The language difficulty of Spanish-American children. *Journal of Applied Psychology* 15:92–95.

Hayes, F. 1949. Anglo-Spanish speech in Tampa, Florida. *Hispania* 32:48–52.

Hendricks, G. 1974. *The Dominican diaspora: from the Dominican Republic to New York City. Villagers in transition.* New York: Teachers' College Press.

Henríquez Ureña, P. 1938. *El español en Méjico, los Estados Unidos y la América Central.* Buenos Aires: Biblioteca de Dialectología Hispanoamericana 4.

————. 1939. Ello. *Revista de Filología Hispánica* 1:209–29.

————. 1940. *El español en Santo Domingo.* Buenos Aires: Biblioteca de Dialectología Hispanoamericana, v. 5.

Hensey, F. 1973. Grammatical variation in Southwest American Spanish. *Linguistics* 108:5–26.

————. 1976. Toward a grammatical analysis of Southwest Spanish. Ed. Bowen and Ornstein, 29–44.

Hernández, J. E. 2002. Accommodation in a dialect contact situation. *Filología y Lingüística* 28(2):93–100.

————. 2007. *Ella me dijo, seguí adelante, sigue estudiando:* social and semantic differentiation in casual form of address variation. *Bulletin of Hispanic Studies* 84:703–24.

Hernández Alvarez, J. 1967. *Return migration to Puerto Rico.* Berkeley: Institute of International Studies, University of California, Berkeley.

Hernández Aquino, L. 1977. *Diccionario de voces indígenas de Puerto Rico.* Río Piedras: Editorial Cultural, 2nd ed.

Hernández-Chávez, E., G. Bills, and A. Hudson. 1996. El desplazamiento del español en el soroeste de EEUU. según el censo de 1990. In *Actas del X Congreso Internacional de la Asociación de Lingüística y Filología de la América Latina (ALFAL),* ed., M. A. Iglesis, 664–72. México: Universidad Nacional Autónoma de México.

Hernández-Chávez, E., A. Cohen, and A. Beltramo, eds. 1975. *El lenguaje de los chicanos.* Arlington, VA: Center for Applied Linguistics.

Hernández-Chávez, E., and G. Pérez. 1991. Paragoge en el español de Nuevo México. Presented at the XI Conference on Spanish in the United States, Los Angeles, November 1991.

Hernández Cruz, J., ed. 1994. *Corrientes migratorias en Puerto Rico/migratory trends in Puerto Rico.* San Germán: Centro de Investigaciones del Caribe y Latinoamérica, Universidad Interamericana de Puerto Rico.

Herranz, A. 1990. El español de Honduras a través de su bibliografía. *Nueva Revista de Filología Hispánica* 38:15–61.

Herranz, A., ed. 1990. *El español hablado en Honduras.* Tegucigalpa: Guaymuras.

Herriman, G. W. 1932. An investigation concerning the effect of language handicap on mental development and educational progress. MA thesis, University of Southern California.

Hidalgo, M. 1987. Español mexicano y español chicano: problemas y propuestas fundamentales. *Language Problems and Language Planning* 11:166–93.

———. 1990. Sobre las variantes de /s/ en Mazatlán, Sinaloa. Hispania 73:526–29.

———. 1993. The dialectics of language maintenance and language loyalty in Chula Vista, CA. Ed. Roca and Lipski, 47–71.

———. 1995. Language and ethnicity in the "taboo" region: the U.S.-Mexico border. *International Journal of the Sociology of Language* 114:29–42.

———. 2001. Spanish language shift reversal on the U.S.-Mexico border and the extended third space. *Language and Intercultural Communication* 1:57–75.

Hill, J. 1993a. Hasta la vista baby: Anglo Spanish in the American Southwest. *Critique of Anthropology* 13:145–76.

———. 1993b. Is it really "no problemo"? Junk Spanish and Anglo racism. *Texas Linguistic Forum* 33:1–12.

———. 1998. Language, race, and white public space. *American Anthropologist* 100:680–89.

Hills, E. C. 1906. New Mexican Spanish. *P. M. L. A.* 21:706–753. Spanish translation "El español de Nuevo Méjico" in *Biblioteca de Dialectología Hispanoamericana* 4 (1938):1–73.

Hoben, N., and J. Hood. 1937. Help the language handicapped. *Texas Outlook* 21 (June), 38–39.

Hochberg, J. 1986. Functional compensation for /s/ deletion in Puerto Rican Spanish. *Language* 62:609–21.

Hoffman, G. 1975. Puerto Ricans in New York: a language-related ethnographic summary. Ed. Fishman et al., 13–42.

Hoffman, M. 2004. Sounding Salvadorean: phonological variation in the Spanish of Salvadorean youth in Toronto. PhD dissertation, University of Toronto.

Holloway, C. 1997. *Dialect death: the case of Brule Spanish.* Amsterdam and Philadelphia: John Benjamins.

Holm, J. 1988. *Pidgins and creoles, volume I: theory and structure.* Cambridge: Cambridge University Press.

———. 2000. *An introduction to pidgins and creoles.* Cambridge: Cambridge University Press.

Hudson, A., E. Hernández-Chávez, and G. Bills. 1992. English language proficiency, Spanish language maintenance, and the socioeconomic characterics of the Spanish Origin population. Paper presented at the 13th conference El español en los Estados Unidos, University of Minnesota.

———. 1995. The many faces of language maintenance: Spanish language claiming in five southwestern states. In *Spanish in four continents: Studies in language contact and bilingualism,* ed. C. Silva-Corvalán, 165–83. Washington, DC: Georgetown University Press.

Humphrey, N. 1943–44. The education and language of Detroit Mexicans. *Journal of Educational Psychology* 17:534–42.

Ibarz, J. 2002. In un placete de La Mancha. *El Espectador* (Bogotá), 3 de julio de 2002.

Isbašescu, C. 1965. Algunas peculiaridades fonéticas del español hablado en Cuba. *Revue Roumaine de Linguistique* 10:575–94.

———. 1968. *El español en Cuba: observaciones fonéticas y fonológicas.* Bucharest: Sociedad Rumana de Lingüística Románica.

Jackson, L. 1938. An analysis of the language difficulties of the Spanish-speaking children of the Bowie High School, El Paso, Texas. MA thesis, University of Texas.

Jacobson, R. 1977a. How to trigger code-switching in a bilingual classroom. *Southwest Areal Linguistics Then and Now,* ed. B. Hoffer, B. Dubois, 16–39. San Antonio: Trinity University.

———. 1977b. The social implications of intra-sentential code-switching. In *New Directions in Chicano Scholarship,* ed. R. Romo and R. Paredes. Special issue of *The New Scholar,* 227–56.

———. 1978a. Anticipatory embedding and imaginary content: two newly identified codeswitching variables. *SWALLOW VII,* ed. A. Lozano, 16–25. Boulder: University of Colorado.

———. 1978b. Code-switching in south Texas: sociolinguistic considerations and pedagogical applications. *Journal of the Linguistic Association of the Southwest* 3:20–32.

Jaramillo, J. 1986. Variation of /ch/ and second person address in the Spanish of Tomé, New Mexico. PhD dissertation, University of New Mexico.

———. 1990. Domain constraints on the use of TÚ and USTED. Ed. Bergen, 14–22.

———. 1995. Social variation in personal address etiquette. *Hispanic Linguistics* 6/7: 191–224.

Jaramillo, J., and G. Bills. 1982. The phoneme /ch/ in the Spanish of Tomé, New Mexico. *Bilingualism and language contact,* ed. Florence Barkin, Elizabeth Brandt, Jacob Ornstein-Galicia, 154–65. New York: Teachers' College Press.

Jensen, L., J. Cohen, A. J. Toribio, G. DeJong, and L. Rodríguez. 2006. Ethnic identities, language and economic outcomes among Dominicans in a new destination. *Social Science Quarterly* 87:1088–99.

Jiménez Sabater, M. 1975. *Más datos sobre el español en la República Dominicana.* Santo Domingo: Ediciones Intec.

————. 1977. Estructuras morfosintácticas en el español dominicano: algunas implicaciones sociolingüísticas. *Ciencia y Sociedad* 2:5–19.

————. 1978. Estructuras morfosintácticas en el español dominicano: algunas implicaciones sociolingüísticas. Ed. López Morales, 165–80.

————. 1986. La neutralización de /-r/ y /-l/ en el dialecto dominicano. Puesta al día sobre un tema a debate. *Anuario de Lingüística Hispánica* (Valladolid) 2:119–52.

Johnson, L. 1938. A comparison of the vocabularies of Anglo-American and Spanish-American high school pupils. *Journal of Educational Psychology* 29:135–44.

Jonas, S. 2000. *Of centaurs and doves: Guatemala's peace process.* Boulder, CO: Westview Press.

Jones, J. 1994. Political development of the Salvadoran community living in the Washington, DC, metropolitan area. MA thesis, University of Florida.

Jones, O. L., Jr. 1966. *Pueblo warriors and Spanish conquest.* Norman: University of Oklahoma Press.

————. 1979. *Los Paisanos: Spanish settlers on the northern frontier of New Spain.* Norman: University of Oklahoma Press.

Jorge Morel, E. 1974. *Estudio lingüístico de Santo Domingo.* Santo Domingo: Editorial Taller.

Joshi, A. 1985. Processing sentences with intrasentential code-switching. In *Natural language parsing: Psychological, computational and theoretical perspectives,* ed. D. Dowty, L. Karttunen, and A. Zwicky, 190–204. Cambridge: Cambridge University Press.

Kamwangamalu, N. M. 1987. French/vernacular code mixing in Zaire: implications for syntactic constraints on code mixing. *CLS* (Proceedings of the Chicago Linguistics Society) 23(1):166–80.

Kayal, P. 1978. The Dominicans in New York. *Migration Today* 6:10–15.

Keller, G., R. Teschner, and S. Viera, eds. 1976. *Bilingualism in the bicentennial and beyond.* Jamaica, NY: Queen's University Press.

Kelly, V. 1935. The reading ability of Spanish and English speaking pupils. *Journal of Educational Research* 29:209–11.

Keniston, H. 1942. Notes on research in the Spanish spoken in the United States. *Bulletin of the American Council of Learned Societies* 34:64–67.

Kercheville, F. M. 1934. A preliminary glossary of New Mexican Spanish. *University of New Mexico Bulletin* 5(3):9–69.

Kirschner, C. 1992. The Spanish subjunctive and the Spanish-English bilingual: a semantically-motivated functional shift. *Hispanic Linguistics* 5:89–108.

Kirschner, C., and T. Stephens. 1988. Copula choice in the Spanish-English bilingual. In *On spanish, portuguese, and catalan linguistics,* ed. J. Staczek, 128–34. Washington, DC: Georgetown University Press.

Klein, F. 1980. A quantitative study of syntactic and pragmatic indication of change in the Spanish of bilinguals in the U.S. In *Locating language in time and space,* ed. W. Labov, 69–82. New York: Academic Press.

Kohpahl, G. 1998. *Voices of Guatemalan women in Los Angeles: understanding their immigration.* New York and London: Garland.

Kravitz, M. 1985. Sociolinguistic perspectives on decisions for correctness in New Mexico Spanish. PhD dissertation, University of New Mexico.

Kreidler, C. 1958. A study of the influence of English on the Spanish of Puerto Ricans in Jersey City, New Jersey. PhD dissertation, University of Michigan.

Lacayo, H. 1954. Apuntes sobre la pronunciación del español en Nicaragua. *Hispania* 37:267–68.

———. 1962. *Cómo pronuncian el español en Nicaragua.* Mexico: Universidad Iberoamericana.

Lamb, A. 1968. A phonological study of the Spanish of Havana, Cuba. PhD dissertation, University of Kansas.

Lance, D. 1975a. Dialectal and nonstandard forms in Texas Spanish. Ed. Hernández-Chávez et al., 37–51.

———. 1975b. Spanish-English code switching. Ed. Hernández-Chávez et al., 138–53.

Lantolf, J. 1978. Evolutive change in syntax: interrogative word order in Puerto Rican Spanish. In *Proceedings of the Eighth Annual Linguistic Symposium on Romance Languages,* ed., F. Nuessel, Jr. Rowley: Newbury House.

———. 1980. Constraints on interrogative word order in Puerto Rican Spanish. *Bilingual Review* 7:113–22.

Larzelere, A. 1988. *The 1980 Cuban boatlift.* Washington, DC: National Defense University Press.

Láscaris, C. 1977. *El costarricense.* San José: EDUCA.

Lastra de Suárez, Y. 1975. El habla y la educación de los niños de origen mexicano en Los Angeles. Ed. Hernández-Chávez et al., 61–69.

———. 1992. *Sociolingüística para hispanoamericanos.* México: El Colegio de México.

Lawton, D. 1971. The question of creolization in Puerto Rican Spanish. In *Pidginization and creolization of languages,* ed. D. Hymes, 193–94. Cambridge: Cambridge University Press.

Lentzner, K. 1938. Observaciones sobre el español de Guatemala. *Biblioteca de Dialectología Hispanoamericana* 4:227–34.

Lestrade, P. M. 1999. Trajectories in Isleño Spanish with special emphasis on the lexicon. PhD dissertation, University of Alabama.

Lewis, O. 1966. *La vida: a Puerto Rican family in the culture of poverty—San Juan and New York.* New York: Vintage Books.

Lipski, J. 1975. The language battle in Puerto Rico. *Revista Interamericana* 5:346–54.

———. 1977a. Code-switching and the problem of bilingual competence. In *Fourth LACUS Forum,* ed. M. Paradis, 263–77. Columbia, SC: Hornbeam Press.

———. 1977b. Preposed subjects in questions. *Hispania* 60:61–67.

———. 1978. Code-switching and bilingual competence. Ed. Paradis , 250–64.

———. 1979. Bilingual competence and code-switching. *Langue et l'Homme* 42: 30–39.

———. 1982. Spanish-English language switching in speech and literature: Theories and models. *Bilingual Review* 9:191–212.

———. 1983a. La norma culta y la norma radiofónica: /s/ y /n/ en español. *Language Problems and Language Planning* 7:239–62.

———. 1983b. Reducción de /s/ en el español de Honduras. *Nueva Revista de Filología Hispánica* 32:273–88.

———. 1984a. On the weakening of /s/ in Latin American Spanish. *Zeitschrift für Dialektologie und Linguistik* 51:31–43.

———. 1984b. Spanish world-wide: Toward a more perfect union. *Revista Chicano-Riqueña* 12(1):43–56.

———. 1984c. The impact of Louisiana *isleño* Spanish on historical dialectology. *Southwest Journal of Linguistics* 7(1984–87):2–15

———. 1985a. Creole Spanish and vestigial Spanish: evolutionary parallels. *Linguistics* 23:963–84.

———. 1985b. *Linguistic aspects of Spanish-English language switching.* Tempe: Arizona State University, Center for Latin American Studies.

———. 1985c. Reducción de /s/ y /n/ en el español *isleño* de Luisiana: vestigios del español canario en Norteamérica. *Revista de Filología de La Laguna* 4:125–33.

———. 1985d. /s/ in Central American Spanish. *Hispania* 68:143–49.

———. 1985e. The construction *pa(ra) atrás* in bilingual Spanish-English communities. *Revista/Review Interamericana* 15:91–102.

———. 1986a. Central American Spanish in the United States: El Salvador. *Aztlán* 17: 91–124.

———. 1986b. El español vestigial de los Estados Unidos: características e implicaciones teóricas. *Estudios Filológicos* 21:7–22.

———. 1986c. English-Spanish contact in the United States and Central America: sociolinguistic mirror images? In *Focus on the Caribbean,* ed. M. Görlach and J. Holm, 191–208. Amsterdam: John Benjamins.

———. 1986d. Instability and reduction of /s/ in the Spanish of Honduras. *Revista Canadiense de Estudios Hispánicos* 11:27–47.

———. 1986e. Realización de /s/ y /n/ en el dialecto *ISLEÑO* de luisiana: remanentes del español canario en Norteamérica. In *Actas del II Congreso Internacional sobre el Español de América,* ed. J. Moreno de Alba, 321–26. Mexico: Universidad Nacional Autónoma de México.

———. 1986f. Reduction of Spanish word-final /s/ and /n/. *Canadian Journal of Linguistics* 31:139–56.

———. 1986g. Sobre el bilingüismo anglo-hispánico en Gibraltar. *Neuphilologische Mitteilungen* 87:414–27.

_____. 1987a. El español del Río Sabinas: vestigios del español mexicano en Luisiana y Texas. *Nueva Revista de Filología Hispánica* 35:111–28.

_____. 1987b. *Fonética y fonología del español de Honduras.* Tegucigalpa: Guaymuras.

_____. 1987c. Language contact phenomena in Louisiana *isleño* Spanish. *American Speech* 62:320–31.

_____. 1987d. The construction *pa(ra) atrás* among Spanish-English bilinguals: parallel structures and universal patterns. *Ibero Americana* 28/29:87–96.

_____. 1988a. Central American varieties, Mexican and Chicano Spanish. In *Research Issues and Problems in United States Spanish,* ed. J. Ornstein, G. Green, and D. Bixler-Marquez, 157–69. Brownsville: Pan American University.

_____. 1988b. La discontinuidad fonética como criterio dialectológico. *Thesaurus* 43:1–17.

_____. 1988c. Sabine River Spanish: vestigial 18th century Mexican Spanish in Texas and Louisiana. *Southwest Journal of Linguistics* 8:5–24

_____. 1989a. Houston Spanish or Spanish in Houston? In *Hispanics in Houston and Harris County 1519–1986, a sesquicentennial celebration,* ed. Dorothy Caram, Anthony Dworkin, Néstor Rodríguez, 69–74. Houston: Houston Hispanic Forum.

_____. 1989b. /s/ in the Spanish of Nicaragua. *Orbis* 33:171–81.

_____. 1989c. Salvadorans in the United States: patterns of sociolinguistic integration. *National Journal of Sociology* 3(1):97–119.

_____. 1990a. Elision of Spanish intervocalic /y/: toward a theoretical account. *Hispania* 73:797–804.

_____. 1990b. Sabine River Spanish: a neglected chapter in Mexican-American dialectology. Ed. Bergen, 1–13.

_____. 1990c. *The language of the isleños: vestigial Spanish in Louisiana.* Baton Rouge: Louisiana State University Press.

_____. 1991a. Clandestine broadcasting as a sociolinguistic microcosm. In *Sociolinguistics of the Spanish-speaking world,* ed. C. Klee and L. Ramos-García, 113–37. Tempe: Bilingual Press.

_____. 1991b. In search of the Spanish "personal infinitive." In *New analyses in Romance linguistics, papers from the XVIII Linguistic Symposium on Romance Languages,* ed. D. Wanner and D. Kibbie, 201–20. Amsterdam: John Benjamins.

_____. 1992. Language—varieties of Spanish spoken, English usage among Hispanics, Spanish in business, the media and other social environments, bilingualism and code-switching. In *The Hispanic-American almanac,* ed. N. Kanellos, 209–27. Detroit: Gale Research Inc.

_____. 1993a. Creoloid phenomena in the Spanish of transitional bilinguals. Ed. Roca and Lipski, 155–82.

_____. 1993b. Syllabic consonants and New Mexico Spanish: the geometry of syllabification. *Southwest Journal of Linguistics* 12;109–27 [published 1998].

_____. 1994a. *A new perspective on Afro-Dominican Spanish: the Haitian contribution.* Research Paper No. 26, University of New Mexico Latin American Institute.

————. 1994b. *Latin American Spanish*. London: Longman.

————. 1994c. Tracing Mexican Spanish /s/: a cross-section of history. *Language Problems and Language Planning* 18:223–41.

————. 1996a. Contactos de criollos en el Caribe hispánico: contribuciones al español *bozal. América Negra* 11:31–60.

————. 1996b. Los dialectos vestigiales del español en los Estados Unidos: estado de la cuestión. *Signo y Seña* 6:459–89.

————. 1996c. Patterns of pronominal evolution in Cuban-American bilinguals. Ed. Roca and Jensen, 159–86.

————. 1997. Linguistic consequences of the Sandinista revolution and its aftermath in Nicaragua. In *Undoing and redoing corpus planning,* ed. M. Clyne and J. Fishman, 61–93. Berlin: Mouton De Gruyter.

————. 2000a. El español que se habla en El Salvador y su importancia para la dialectología hispanoamericana. *Científica* (Universidad Don Bosco, San Salvador) 1(2):65–88.

————. 2000b. The linguistic situation of Central Americans. In *Language diversity: problem or resource?* 2nd ed. Ed. S. McKay and S. C. Wong, 189–215. Cambridge: Cambridge University Press.

————. 2001a. Back to zero or ahead to 2001?: Issues and challenges in U.S. Spanish research. In *Research on Spanish in the United States: Linguistic issues and challenges,* ed., A. Roca, 1–41, Somerville, MA: Cascadilla Press.

————. 2001b. From *bozal* to *boricua:* implications of Afro Puerto Rican language in literature. *Hispania* 82:850–59.

————. 2002. Rethinking the place of Spanish. *PMLA (Publications of the Modern Language Association)* 117:1247–51.

————. 2004a. El español de América y los contactos bilingües recientes: apuntes microdialectológicos. *Revista Internacional de Lingüística Iberoamericana* 4:89–103.

————. 2004b. La lengua española en los Estados Unidos: avanza a la vez que retrocede. *Revista Española de Lingüística* 33:231–60.

————. 2004c. Nuevas perspectivas sobre el español afrodominicano. In *Pensamiento lingüístico sobre el Caribe insular hispánica,* ed. Sergio Valdés Bernal, 505–52. Santo Domingo: Academia de Ciencias de la República Dominicana.

————. 2005. Code-switching or Borrowing? No sé *so* no puedo decir, *you know.* In *Selected Proceedings of the Second Workshop on Spanish Sociolinguistics,* ed. L. Sayahi and M. Westmoreland, 1–15. Somerville, MA: Cascadilla Press.

Lizardi, C. 1993. Subject position in Puerto Rican WH-questions: syntactic, sociolinguistic, and discourse factors. PhD dissertation, Cornell University.

Llanes, J. 1982. *Cuban-Americans: Masters of Survival.* Cambridge, MA: ABT Press.

Lloréns, W. 1971. *El habla popular de Puerto Rico.* 2nd ed. Río Piedras: Editorial Edil.

Lope Blanch, J. 1964. Estado actual del español en México. *Presente y futuro de la lengua española,* t. I, 79–91. Madrid: Oficina Internacional de Información y Observación del Español.

_____. 1987. El estudio del español hablado en el suroeste de los Estados Unidos. *Anuario de Letras* 25:201–8.

_____. 1990a. *El español hablado en el suroeste de los Estados Unidos.* Mexico: Universidad Nacional Autónoma de México.

_____. 1990b. El estudio coordinado del español del suroeste de los Estados Unidos (memoria de un coloquio). *Anuario de Letras* 28:343–54.

_____. 1990c. La estructura del discurso en el habla de Mora, Nuevo México. *Romance Philology* 65:26–35.

Lope Blanch, J., ed. 1990. *Atlas lingüístico de México,* vol. I. Mexico City: Colegio de México/ Fondo de Cultura Económica.

López Chávez, J. 1977. El fonema /s/ en el habla de La Cruz, Sinaloa. *Nueva Revista de Filología Hispánica* 26:332–40.

López Morales, H. 1970. *Estudio sobre el español de Cuba.* New York: Las Américas.

_____. 1971. Transculturalización e interferencia lingüística en el Puerto Rico contemporáneo: cuestiones de método. *Revista de Filología Española* 54:317–25.

_____. 1974. Anglicismos en Puerto Rico: en busca de los índices de permeabilización del diasistema. In *Omagiu profesorului D. Gazdaru: miscellanea din studiile sale inedite sau rare,* 77–83. Freiburg: Br. Germania, Institutul Român de Cercetari.

_____. 1979a. *Dialectología y sociolingüística: temas puertorriqueños.* Madrid: Hispanova.

_____. 1979b. Velarización de /rr/ en el español de Puerto Rico: índices de actitud y creencias. In *Homenaje a Fernando Antonio Martínez: estudios de lingüística, filología, literatura e historia cultural,* 193–214. Bogotá: Instituto Caro y Cuervo.

_____. 1980. Velarización de /n/ en el español de Puerto Rico. *Lingüística Española Actual* 2:203–17.

_____. 1981. Velarization of /n/ in Puerto Rican Spanish. In *Variation omnibus,* ed. D. Sankoff and H. Cedergren, 105–13. Edmonton: Linguistic Research.

_____. 1983a. *Estratificación social del español de San Juan de Puerto Rico.* Mexico: Universidad Nacional Autónoma de México.

_____. 1983b. Lateralización de -/r/ en el español de Puerto Rico: sociolectos y estilos. *Philologica hispaniensia in honorem Manuel Alvar,* t. I, 387–98. Madrid: Gredos.

_____. 1984. El fenómeno de lateralización en las Antillas y en Canarias. In *II Simposio Internacional de Lengua Española* (1981), ed. M. Alvar, 215–28. Las Palmas: Excmo. Cabildo Insular.

López Morales, H., ed. 1978. *Corrientes actuales en la dialectología del Caribe hispánico.* Río Piedras: Editorial Universitaria.

López Scott, L. 1983. A sociolinguistic analysis of /s/ variation in Honduran Spanish. PhD dissertation, University of Minnesota.

Lozano, A. 1961. Intercambio de español e inglés en San Antonio, Texas. *Archivum* 11:111–38.

Lungo Uclés, M. 1990. *El Salvador en los 80: Contrainsurgencia y revolución.* San José: EDUCA-FLASCO.

Ma, R., and E. Herasimchuk. 1975. The linguistic dimensions of a bilingual neighborhood. Ed. Fishman et al., 347–464.

MacCurdy, R. 1947. Un romance tradicional recogido en Luisiana: las señas del marido. *Revista Hispánica Moderna* 13:164–66.

———. 1948. Spanish riddles from St. Bernard Parish, Louisiana. *Southern Folklore Quarterly* 12:129–35.

———. 1949. Spanish folklore from St. Bernard Parish, Louisiana. *Southern Folklore Quarterly* 13:180–91.

———. 1950. *The Spanish Dialect of St. Bernard Parish, Louisiana.* Albuquerque: University of New Mexico.

———. 1952. Spanish folklore from St. Bernard Parish, Louisiana. *Southern Folklore Quarterly* 16:227–50.

———. 1959. A Spanish word-list of the "brulis" dwellers of Louisiana. *Hispania* 42:547–54.

———. 1975. Los *isleños* de Luisiana: supervivencia de la lengua y folklore canarios. *Anuario de Estudios Atlánticos* 21:471–591.

Macías, J. M. 1885. *Diccionario cubano etimológico, crítico, razonado y comprensivo.* Veracruz: Imprenta de C. Trowbridge.

Macnamara, J., and S. Kushnir. 1971. Linguistic independence of bilinguals: the input switch. *Journal of Verbal Learning and Verbal Behavior* 10:480–87.

MacSwan, J. 1999. *A minimalist approach to intrasentential code switching.* New York: Garland.

Magoffin, S. S. 1926. *Down the Santa Fe Trail and into Mexico.* Ed. S. M. Drumm. New Haven: Yale University Press.

Mahikian, C. 1939. Measuring the intelligence and reading capacity of Spanish-speaking children. *Elementary School Journal* 39:760–68.

Malaret, A. 1955. *Vocabulario de Puerto Rico.* New York: Las Américas.

Mántica, C. 1973. *El habla nicaragüense.* San José: EDUCA.

———. 1989. *El habla nicaragüense y otros ensayos.* San José: Libro Libre.

Manuel, H., and C. Wright. 1929. The language difficulty of Mexican children. *Pedagogical Seminary and Journal of Genetic Psychology* Sept. 1929:458–68.

Marasigan, E. 1983. *Code-switching and Code-mixing in Multilingual Societies.* Singapore: Singapore University Press.

Maravilla, F. 1955. Los anglicismos en el español de Indiana Harbor, Indiana. MA thesis, University of Chicago.

Marcoux, F. 1961. Handicaps of bi-lingual Mexican children. MA thesis, University of Southern California.

Marqués, R. 1963. *La carreta: drama en tres actos.* Río Piedras: Editorial Cultural.

Marqués, S. 1986. *La lengua que heredamos: curso de español para bilingües.* New York: Wiley.

Martin, L. 1978. Mayan influence on Guatemalan Spanish: a research outline and test case. In *Papers in Mayan Linguistics,* ed. N. England, 106–26. Columbia: University of Missouri Press.

———. 1985. Una mi tacita de café: the indefinite article in Guatemalan Spanish. *Hispania* 68:383–87.

———. 1986. Eskimo words for snow: a case study in the genesis and decay of an anthropological example. *American Anthropologist* 88:418–22.

Martínez, E. 1993. *Morpho-syntactic erosion between two generational groups of Spanish speakers in the U.S.* New York: Peter Lang.

Marx, M. 1953. *The problem of bi-lingualism among Spanish speaking groups in the United States: a review of the literature.* Project Report, University of Southern California, August 1953.

Matluck, J. 1961. Fonemas finales en el consonantismo puertorriqueño. *Nueva Revista de Filología Hispánica* 15:332–42.

———. 1963. La *e* trabada en la ciudad de México. *Anuario de Letras* 3:5–34.

Matus Lazo, R. 1982. *Léxico de la ganadería en el habla popular de Chontales.* Managua: Ministerio de Educación.

Matus-Mendoza, María de la Luz. 2002. In *Linguistic variation in Mexican Spanish as spoken in two communities—Moroleón, Mexico and Kennett Square, Pennsylvania.* Lewiston, NY: Edwin Mellen Press.

———. 2004. Assibilation of /-r-/ and migration among Mexicans. *Language Variation and Change* 16:17–30.

———. 2005. Gender roles and the variations of /r/. In *Selected proceedings of the second workshop on Spanish sociolinguistics,* ed. L. Sayahi and M. Westmoreland, 120–26. Somerville, MA: Cascadilla Proceedings Project.

Maura, G. V. 1984. *Diccionario de voces coloquiales de Puerto Rico.* San Juan: Editorial Zemí.

May, D. 1966. Notas sobre el tex-mex. *Boletín del Instituto Caro y Cuervo* 70:17–19.

McClure, E., and J. Wentz. 1975. Functions of code-switching among Mexican-American children. In *Papers from the parasession on functionalism, Chicago Linguistic Society,* ed. R. Grossman, L. San, and T. Vance, 421–32.

McHale, C. 1976. Discurso de D. Carlos McHale al instalarse la Academia Norteamericana de la Lengua Española. *Boletín de la Academia Norteamericana de la Lengua Española* 1:89–94.

McKay, S., and S. C. Wong, eds. 1988. *Language diversity: problem or resource?* Cambridge and New York: Newbury House.

———. 2000. *New immigrants in the United States.* Cambridge: Cambridge University Press.

McKinstry, H. E. 1930. The American language in Mexico. *American Mercury* 1975 (March):336–38.

McMenamin. J. 1973. Rapid code-switching among Chicano bilinguals. *Orbis* 22:474–87.

McSpadden, G. 1934. Some semantic and philolgical facts of the Spanish spoken in Chilili, New Mexico. *University of New Mexico Bulletin* 5(2):72–102.

Medina-Rivera, A. 1999. Variación fonológica y estilística en el español de Puerto Rico. *Hispania* 82:529–41.

Megenney, W. 1982. Elementos subsaháricos en el español dominicano. In *El español del Caribe,* ed. O. Alba, 183–201. Santiago de los Caballeros: Universidad Católica Madre y Maestra.

———. 1990. *Africa en Santo Domingo: la herencia lingüística.* Santo Domingo: Museo del Hombre Dominicano.

Mejías, H., and G. Garza-Swan. 1981. *Nuestro español: curso para estudiantes bilingües.* New York: Macmillan.

Membreño, A. 1895. *Hondureñismos.* Tegucigalpa: Tipografía Nacional. Reprinted in 1982 by Editorial Guaymuras, Tegucigalpa.

_____. 1901. *Nombres geográficos indígenas de la República de Honduras.* Tegucigalpa: Tipografía Nacional.

_____. 1907. *Aztequismos de Honduras.* Mexico: Imprenta de P. Escalante.

Mencken, H. L. 1962. *The American language.* 4th ed. New York: Alfred A. Knopf.

Mendieta, E. 1999. *El préstamo en el español de los Estados Unidos.* New York: Peter Lang.

Mendoza-Denton, N. 1994. Language attitudes and gang affiliation among California Latina girls. *Proceedings of the Third Annual Berkeley Women and Language Conference,* ed. M. Bucholtz, A. C. Liang, and L. A. Sutton. Berkeley: Berkeley Women and Language Group.

_____. 1996. Muy "macha": gender and ideology in gang girls' discourse about makeup. *Ethnos* 61:47–63.

_____. 1997. Chicana/Mexicana identity and and linguistic variation: an ethnographic and sociolinguistic study of gang affiliation in an urban high school. PhD dissertation, Stanford University.

_____. 1999. Sociolinguistics and linguistic anthropology of U.S. Latinos. *Annual Review of Anthropology* 28:375–95.

Menéndez, C. 1928. *Historia del infame y vergonzoso comercio de indios vendidos a los esclavistas de Cuba por los políticos yucatecos, desde 1848 hasta 1861.* Mérida: Tallers de la Compañía Tipográfica Yucateca, S. A.

_____. 1932. *Las memorias de D. Buenaventura Vivó y la venta de indios yucatecos en Cuba.* Mérida: Tallers de la Compañía Tipográfica Yucateca, S. A.

Meyers-Scotton, C. 1992. Comparing codeswitching and borrowing. *Codeswitching,* ed. C. Eastman, 19–39. Clevedon: Multilingual Matters.

Milán, W. 1982. Spanish in the inner city: Puerto Rican speakers in New York. In *Bilingual Education for Hispanic Students in the United States,* ed. J. Fishman and G. Keller, 191–206. New York: Columbia University, Teacher's College.

Mondéjar, J. 1970. *El verbo andaluz.* Madrid: Consejo Superior de Investigación Científica.

Monteforte Toledo, M. 1959. *Guatemala, monografía sociológica.* México: Instituto de Investigaciones Sociales, Universidad Nacional Autónoma de México.

Montero de Pedro, J. 1979. *Españoles en Nueva Orleans y Luisiana.* Madrid: Ediciones Cultura Hispánica del Centro Iberoamericano de Cooperación.

Montes, M. 2003. *Get ready for Gabí! A crazy mixed-up Spanglish day.* New York: Scholastic Press.

Montes, S. 1986. La situación de los salvadoreños desplazados y refugiados. *El Salvador: Centro de Investigación y Acción Social,* (1986): 55–71.

_____. 1987. *El Salvador 1987: salvadoreños refugiados en los Estados Unidos.* San Salvador: Instituto de Investigaciones, Universidad Centroamericana José Simeón Cañas.

Montes Mozo, S. and J. J. García Vásquez. 1988. *Salvadoran Migration to the United States: An Exploratory Study.* Washington, DC: Hemispheric Migration Project, Center for Immigration Policy and Refugee Assistance, Georgetown University.

Montori, A. 1916. *Modificaciones populares del idioma castellano en Cuba.* Havana: Imp. de Cuba Pedagógica.

Montoya, A. 1932. Removing the language difficulty. *American Childhood* 17:12–15.

Moore, J., and H. Pachon. 1985. *Hispanics in the United States.* Englewood Cliffs, NJ: Prentice-Hall.

Moorhead, M. 1958. *New Mexico's Royal Road: Trade and Travel on the Chihuahua Trail.* Norman: University of Oklahoma Press.

———. 1975. *The presidio: bastion of the Spanish borderlands.* Norman: University of Oklahoma Press.

Morales, A. 1980. La expresión de sujeto pronominal, primera persona, en el español de Puerto Rico. *Boletín de la Academia Puertorriqueña de la Lengua Española* 8:91–102.

———. 1986a. *Gramáticas en contacto: análisis sintácticos sobre el español de Puerto Rico.* Madrid: Editorial Playor.

———. 1986b. La expresión de sujeto pronominal en el español de Puerto Rico. *Anuario de Letras* 24: 71–85.

———. 1988. Infinitivo con sujeto expreso en el español de Puerto Rico. In *Studies in Caribbean Spanish dialectology*, ed. R. Hammond and M. Resnick, 85–96. Washington, DC: Georgetown University Press.

———. 1989. Preposición "para" mas infinitivo: implicaciones en el español de Puerto Rico. *Actas del VII Congreso de la ALFAL,* 217–30. Santo Domingo: Asociación de Lingüística y Filología de América Latina.

Morales, A., and M. Vaquero, eds. 1990. *El habla culta de San Juan.* Río Piedras: Editorial Universitaria.

Morales, E. 2002. *Living in Spanglish: the search for Latino identity in America.* New York: St. Martin's Press.

Morales, J. 1986. *Puerto Rican poverty and migration: we just had to try elsewhere.* New York: Praeger.

Morales Hidalgo, I. 1978. *Vocabulario del calibre o caliche.* Guatemala City: Sociedad de Geografía e Historia.

Morel, A. 1991. *Refugiados salvadoreños en Nicaragua.* Managua: ACRES.

Moreno de Alba, J. 1988. *El español en América.* Mexico City: Fondo de Cultura Económica.

———. 1994. *La pronunciación del español en México.* Mexico: El Colegio de México.

Morrill, D. B. 1918. The Spanish language problem. *New Mexico Journal of Education* 14 (May): 6–7.

Moya Pons, F. 1981. *Dominican national identity and return migration.* Occasional Papers 1, Center for Latin American Studies, University of Florida.

Moyer, M. 1992. Analysis of code-switching in Gibraltar. PhD dissertation, Universitat Autònoma de Barcelona.

Mühlhäusler, P. 1986. *Pidgin and creole linguistics.* Oxford: Basil Blackwell.

Murphy, R. P. 1972. Integration of English lexicon in Albuquerque Spanish. PhD dissertation, University of New Mexico.

Muysken, P. 1997. Media Lengua. In *Contact languages: a wider perspective*, ed. S. G. Thomason, 365–426. Amsterdam and Philadelphia: John Benjamins.

_____. 2000. *Bilingual speech: a typology of code-mixing.* Cambridge: Cambridge University Press.

Nackerud, L. 1993. *The Central American refugee issue in Brownsville, Texas.* San Francisco: Mellen Research University Press.

Nartey, J. 1982. Code-switching: interference or faddism? *Anthropological Linguistics* 24:183–92.

Nash, R. 1970. Spanglish: language contact in Puerto Rico. *American Speech* 45:223–33.

_____. 1971. Englañol: more language contact in Puerto Rico. *American Speech* 46: 106–22.

Natal, C. R. 1983. *Exodo puertorriqueño (las migraciones al Caribe y Hawaii: 1900–1915).* San Juan: Carmelo Rosario Natal.

Navarro Tomás, T. 1948. *El español en Puerto Rico.* Río Piedras: Editorial Universitaria.

Navas, T. (director) and A. Thomas (producer). 1984. *El norte.* Cinecom International Films, distributed by CBS/Fox, Farmington, MI.

Nieto, E. M. 1986. *Léxico del delincuente houdnreño: diccionario y análisis lingüístico.* Tegucigalpa: Universidad Nacional Autónoma de Honduras.

Nishimura, M. 1986. Intrasentential code-switching: the case of language assignment. In *Language processing in bilinguals: psycholinguistic and neuropsychological perspectives,* ed. Jyotsna Vaid, 123–43. Hillsdale, NJ: Lawrence Erlbaum Associates.

North, L., and A. Simmons, eds. 1999. *Journeys of fear: refugee return and national transformation in Guatemala.* Montreal and Kingston: McGill-Queen's University Press.

Nortier, J. 1990. *Dutch-Moroccan Arabic code switching among Moroccans in the Netherlands.* Dordrecht: Foris.

Núñez Cedeño, R. 1980. *La fonología moderna y el español de Santo Domingo.* Santo Domingo: Editorial Taller.

_____. 1983. La pérdida de transposición de sujeto en interrogativas pronominales del español del Caribe. *Thesaurus* 38:1–24.

_____. 1986. La /s/ ultracorrectiva en dominicano y la estructura silábica. *Actas del II Congreso Internacional sobre el Español de América,* ed. J. M. de Alba, 337–47. Mexico: Universidad Nacional Autónoma de México.

_____. 1987a. Alargamiento vocálico en cubano: re-análisis autosegmental. *Actas del VII Congreso de ALFAL (Asociación de Lingüística y Filología de América Latina,* t. I, 623–30. Santo Domingo: ALFAL.

_____. 1988a. Alargamiento vocálico compensatorio en el español cubano: un análisis autosegmental. In *Studies in Caribbean Spanish dialectology,* ed. R. Hammond and M. Resnick, 97–102. Washington, DC: Georgetown University Press.

_____. 1988b. Structure-preserving properties of an epenthetic rule in Spanish. *Advances in Romance linguistics,* ed. D. Birdsong and J.-P. Montreuil, 319–35. Dordrecht: Foris.

O'Brien, M. 1937. A comparison of the reading ability of Spanish-speaking with non-Spanish-speaking pupils in grade 6A of the Denver Public Schools. MA thesis, University of Denver.

Ocampo, F. 1990. El subjuntivo en tres generaciones de hablantes bilingües. *Spanish in the United States: sociolinguistic issues*, ed. J. Bergen, 39–48. Washington, DC: Georgetown University Press.

Olivier, C. 1967. *De nuestro lenguaje y costumbres.* Santo Domingo: Editorial Arte y Cine.

Olson, James, and Judith Olson. 1995. *Cuban Americans: from trauma to triumph.* New York: Twayne.

Ornstein, J. 1951. The archaic and the modern in the Spanish of New Mexico. *Hispania* 34:137–42.

———. 1972. Toward a classification of Southwest Spanish non-standard variants. *Linguistics* 93:70–87.

———. 1975a. Sociolinguistics and the study of Spanish and English language varieties and their use in the U.S. Southwest: a state of the art paper. *Three essays on linguistic diversity in the Spanish-speaking world,* ed., J. Ornstein, 9–45. The Hague: Mouton.

———. 1975b. The archaic and the modern in the Spanish of New Mexico. In *El lenguaje de los chicanos,* ed. Hernández-Chávez et al., 6–12. Arlington, Virginia: Center for Applied Linguistics,

Ornstein-Galicia, J. 1987. Chicano caló: description and review of a border variety. *Hispanic Journal of Behavioral Sciences* 9:359–73.

Ornstein-Galicia, J., G. Green, and D. Bixler-Márquez, eds. 1988. *Research issues and problems in United States Spanish: Latin American and southwestern varieties.* Brownsville: Pan American University at Brownsville.

Oroz, R. 1966. *La lengua castellana en Chile.* Santiago: Universidad de Chile.

Ortega, M. 1991. *Reintegration of Nicaraguan refugees and internally displaced persons.* Washington, DC: Hemispheric Migration Project, Center for Immigration Policy and Refugee Assistance, Georgetown University.

Ortiz, C. 1947. English influences on the Spanish of Tampa. MA thesis, University of Florida.

———. 1949. English influence on the Spanish of Tampa. *Hispania* 32:300–304.

Ortiz, F. 1974. *Nuevo catauro de cubanismos.* Havana: Editorial de Ciencias Sociales.

Ortiz, L. 1975. A sociolinguistic study of language maintenance in the northern New Mexico community of Arroyo Seco. PhD dissertation, University of New Mexico.

———. 1981. Language maintenance in the northern New Mexican community of Arroyo Seco. In *Areal Language and Linguistics Workshop,* ed., C. Elerick, 240–57. El Paso: Department of Linguistics, University of Texas El Paso.

Otheguy, R. 1993. A reconsideration of the notion of loan translation in the analysis of U.S. Spanish. In *Spanish in the United States: Linguistic contact and diversity,* ed. Roca and Lipski, 21–45. Berlin: Mouton de Gruyter.

Páez Urdaneta, I. 1981. *Historia y geografía hispanoamericana del voseo.* Caracas: Casa de Bello.

Page, D. 1931. Performance of Spanish-American children on verbal and non-verbal intelligence tests. MA thesis, University of New Mexico.

Pandit, I. 1987. Grammaticality in code switching. *Codeswitching as a worldwide phenomenon,* ed., R. Jacobson, 33–69. New York: Peter Lang.

Paradis, M. 1980. The language switch in bilinguals: psycholinguistic and neurolinguistic perspectives. In *Sprachkontakt und Sprachkonflict = Languages in contact and conflict = Langues en contact et en conflit,* ed. P. Nelde, 501–6. Weisbaden: Franz Steiner.

Park, J.-E. 1990. Korean/English intrasentential code-switching: matrix language assignment and linguistic constraints. PhD dissertation, University of Illinois.

Parks, R. 1989. The survival of Judeo-Spanish cultural and linguistic traits among descendents of the crypto-Jews of New Mexico. MA thesis, University of New Mexico.

Patín Maceo, M. 1947. *Dominicanismos.* Ciudad Trujillo: Librería Dominicana.

Patterson, M. 1946. Some dialectal tendencies in popular Spanish in San Antonio. MA thesis, Texas Women's University.

Paz Pérez, C. 1988. *De lo popular y lo vulgar en el habla cubana.* Havana: Editorial de Ciencias Sociales.

Peña Hernández, E. 1992. El español en Nicaragua a principios de los 90. In *El español de Nicaragua.,* ed. Arellano, 71–78. Managua: Instituto Nicaraguense de Cultura Popular

Peñalosa, F. 1975. Chicano multilinguism and multiglossia. Ed. Hernández-Chávez et al., 164–69.

———. 1980. *Chicano sociolinguistics.* Rowley: Newbury House.

———. 1984. *Central Americans in Los Angeles: background, language, education.* Los Alamitos, CA: National Center for Bilingual Research.

Peñuelas, M. 1964. *Lo español en el suroeste de los Estados Unidos.* Madrid: Ediciones Cultura Hispánica.

———. 1978. *Cultura hispánica en Estados Unidos: los chicanos.* 2nd ed. Madrid: Ediciones Cultura Hispánica del Centro Iberoamericano de Cooperación.

Peralta Lagos, J. M. 1961. *Brochazos.* 2nd ed. San Salvador: Ministerio de Educación.

Pérez, L. 1986. Cubans in the United States. *Annals of the American Academy of Political and Social Science* 487:126–37.

———. 1988. *Cuba: Between reform and revolution.* New York: Oxford University Press.

Pérez Firmat, G. 1994. *Life on the hyphen: The Cuban-American way.* Austin: University of Texas Press.

Pérez Guerra, I. 1991. Un caso de prestigio encubierto en el español dominicano: la "vocalización cibaeña." In *Paragoge en el español de Nuevo México,* ed. E. Hernández-Chávez and I. Pérez Guerra, t. III, 1185–91. Presented at the XI Conference on Spanish in the United States, Los Angeles, November 1991.

Pérez Sala, P. 1973. *Interferencia lingüística del inglés en el español hablado en Puerto Rico.* Hato Rey: Inter American University Press.

Perrigo, L. 1982. *Gateway to Glorieta: a history of Las Vegas, New Mexico.* Boulder, CO: Pruett Publishing Company.

Peterson, L. 1986. *Central American migration: past and present.* Washington, DC: Center for International Research, U.S. Bureau of the Census, CIR Staff Paper 25.

Pfaff, C. 1979. Constraints on language mixing. *Language* 55:291–318.

Phillips, R. 1967. Los Angeles Spanish: a description analysis. PhD dissertation, University of Wisconsin.

_____. 1972. The influence of English on the /v/ in Los Angeles Spanish. *Studies in language and linguistics, 1969–70,* ed. R. W. Ewton and J. Ornstein, 201–12. El Paso: Texas Western Press.

_____. 1975. Variations in Los Angeles Spanish phonology. In *El lenguaje de los chicanos.* Arlington, Virginia: Center for Applied Linguistics, ed. Hernández-Chávez et al., 52–60.

_____. 1976. The segmental phonology of Los Angeles Spanish. In *Studies in Southwest Spanish,* ed. Bowen and Ornstein, 74–92. Rowley, MA: Newbury House.

Pichardo, E. 1976. *Diccionario provincial casi razonado de vozes y frases cubanas.* 5th ed. [1st ed. 1836]. Havana: Editorial de Ciencias Sociales.

Pinkerton, A. 1986. Observations on the *tú/vos* option in Guatemalan *ladino* Spanish. *Hispania* 69:690–98.

Piñeros, C.-E. 2005. Syllabic consonant formation in traditional New Mexico Spanish. *Probus* 17:253–301.

Plann, S. 1979. Morphological problems in the acquisition of Spanish in an immersion classroom. In *The acquisition and use of Spanish and English as first and second languages,* ed. R. Andersen, 119–32. Washington, DC: TESOL.

Poplack, S. 1979a. Function and process in a variable phonology. PhD dissertation, University of Pennsylvania.

_____. 1979b. Sobre la elisión y la ambigüedad en el español puertorriqueño: en el caso de la /n#/ verbal. *Boletín de la Academia Puertorriqueña de la Lengua Española* 7:129–43.

_____. 1980a. Deletion and disambiguation in Puerto Rican Spanish. *Language* 56:371–85.

_____. 1980b. Sometimes I'll start a sentence in English y termino en español. *Linguistics* 18:581–618.

_____. 1980c. The notion of the plural in Puerto Rican Spanish: competing constraints on (s) deletion. *Locating Language in Time and Space,* ed. W. Labov, 55–67. New York: Academic Press.

_____. 1981. Mortal phonemes as plural morphemes. *Variation omnibus,* ed. D. Sankoff and H. Cedergren, 59–71. Edmonton: Linguistic Research.

_____. 1983. Bilingual competence: linguistic interference or grammatical integrity? In *Spanish in the U.S. setting: beyond the southwest,* ed. Elías-Olivares, 107–29. Rosslyn, VA: National Clearinghouse for Bilingual Education.

_____. 1988. Contrasting patterns of code-switching in two communities. In *Code-switching: anthropological and sociolinguistic perspectives,* ed. M. Heller, 215–44. The Hague: Mouton de Gruyter.

Poplack, S., D. Sankoff, and C. Miller. 1988. The social correlates and linguistic process of lexical borrowing and assimilation. *Linguistics* 26:47–104.

Poplack, S., S. Wheeler, and A. Westwood. 1989. Distinguishing language contact phenomena: evidence from Finnish-English bilingualism. *World Englishes* 8:389–406.

Porges, A. 1949. The influence of English on the Spanish of New York. MA thesis, University of Florida.

Portes, A., and R. Bach. 1985. *Latin journey: Cuban and Mexican immigrants in the United States.* Berkeley and Los Angeles: University of California Press.

Portes, A., and A. Stepick. 1985. Unwelcome immigrants: the labor market experiences of 1980 (Mariel) Cuban and Haitian refugees in south Florida. *American Sociological Review* 50(4):493–514.

Post, A. 1931. Some aspects of Arizona Spanish. *Hispania* 16:35–42.

Potowski, K. 2004. Spanish language shift in Chicago. *Southwest Journal of Linguistics* 21:87–116.

Pousada, A., and S. Poplack. 1982. No case for convergence: the Puerto Rican Spanish verb system in a language-contact situation. In *Bilingual Education for Hispanic Students in the United States,* ed. J. Fishman and G. Keller, 207–40. New York: Columbia University, Teacher's College Press.

Pratt, Comfort. 2004. *El español del noroeste de Luisiana: Pervivencia de un dialecto amenazado.* Madrid: Editorial Verbum.

Predmore, R. 1945. Pronunciación de varias consonantes en el español de Guatemala. *Revista de Filología Hispánica* 7:277–80.

Prohias, R., and L. Casal. 1980. *The Cuban minority in the U.S., vol. 1.* New York: Arno Press.

Pullum, G. 1991. *The great Eskimo vocabulary hoax and other irreverent essays on the study of language.* Chicago: University of Chicago Press.

Quilis, A., and M. Vaquero. 1973. Realizaciones de /č/ en el área metropolitana de San Juan de Puerto Rico. *Revista de Filología Española* 56:1–52.

Quintanilla, G., and J. Silman. 1978. *Español: lo esencial para el bilingüe.* Washington, DC: University Press of America.

Rabella, J., and C. Pallais. 1994. *Vocabulario popular nicaragüense.* Managua: Imprenta El Amanecer.

Rael, J. 1934. *Cosa nada* en el español nuevomejicano. *Modern Language Notes* 49:31–32.

———. 1937. A study of the phonology and morphology of New Mexico Spanish based on a collection of 400 folktales. PhD dissertation, Stanford University.

———. 1939. Associative interference in New Mexican Spanish. *Hispanic Review* 7 (1939): 324–36.

———. 1940. Associative interference in Spanish. *Hispanic Review* 8:346–49.

———. 1975. Associative interference in New Mexico Spanish. Ed. Hernández Chávez et al., 19–29.

Ramírez, A. 1992. *El español de los Estados Unidos: el lenguaje de los hispanos.* Madrid: MAPFRE.

Ramírez Fajardo, C. 1993. *Lengua madre.* Managua: Lithorama Industrial.

Ramírez, M. 1939. Some semantic and linguistic notes on the Spanish spoken in Tampa, Florida. *Revista Inter-Americana* 1:25–33.

Ramos Huerta, O. 1997. *Diccionario popular cubano.* Madrid: Agualarga.

Ranson, H. 1954. Viles pochismos. *Hispania* 37:285–87.

Redlinger, W. 1976. A description of transference and code-switching in Mexican-American English and Spanish. In *Bilingualism in the bicentennial and beyond,* ed. Keller et al., 41–52. Jamaica, NY: Queen's University Press.

Rey, A. 1994. The use of *usted* in three societies: Colombia, Honduras, and Nicaragua. *Language Quarterly* 32(1–2):193–204.

Reyes, R. 1976a. Language mixing in Chicano bilingual speech. In *Studies in Southwest Spanish,* ed. Bowen and Ornstein, 183–88. Rowley, MA: Newbury House.

――――. 1976b. Studies in Chicano Spanish. PhD dissertation, Harvard University.

――――. 1981. Independent convergence in Chicano and New York City Puerto Rican bilingualism. *Latino Language and Communicative Behavior,* ed. R. Durán, 439–48. Norwood, NJ: ABLEX.

Rideling, W. 1876. A trail in the far southwest. *Harper's New Monthly Magazine* 53:15–24.

Rivas Bonilla, A. 1958. *Me monto en un potro.* 3rd ed. San Salvador: Ministerio de Cultura.

Rivera-Mills, S. 2000. *New perspectives on current sociolinguistic knowledge with regard to language use, proficiency, and attitudes among Hispanics in the U.S.: the case of a rural Northern California community.* Lewiston, NY: E. Mellen Press.

――――. Unpublished manuscript. The Use of the Voseo as an Identity Marker among Second and Third Generation Salvadorans in the U.S.

――――. Unpublished manuscript. Un análisis comparativo del voseo salvadoreño.

Roca, A. 1986. Pedagogical and sociolinguistic perspectives on the teaching of Spanish to Hispanic bilingual college students in South Florida. DA dissertation, University of Miami.

――――. 1999. *Nuevos mundos.* New York: Wiley.

Roca, A., and J. Jensen, eds. 1996. *Spanish in contact: issues in bilingualism.* Somerville, MA: Cascadilla Press.

Roca, A., and J. Lipski, eds. 1993. *Spanish in the United States: linguistic contact and diversity.* Berlin: Mouton de Gruyter.

Rodríguez Demorizi, E. 1975. *Lengua y folklore de Santo Domingo.* Santiago de los Caballeros: Universidad Católica Madre y Maestra.

――――. 1983. *Del vocabulario dominicano.* Santo Domingo: Editorial Taller.

Rodríguez Herrera, E. 1958–9. *Léxico mayor de Cuba.* Havana: Editorial Lex.

――――. 1977. Nuestro lenguaje criollo. *Antología de lingüística cubana, tomo II,* ed. G. Alonso, A. L. Fernández, 245–63. Havana: Editorial de Ciencias Sociales.

Rodríguez Herrera, E., E. Rogg, and R. Cooney. 1980. *Adaptation and adjustments of Cubans: West New York, New Jersey.* New York: Hispanic Research Center.

Rodríguez Ruíz, N. 1960. *El janiche y otros cuentos.* San Salvador: Ministerio de Cultura.

――――. 1961. *Las quebradas chachas.* San Salvador: Editorial Universitaria.

――――. 1968. *Jaraguá: novela de las costas de El Salvador.* 3rd ed. San Salvador: Ministerio de Educación.

Rojas, N. 1982. Sobre la semivocalización de las líquidas en el español cibaeño. In *El español del Caribe,* ed. Alba, 271–87. Santiago de los Caballeros: Universidad Católica Madre y Maestra.

Romaine, S. 1988. *Pidgin and creole languages.* London: Longman.

Romick, J. 1984. Are there universal constraints on borrowing in language contact situations? *Working Papers in Linguistics 16,* University of Hawaii.

Rona, J. P. 1967. *Geografía y morfología del voseo.* Porto Alegre: Pontificia Universidade Católica do Rio Grande do Sul.

Rosario, R. de. 1965. *Vocabulario puertorriqueño.* Sharon, CT: Troutman Press.

Rosengren, P. 1974. *Presencia y ausencia de los pronombres personales sujetos en español moderno.* Stockholm: University Gothobur.

Ross, J. R. 1975. La lengua castellana en San Luis, Colorado. PhD dissertation, University of Colorado.

————. 1980. La supresión de /y/ en el español chicano. *Hispania* 63:552–54.

Roy, M.-M. 1979. Les conjonctions anglaises "but" et "so" dans le français de Moncton. MA thesis, Université du Québec à Montréal.

Rubio, J. F. 1982. *Diccionario de voces usadas en Guatemala.* Guatemala City: Editorial Piedra Santa.

Ruíz Hernández, V., and E. M. Bermúdez. 1984. *El consonantismo en Cuba.* Havana: Editorial de Ciencias Sociales.

Saciuk, B. 1977. Las realizaciones múltiples o polimorfismo del fonema /y/ en el español puertorriqueño. *Boletín de la Academia Puertorriqueño de la Lengua Española* 5:133–53.

————. 1980. Estudio comparativo de las realizaciones fonéticas de /y/ en dos dialectos del Caribe hispánico. In *Dialectología hispanoamericana, estudios actuales,* ed. G. Scavnicky, 16–31. Washington, DC: Georgetown University Press.

Salarrué (Salvador Salazar Arrué). 1970. *Obras completas.* San Salvador: Editorial Universitaria, 2 vol.

Salazar García, S. 1910. *Diccionario de provincialismos y barbarismos centro-americanos, y ejercicios de ortología clásica.* 2nd ed. San Salvador: Tipografía "La Unión."

Salcines, D. 1957. A comparative study of dialects of Cuba. MA thesis, Georgetown University.

Saltarelli, M. 1975. Leveling of paradigms in the Southwest. In *Colloquium on Spanish and Portuguese linguistics,* ed. W. Milan et al., 123–31. Washington, DC: Georgetown University Press.

Sánchez, G. 1931. A study of the scores of Spanish-speaking children on repeated tests. MA thesis, University of Texas.

————. 1934a. Bilingualism and mental measurement. *Journal of Applied Psychology* 18:765–72.

————. 1934b. The implications of a basal vocabulary to the measurement of the abilities of bilingual children. *Journal of Social Psychology* 5:395–402.

Sánchez, R. 1972. Nuestra circunstancia lingüística. *El Grito* 6:45–74.

————. 1978. Denotations and connotations in Chicano code-switching. *SWALLOW VII,* ed. A. Lozano, 187–98. Boulder: University of Colorado.

————. 1983. *Chicano discourse.* Rowley, MA: Newbury House.

Sánchez-Boudy, J. 1978. *Diccionario de cubanismos más usuales.* Miami: Ediciones Universal.

Sandoval, L. 1941–42. *Semántica guatemalense.* Guatemala City: Tipografía Nacional.

Sankoff, D., and S. Poplack. 1981. A formal grammar for code-switching. *Papers in Linguistics* 14:1–25.

Sankoff, D., S. Poplack, and S. Vanniarajan. 1990. The case of the nonce loan in Tamil. *Language Variation and Change* 2:71–101.

Santiesteban, A. 1982. *El habla popular cubana de hoy.* Havana: Editorial de Ciencias Sociales.

Saragoza, A. 1995. *Central American immigrant children in the classroom.* San Francisco: Many Cultures Publishing.

Sassen-Koob, S. 1987. Formal and informal associations: Dominicans and Colombians in New York. In *Caribbean life in New York City: sociocultural dimensions,* ed. Sutton and Chaney, 278–296. New York: Center for Migration Studies of New York.

Sawyer, J. 1958. A dialect study of San Antonio, Texas: a bilingual community. PhD dissertation, University of Texas.

———. 1964. Spanish-English bilingualism in San Antonio, Texas. *Publications of the American Dialect Society* 41:7–15.

Schirmer, J. 1998. *The Guatemalan military project: a violence called democracy.* Philadelphia: University of Pennsylvania Press.

Schlesinger, S., and S. Kinzer. 1982. *Bitter fruit: the untold story of the American coup in Guatemala.* Garden City, NY: Doubleday & Company.

Schmitt, C. 1997. *Nosotros y nuestro mundo.* New York: Glencoe/McGraw Hill.

Schneider, H. 1961. Notas sobre el lenguaje popular y caló salvadoreños. *Romanistisches Jahrbuch* 12:373–92.

———. 1962. Notas sobre el lenguaje popular y caló salvadoreños. *Romanistisches Jahrbuch* 13:257–72.

———. 1963. Notas sobre el lenguaje popular y caló salvadoreños. *Romanistisches Jahrbuch* 14:231–44.

Schwegler, A. 1996. La doble negación dominicana y la génesis del español caribeño. *Hispanic Linguistics* 8:247–315.

Scotton, C., and J. Okeju. 1973. Neighbors and lexical borrowings. *Language* 49:871–89.

Sebba, M. 1997. *Contact languages: pidgins and creoles.* New York: St. Martin's Press.

Shoban, G., and P. Singer. 1970. The degeneration of the spoken language of San Miguel County. MA thesis, New Mexico Highlands University.

Shoemaker, J. 1988. The "broken" Spanish of Ebarb: a study in language death. MA thesis, Louisiana State University.

Silva-Corvalán, C. 1982. Subject expression and placement in Mexican-American Spanish. In *Spanish in the United States: Sociolinguistic Aspects,* ed. J. Amastae and L. Elías-Olivares, 93–120. Cambridge: Cambridge University.

———. 1983. Tense and aspect in oral Spanish narrative. *Language* 59:760–80.

———. 1986. Bilingualism and language change: the extension of *estar* in Los Angeles Spanish. *Language* 62:587–608.

———. 1988. Oral narrative along the Spanish-English bilingual continuum. In *On Spanish, Portuguese, and Catalan linguistics,* ed. J. Staczek, 172–84. Washington, DC: Georgetown University Press.

———. 1990. Current issues in studies of language contact. *Hispania* 73:162–76.

————. 1991a. Cross-generational bilingualism: theoretical implications of language attrition. In *Crosscurrents in second language acquisition,* ed. T. Huebner and C. Ferguson, 325–45. Amsterdam: John Benjamins.

————. 1991b. Spanish language attrition in a contact situation with English. In *First language attrition: structural and theoretical perspectives,* ed. H. W. Seliger and R. Vago, 151–71. Cambridge: Cambridge University Press.

————. 1993. On the permeability of grammars: evidence from Spanish and English contact. In *Linguistic perspectives on the Romance languages,* ed. W. Ashby, M. Mithun, G. Perissinotto, and E. Raposo, 19–43. Amsterdam: John Benjamins.

————. 1994. *Language contact and change: Spanish in Los Angeles.* Oxford: Clarendon Press.

————. 1997. El español hablado en Los Angeles: aspectos sociolingüísticos. In *La enseñanza del español a hispanohablantes: praxis y teoría,* ed. Colombi and Alarcón, 140–55. Boston and New York: Houghton Mifflin.

Silva-Corvalán, C., ed. 1995. *Spanish in four continents: studies in language contact and bilingualism.* Washington, DC: Georgetown University Press.

Simmons, M. 1968. *Spanish government in New Mexico.* Albuquerque: University of New Mexico Press.

Singh, R. 1981. Grammatical constraints on code-switching. *Recherches Linguistiques à Montréal* 17:155–63.

————. 1985. Grammatical constraints on code-mixing: evidence from Hindi-English. *Canadian Journal of Linguistics* 30:33–45.

Sobin, N. 1984. On code-switching inside NP. *Applied Psycholinguistics* 5:293–303.

Solé, C. 1970. *Bibliografía sobre el español en América, 1920–1967.* Washington, DC: Georgetown University Press.

————. 1979. Selección idiomática entre la nueva generación de cubano-americanos. *Bilingual Review/Revista Bilingüe* 6:1–10.

————. 1980. Language usage patterns among a young generation of Cuban-Americans. In *Festschrift for Jacob Ornstein,* ed. E. Blansitt and R. Teschner, 274–81. Rowley, MA: Newbury House.

————. 1982. Language loyalty and language attitudes among Cuban-Americans. In *Bilingual education for Hispanic students in the United States,* ed. J. Fishman and G. Keller, 254–68. New York: Columbia University Teachers College Press.

Solé, Y. 1975. Language maintenance and language shift among Mexican American college students. *Journal of the Linguistic Association of the Southwest* 1(1):22–48.

————. 1990. Bilingualism: stable or transitional? The case of Spanish in the United States. *International Journal of the Sociology of Language* 84:35–80.

Sosa, F. 1974. Sistema fonológico del español hablado en Cuba. PhD dissertation, Yale University.

Soto, P. J. 1956. *Spiks.* Mexico: Los Presentes.

Speed, S. 1992. The Salvadoran refugee experience: humanizing our understanding of the migration process. MA thesis, University of Texas at Austin.

Sridhar, S., and K. Sridhar. 1980. The syntax and psycholinguistics of bilingual code-mixing. *Canadian Journal of Psychology* 34:407–16.

Stark, L. 1980. Notes on a dialect of Spanish spoken in northern Louisiana. *Anthropological Linguistics* 22(4):163–76.

Stavans, I. 2000. *Spanglish para millones*. Madrid: Colección Apuntes de Casa de América.

———. 2002. Translation of the *Quijote* into "spanglish." *La Vanguardia* (Barcelona) (July 3):5–6.

———. 2003. *Spanglish: the making of a new American language*. New York: Harper-Collins.

Stoll, O. and A. G. Carrera. 1958. *Etnografía de Guatemala*. 2nd ed. Guatemala: Editorial del Ministerio de Educación Pública.

Suárez, C. 1921. *Vocabulario cubano*. Havana: R. Velsos.

Sutton, C., and E. Chaney, eds. 1987. *Caribbean life in New York City: sociocultural dimensions*. New York: Center for Migration Studies of New York.

Tejera, E. 1951. *Palabras indíjenas de la isla de Santo Domingo*. Ciudad Trujillo: Editora del Caribe.

Terrell, T. 1977. Constraints on the aspiration of final /s/ in Cuba and Puerto Rico. *Bilingual Review/Revista Bilingüe* 4:35–51.

———. 1979. Final /s/ in Cuban Spanish. *Hispania* 62:599–612.

———. 1980. The problem of comparing variable rules across dialects: some examples from Spanish. In *Festschrift for Jacob Ornstein*, ed. E. Blansitt, Jr. and R. Teschner, 303–13. Rowley: Newbury House.

———. 1981. Diachronic reconstruction by dialect comparison of variable constraints: s-aspiration and deletion in Spanish. In *Variation omnibus*, ed. D. Sankoff and H. Cedergren, 115–24. Edmonton: Linguistic Research.

———. 1982. Relexificación en el español dominicano: implicaciones para la educación. In *El español del Caribe*, ed. Alba, 301–318. Santiago de los Caballeros: Universidad Católica Madre y Maestra,

———. 1983. Sound change: the explanatory value of the heterogeneity of variable rule application. In *Spanish in the U.S. setting: beyond the southwest*, ed. Elías-Olivares, 133–48. Rosslyn, VA: National Clearinghouse for Bilingual Education.

———. 1986. La desaparición de /s/ posnuclear a nivel léxico en el habla dominicana. In *Estudios sobre el español del Caribe*, ed. R. N. Cedeño, I. P. Urdaneta, and Jorge Guitart, 117–34. Caracas: Casa de Bello.

Teschner, R. 1972. Anglicisms in Spanish: a crossreferenced guide to previous findings, together with English lexical influence on Chicago Mexican Spanish. PhD dissertation, University of Wisconsin.

Teschner, R., G. Bills, and J. Craddock. 1975. *Spanish and English of United States Hispanos: a critical, annotated, linguistic bibliography*. Arlington, Virginia: Center for Applied Linguistics.

Thiemer, E. 1989. El voseo ante la polémica y la práctica: a propósito de algunos datos recogidos en Nicaragua. In *Homenaje a Alonso Zamora Vicente, t. II: dialectología, estudios sobre el romancero*, 299–306. Madrid: Castalia.

Thomason, S. G., and T. Kaufman. 1988. *Language contact, creolization, and genetic linguistics.* Berkeley: University of California Press.

Thompson, R. 1974. Mexican American language loyalty and the validity of the 1970 census. *Southwest areal linguistics,* ed. G. Bills, 65–78. San Diego: Institute for Cultural Pluralism.

Timm, L. 1975. Spanish-English code-switching: el porque y how-not-to. *Romance Philology* 28:473–82.

Tió, S. 1954. Teoría del espanglish. *A fuego lento, cien columnas de humor y una cornisa,* 60–65. Rio Piedras: University of Puerto Rico.

———. 1992. *Lengua mayor: ensayos sobre el español de aquí y de allá.* Madrid: Editorial Plaza Mayor.

Toribio, A. J. 2000a. Language variation and the linguistic enactment of identity among Dominicans. *Linguistics* 38:1133–59.

———. 2000b. Setting parametric limits on dialectal variation in Spanish. *Lingua* 110: 315–41.

———. 2001a. Accessing billingual code-switching competence. *International Journal of Bilingualism* 5:403–36.

———. 2001b. Minimalist ideas on parametric variation. In *North East Linguistics Society (NELS) 30,* ed. M. Hirotari, A. Coetzle, N. Hall, and J.-Y. Kim, 627–38. Amherst, MA: University of Massachusetts GLSA.

———. 2001c. On the emergence of bilingual code-mixing competence. *Bilingualism, language and cognition* 4:203–31.

———. 2002. Focus on clefts in Dominican Spanish. In *Structure, meaning, and acquisition in Spanish,* ed. J. Lee, K. Geeslin, and J. C. Clements, 130–46. Somerville, MA: Cascadilla Press.

———. 2003. The social significance of language loyalty among Black and White Dominicans in New York. *The Bilingual Review/La Revista Bilingüe* 27(1):3–11.

———. 2006. Linguistic displays of identity among Dominicans in national and diasporic settlements. *English and ethnicity,* ed. C. Davies and J. Brutt-Griffler. New York: Palgrave.

Torres, L. 1989. Code-mixing and borrowing in a New York Puerto Rican community: a cross-generational study. *World Englishes* 8:419–32.

———. 1990. Mood selection among New York Puerto Ricans. *International Journal of the Sociology of Language* 79:67–79.

———. 1992. Code-mixing as a narrative strategy in the Puerto Rican community. *World Englishes* 11:183–94.

———. 1997. *Puerto Rican discourse: a sociolinguistic study of a New York suburb.* Mahwah, NJ: Lawrence Erlbaum.

———. 2002. Bilingual discourse markers in Puerto Rican Spanish. *Language in Society* 31:65–83.

Torres Rivas, E. 1986. Informe sobre el estado de la migración en Centroamérica. *Centro de Investigación y Acción Social* (1986): 4–53.

Torres-Saillant, S. 1989. Dominicans as a New York community: a social appraisal. *Punto 7 Review* 2(1):7–25.

Tovar, E. 1945. Un puñado de gentilicios salvadoreños. *Boletín del Instituto Caro y Cuervo* 1:547–57.

———. 1946. Contribución al estudio del lenguaje salvadoreño: algo sobre el léxico de flora. *Boletín del Instituto Caro y Cuervo* 2:421–59.

Trager, George and Genevieve Valdez. 1937. English loans in Colorado Spanish. *American Speech* 12:34–44.

Travis, C. 2004. Subject expression in two dialects: New Mexican and Colombian Spanish. Paper presented at the *34th Annual Linguistic Symposium in Romance Languages*. The University of Utah.

Treffers-Daller, J. 1991. Towards a uniform approach to code-switching and borrowing. *Papers for the workshop on constraints, conditions and models: London, 27–29 Sept. 1990*, 257–79. Strasbourg: European Science Foundation.

Trista, A. M., and S. Valdés. 1978. *El consonantismo en el habla popular de La Habana*. Havana: Editorial de Ciencias Sociales.

Trujillo, L. 1982. Diccionario del español del Valle de San Luis de Colorado y del norte de Nuevo México. PhD dissertation, University of New Mexico. Also 1983 [Alamosa, Colorado: O & V Printing].

Tsuzaki, S. 1963. English influences in the phonology and morphology of the Spanish spoken in the Mexican colony in Detroit, Michigan. PhD dissertation, University of Michigan.

———. 1971. *English influence on Mexican Spanish in Detroit*. The Hague: Mouton.

Uber, Diane Ringer. 1984. Phonological implications of the perception of -s and -n in Puerto Rican Spanish. *Papers from the XIIth linguistic symposium on Romance languages*, ed. P. Baldi, 287–299. Amsterdam: John Benjamins.

———. 1986. Los procesos de retroflexión y geminación de líquidas en el español cubano: análisis sociolingüístico y dialectológico. *Actas del II Congreso Internacional sobre el Español de América*, ed. José Moreno de Alba, 350–56. Mexico: Universidad Nacional Autónoma de México.

Ugalde, A., F. Bean, and G. Cárdenas. 1979. International migration from the Dominican Republic: findings from a national survey. *International Migration Review* 13(2):253–54.

Universidad para la Paz. 1987. *Los refugiados centroamericanos*. Heredia, Costa Rica: Universidad para la Paz, Universidad Nacional.

Urciuoli, B. 1996. Exposing prejudice: Puerto Rican experiences of language, race, and class. Boulder, CO: Westview Press.

U.S. Office of Education. 1972. *Teaching Spanish in school and college to native speakers of Spanish*. Washington, DC: Department of Health, Education and Welfare.

Valdés, G. 1988. The language situation of Mexican Americans. In *Language diversity: problem or resource?*, ed. McKay and Wong, 111–39. Cambridge and New York: Newbury House.

———. 2000. Bilingualism and language use among Mexican-Americans. In *New immigrants in the United States*, ed. McKay and Wong, 99–136. Cambridge: Cambridge University Press.

Valdés, G., and R. García-Moya, eds. 1976. *Teaching Spanish to the Spanish speaking: theory and practice.* San Antonio: Trinity University.

Valdés, G., and M. Geoffrion-Vinci. 1998. Chicano Spanish: the problem of the "under-developed" code in bilingual repertoires. *Modern Language Journal* 82:473–501.

Valdés, G, A. Lozano, and R. García-Moya, eds. 1981. *Teaching Spanish to the Hispanic Bilingual.* New York: Columbia University, Teacher's Press.

Valdés-Fallis, G. 1975. Code-switching in bilingual Chicano poetry. In *Southwest languages and linguistics in educational perspective,* ed. G. Cantoni Harvey and M. Heiser, 143–70. San Diego: Institute for Cultural Pluralism, San Diego State University.

———. 1976a. Code-switching in bilingual Chicano poetry. *Hispania* 59:877–85.

———. 1976b. Social interaction and code-switching patterns: a case study in Spanish/English alternatives. In *Bilingualism in the bicentennial and beyond,* ed. Keller et al., 53–85. Jamaica, NY: Queen's University Press.

———. 1978. Code-switching and language dominance: some initial findings. *General Linguistics* 18:90–104.

———. 1979. Is code-switching interference, integration or neither? In *Festschrift for Jacob Ornstein,* ed. Blansitt and Teschner, 314–25. Rowley, MA: Newbury House.

Valdés, G., and R. Teschner. 1977a. *Español escrito: curso para hispanoparlantes bilingües.* New York: Scribner's.

———. 1977b. *Spanish for the Spanish speaking: a descriptive bibliography of materials.* Austin: National Educational Laboratory.

Valdés Bernal, S. y N. G. Torada. 2001. Identidad, uso y actitudes lingüísticas de la comunidad cubana en Miami. *Unidad y diversidad, programa informativo sobre la lengua castellana 4 de abril de 2001.*

Valle, A. 1948. *Diccionario del habla nicaragüense.* Managua: Ed. "La Nueva Prensa."

———. 1972. *Diccionario del habla nicaragüense.*2nd ed. Managua: Editorial Unión.

———. 1976. *Filología nicaragüense.* 2nd ed. Managua: Editorial Unión.

Vallejo-Claros, B. 1970. La distribución y estratificación de /r/, /rr/ y /s/ en el español cubano. PhD dissertation, University of Texas.

Vallejo, B. 1976. Linguistic and socio-economic correlations in the spoken language of Mexican-American children. In *Studies in Southwest Spanish,* ed. Bowen and Ornstein, 165–82. Rowley, MA: Newbury House.

Van Wijk, H. 1969. Algunos aspectos morfológicos y sintácticos del habla hondureña. *Boletín de Filología* (Universidad de Chile) 30:3–16.

Vaquero, M. 1972. Algunos fenómenos fonéticos señalados por Navarro Tomás en *El español en Puerto Rico* a la luz de las investigaciones posteriores. *Revista de Estudios Hispánicos* 2:243–51.

———. 1978. Hacia una espectografía dialectal: el fonema /č/ en Puerto Rico. In *Corrientes actuales en la dialectología del Caribe hispánico,* ed. López Morales, 239–47. Río Piedras: Editorial Universitaria.

———. 1991. El español de Puerto Rico en su contexto antillano. In *Paragoge en el español de Nuevo México,* ed. Hernández-Chávez et al., t. I, 117–139. Presented at the XI Conference on Spanish in the United States, Los Angeles, November 1991.

Vaquero, M., and A. Quilis. 1989. Datos acústicos de /rr/ en el español de Puerto Rico. *Actas del VII Congreso de la ALFAL,* 115–42. Santo Domingo: Asociación de Lingüística y Filología de América Latina.

Varela, B. 1974. La influencia del inglés en los cubanos de Miami y Nueva Orleans. *Español Actual* (abril):16–25.

———. 1978. Observaciones sobre los isleños, los cubanos y la importancia del bilingüismo. *New Orleans Ethnic Cultures* 1:63–8.

———. 1979. Isleño and Cuban Spanish. *Perspectives on Ethnicity in New Orleans* 2:42–7.

———. 1992. *El español cubano-americano.* New York: Senda Nueva de Ediciones.

———. 1998–99. Discurso de incorporación: el español centroamericano de Luisiana. *Boletín de la Academia Norteamericana de la Lengua Española* 9–10:1–40.

Vargas, C. A. 1974. El uso de los pronombres "vos" y "usted" en Costa Rica. *Revista de Ciencias Sociales* 8:7–30.

Varo, C. 1971. *Consideraciones antropológicas y políticas en torno a la enseñanza del "spanglish" en Nueva York.* Río Piedras: Ediciones Librrería Internacional.

Vázquez, I. 1986. Los tiempos de subjuntivo en el español de Puerto Rico. *Actas del II Congreso Internacional sobre el Español de América,* ed. J. M. de Alba, 487–93. Mexico: Universidad Nacional Autónoma de México.

Veltman, C. 1988. *The future of the Spanish language in the United States.* New York and Washington, DC: Hispanic Policy Development Project.

Vigil, L. 1990. Fidelidad lingüística en una población del norte de Nuevo México. *Anuario de Letras* 28:285–90.

———. 1993. The traditional Spanish of Mora, New Mexico. PhD dissertation, University of New Mexico.

Vigil, N., and G. Bills. 1997. A methodology for rapid geographical mapping of dialect features. *Issues and methods in dialectology,* ed. Alan Thomas, 247–55. Bangor, Wales: University of Wales, Department of Linguistics.

Vigil, N., G. Bills, Y. Bernal-Enríquez, and R. Ulibarrí. 1996. El atlas lingüístico de Nuevo México y el sur de Colorado: algunos resultados preliminares. *Actas del X Congreso Internacional de la Asociación de Lingüística y Filología de la America Latina,* ed. M. Arjona Iglesias, J. López Chávez, A. Enríquez Ovando, G. López Lara, and M. A. Novella Gómez, 651–63. Mexico: Universidad Nacional Autónoma de México.

Villegas, F. 1965. The voseo in Costa Rican Spanish. *Hispania* 46:612–15.

Vincent, H. 1933. A study of performance of Spanish-speaking pupils on Spanish tests. MA thesis, New Mexico State Teachers College.

Wagner, M. 1953. Ein mexicanisch-amerikanischer Argot: das Pachuco. *Romanistisches Jahrbuch* 6:237–66.

Walz, T. 1964. *Favorite idioms and expressions used in Honduras.* Tegucigalpa: n.p.

Webb, J. 1976. A lexical study of "calo" and non-standard Spanish in the Southwest. PhD dissertation, University of California, Berkeley.

———. 1980. Pidgins (and creoles?) on the U.S.-Mexican Border. In *Festschrift for Jacob Ornstein,* ed. Blansitt and Teschner, 326–31. Rowley, MA: Newbury House.

Weinreich, U. 1953. *Languages in contact: findings and problems.* New York: The Linguistic Circle of New York.

Whetten, N. 1961. *Guatemala, the land and the people.* New Haven: Yale University Press.

Wherritt, I., and O. García, eds. 1989. U.S. Spanish: the language of the Latinos. *International Journal of the Sociology of Language,* 79 [special issue].

Whitney, W. D. 1881. On mixture in language. *Transactions of the American Philological Association* 12:5–26.

Whittier Union High School District. 1966. *Spanish for the bilingual student.* Whittier, CA: District.

Wilkinson, D. 2002. *Silence on the mountain: stories of terror, betrayal, and foretting in Guatemala.* Boston and New York: Houghton Mifflin.

Woodbridge, H. 1954. Spanish in the American South and Southwest: a bibliographical survey for 1940–1953. *Orbis* 3:236–44.

Woolford, E. 1983. Bilingual code-switching and syntactic theory. *Linguistic Inquiry* 13:519–35.

Ycaza Tigerino, J. 1980. *Situación y tendencias actuales del español en Nicaragua.* Managua: Ediciones Lengua.

———. 1992. Términos políticos y deportivos en el habla nicaragüense. In *El español de Nicaragua,* ed. Arellano, 63–70. Managua: Instituto Nicaraguense de Cultura Popular.

Zentella, A. C. 1981a. Hablamos los dos. We speak both: growing up bilingual in El Barrio. PhD dissertation, University of Pennsylvania.

———. 1981b. Language variety among Puerto Ricans. *Language in the U.S.A.,* ed. C. Ferguson, S. B. Heath. Cambridge: Cambridge University Press.

———. 1981c. Tá bien: you could answer me in cualquier idioma: Puerto Rican code-switching in bilingual classrooms. In *Latino language and communicative behavior,* ed. R. Durán, 109–31. Norwood, N.J.: ABLEX.

———. 1983. Spanish and English in contact in the U.S.: the Puerto Rican experience. *Word* 33(1–2):42–57.

———. 1985. The fate of Spanish in the United States: the Puerto Rican experience. *The language of inequality,* ed. N. Wolfson and J. Manes, 41–59. The Hague: Mouton.

———. 1988. The language situation of Puerto Ricans. In *Language diversity: problem or resource?,* ed. McKay and Wong, 140–65. Cambridge and New York: Newbury House.

———. 1997. *Growing up bilingual: Puerto Rican children in New York.* Malden, MA: Blackwell.

———. 2000. Puerto Ricans in the United States: confronting the linguistic repercussions of colonialism. Language diversity: problem or resource? In *New immigrants in the United States,* ed. McKay and Wong, 137–64. Cambridge: Cambridge University Press.

Index

Note: A page number followed by "t" indicates a table; "f" indicates a figure; a page number followed by "n" indicates a footnote.

sugar plantations in, 133
U.S. control of, 133–34
Dominicans, in the U.S.
census data, 135
demographics, 9, 132, 134–35
immigration of, 6, 134
literacy of, 138
undocumented, 135, 140n.5
Dominican Spanish
Haitian Creole, impact of, 139n.3
lexical characteristics, 137–38
linguistic characteristics of, 136–38
morphological characteristics, 137
phonetics and phonology, 136, 138
and Puerto Rican Spanish compared,
122–23, 132
scholarship on in the United States,
34, 139
syntactic characteristics, 137
in the United States, 3, 138–39
Duarte, José Napoleón, 151–52
Duncan, Quince, 145
Durán, Roberto, 31
Durango, 193

Ecuadorians, 9
Elephant Butte Reservoir, 195–96
*El español de los Estados Unidos: el lenguaje
de los hispanos*, 34
El español y su estructura, 31
El Grito, 80
El lenguaje de los chicanos, x, 26
El Paso del Norte, 193, 195
El Salvador, 34, 180. *See also*
Salvadorans, in the U.S.; Salvadoran Spanish
civil war in, 3, 151–52, 181
"death squads," 151, 153
history of, 150–52
population density, 150
"soccer war" with Honduras, 151
vos, use of, 146

Elías-Olivares, Lucia, 31
Englañol, 48
English only movements, 5
English-speaking "self," 15
Espanglish, 38
Español escrito, 29
Español para los hispanos, 19
Española, 133. *See also* Dominican
Republic; Haiti
Espejo, Antonio de, 194
Espinosa, Aurelio, 15–16, 17, 209
Estampas del Valle, 22
Estar, 87
Ethnic assimilation, 5
Ethnic mixing, 38
Ethnic slurs, 66
Ethnolinguistic identity, 39, 72

Fagoth, Steadman, 169
Fallas, Carlos Luis, 145
False cognates, 44
Fernández, Roberto, 50
Fishman, Joshua, x, 22, 31
Floricanto en Aztlán, 22
Fluent bilingual speakers
code switching among, 88, 223,
234–35
semifluent heritage language speakers
compared, 71
semi-speakers, 58
transitional bilinguals (TBs)
compared, 58
Fluent Spanish speakers, structural
features of, 63f
Foraker Act, 117
Foreign languages, teaching of in the U.S.
enrollment percentages, 11f
Spanish, growth of, 10–12
Franglais, 40
Frente Farabundo Martí para la
Liberación Nacional (FMLN),
151, 152, 181

CPSIA information can be obtained
at www.ICGtesting.com
Printed in the USA
BVOW11s0728151117
500435BV00001B/60/P